David G. White, Jr. maps out a provocative journey into the multidisciplinary possibility of holding an integral understanding that finds new meanings in useful theories. Supported by an extremely thought-provoking framework, White insists on a more up-to-date and unified approach to culture and change. This exciting and well-researched book steps beyond the thought boundaries within which organizational culture and cognition are usually confined. He is not willing to accept today's challenges and conflicts as intractable. And he doesn't want us to accept them either.
—Brenda B Jones, Co-editor, *NTL Handbook for Organization Development and Change*; recipient of the *OD Network's Lifetime Achievement Award*

Imagine an anthropologist studied your culture through the eyes of your employees and asked them to describe the purpose and workings of your organization. David J. White, Jr. did just that, and he shows how those descriptions reveal that many "cultures" exist in every organization, and they may not be as "manageable" as you think. His scholarly argument suggests evidence that culture emerges from the logic models or "schemas" that help people make sense of the organization and their place in it. For example, is your organization a "machine" or an "organism?" Is something "true" only when experienced, or can truth emerge from extrapolation? This perspective on culture has profound implications for whether and how culture can be shaped and directed, and takes you beyond the hype that culture can be everything and anything.
—Dr. John W. Boudreau, Professor and Research Director, Center for Effective Organizations, University of Southern California

David G. White, Jr. charges into the crowded morass of organizational culture with a keen eye and a sharp machete in hand. This thorough and provocative book offers no easy answers or quick fixes. Rather it challenges the reader to explore the terrain of cognition, practice and language, which are the most perceivable and visible instantiations of true (not espoused) organizational culture. Like Gideon Kunda, White seeks out the deeper structures of culture and thus presents a very innovative and compelling perspective on this most impactful dimension of organizational life.

—Eric Rait, Principal, Honeycomb Development

David G. White, Jr.'s thoughtful, hard-working and intelligent treatise sounds a cautionary note to current thinking about 'organizational culture,' and opens up a fresh, provocative perspective on this popular topic."

—Robert Kegan, Meehan Research Professor of Adult Learning, Harvard University Graduate School of Education, and Co-author, *An Everyone Culture: Becoming a Deliberately Developmental Organization*

Rethinking Culture

Organizational or corporate 'culture' is the most overused and least understood word in business, if not society. While the topic has been an object of keen academic interest for nearly half a century, theorists and practitioners still struggle with the most basic questions: *What is organizational culture? Can it be measured? Is it a dependent or independent variable? Is it causal in organizational performance, and, if so, how?* Paradoxically, managers and practitioners ascribe cultural explanations for much of what constitutes organizational behavior in organizations, and, moreover, believe culture can be engineered to their own designs for positive business outcomes. What explains this divide between research and practice?

While much academic research on culture is challenged by ontological, epistemic and ethical difficulties, there is little empirical evidence to show culture can be deliberately shaped beyond espoused values. The gap between research and practice can be explained by one simple reason: the science and practice of culture has yet to catch up to managerial intuition. Managers are correct in suspecting culture is a powerful normative force, but, until now, current theory and research is not able to adequately account for cultural behavior in organizations.

Rethinking Culture describes and presents evidence for a new framework of organizational culture based on the cognitive science of the so-called cultural mind. It will be of relevance to academics and researchers with an interest in business and management, organizational culture, and organizational change, as well as cognitive and cultural anthropologists and sociologists interested in applications of theory in organizational and institutional settings.

David G. White, Jr., Ph.D., is a cognitive anthropologist who has spent his career working in large organizations as well as entrepreneurial start ups. He is a co-founder of and principal in ONTOS Global, a boutique consulting firm in the alignment of business strategy, change and organizational culture.

Routledge Studies in Organizational Change & Development

Series Editor: Bernard Burnes

For a full list of titles in this series, please visit www.routledge.com

Rethinking Culture

Embodied Cognition and the Origin
of Culture in Organizations

David G. White, Jr.

Routledge
Taylor & Francis Group

LONDON AND NEW YORK

First published 2017 by Routledge

2 Park Square, Milton Park, Abingdon, Oxfordshire OX14 4RN
52 Vanderbilt Avenue, New York, NY 10017

Routledge is an imprint of the Taylor & Francis Group, an informa business

First issued in paperback 2019

Library of Congress Cataloging-in-Publication Data
A catalog record for this book has been requested

ISBN: 978-1-138-21058-5 (hbk)
ISBN: 978-0-367-24289-3 (pbk)

Typeset in Sabon
by Apex CoVantage, LLC

Contents

Figures and Tables

Figures

Tables

Foreword

'Culture' is a surprisingly slippery construct. Even in my field of sociocultural anthropology, the social science dedicated to the study of culture, there are multiple definitions. Yes, although we do not agree about what culture is, we tend to agree about what it is not. One problematic approach found among scholars in other fields is to treat culture as a single variable rather than a complex of ideas, social structures, artifacts, and practices that are variably distributed in social groups. Another problematic approach focuses on espoused values alone. Articulated values do play an important role in society, but culture also lies in what people do and in understandings that are so taken for granted that members feel no need to voice them because they cannot imagine anyone thinking differently.

In this valuable book David White shows what happens when problematic applications of the culture construct are put into practice, and he presents a better alternative. Why are there so many failed attempts to change organizational culture? As White explains, the failures are inevitable given misunderstandings of what culture is. For example, if culture is equated with espoused values, it should be easy to create a strong culture by insistently repeating slogans articulating those values. It should also be easy to change a culture: Simply replace the old slogans with newer and better slogans. That way of thinking about culture emphasizes the role of leaders; it exemplifies what I call a height metaphor for culture. In the height metaphor, culture emanates from on high. A corollary of the height metaphor is that a new culture can be promulgated by leaders, much like God handing Moses the Ten Commandments.

The research cited by White shows this understanding of culture as handed down by leaders does not work. It is particularly ineffective in the large corporations that are most likely to spend a lot of money on 'values engineering' to change the organizational climate and foster greater employee engagement. Middle managers and workers become skilled at repeating the slogans, but nothing else changes.

A better metaphor for culture is one of depth rather than height. Authentic company cultures are rooted in what White nicely calls *unthought knowns*. Unthought knowns are cognitive schemas so fundamental that they are not thought about. A key contribution of *Rethinking Culture* is to ground these schemas in two fundamental factors shaping employee socialization and corporate behavior. The first is the professional training and identity of those employees whose work is central to the functioning of organization—software engineers for Internet technology companies, professors for colleges and universities, construction workers for construction companies. Their years of learning how to identify problems and solutions and the key constructs that are the basis of their problem-solving analogies are deep assumptions not readily changed by sloganeering. The second crucial factor White identifies is the *strategic task context:* what the organization does, the technology it uses, and the legal and social environment in which it works. These are external affordances for behavior, but they also become internalized in habits and assumptions.

Given this analysis of culture, White attends to both ideas and situated practices. In my subfield of cognitive anthropology, some scholars focus on cultural understandings implicit in what people say and others on cognition as observed in practice when people interact in specific settings. One of White's achievements is to integrate these distinct approaches and to recognize that both are forms of embodied knowledge.

That is not to say that organizational change is impossible or that leaders have no effect on the culture of the organization. Building upon his rethinking of the foundations of organizational culture, White proposes that leaders can foster greater coherence by recognizing the schemas that already make sense to their employees, then selectively reinforcing the ones that align with the organization's strategy. Reinforcement is not just verbal repetition. White suggests techniques for helping leadership groups recognize the schemas that are implicit in their practices. Awareness of these schemas is a necessary first step; after that, cultural change requires changing an organization's technology, its behavioral routines, and the larger setting in which it operates, including occupational training. Such changes will eventually yield new unthought knowns.

This book provides insight into what culture is—a reality check that is needed before attempting to change culture from on high. Beyond its application to organizations, White's sophisticated rethinking of culture is valuable for any scholar or practitioner who relies upon that elusive notion.

Claudia Strauss
Pitzer College,
October 2016

Acknowledgments

As with any significant endeavor, what takes shape as a finished product is really the accumulation of false starts, clever procrastinations, blind alleys, seductive detours, and stubborn persistence. This has truly been a journey of intellectual passion dating more than 30 years to my undergraduate days as a philosophy student and my discovery of Lakoff and Johnson's *Metaphors We Live By*. To this I owe a debt to Jay Atlas at Pomona College.

I owe much to my employers, mentors, and colleagues over the years, notably Jan Miller, Tanya Clemons, Joe Whittinghill, Carrie Olesen, Eric Rait, and many others who within the context of complex systems such as Lotus (IBM) and Microsoft allowed or encouraged me to experiment and refine ideas about culture and change. I owe a special thanks to my clients at 'IMCO' for granting access and allowing me to locate this work within their own culture change journey.

My thanks to my dissertation committee members Dorothy Agger-Gupta, Fred Steier and, especially, Bob Silverman, who as a mentor placed alternative perspectives and formulations in front of me long before I could understand why they mattered. My thanks also to Claudia Strauss, an intellectual guiding light long before I had the privilege of working with her.

Lastly, a large debt is owed to my father who indulged many papers along the way. And to Lisa, my business and life partner and love of my life, who shouldered the business of our business and life while putting her own academic journey on hold to support mine. Her questions, comments, and insights are the fuel for this project, returning me to what is most relevant for those who stand to benefit most, the employees and managers of complex organizational systems. Without her, these words would not have been possible, nor matter as much. *Thank you.*

Introduction

If everywhere it is the inarticulate which has the last word, unspoken and yet decisive, then a corresponding abridgement of the status of spoken truth itself is inevitable. The ideal of an impersonally detached truth would have to be reinterpreted, to allow for the inherently personal character of the act by which truth is declared.

—Michael Polanyi (*Personal Knowledge*, 1958)

Venereal disease in the Middle Ages and early Renaissance was thought by the scientists of the day to be caused by the sin of fornication, seen as just punishment for sexual transgression. Such a diagnostic frame could have only been possible in an age where religion explained most natural phenomena (Fleck, 1979). In a similar fashion, the recent ethical lapses apparent at General Motors leading to the recall of 2.5 million cars has been likened to a failure of GM's corporate culture (Norris, 2014). The scandal at Volkswagen in 2015, the failure of Enron in the early 2000s, and many other firms is similarly attributed.[1] Failures of corporate culture, it seems, are the summary explanation for executive malfeasance, poor performance, low morale, failed strategy, and other shortcomings, as well as the source of enduring corporate success and un-replicable competitive advantage (for example, see Bates, Amundson, Schroeder, & Morris,1995; Deal & Kennedy, 1982; Denison, 1990; Kotter & Heskett, 1992)

So it is odd that the much of the academic community has such difficulty with the concept. John Van Maanen and Stephen Barley (1984) characterized the study of human behavior in organizations as a field "already choking on assorted frameworks, hypotheses, methods, variables, and other objects of intellectual passion" (p. 1). Organizational culture theory and practice exemplifies the case.

Organizational culture as an object of academic and management interest is a relatively recent phenomenon, traceable to the 1970s (Kunda, 1992) when organizations were acknowledged to be "culture-bearing milieus" (Frost, Moore, Louis, Lundberg, & Martin, 1985, p. 19). The concept powerfully holds the imagination of corporate executives and consultants. As put by recently by *The Economist*:

> 'Culture' is the *mot du jour* in the business world. Why do the wolves of Wall Street howl? Because Wall Street has a wolverine culture. Why do mergers fail? Because the cultures of the companies doing the merging often clash. Why do some companies succeed and others fail? Because they have either supportive or toxic cultures.
>
> (January 11, 2014)

Despite its attraction, after nearly half a century of keen effort and focus the culture field today is in a state of paradox. While the academic community wrestles with even the most basic questions, such as *what is culture, can it be measured, is it a dependent or independent variable, is it causal in organizational performance, and, if so, how* (Martin, 2002), or sidesteps them altogether with reductionist approaches, managers and practitioners impugn cultural explanations for much of what constitutes behavior in organizations, and, moreover, believe with almost evangelical fervor organizational culture can be engineered to their own designs for positive business outcomes.

This is a remarkable paradox. While much of the academic research on culture is challenged by ontological, epistemic and ethical difficulties, and while there is little empirical evidence to show culture can be deliberately shaped beyond espoused values in any organization larger than about 150 people, both camps are not misguided. They are simply ignoring each other, for a simple reason: the science of organizational culture is not yet able to fully or adequately account for culture in organizations. The science has yet to catch up to the intuition of managers that culture is a potentially powerful normative force.

This is why in the pages that follow I will argue the research and practice of organizational culture are badly in need of a fresh approach. This new approach is based on what we are learning about the mind through the last 30 years of cognitive science, and in particular the so-called 'cultural mind' and its embodied basis.

Within the academy the organizational culture field is characterized by an ongoing struggle for intellectual relevance, a struggle Joanne Martin and Peter Frost (2011) labeled the "culture wars" (p. 599). Beyond superficial agreement that culture is something shared, the field is characterized by intellectual silos marking the various academic traditions within management, such as economics, industrial-organizational psychology, and social psychology, that claim culture as their own. Within each, underlying positivist or constructivist worldviews muddle the debate. This results in a proliferation of definitions and epistemologies (see Chapter 1), with a corresponding tendency to promulgate theory within relatively narrow hermeneutic confines (Martin, 2002), which serves to preclude consensus. Ironically, the one field that places culture at the center of its intellectual agenda, cultural and cognitive anthropology, has had relatively little influence in management (Stewart & Aldrich, 2015). Which means its many insights accrued over the last 30 years have not found their way into the culture praxis mainstream.

The fact managers and practitioners find the culture concept so compelling is perhaps ironic but not surprising. Given fragmented or contradictory schools, theories, epistemologies, and frameworks, the resulting lack of academic consensus leads managers and practitioners to either greatly oversimplify culture, reducing it to one or two variables, or conceptualize it as a muddle of competing constructs (Martin & Frost, 2011). Almost any notion concerning what people believe or how they habitually behave within social milieus can be operationalized as culture ('a culture of leadership', 'a culture of continuous improvement', 'a culture of trust', etc.). At times it is confused with other concepts such as strategy (for example, see Bates et al., 1995). Culture diagnostic frameworks and intervention strategies are often crafted from untested theories, a single case study, or employee opinion surveys, which leads to change programs that typically impact little more than espoused values while wasting a significant amount of resources.

Yet many managers passionately believe organizational culture can be built and shaped, often as an expression and projection of their own values and desired norms (Alvesson & Sveningsson, 2008; Kunda, 1992; Martin & Frost, 2011). One need look no further than the Sunday Business section of the *New York Times* to witness how unencumbered business leaders are by academic research (Bryant, 2009–2015) and see Chapter 1). The amount of energy focused on one's culture is justified by the search for 'competitive advantage', which leads managers to seek out new variables to manage and control. This belief is so widespread that 'culture work' is taken as self evident, no matter what the science might have to say.

As beguiling as the concept is, I will argue it is flawed. While not denying the existence of culture or its normative and psychological force, I suggest in all its intellectual heterogeneity and pragmatic simplification the concept as applied in organizations is still immature in conceptualization, measurement, and application. It fails to provide an adequate explanatory framework for cultural behavior and change in organizations and therefore is incapable of delivering on the promises and benefits that ostensibly accrue based on the prescriptions offered by its proponents.

A new approach is needed, for several reasons. For one, there is little empirical evidence of successful culture change. The few serious studies focused on culture change effectiveness suggest ambiguous results, anecdotal evidence, or no major effects on anything other than espoused values (Alvesson & Sveningsson, 2008; Ogbonna & Wilkinson, 2003; Siehl, 1985). Planned change efforts involving culture often fail (Balogun & Johnson, 2005). And while part of the goal of most culture change programs is to improve employee engagement (for example, Corporate Leadership Council, 2004; Lockwood, 2007), a recent Gallup survey finds 70% of U.S. workers do not feel engaged at work, with the problem most pronounced in larger companies (Gallup, 2016).

Another domain where enriched knowledge of culture could add insight is in mergers and acquisitions (M&A), yet culture as a variable in M&A remains even more opaque. The culture–performance relationship in M&A is contradictory and yet to be adequately explained (Bruner, 2001; Kelly, Cook, & Spitzer, 1999; Vaara, 2003).[2] Companies that produce similar services or products appear to have difficulties in merger integration (Larsson & Finkelstein, 1999), and those in dissimilar industries have severe difficulties (Ralls & Web, 1999).

Beyond culture change, employee engagement and M&A, much of the academic research on organizational culture suffers from ontological and epistemic challenges ranging from assumptions of culture as a natural kind to issues of boundaries, measurement and interpretation. These issues remain unresolved. If adequate theory and explanatory frameworks for culture and change existed, the number of failed cultural adaptions and change efforts in practice would be fewer, and consensus in the academic literature, 40 years after the introduction of the concept, would be clear. Instead, what is evident in practice is the actual value of culture as a resource disappears behind thin and superficial descriptions, slogans, and wishful thinking (Alvesson & Sveningsson, 2008), often at great effort and financial cost. In its popularity the concept has been untethered from its intellectual foundations to such an extent that, ironically, its potential as a domain for organizational improvement is seriously in doubt. At some point the culture fad will give way to disillusionment, resulting in its abandonment altogether.

1. Functionally Embodied Culture

Against these notions I will propose an alternative, one that offers the possibility of bridging intellectual divides by providing a framework that fully accounts for cultural phenomena in organizations. This framework shifts the lens through which culture is analyzed and, as a result, offers the possibility of more robust, systemic, precise and sustainable interventions.

In this new framework, culture *does* consist of values, norms, habits and practices and so forth, but these are culture's manifestations, not its roots. It is first and foremost a *cognitive* phenomenon whose affordances manifest in human systems through a myriad of structures, practices, language and behavior. Culture is a pervasive phenomenon of human communities, manifesting as cognitive codifications of ecological and physical contingencies that are mostly *invisible* as ontological objects. This pervasiveness accounts for its popularity. Managers and practitioners have the correct intuition in imagining culture's influence on collective behavior. But their intuition is akin to quantum physicists' study of dark matter: they know something is there, but they cannot yet fully explain what it is or why it is there. Thus, their interventions are surface ones, consequently limited and incapable of imparting sustained change. Culture is also not a purely social construction, a subject of the hegemonic or narcissistic impulses of those in power. Instead, it is loosely but distinctively ecological, underwritten by human cognition grounded in the functional, technological and social forces inherent in work, and the production of systems of meaning accompanying work. This foundation is strongly suggested by recent advances in cognitive science and represents an exciting, and to date untapped basis for understanding where culture in organizations comes from. As such it offers promise for practitioners while helping to unify diverse theoretical perspectives.

Dynamic Embodiment

This new framework begins with the idea people are a part and product of their environments, in the sense human ontogenesis is not only the result of a genetic program but occurs in a developmental system in which cognitive development is at least partially 'scaffolded' by the external environment (Griffiths & Stotz, 2000, p. 29; Bolender, 2008). Theory and evidence put forth by the so-called embodiment school of modern cognitive science supports the idea that cognition is dynamically embodied, emerging from the kinesthetic, social and cultural experience of the human organism in its surroundings (for example, see de Bruin & Kastner, 2012; Hutchins, 2010; Johnson, 1987; Kitayama & Park, 2010; Stewart, 2010; Varela, Thompson, & Rosch, 1991).[3] How we think, reason and make sense of the world is mediated and structured by our embodied minds, embodied not only in the literal sense of our brains encased within our own skulls but also in the sense of being embedded, interconnected and actively mediated by the physical, social and cultural worlds of which we are a part (Hutchins, 2000). To accept this, then, is to accept these dynamics are no less a part of human experience in *organizational settings* as they are in any other realm.

Culture under this view is the product of shared cognitive representations, in the form of shared schemas and mental models that arise through, or are induced by, repeated and sustained experience working in and making meaning in particular task, technology and sociocultural environments. Specifically, these are the environments associated with *professionalization*, and (or) *strategic task contexts*. As such, all organizations have cultures. To the extent organizations manifest distinctly discernible and relatively unified cultures is, I suggest, the product of these two interrelated processes. The sustained experience involved in becoming a professional, as well as the tasks, technologies, routines, and normative environments people experience in accomplishing work, especially in contexts with highly differentiated and meaningful missions, provides the cognitive grounding for culture. This occurs via cognitive representations neurologically induced by repeated and sustained exposure and interaction with the material and social environment that are analogically but (mostly) unconsciously applied to new situations through sensemaking, a dynamic that reinforces the prevailing sense of culture or cultures. I call this dynamic the *functionally embodied framework* for organizational culture. Culture, thus, is the product of collective minds making meaning in dynamic worlds. In this way culture is less a dependent variable or object of control and more ecologically contingent, a phenomenon only *partially* available for enactment and change.

2. Foundations

To put forth a new framework for organizational culture is, of course, ambitious. My hope here is to not recreate another culture study extolling its own literature, tradition, and appeals to authority. Counteracting this will require casting a wide net, drawing from disciplines well beyond management and organization or industrial–organizational psychology, the traditional provinces of organizational culture research.

The theoretical launching point here is embodied cognition, a branch of cognitive science that emerged in the last 30 years representing a departure from traditional computational theories of mind that dominated the mid 20th century (Hutchins, 2000). And while this project is rooted, in spirit if not in epistemology, in cognitive anthropology, it falls into liminal space between disciplines as I synthesize, translate and apply diverse literatures and perspectives. The lack of a narrowly drawn intellectual home base may trouble some readers intent on locating this project in a particular camp. But the only way to penetrate intellectual silos is to search farther afield. The broad insights of cognitive science provide a way to do just that; theory and research on embodied cognition unifies disparate approaches to culture by refocusing on what gives rise to cultural meaning systems to begin with— the embodied and situated mind. By definition this requires synthesizing the perspectives emerging from cognitive neuroscience, psychology, linguistics, anthropology, and sociology.

Such a synthesis carries some risk. For one, I do not claim expertise in all of the fields upon which this work is based. I have been formally researching and developing the theoretical foundation and framework for this book for over 10 years, longer if one counts my many years as a practitioner, but this hardly qualifies me as an expert outside of anthropology and management. I rely on other scholars, and on scholarly intuition and triangulation, on which to privilege research. On the other hand, I suggest it takes—for lack of better—a relative generalist, a scholar–practitioner at that, to synthesize research across disciplines so as to overcome the inertia of narrowly drawn organizational culture theory. The intense focus on culture over the last 40 years has yet to produce consensus on even its most basic questions. Meanwhile, the state of practice can be characterized as *The Wild West*: just about anything that can be operationalized as culture, is. It would be an understatement to say the field is ready—the practitioner in me would say *clamoring*—for something substantive and new. The functionally embodied approach is just that.

For what is the alternative? Would a neuroscientist or cognitive psychologist have the practical orientation, or interest, to tackle this subject? Certainly cognitively-oriented management scholars (for example, Bingham & Kahl; Argyris & Schon, 1996; Erez & Earley, 1993; Harris, 1994; Johnson, 1990; Steiger & Steiger, 2008; Walsh, 1995) have been working with schema theory for a number of years, but few except for the pioneers Harris and Erez and Earley tilted at the organizational culture windmill. Perhaps it takes the odd duck to move the conversation forward. Waiting for sufficient expertise across all disciplines to emerge will mean waiting a long time. And only a multi-disciplinary approach is broad enough to sustain a new kind of praxis. And as Martin and Frost (2011) point out, what the organizational culture field needs more of now is imagination, and courage.

The best way I know to address this risk is to maintain a reflexive stance, what Alvesson and Skoldberg (2009) see as "the very ability to break away from a frame of reference to look at what it is *not* capable of saying" (p. 271). This means being engaged in a dialog with one's own material, broad as it may be, to state clearly one's assumptions and biases, and to condition theory and findings. In the tradition of Dewey and James, it means viewing theory through the lens of practice to ask 'to what use could this theory be put', and 'how does this phenomenon manifest in practice in my experience?' This kind of phenomenology admittedly is ambitious, but I suggest is the most effective mitigation to the challenges posed.

Cognitive anthropology itself is a field characterized by a diversity of thought and fuzzy boundaries with related fields such as cognitive developmental psychology and linguistics. The concept of an embodied and ecologically embedded culture in anthropology is not new. It is built upon the structural anthropology of Levi Strauss (1985) and Bourdieu's *habitus* (1990), although the idea of cultural structuring can be traced to Ruth Benedict (1934) and later Hallowell (1976) and Goodenough (1981). More directly, this project is guided by the work of Philippe Descola (2013), whose conception of cultures as "governed" by "cognitive and corporeal" templates, or "schemas of practice" provides much of the theoretical brick and mortar for this work (p. 92). Schemas "might make it possible to take account of the whole gamut of relations to existing beings" (p. 94). In positing the existence of so-called "integrating" schemas (p. 110) as structuring dynamics underpinning cultures, my argument is a kind of extended case study utilizing his framework, but instead of the Achuar of Amazonia one situated within a modern, global manufacturing organization.

Pragmatically, the pioneering work of Naomi Quinn and Claudia Strauss (1997) and the so-called 'cultural models' school of cognitive anthropology provide the project's inspiration and method. I also use research from cognitive anthropologists who study cognition in practice (notably Bennardo, 2011; Hutchins, 2005, 2010), as well those who use quantitative methods for establishing the validity of cultural schemas (D'Andrade, 1995; Handwerker, 2002).

Within the management cognition literature, of course, the notion of schemas and cognitive representation has a 30-year tradition (for example, see Bartunek & Moch, 1987; Bingham & Kahl, 2013; Gordon, 1991; Ravasi & Schultz, 2006; Rentsch & Klimoski, 2001; Senge, 1992; Sieck, Rasmussen & Smart, 2010) But much of it suffers from a lack of definitional clarity that dilutes its efficacy in practice.[4] There are over 100 distinct but closely related definitions of schemas and similar constructs in this literature (Walsh, 1995), and this has implications. A small difference in definition, such as defining schemas as "frameworks that give meaning to experience" (Labianca, Gray, & Brass, 2000, p. 235) rather than, say, "firm knowledge" (Gertler, 2004) has large impacts on the assertions and conclusions drawn, as well as what is privileged in practice. The lack of precision and consensus in the literature contributes to schema theory remaining in a kind of prolonged idle. Little of it has yet to find its way into the practitioner mainstream.

And with few exceptions, this literature is not directly concerned with culture. One exception is Harris (1994), who saw schemas as containers for cultural knowledge and the source of sensemaking, and identified schemas as maps that create cultural experiences. He also suggested schemas are a source of emotional attachment. I follow the path blazed by Harris but believe he does not go far enough in establishing their salience and pervasiveness as underpinnings of culture. Similarly, while my claim of cognitive processes playing a pivotal role in organizations can be traced to the work of Erez and Earley (1993), they posit these processes reside within a static and monolithic culture whereas I see culture as ecologically contingent and the negotiated product of collective sense and meaning-making. Moreover, this work is the first I know of that offers a comprehensive view of *how and why* schemas and cultural models underwrite culture, *and what that means for theory practice.*

My thinking on professional culture has been influenced by Gordon (1991) and Chatman and Jehn (1994), as well as by researchers focused on the relationship between work and meaning, a generally neglected sub-field (Barley, 1990, 1996; Louis, 1985). As Van Maanen and Barley (1984) observe, "social worlds coalesce around the objects produced and the services rendered by people at work" (pp. 4–5):

> Organization researchers largely disregard the phenomenological boundaries recognized by members of particular work worlds. Descriptions of these intersubjective boundaries and the shared activities, social interactions, and common understandings established by those who fall within these boundaries . . . represent lively, rich accounts of occupational ways of life; accounts we believe must be reckoned with if organizational theories are to locate and explain more of the behavioral variability of the workplace than has been the case to date.
>
> (p. 1)

Edgar Schein (1984, 1992) presaged the concept of schemas underwriting culture in his idea "basic assumptions" (see also Heskett, 2011). His model is entirely compatible with the idea of functionally embodied culture.[5] The functionally embodied framework adds explanatory power to Schein's model by explaining *how* basic assumptions underpin and endow cultures with their sense of pervasiveness. And yet while this work is, in part, an elaboration of his model, this is the first attempt, to my knowledge, to weave theories of embodiment, schema induction and analogical transfer, cultural models and sensemaking together into a comprehensive framework for organizational culture and change.

IMCO: A Theory-Based Case

The site of the research for this book is IMCO, a Fortune 1000 diversified manufacturer of highly engineered components and technology for the energy, transportation and industrial markets.[6] IMCO undertook a culture-'shaping' program in 2013, thus this book can be read as a contrapuntal line illustrating the functionally embodied framework underneath IMCO's culture-shaping effort. I was not in any way involved in the culture-shaping project but was fortunate to have observed it during the course of my own research at the company. That IMCO is my client as well as my research site, of course, has interesting interpretive implications that I discuss in some detail.

In positing an alternative to culture-shaping, I will show how the program undertaken by IMCO executives may not yield the hoped-for benefits because it will clash with more deeply held shared schemas and cultural models manifesting at all levels of the organization. These will act as barriers to fully adopting the aspired values and norms, which, two years after the launch of this program, is proving to be the case. In so far as IMCO's culture shaping is emblematic of the mainstream of culture change practice in most large corporations, this case provides a frame through which to apprehend a fresh approach.

3. How This Book Is Organized

This book is in two parts. In the first I describe the research supporting functionally embodied culture, and lay out the elements of the framework. In the second I address two closely related questions: *How do schemas manifest in organizations?* And *what preliminary evidence is there, if any, for the functional embodied culture framework at IMCO?*

By showing the organization of schemas and how they function in practice at IMCO, the concept of a functionally embodied culture comes to life. The evidence presented is rich and abundant, and acquired through multiple means. By validating thethrough quantitative methods with a broader sample the schemas identified though informant interviews, as well as by tracing schema affordances in practice within IMCO, preliminary evidence for functional embodiment is seen. Specifically, I show how schemas and models themselves tend not to be directly discernible but become visible through their 'affordance structures': Their manifestations in tasks, processes and patterns of organizational behavior.

Identifying schemas, of course, presents several epistemological and methodological challenges. At the same time, if these challenges can be bridged, new vistas for research and practice open up because, following Descola, they represent the 'deep structures' that unify social domains. Intervention in these deep structures, and their manifestations in practice, I suggest, will yield sustainable solutions to the many seemingly intractable problems of social and cultural conflict and change that today seem out of reach.

Chapters

Chapter 1 addresses issues in organizational culture theory and practice. I review the major tenets of positivist (or 'objectivist') and constructivist (or 'subjectivist') approaches. With respect to the former, while there is an important need for verifiable and generalizable knowledge about culture in organizations, objectivist approaches tend to suffer from problems of ontology, epistemology, and ideation. Within these I focus on two popular reductive conceptions of culture: as personality traits, and as values, and discuss the shortcomings of each. I also show how the functionally embodied approach may better explain cultural phenomena observed at some well-known cases.

Conversely, subjectivist approaches, while in the minority, suffer from a lack of pragmatic relevance. I suggest it is the divide between these orientations that is partially to blame for how culture is operationalized in practice by describing two prevalent issues: Construct oversimplification and managerial self-enhancement.

Embodiment poses a significant challenge to the popular narrative of culture willfully imposed by top management. Chapter 2, thus, establishes the foundation for a functionally embodied theory of organizational culture by working through the research on embodiment and its corollaries. I provide a review of the theoretical positions making up the embodiment thesis, and explore the extensive neuroscientific, experimental, developmental and linguistic evidence supporting embodied cognition, theories of representation (schemas) and analogical transfer.

Radical embodiment, or 'enacted', cognition challenges traditional cognitivism by claiming little or no role for mental representation (de Bruin & Kastner, 2012, Stewart, Gapenne, & Di Paolo, 2010). While the notion of a non-representational, dynamically emerging and socioculturally situated theory of cognition offers a compelling reorientation to computational theories of mind, a more modest view holds that representation is essential for much 'off-line' processing, including abstract and analogical reasoning as well as artistic and moral imagination (de Bruin & Kastner, 2012; Johnson, 1993). The functionally embodied framework for culture draws from this more modest representationalist framework. I close with a review of some of the challenges to embodiment and schema theory.

Embodiment does not fully explain how schemas and cultural models function as 'culture'. Thus Chapter 3 is devoted to how this happens. Meaning-making in general, and sensemaking effort in particular, I suggest, are the principal drivers of culture formation in organizations and how cultural schemas and models, as meaning-generating devices, come to constitute culture. I outline a schema-model hierarchy that explains how abstract models are built up from more concrete, foundational ones (D'Andrade, 1995). I then focus on how schemas are treated in the management cognition literature, including what (little) has been done in relation to organizational culture. In particular, I draw upon the neglected work of Fred Steele (1972) to show how organizational 'overlearning' may be a manifestation of schema transposition from core professional orientation or purpose to delimit and constrain other areas of organizational functioning.

It is one thing to suggest embodied cognition and cultural schemas play a role in organizational culture. It is quite another to establish a theory for what gives rise to culture in organizations to begin with. Chapter 4 does just that. 'Functional' embodiment refers to the structuring of cognition on the basis of social and task work experience at what Gallagher (2005) calls a *prenoetic* stage, at a level below phenomenal or conscious experience. Its important to note here that 'functional' does not refer to *functionalism*. The latter is a strategy that views cognition as reducible to computation and silicon-based processes (Gallagher, 2005). The sense of functional I intend is in relation to task and work, that is, in the production of *things* material, and in social experience. What is being claimed is not simply that embodied and situated experience shapes mental content, but that it structures *how* people think and behave, and what they find meaningful. This has profound implications for theory and practice.

In its most basic terms, the idea is simple: organizations develop cultures by doing work and producing goods and services. This comes about either through their dominant professional orientations or through strategic task context. Task context refers to the tasks, routines, technologies, practices, and social norms enrolled in the fulfillment of the firm's basic mission and strategy. Professionalization and strategic task contexts tend to be highly meaningful for their constituents; their very meaningfulness is what induces schemas, although how this happens is obviously quite complex. Organizations that have highly differentiated task contexts in the form of unique missions and purpose will tend to have particularly strong grounding contexts.

Of course, most large organizations are comprised of many different professional communities and most, at the surface, do not show evidence of a single distinct professional culture. More than just a dominant professional group or a strategic task context is needed to enable the formation of an identifiable culture. The 'yeast' in culture formation, thus, is sensemaking. Sensemaking draws from the available reservoirs of cultural schemas, reservoirs endowed by prevailing cognitive predispositions and orientations. If the available schemas are robust enough in their sensemaking utility and motivational force, and are continually reinforced through aligned structures and processes, they will come to make up a definable and palpable organizational culture.

Chapter 5 is devoted to a discussion of the research methods used to uncover schemas and establish their valance within a social community. Research into schemas is fraught with ontological and epistemic issues; thus I begin with an examination of these issues and the strategies used to neutralize them. As my research involves discourse, I include a brief incursion into the issue of linguistic relativity. I review Quinn's (2005) method for adducing schemas, as well as secondary methods involving conceptual metaphor and metonymy (Radden, 2003). I then outline the quantitative methods involving factor and principal components analysis used to validate the findings adduced through the qualitative study.

In Chapter 6 I present the results from the IMCO research. While provisional, the results are promising. Evidence of functional grounding is visible in both qualitative and quantitative results. The chapter offers comprehensive and detailed accounts of how schemas are visualized in causal logic, and how metaphor source domain analysis is used to support the schema findings, along with the quantitative studies. Notable also is an analysis of how certain conventional metonymies function as cognitive artefacts, which lends further support to functional grounding.

Chapter 7 describes the locus of functional grounding at IMCO, as well as schema affordance structures. Affordances are the many ways in which schemas manifest as practices and adaptations. For example, one of the most prevalent schemas identified has to do with the virtue of first-hand experience: What is not known first-hand by management tends not to be thought of as valuable or trustworthy. Many formal and informal practices at IMCO reify practices emphasizing first-hand experience, which results in adaptations of excessive control and low trust. Affordances in this way illuminate the links between schemas and practice, highlighting the particular logic embedded in practices that is often difficult to discern until one beholds all practices at once. In tracing these linkages, this chapter fully exposes how functionally grounded cognition underpins culture and helps explain why, for example, it is difficult for a manufacturing company to function, culturally speaking, as a data science or Internet company, as many today seek to do.

The functionally embodied framework also explains why culture shaping is difficult. And yet there appear to be counterexamples. Chapter 8 explores a few of these provided by so-called *Deliberately Developmental Organizations* (Kegan & Lahey, 2016), concluding that functional grounding also can account for these examples. I then discuss the broader implications of these findings in light of IMCO's culture-shaping project, including how it enriches theory and practice. With respect to the latter, I conclude with a brief discussion of schema elicitation techniques for managers and practitioners.

The functionally embodied approach establishes culture as the product of shared schemas and sensemaking. Change work using this approach, by definition, requires interventions at all levels of an organizational system, illuminating and targeting affordance structures close to a firm's core means of production and its most revered practices. While the call for systemic interventions is by no means unique, the functionally embodied perspective explains *why* change is so hard, and why efforts that deal with surface effects or rely on top-down programs are non-starters. This means leaders in complex organizations cannot expect to 'set' their own culture. That is not to say leadership does not matter, but leadership in the cognitive-cultural world requires much more knowledge of how culture actually takes shape in human minds and practices, and far greater sophistication in knowing what to do about it.

4. Contributions

To paraphrase Bennardo and Kronnenfeld (2011), our explorations in the cultural mind are just beginning. Nowhere is this truer than in the domain of organizational culture. This book represents several first ascents: it is the first to show how theories of schema induction and transposability, eloquently described by Descola (2013) but with substantive bases in cognitive psychology and linguistics, exist in organizational and institutional settings. This is the first fully elaborated account of culture that shows how, and why, professional and task grounding are its cognitive roots.[7] This book is also first documented use of Naomi Quinn's (2005) method for schema elicitation, opening up her pioneering work to a new domain of praxis. Following D'Andrade (1995), this work provides further evidence for understanding cultural models as hierarchies of meaning, which may be of interest to cognitive linguists and anthropologist, as well as organizational change practitioners interested in systemic interventions.

While sensemaking is widely studied in the literature (Weick, 1995; Weick, Sutcliffe, & Obstfeld, 2005), much of it does not account for how knowledge structures are formed, where schemas come from (Mohammed, Ferzandi, & Hamilton, 2010; Walsh, 1995), or what makes these structures meaningful to begin with. This work also introduces the idea of a so-called sensemaking boundary to explain the conditions under which schemas are revised.

I suspect some readers may have a 'so what' reaction to this book. Practitioners might be liable to say 'that's just simply engineering culture or manufacturing culture'. To a large extent they will be right, but their observations will be incomplete. Because while what is presented in these pages may feel intuitively correct, there is little understanding of why it is correct. What are the mechanisms that underpin culture? What is the nature of the structural logic that gives a particular organizational or occupational milieu its character and distinctness rendering it categorically different from another? This is the central question motivating this book.

For some, functionally embodied culture may appear not only as new but also as problematic because its locus is the realm of implicit knowledge and learning. How do we know what we cannot see or directly measure? Yet cognitive anthropology is well ahead of management science on the topic of culture. Beyond the many ways illustrated here, the most important is that it bridges objectivist–subjectivist dualism by accepting culture's embodied and situated basis while accounting for its co-constructed manifestations.

The functionally embodied alternative represents a cognitive and embodied turn in organizational theory and practice, with exciting implications. The grounding of culture recasts theory in ecologically, technologically, functionally and socially situated terms while opening up new research and intervention possibilities based on the fabric of collective meaning. As put by Descola (2013):

> It seems that what a structural analysis reveals, when well conducted, is a way of assessing an understanding of the schematization of experience carried out by the members of a collectivity and the manner in which this serves as a framework for the explicit codification systems to which its members adhere.
>
> (p. 110)

Most of all, a framework that unifies subjective experience with material reality allows a shift to be made in how we study and intervene in culture. That shift is from thinking of systems and bureaucracies as either wholly autonomous, the result of powerful individual actors causally shaping their environments, or wholly intersubjective hermeneutic milieus of arbitrariness, to thinking of cultures as cognitively embodied in actors who themselves are dynamically situated and embedded in social, historical, technological and wider cultural contexts in which they only partially have agency. This brings to mind Descola's (2013) assertion that the task of anthropology is to understand how ontologies come to be considered "self evident to some people in certain places and at certain epochs" (p. 68). Such is the challenge confronting the investigator of organizational culture. It is difficult to jump into the cultural divide without potentially undermining the concept altogether, since my argument is set in relief against both objectivist and subjectivist camps. And yet what is at stake, I submit, is the very existence of the concept. Managers, after all, are pragmatists (Spender, 1996). Failures in theory already manifest as failures in practice; without better frameworks, the culture concept will eventually be abandoned. We clearly need a more up-to-date, comprehensive and sustainable approaches to culture and change, an approach capable of addressing challenges and conflicts that today are thought of as intractable. What comes forth in these chapters offers that alternative.

Notes

1 A recent search on Google Scholar on the terms "Enron" and "corporate culture" returned 8,110 results. While not every article of course will attempt to establish a causal link between Enron's culture and the company's demise, the fact the two concepts appear together so often is suggestive of how prevalent and popular it is to link the two terms. If the search is narrowed to "Enron failure" and "corporate culture," a search returns 94 results (for the Volkswagen example, see J.B. Stewart, *New York Times*, September 25, 2015).
2 For example, managers in mergers are often confronted with contradictory frames of reference that create impediments to integration and a cause of irrational decision making (Vaara, 2003).
3 The term "dynamic embodied cognition" is de Bruin and Kastner's (2012).
4 It should be noted this lack of clarity mirrors the general lack of definitional clarity for schemas found in the broader cognitive psychology, linguistics and anthropology literature. See Chapter 2.
5 However, it should be noted Schein believed cultures could be shaped. I am more skeptical. See also Chapter 2.
6 Not the company's real name.
7 Swidler (2001), for example, offers an excellent treatment of schemas as "toolkits" for cultural practice, but does not go as far as to suggest these are underwriters of culture.

Bibliography

Alvesson, M., & Skoldberg, K. (2009). *Reflexive methodology: New vistas for qualitative research*. Los Angeles: Sage.
Alvesson, M., & Sveningsson, S. (2008). *Changing organizational culture: Cultural change work in progress*. Abingdon: Routledge.
Argyris, C. S., & Schön, D. (1996). *Organizational learning II: Theory, method and practice*. Reading, PA: Addison-Wesley.
Balogun, J., & Johnson, G. (2005). From intended strategies to unintended outcomes: The impact of change recipient sensemaking. *Organization Studies*, 26(11), 1573–1601.
Barley, S. R. (1990). The alignment of technology and structure through roles and networks. *Administrative Science Quarterly*, 35(1), 61–103.
Barley, S. R. (1996). Technicians in the workplace: Ethnographic evidence for bringing work into organization studies. *Administrative Science Quarterly*, 41(3), 404–441.
Bartunek, J., & Moch, M. (1987). First order, second order, and third order change and organizational development interventions: A cognitive approach. *The Journal of Applied Behavioral Science*, 23, 483–500. Retrieved from http://scholar.google.com/.
Bates, K. A., Amundson, S. D., Schroeder, R. G., & Morris, W. T. (1995). The crucial interrelationship between manufacturing strategy and organizational culture. *Management Science*, 41(10), 1565–1580.

Benedict, R. (1934). *Patterns of culture* (Vol. 8). New York: Houghton Mifflin Harcourt.

Bennardo, G. (2011). A foundational cultural model in Polynesia: Monarchy, democracy, and the architecture of the mind. In D. Kronenfeld, G. Bennardo, V. de Munck, & M. Fischer (Eds.), *A companion to cognitive anthropology* (pp. 471–488). Malden, MA: Wiley-Blackwell.

Bennardo, G., & Kronnenfeld, D. (2011). Types of collective representations: Cognition, mental architecture, and cultural knowledge. In D. Kronenfeld, G. Bennardo, V. de Munck, & M. Fischer (Eds.), *A companion to cognitive anthropology* (pp. 82–101). Malden, MA: Wiley-Blackwell.

Bingham, C., & Kahl, S. (2013). The process of schema emergence: Assimilation, deconstruction, utilization, and the plurality of analogies. *Academy of Management Journal, 56,* 14–34. Retrieved from http://dx.doi.org.10.5465/amj.2010.0723.

Bolender, J. (2008). Hints of beauty in social cognition: Broken symmetries in mental dynamics. *New Ideas in Psychology, 26*(1), 1–22.

Bourdieu, P. (1990). *The logic of practice.* Stanford: Stanford University Press.

Bruner, R. (2001). *Does M&A pay? A survey of evidence for the decision-maker.* Retrieved from http://scholar.google.com/scholar?hl=en&q=M%26A&btnG=&as_sdt=1%2C5&as_sdtp=.

Bryant, A. (2009–2015). The corner office. *The New York Times (2009–2012).* Retrieved from http://projects.nytimes.com/corner-office.

Chatman, J., & Jehn, K. (1994). Assessing the relationship between industry characteristics and organizational culture. How different can you be? *Academy of Management Journal, 37,* 522–553. Retrieved from http://scholar.google.com/.

Corporate Leadership Council. (2004). *Driving performance and retention through employee engagement.* Washington, DC: Corporate Executive Board.

D'Andrade, R. (1995). *The development of cognitive anthropology.* Cambridge: Cambridge University Press.

de Bruin, L. C., & Kästner, L. (2012). Dynamic embodied cognition. *Phenomenology and the Cognitive Sciences, 11*(4), 541–563.

Deal, T., & Kennedy, A. (1982). *Corporate cultures: The rites and rituals of corporate life.* Cambridge, MA: Perseus Publishing.

Denison, D. (1990). *Corporate culture and organizational effectiveness.* New York: John Wiley & Sons.

Descola, P. (2013). *Beyond nature and culture.* Chicago: University of Chicago Press.

Erez, M., & Earley, P. (1993). *Culture, self identity, and work.* Oxford: Oxford University Press.

Fleck, L. (1979). *Genesis and development of a scientific fact* (Fred Bradley and Thaddeus Trenn, Trans.). Chicago: University of Chicago Press. (Original work published 1935.)

Frost, P. J., Moore, L. F., Louis, M. R., Lundberg, C. C., & Martin, J. (1985). An allegorical view of organizational culture. In P. J. Frost, L. F. Moore, M. R. Louis, C. C. Lundberg, & J. Martin (Eds.), *Organizational culture* (pp. 13–25). Newbury Park, CA: Sage.

Gallagher, S. (2005). *How the body shapes the mind.* New York: Oxford University Press.

Gallup. (2016). State of the American workplace. Retrieved from www.gallup.com/services/178514/state-american-workplace.aspx?g_source=EMPLOYEE_ENGAGEMENT&g_medium=topic&g_campaign=tiles.

Gertler, M. (2004). *Manufacturing culture: The institutional geography of industrial practice.* Oxford: Oxford University Press.

Goodenough, W. (1981). *Culture, language and society* (2nd ed.). Menlo Park: Benjamin/Cummings.

Gordon, G. G. (1991). Industry determinants of organizational culture. *Academy of Management Review, 16*(2), 396–415.

Griffiths, P., & Stotz, K. (2000). How the mind grows: A developmental perspective on the biology of cognition. *Synthese, 122,* 29–51.

Hallowell, I. (1976). *Selected papers of irving Hallowell.* Chicago: University of Chicago Press. (Originally published in 1954.)

Handwerker, W. P. (2002). The construct validity of cultures: Cultural diversity, culture theory, and a method for ethnography. *American Anthropologist, 104*(1), 106–122.

Harris, S. (1994). Organizational culture and individual sensemaking: A schema-based perspective. *Organization Science, 1,* 309–321. Retrieved from http://scholar.google.com/.

Heskett, J. (2011). *The culture cycle: How to shape the unseen force that transforms performance.* Upper Saddle River, NJ: FT Press.

Hutchins, E. (2000). Distributed cognition. International Encyclopedia of the Social & Behavioral Sciences (4th ed., pp. 2068–2072). Amsterdam: Elsevier.

Hutchins, E. (2005). Material anchors for conceptual blends. *Journal of Pragmatics, 37,* 1555–1577. Retrieved from http://scholar.google.com/

Hutchins, E. (2010). Enaction, imagination, and insight. In J. Stewart, O. Gapenne, & A. Di Paolo (Eds.), *Enaction: Toward a new paradigm for cognitive science* (pp. 425–450). Cambridge, MA: MIT Press.

Johnson, G. (1990). Managing strategic change: The role of symbolic action. *British Journal of Management, 1,* 183–200.

Johnson, M. (1987). *The body in the mind.* Chicago: University of Chicago Press.

Johnson, M. (1993). *Moral imagination: The implications of cognitive science for ethics.* Chicago: University of Chicago Press.

Kegan, R., & Lahey, L. L. (2016). *An everyone culture: Becoming a deliberately developmental organization.* Cambridge, MA: Harvard Business School Publishing.

Kelly, J., Cook, C., & Spitzer, D. (1999). *Unlocking shareholder value: The keys to success.* Mergers and Acquisitions: A Global Research Report. A Study by KPMG.

Kitayama, S., & Park, J. (2010). Cultural neuroscience of the self: Understanding the social grounding of the brain. *Social Cognitive and Affective Neuroscience, 5,* 111–129. doi: 10.1093/scan/nsq052.

Kotter, J. P., & Heskett, J. L. (1992). *Corporate culture and performance.* New York: The Free Press.

Kunda, G. (1992). *Engineering culture: Control and communication in a high-tech corporation.* Philadelphia: Temple University Press.

Labianca, G., Gray, B., & Brass, D. J. (2000). A grounded model of organizational schema change during empowerment. *Organization Science, 11*(2), 235–257.

Larsson, R., & Finkelstein, S. (1999). Integrating strategic, organizational, and human resource perspectives on mergers and acquisitions: A case survey of synergy realization. *Organization Science, 10*(1), 1–26.

Learning the lingo. (2014, January 11). *The Economist,* p. 72.

Levi-Strauss, C. (1985). *The view from afar.* New York: Basic Books.

Lockwood, N. R. (2007). Leveraging employee engagement for competitive advantage. *Society for Human Resource Management Research Quarterly, 1*, 1–12.

Louis, M. R. (1985). An investigator's guide to workplace culture. In P. Frost, L. Moore, M. R. Louis, C. Lundberg, & J. Martin (Eds.), *Organizational culture* (pp. 73–94). Newbury Park, CA: Sage.

Martin, J. (2002). *Organizational culture: Mapping the terrain.* Thousand Oaks, CA: Sage.

Martin, J., & Frost, P. (2011). The organizational culture war games: A struggle for intellectual dominance. In M. Godwin & J. Hoffer Gittell (Eds.), *Sociology of organizations: Structures and relationships* (pp. 559–621). Thousand Oaks, CA: Sage. Retrieved from http://scholar.google.com/.

Mohammed, S., Ferzandi, L., & Hamilton, K. (2010). Metaphor no more: A 15-year review of the team mental model construct. *Journal of Management, 36*(4), 876–910.

Norris, F. (2014, March 28). History gives other cases of G.M.'s behavior. *The New York Times*, pp. B1, B8.

Ogbonna, E., & Wilkinson, B. (2003). The false promise of organizational culture change: A case study of middle managers in grocery retailing. *Journal of Management Studies, 40*(5), 1151–1178.

Polanyi, M. (1958). *Personal knowledge.* Chicago: University of Chicago Press.

Quinn, N. (2005). How to reconstruct schemas people share, from what they say. In N. Quinn (Ed.), *Finding culture in talk* (pp. 35–84). New York: Palgrave Macmillan.

Radden, G. (2003). How metonymic are metaphors? In R. Dirven & R. Pörings (Eds.), *Cognitive linguistics research: Metaphor and metonymy in comparison and contrast* (pp. 419–445). Berlin: Mouton de Gruyter.

Ralls, J. G., & Webb, K. A. (1999). *The nature of chaos in business: Using complexity to foster successful alliances and acquisitions.* Houston, TX: Gulf Publishing.

Ravasi, D., & Schultz, M. (2006). Responding to organizational identity threats: Exploring the role of organizational culture. *Academy of Management Journal, 49*(3), 433–458.

Rentsch, J. R., & Klimoski, R. J. (2001). Why do 'great minds' think alike? Antecedents of team member schema agreement. *Journal of Organizational Behavior, 22*(2), 107–120.

Schein, E. H. (1984). Coming to a new awareness of organizational culture. *Sloan Management Review, 25*(2), 3–16.

Schein, E. H. (1992). *Organizational culture and leadership* (2nd ed.). San Francisco: Jossey-Bass.

Senge, P. M. (1992). Mental models. *Planning Review, 20*(2), 4–44.

Sieck, W., Rasmussen, L., & Smart, P. R. (2010). Cultural network analysis: A cognitive approach to cultural modeling. In V. Dinesh (Ed.), *Network science for military coalition operations: Information extraction and interaction* (pp. 237–255). Hershey, PA: ICI Global.

Siehl, C. (1985). After the founder: An opportunity to manage culture. In P. Frost, L. Moore, M. R. Louis, C. Lundberg, & J. Martin (Eds.), *Organizational culture* (pp. 125–140). Newbury Park, CA: Sage.

Spender, J. C. (1996). Making knowledge the basis of a dynamic theory of the firm. *Strategic Management Journal, 17*, 45–62.

Steele, F. I. (1972). Organizational overlearning. *Journal of Management Studies,* *9*(3), 303–313.

Steiger, D., & Steiger, N. (2008). Instance-based cognitive mapping: A process for discovering a knowledge worker's tacit mental model. *Knowledge Management Research & Practice, 6,* 312–321.

Stewart, A., & Aldrich, H. (2015). Collaboration between management and anthropology researchers: Obstacles and opportunities. *The Academy of Management Perspectives, 29*(2), 173–192.

Stewart, J. (2010). Introduction. In J. Stewart, O. Gapenne, & A. Di Paolo (Eds.), *Enaction: Toward a new paradigm for cognitive science* (vii–xvi). Cambridge, MA: MIT Press.

Strauss, C., & Quinn, N. (1997). *A cognitive theory of cultural meaning.* Cambridge: Cambridge University Press.

Swidler, A. (2001). What anchors cultural practices. In T. Schatzki, K. Knorr-Cetina, & E. Von Savigny (Eds.), *The practice turn in contemporary theory* (pp. 74–92). London: Routledge.

Vaara, E. (2003). Post-acquisition integration as sensemaking: Glimpses of ambiguity, confusion, hypocrisy, and politicization. *Journal of Management Studies, 40*(4), 859–894.

Van Maanen, J., & Barley, S. (1984). *Occupational communities: Culture and control in organizations* (No. TR-ONR-10). Cambridge, MA: Alfred P. Sloan School of Management.

Varela, F. J., Thompson, E., & Rosch, E. (1991). *The embodied mind.* Cambridge, MA: MIT Press.

Walsh, J. P. (1995). Managerial and organizational cognition: Notes from a trip down memory lane. *Organization Science, 6*(3), 280–321.

Weick, K. E. (1995). *Sensemaking in organizations.* Thousand Oaks, CA: Sage.

Weick, K. E., Sutcliffe, K. M., & Obstfeld, D. (2005). Organizing and the process of sensemaking. *Organization Science, 16*(4), 409–421.

Part I

Functionally Embodied Culture

1 What's Wrong with Organizational Culture?

On April 1, 2014, IMCO,[1] a nearly 100 year-old diversified manufacturer of highly engineered components and technology for the energy, transportation and industrial markets, held a three-day Leadership Summit for its top 200 managers at the Ritz Carlton in Battery Park, New York City. This was a significant moment in IMCO's history. Never had this company sponsored an event solely dedicated to shaping its own culture. As a consultant working with the company for over five years, I felt privileged to be invited.

IMCO was founded in 1920. During the 1960s and 1970s the company was known as the quintessential conglomerate, acquiring hundreds of companies across different industries, from telecommunications to casinos. Over time, the company divested, and in 1995 spun off its non-manufacturing divisions. In 2011 the company split itself into three: one focused on technology for the defense market, one on water treatment and transport and related technologies, and one retaining the IMCO brand focused on industrial technology. This 'new' IMCO went from a $12 billion, multi-industry conglomerate with close to 25,000 employees to a '$2 billion start up', as IMCO managers like to characterize it, with 9,000 employees, sales in 120 countries, and operations in 35.[2] As stated in the IMCO Factbook:

IMCO makes products and technologies that make other products operate:

> Our goal is to make an enduring impact on the world. While many of our products operate in the background as part of larger systems, they are essential. Cars stop, planes fly, factories run, cell phones ring, and computers hum—all because they use critical components from IMCO.
> (IMCO Corporation, 2014)

Conglomerates are characterized by diversification of assets in attempts to deliver better financial returns (Smith & Schreiner, 1969). They are not known for investments in human resource management (HRM) or culture; indeed, when construed as a portfolio of independent companies and brands, there is little need to integrate products, technologies, operations, or people. As such, the Leadership Summit represented a major event for this new entity, an opportunity to talk about and champion what the company aspired to become as a newly independent, smaller and more focused enterprise.

Through many hours of multi-media events, speeches, and breakout sessions, IMCO executives unveiled what they had been working on: the values and norms associated with a new aspired 'culture'. The event was prompted by recent employee survey results that showed significant morale issues as many employees felt overworked and under-valued. The new cultural 'behaviors' (Figure 1.1) were thus targeted at changing how people in the company should behave.

Culture 'Shaping'

The new cultural behaviors were part of a comprehensive culture-'shaping' program. Designed by a consulting firm retained to lead this effort, the Leadership Summit was the unveiling of work begun a year earlier with the employee survey and focus groups, followed by meetings with executives to present the survey results and define the new aspired values (see Figure 1.1). The Summit allowed me to witness first-hand what culture shaping, or "value engineering" (Martin & Frost, 2011, p. 602) looks like in action.

IMCO's culture-shaping program, drawn from the marketing material of the culture consultant, is described in Table 1.1. Accompanying it is a list of assumptions upon which this program, and others like it, is based.

Impeccabl character	Bold thinking	Collective know-how
Our behaviors: • We demonstrate our values of respect, responsibility and integrity in all we do • We are accountable for results and actions • We take care of ourselves and each other • We practice appreciation and gratitude	Our behaviors: • We challenge the status quo and are willing to do things differently • We are curious and agile • We communicate with courage • We are biased for action and speed, while recognizing safety and quality are critical for our success	Our behaviors: • We listen to our customers and create enduring relationships • We continuously learn from each other by valuing different ideas, opinions and experiences • We are passionate about each other's success and create more success together as a team • We contribute to a positive and purposeful environment

Figure 1.1 New cultural behaviors, IMCO.

These assumptions can be said to represent the mainstream view of organizational culture and change as taught and practiced in the United States and Europe.[3] The basis of these assumptions is that 'getting your culture right' is a prescription for business success. What is curious about this view is that the cultural and cognitive anthropology literature, arguably the one discipline that puts culture at the center of its intellectual agenda, has very little to say about culture 'shaping'.

Normative Control

Organizational norms, values and ideologies were first referenced in the late 1950s and early 1960s, and organizational culture as a construct has been a direct focus of inquiry since the 1970s. This in part can be attributed to a general interest in normative, or 'Theory Y', management that appeared in the 1960s as an antidote to the traditional 'Theory X' approaches

Table 1.1 Culture change model espoused at IMCO

Culture and change model espoused at IMCO	Underlying assumption(s)
1 *Culture is a source of competitive advantage*	Values such as collaboration, agility, accountability, innovation characterize a 'high performance culture'.
2 *Culture can be 'shaped'*	• Cultures are unitary wholes. • Culture is normative behavior. Norms can be 'engineered' by leaders for a positive outcome. This starts with establishing 'core principles'.
3 *Culture change must be 'led from the top'*	• 'If change does not start from the top, the effort will fail'. Leadership must be 'purposeful' and entirely committed to the culture change. • Top leaders must 'internalize' the change.
4 *Culture change requires new behavior*	• People change through 'insights' that come from their own experience. • In order to change culture, people must have a 'profound' experience of the new culture.
5 *Culture change must happen quickly*	• 'The faster people are engaged in the process of culture change, the higher the probability the culture will shift'. • The change effort must reach every employee in 10–12 months. • Leaders must be active and involved.
6 *Culture change must be reinforced to be sustainable*	'Systematic reinforcement' is needed at all levels of the organizational system (individual, team, organization). All 'institutional practices, systems, performance drivers and capabilities' need to drive toward the desired change.

(McGregor, 1960). The assumptions of the traditional approach were that people inherently dislike work and are unmotivated, thus control, coercion, and close direction is needed to achieve organizational outcomes. In response, Theory Y held that creative capacity of people in organizations is underutilized. Most people seek autonomy and responsibility and want to exercise creativity and imagination in problem solving. Theory Y shifted the focus from top-down to normative means of control, and with this came a corresponding interest in corporate culture (Kunda, 1992). However, underneath this new orientation remained an unstated assumption of managerial agency and control. The shift from overt to more indirect or covert forms of control retained the presumption of *control*. This is one reason why managerial control remains to this day an (unspoken) assumption underlying popular conceptions of culture.

While organizational culture has remained a focus of research since the 1970s, beyond what I call the culture 'industry'—management consulting firms and organizational development (OD) practitioners—there remains little consensus on what culture is or whether it can be managed, and, if so, how. Researchers and practitioners still disagree on even the most basic questions: *What is culture? Is it something an organization has or something an organization is? Can it be measured, and, if so, on what basis? Is there relationship between culture and business performance, and, if so, what is it? Is it something management can impose, or is it somehow a part of all organizational actors?* (Alvesson & Svenignsson, 2008; Martin, 2002; Smircich, 1983; Testa & Sipe, 2011). The Economist (2014) is one of the few in the mainstream business press to point out the difficulties in attributing causality to culture, admitting the term is so vague that "culture based explanations are often meaningless" (January 11, p. 72). Yet despite these questions, culture-shaping projects like IMCO's proceed unchecked and unburdened by epistemic doubt. Managers and practitioners impugn cultural explanations for much of what constitutes organizational behavior in organizations, and, moreover, believe culture can be engineered to their own designs for positive business outcomes, no matter what the academic research may say.

What explains this gap between theory and practice? I suggest there is a relatively straightforward explanation. Managers are correct in suspecting culture is a powerful normative force, but current theory is unable to adequately account for it. This does not relieve managers and practitioners (or the popular media) of culpability for wasting resources when they carry out 'quick fix' culture change programs using watered down constructs based on little more than anecdotal evidence, projections of espoused values, or wishful thinking. At the same time, managers may be more sophisticated in their understanding of culture than is appreciated (Ogbonna & Harris, 2002). Rather, the lack of academic consensus is a result of the fact existing theory and research is unable to provide adequate answers to even the most basic questions on culture such as those posed above. Nor is it able to account for why some discourses, symbols, ideologies, and so forth become compelling to actors in some cultural and social systems, and others do not (Strauss, 1992). Simply put, despite many decades of work there is much about organizational culture we have yet to learn. Until better explanatory frameworks are developed, the gap between theory and practice will remain.

In this chapter I examine the principal reasons for this gap. I attempt to explain why culture theory is as impoverished as it is. I begin with a review of the current state of culture research, focusing on problems in both objectivist and subjectivist approaches.[4] I then discuss how these issues impact culture practice, and examine the issues inherent in popular approaches to culture. I end by offering how a functionally embodied alternative to culture provides a way to reconcile divergent approaches while providing a more robust explanatory framework that accounts for the full range of cultural experience in organizations.

1. The Objectivist–Subjectivist Divide

The organizational culture field is characterized by a struggle for intellectual relevance, a struggle Joanne Martin and Peter Frost (2011) labeled the "culture wars" (p. 599). The culture wars cleave on the debate between an objectivist, rationally known world and an arbitrary, subjectively known one, a debate traceable to Descartes and Kant that has caused some anthropologists to abandon the concept of culture altogether (Strauss, personal communication, August 23, 2014; Descola, 2013). On one side are the objectivists, mostly economists, industrial-organizational psychologists and quantitatively oriented social psychologists who approach culture empirically, treating it as a variable to be measured, managed and leveraged.[5] There is also a long tradition in anthropology of quantitative assessments of culture for the purposes of creating cultural typologies and cross-cultural comparisons, traceable to the work or Franz Boas and E.B. Tylor in the early 20th century (Jorgensen, 1979). This approach tends to put forth empirical 'evidence' of culture change by positing culture as one or two dependent variables, such as values or beliefs, and then providing statistical evidence of the state change of those variables. This research has been criticized for being overly reductionist, etic, and stuck in 'paradigm myopia', and yet remains immensely popular, with old and new culture diagnostics, measurements and typologies being invented and invoked with frequency (Baskerville, 2003, p. 5; Martin & Frost, 2011).[6]

On the other side are the "troublemakers" (Alvesson & Skoldberg, 2009, p. 3), subjectivists who challenge objectivist theoretical foundations and methods, and instead locate culture exclusively in symbols (public forms), texts and utterances (semiotic forms), artefacts and other "public phenomena" (Geertz, 1973; Shore, 1996, p. 51). Most culture research in this tradition offers little of pragmatic relevance for the practitioner or executive, which undermines its valuable contributions to methodology and its focus on the cultural subject.

Objectivist Approaches

There is an important need for verifiable and generalizable knowledge about culture in organizations. Nonetheless, objectivist approaches tend to suffer from issues related to *ontology, epistemology*, and *ideation*.

Problems of Ontology

We perceive social categories such as culture existing naturally in the world. As the social historian William Sewell Jr. (2005) puts it, this tendency "ontologizes" culture, giving it the appearance of being something naturally occurring (p. 349). Social categories such as mergers and acquisitions (M&A), for example, are imbued with pervasive power by metaphors such as FIGHTING, MATING or EVOLUTIONARY STRUGGLE. Such metaphors, embedded in multiple narratives, reify the sense that social phenomena such as mergers really *are* a struggle to evolve (Koller, 2005).

This phenomenon is aided by a major feature of human cognition, analogical reasoning, which enables thinking about abstract things by analogy to physical things (Lakoff & Johnson, 1980, 1999). Our language reflects this through the many metaphors we use to talk about culture, metaphors that over time become so conventionalized and routine we take abstractions like cultures to be physical things. Indeed, this has become the dominant mainstream notion of corporate culture, seen and heard abundantly in the CULTURE AS OBJECT metaphors (e.g. *shape the culture; manipulate the culture; a culture of ____*) or CULTURE AS LIVING THING metaphors (e.g. *a family culture; we are an aggressive culture*) conventionalized in business idioms and reinforced in mainstream business publications. For example, the *Corner Office* column in the *New York Times* each Sunday publishes interviews with corporate leaders on, among other things, how they 'view their cultures' and what they are trying to achieve 'with their cultures'. In M&A, culture is usually conceived of as a discrete variable, as in the *acquirer imposes its culture*.

The very posing of these questions, questions so routine the underlying ontological assumption of culture as a natural kind is obscured from all but the most attuned observer, reifies the notion that cultures are 'things' to be managed, manipulated and leveraged. Like 'god', 'society', and 'the economy,' 'culture' is another way of reifying the environment, engendering the sense these abstractions are real and enabling us to organize ourselves as if they are (Vike, 2011, p. 381). Once so conceptualized, culture shaping is easily conceived of as reasonable, even logical.

Objectivist and quantitative management science makes the error of assuming the social world is naturally composed of units that are quantifiable, and that these units are what comprise it (Sewell, 2005). Corollary to conceptualizing culture as things, objectivist researchers often conceive of culture, paradoxically, as stable (for example, see Helfrich, Li, Mohr, Meterko, & Sales, 2007) and able to be seen as it "truly is" (Testa & Sipe, 2011, p. 3). Helfrich and his colleagues stress this point in describing the Competing Values Framework (CVF), a four-factor typology developed by Quinn and Rohrbaugh (1983): "a fundamental supposition of the CVF is that all four cultures operate at an organizational level and remain relatively stable over time" (Helfrich et al., 2007, p. 2). Without assumed stability, quantifiable measurement is impossible. *With* assumed stability, causality can be attributed to the statistical distributions of cultural traits. Such traits will appear as "patterned" and systematic and therefore presumed to be "intentional" (Vike, 2011, p. 381). As Sewell (2005) states, "quantitative reasoning works because semiotic practices" generated by underlying paradigms or schemas "produce regularities in human action" (p. 350). These regularities are hidden in discourses but are made manifest through statistical reasoning. What is measured, by the very fact of its measurement, becomes ontologically real and valid in the minds of actors, and therefore causal. As actors adapt to these patterns this contributes to the idea that culture is real rather than an "epiphenomenon" (Vike, 2011, p. 31). By reducing culture to an object its properties can be identified, quantified and manipulated as variables.

At issue is not quantitative reasoning, nor the idea that culture exerts influence on behavior (or the reverse). At issue is the problematic assumption of culture as a natural kind, the inference of stability that follows from it.

One of the major effects of an ontologized, stabilized and quantified concept of culture is that it is then logical to conceive of it as tool for normative control to define accepted behavior. Viewed this way, culture can be a source of sustained competitive advantage because it presumably increases resource heterogeneity and therefore is hard to duplicate by competitors (for example, see Chan, Shaffer, & Snape, 2004). This was the dominant theme at the IMCO Leadership Summit, with the culture consultant talking about "culture shaping" and the CEO describing the need to "set" and ensure a "healthy," "positive," "fun" and "purposeful" culture.

But cultures are not 'things'. It is only in our minds that we turn them into things (Handwerker, 2002). Ironically, in ontologizing culture, much of its potential value as a resource is lost as it is reduced to simple variables akin to inventory, machinery, or money.

Problems of Epistemology

Capitalist enterprise, by definition, entails an epistemology of certainty based on control, prediction and the management of risk, all competencies employed in the service of attaining and preserving profit. This thinking can be traced all the way to Taylor (1916), who wrote that management knowledge could be reduced to "rules, laws, and in most cases mathematical formulae." It follows then that culture as a domain of inquiry and locus of control should be thought of in the same way. Managers seek tools to succeed at commerce; culture is but another.

Indeed, much of the early literature on culture stressed this very point: culture, when actively managed or made "strong" could enhance profits and productivity (Martin, 2002, p. 8). It is no accident the majority of the culture research has been generated by management and economics-oriented scholars (for example, see Deal & Kennedy, 1982; Denison, 1990; Kotter & Heskett, 1992). These theorists located culture as one or two narrowly defined variables that could be measured, correlated and therefore strengthened and optimized (Martin, 2002). If employees could be encouraged to share the beliefs and values of the organization's leaders and iconic figures, productivity and profitability would result (Deal & Kennedy, 1982).

The evidence, on balance, did not support the promise (Martin, 2002). Perhaps there is more to productivity and profitability than culture. Or perhaps culture, ontologized and reduced to one or two variables, was too narrowly conceived. As consultants and managers tried hard to emulate 'strong cultures' like those of IBM, Johnson & Johnson, Proctor & Gamble or GE, many found the promise of productivity and profitability elusive (Martin, 2002, p. 9). Pointed questions about "missing control and comparison groups" were asked (p. 9). Why did other companies with 'strong cultures', like Apple in the 1990s or Microsoft more recently fare less well? Why did some companies with 'weaker' cultures succeed?

In the effort to establish what makes an 'effective', 'good' or 'strong' culture and thereby provide managers and practitioners with pragmatic tools, objectivist research encounters difficulties. These specifically have to do with boundaries, as well as with methods of measurement and interpretation.

Cultural Boundaries

Consider the fictitious case of an immigrant Bengali chemical engineer living and working in Houston (adapted from Sewell, 2005, pp. 203–204). As Sewell states, such a figure is hardly a "freak in the contemporary world" (p. 205). This person participates simultaneously in American culture when going to the supermarket or dealing with the cable television company or commuting to work, but also in Bengali culture when with his family or raising his children, and with an engineering culture at work when communicating with colleagues or working in a broader community of chemical engineers. Each of the cultures in which he participates has its language, symbols, judgments, authority figures, norms and underlying schemas. The physical, social or political boundaries of each is blurred and overlapping, such as when our engineer is at home with his wife watching TV while working on his laptop on a project for work. The question is when our engineer receives a corporate culture survey with a battery of items linked to etic cultural dimensions (as he is likely to receive at some point if he works in large multinational corporation), which of the many cultures in which he participates will this instrument actually be measuring? And how would those administering such a survey know? What culture, and whose culture, are we measuring when we purport to measure culture in such a way?

Humans exist in environments already considerably shaped by culture; people belong to multiple cultures and communities (Handwerker, 2002; Quinn, 2011; Strauss, 2012). As such, it is difficult to presuppose cultural boundaries. Some anthropologists such as Herzfeld (2001) have gone as far as to doubt the concept of discrete cultures altogether because of the permeability of boundaries. Not surprisingly, studies that treat organizational culture as a monolithic, single variable, or a typology of a few variables obliterate the concept of boundaries altogether (Martin, 2002). While some of these studies acknowledge the imperfection of single-variable models of culture, and some go as far as to posit the need for more comprehensive and non-quantitative approaches (for example, see Hartnell, Ou, & Kinicki, 2011), many of these studies nonetheless proceed to make assertions about culture on the basis of a single or a few variables. For example, the CVF identifies four cultural archetypes hypothesized to permeate all facets of the organization, from management behavior to the values that bind employees together to the priorities the organization pursues.[7] A "dominant" culture thus "manifest(s) in the views of employees at all levels of the organization" (Helfrich et al., 2007, p. 2). Others such as Van den Steen (2009) acknowledge that a model based solely on shared beliefs and values is overly simplistic, but in his study of culture clashes in M&A proceeds to describe a normative model correlating shared beliefs with "more delegation, less monitoring" and "higher execution effort" (p. 2), all elements he characterizes as "culture." It is as if a broad swath of objectivist organizational culture research, and much of the culture industry, is stuck in a literal reading of the classic ethnographies of Mead on Samoa, Benedict on the Zuni, Malinowski on the Trobriands, Evans-Pritchard on the Nuer, and so forth, assuming organizations are distinct, integrated and bounded cultures like these so-called "simple societies" (Sewell, 1999).

Of course, a few objectivist studies do recognize the issue of cultural boundaries, but these studies are a minority. Guldenmund's (2007) research on the degree to which a "safety culture" concept was shared across a manufacturer found that a survey on employee attitudes exposed only those shared throughout the whole organization, not necessarily the ones espoused by top management (Guldenmund, 2007). Similarly, Helfrich and his colleagues (2007) suggest there may be problems applying CVF subscales to non-supervisors, and underscore the importance of assessing the psychometric properties of instruments in each new context and population to which they are applied.

Objectivist methodologies require that levels of analysis be properly recognized with respect to inherent boundaries such as job grade or level (e.g. executive vs. middle management vs. non-management), function, region, nation, gender, ethnicity, and so forth. This is one reason why many organizational culture researchers see culture as necessarily fragmented, comprised of multiple sub cultures (Gregory, 1983; Kunda, 1992; Martin, 2002).

Language, Nation & Region

Cultural boundaries are porous. With respect to regional cultures, for example, Gertler (2004) showed how economic behavior and practices embedded within particular geographies shaped firm practices in those regions. 'Silicon Valley culture' in the San Francisco Bay Area was attributed to a general environment of cooperation and labor mobility among firms in that region, as opposed to 'Route 128 culture' in the greater Boston area in Massachusetts, which discouraged information sharing and labor mobility (Gertler, 2004). Similarly, firms in Emilia-Romagna in Italy share an artisan culture with deeply ingrained social interaction and cultural affinity based on language and trust built up over centuries. In Baden-Wurttemberg in Germany, a longstanding predominant culture of engineering and problem solving allows small firms to compete with much larger ones in worldwide markets (Gertler, 2004).[8]

These issues are amplified when language and political boundaries are considered. Levitt and Schiller (2004) outlined several concerns about national culture that can be extended to organizational cultures: generalizations about culture ignore differences of race, class, gender, or professional orientation. Societies and cultures are not bounded—culture does not end once you step across national borders or off corporate property. Systems of values are not unchanging; they are in flux as actors draw on different resources and repertoires of knowledge to make sense of and function within their environments. Majority groups in nations (linguistic, ethnic or religious) likely develop a stronger sense of attachment to the concept of a nation as a whole than minorities (Sidanius, Feshbach, Levin, & Pratto, 1997). The same phenomenon may exist in large organizations. Top managers or members of dominant professional groups may feel more affinity for the notion of a unified organizational culture than others in the organization.

Nowhere is this better illustrated than the debate over Hofstede's (1998) research on national and organizational culture. Hofstede's' deeply influential work was based on attitude surveys conducted between 1967 and 1983 with 88,000 IBM employees. These surveys yielded 117,000 responses and resulted in the development of indices describing four dimensions of national culture: *power distance, individual–collectivism, uncertainty avoidance* and *masculinity–femininity*. These indices have been among the most influential in measuring organizational culture as well (Baskerville, 2003).

Not surprisingly, researchers have had difficulty replicating Hofstede's work across national boundaries. Hofstede's *uncertainty avoidance* dimension was not observed in China (Smith & Dugan, 1996). Chanchani (1998) tried to replicate Hofstede's indices in India and New Zealand, but found rankings on three out of the five dimensions were opposite to Hofstede's original (in Baskerville, 2003). In deference to Hofstede, one problem might have been the simplicity of the items in the constructs used. Triandis (1996), for example, found over 60 attributes that define individualist or collectivist cultures.[9] Merritt (2000) was only able to partially replicate Hofstede's results in an occupational culture study of airline pilots, although when she removed the constraint of item equivalence she was able to replicate all of his results, from which she concluded "national culture exerts an influence on cockpit behavior over and above the professional culture of pilots" (p. 283). However, as I elaborate below, her results may be better explained by language since the majority of her pilot subjects were English speakers.

Item equivalence as well proves to be important in studies involving national culture because the way people interpret rating scales is substantially different across cultures (for example, see Riordan & Vandenberg, 1994; Van Herk, Poortinga, & Verhallen, 2004). Riordan and Vandenberg (1994) found cultural groups used different conceptual frames of reference when responding to rating scales.[10] There is evidence of respondent bias in understanding rating scales between Koreans and Americans (Chun, Campbell, & Yoo, 1974; Hui & Triandis, 1989), and Japanese and American respondents (Stening & Everett, 1984).[11] Differences in response styles produce systematic differences in cross-cultural survey results, thus the assumption of measurement equivalence of survey instruments across cultures may not be supported (Beuckelaer, Lievens, & Swinnen, 2007).

Similarly, objectivist studies that attempt to posit normative effects for various aspects of organizational behavior such as motivation, goal attainment, feedback, rewards, job satisfaction, organizational commitment, teaming and leadership have had trouble replicating consistent results across national boundaries (Gelfand, Erez, & Aycan, 2007). While each of these domains of organizational behavior are diverse and supported by substantial bodies of literature, organizational culture researchers or practitioners who promulgate the normative and unifying effects of monolithic or strong organizational cultures tend to ignore or sideline these inconvenient data. In multinational or global companies, such normative effects may be difficult to measure, let alone attain. One reason for this may be due to the fact most intercultural measures are based on values, whereas differences across cultures (national, regional or organizational) are also a function of social norms, occupational roles, and basic beliefs, assumptions and theories about the world (Gelfand et al., 2007).

Language may be a bigger factor in assessing cultural boundaries and influence than geography. Beuckelaer and his associates (2007) examined the measurement equivalence of a global organizational survey measuring six work climate factors administered across 25 countries in all regions of the world. They concluded that cultures using the same language exhibit higher levels of human values item equivalence. They state: "Across all countries, the survey instrument exhibited 'form equivalence' and 'metric equivalence', suggesting that respondents completed the survey using the same frame-of-reference and interpreted the rating scale intervals similarly" (Beuckelaer et al., 2007, p. 575. Also see Liu, Borg, & Spector, 2004; Ryan, Chan, Ployhart, & Slade, 1999). English-speaking regions appears to be the only ones where empirical evidence for measurement equivalence of national culture items is to be found (Beuckelaer et al., 2007). Perhaps what support there is for item consistency and validation is being artificially sustained by the prevalence of English in the business world. For all of these reasons, the idea of culture as rigidly defined by organizational boundaries must be considered highly suspect.

Measures and Interpretations

There is wide agreement among culture theorists that culture is something shared (Freeman, Romney, & Freeman, 1987; Straus & Quinn, 1997; Triandis, 1996). Yet cultural sentiments collected through objectivist surveys, ever popular among researchers and practitioners, are usually classified according to categories imposed by the researcher, such as attitudes and values (for example, Hofstede, 1998). This etic approach presupposess the dimensions under study are shared by all members of the targeted community. For example, Bates (1995) and her colleagues posited culture as "shared meanings" then imposed an etic typology (the CVF) to assess it. This position is inherently contradictory. A researcher cannot argue on the one hand that culture consists of shared meanings and then attempt to measure and describe that culture through a set of finite constructs imposed by the researcher. What if what is shared in that community is different than what the researcher posits? Cultural meaning is a matter of context, and is dynamic; it cannot simply be imposed (Sayer, 1992).

Since most objectivist organization culture research is based on etic surveys where respondents retrospectively rate items based on values, attitudes, traits or observed events, memory and distortion effects are also important considerations in evaluating result efficacy. Memory can be subject to social interaction. And false recall can be triggered by group discussion of events that individuals did not actually experience. Neural systems do not operate in isolation from the environment; context matters greatly in recall (Barnier, Sutton, Harris, & Wilson, 2008).

One can also ask to what extent are classifications imposed by etic surveys supported by the distinctions respondents make in their own minds on these items, and whether these distinctions predict how they will behave. As Freeman et al. (1987) state, "what correlates with what in memory-based ratings tells us more about preexisting ideas of what is like what than about what correlated with what in actual behavior" (p. 89). Individual behavior in certain situations may not reflect a person's values, attitudes, or beliefs (Peng, Nisbett, & Wong, 1997).

Research on attitudes as predictors of behavior illustrates this issue. For example, one study of people's self-reports about their own attitudes and observed behavior correlated at no better than .56, which is to say nearly half of observed behavior did not correlate to self reports (Bernard, Kilworth, Kronenfeld, & Sailer, 1984). Hofstede (1998) admits employee attitudes were found to be clearly distinct from employee values: perceptions of organizational practices were unrelated to values and organizational practices did not form recognizable clusters at the level of individuals, only at the level of organizational (sub) units. Memory bias on such ratings, however, is not random: the bias is in the direction of some kind of norm. People seem to remember a system of rules or an abstract underlying pattern better than actual facts or events, lending support to schema-based theories of culture (D'Andrade, 1995; Freeman et al., 1987).

Another issue with etic approaches is that they are incapable of surfacing unanticipated findings beyond the categorization scheme imposed by the researcher (Mallak, Lyth, Olson, Ulshafer, & Sardone, 2003). Many etic studies admit the use of such dimensions is often solely for "practical" reasons (Ogbonna & Harris, 2000), or a reaction to the difficulties in defining and measuring culture. Optimizing for epistemic practicality contributes to much of the difficulty objectivist research encounters in providing adequate explanatory frameworks for culture and change. This research, at best, mostly traffics in culture's surface effects.

Construct validation through factor and principal components analyses are among the techniques researchers can use to counteract construct measurement difficulties (Handwerker, 2002; Helfrich et al., 2007; Hofstede, 1998). These approaches yield correlation coefficients that establish the salience of underlying factors for the range of items under study, although they still cannot identify attitudes or beliefs lying outside that range. Such "nonconforming" frameworks (Strauss, 2012, p. 26) obscure possible ambivalence respondents may hold about an item, or muddy the distinction between those who do not hold a particular belief or attitude and those with beliefs or attitudes that do not fit into the categories being measured. This is the primary reason why the quantitative analyses used in the study presented in this book is built off of emic, or participant-derived, constructs.

Etic surveys that reduce culture to bounded monoliths of one or two variables are among the most popular among practitioners, and yet are fraught with measurement and interpretation difficulties. At the same time, such difficulties should not be read as an indictment of all quantitative methods. Measures of values such as the CVF or desired cultural trait inventories such as the GLOBE study are likely measuring the tip of the culture iceberg, denoting some aspect of culture. What is being contested here is the prevailing assumption that such markers *are* the culture. Whether the variables under study are values, personality traits, desired behavioral norms, habits, or similar construct, studies that employ them should be treated with suspicion unless these constructs can be shown to be antecedent or causal for the items under study. To date this has not been shown to be the case.

Problems of Ideation

When culture is ontologized, bounded and epistemically reduced, the reduction often occurs via two 'ideational' variables that become proxies for culture: *personality* or *values*. These are 'ideational' because they represent projections of individual personality or beliefs onto an ontologized whole. I accord them extra space here because of their popularity in the literature and in practice.

Culture as Personality

Culture conflated with personality has a long tradition in psychology, beginning with Freud who believed cultures could be analyzed, and in anthropology in the work of Sapir and the Culture and Personality school (Lindholm, 2007). Whereas culture and personality theorists saw the relationship between individual personality and culture as analogous, part of a "multi-level integrated system" (Lindholm, 2007, p. 98), organizational researchers tend to see the relationship in literal terms. For example, Schneider and Smith (2004) propose that over time organizations become relatively homogenous based on the personalities of the people in them, and this process of "melding" determines their "observed" and "experienced" cultures. (p. 348). Miller and Droge (1986) suggest the personality traits of the CEO, such as the need for achievement, become manifest within the strategy and structures their organizations adopt. There is a well-established body of research on the relationship between personality and organizational fit.[12] To conflate personality with *culture*, however, requires several leaps of faith.

The first is that personality traits like agreeableness, extroversion or conscientiousness (etc.) reflect underlying psychological realities. The evidence suggests otherwise. D'Andrade (1995), for example, had difficulties replicating the so-called "Big-5" personality factors (D'Andrade, 1995; Norman, 1963).[13] D'Andrade (1965, as cited in D'Andrade, 1995) and later Hakel (1974; as cited in D'Andrade, 1995) showed that personality terms correlated on the basis of similarity in meaning of the terms, or semantic feature overlap.[14] For example, features defining someone as *friendly* were positively correlated with those defining someone as *sociable*. Traits such as *cleverness* correlated with *inventiveness* (D'Andrade, 1995). Using similarity judgments Shweder (1977) also correlated the Minnesota Multiphasic Personality Inventory (MMPI), and he and D'Andrade similarly correlated several other standard personality inventories. What they contested was not the reliability of personality trait ratings, but that these ratings were measuring features of language rather than behavior (D'Andrade, 1995). One wonders whether the scale and sample items in such as well-known trait studies of culture as the GLOBE study of national leadership profiles (for example, *visionary: foresighted, prepared, anticipatory, plans ahead*; *performance oriented: improvement oriented, excellence-oriented*) are measuring observed leadership traits or semantic similarity (from Koopman, Den Hartog, Konrad et al., 1999, p. 513).

Shweder (1991) expanded on this when considering whether such measures in general can be used as the basis for assertions about culture:

> It's troubling that almost all the extant evidence . . . has been collected from interpersonal rating forms, questionnaire interviews, and personality inventories . . . Rating forms, questionnaire interviews and inventories turn out to be quite demanding inferential tasks in which "magical" thought processes are likely to intrude. What seems to happen is that conceptual affiliations (for example, "smiles easily" and "likes parties") and conceptual exclusions (for example, "gentle" and "managerial") dominate the judgment process . . . Items alike in concept are judged to go together even when . . . they do not co-occur in behavior. Thus, the data . . . lends illusory support to the mistaken belief that individual differences can be described in language consisting of context-free global traits, factors or dimensions.
>
> (p. 276)

Another leap of faith is that anthropologists and cultural psychologists have known for many years that attribution and categorization systems, such as those for color, folk biology, kinship, or even conceptions of the self, vary across cultures (D'Andrade, 1995; Hallowell, 1976; 1987; Hutchins, 1995; Lakoff, 1987; Rogoff, 1990; Shweder, 1991). And still another leap is that traits such as achievement are so generalized and well distributed in the CEO population that attribution of them to culture is a tautology (Wood & Vilkinas, 2004). Most CEOs, by their own admission, are achievement oriented; they would not be CEOs otherwise. The issue also hinges on the level of abstraction used to define the construct: the greater a construct's degree of abstraction, the more 'universal' a trait can appear to be (Hui & Triandis, 1986).

Culture as Values

One of the most common items measured by culture researchers are values. Culture understood as values has a long tradition in cross-cultural psychology and anthropology (Peng, Ames, & Knowles, 2000). This perspective, while acknowledged as "imperfect" (p. 248), and contested (Strauss & Quinn, 1997), asserts there are universal and discernible value differences across cultures. For example, causal attribution is shown to vary between

U.S. Americans and Asian cultures: U.S. Americans tend to attribute causality to individual human traits while Asians to social role obligations and situational factors. These differences are thought to lead to differences in espoused values (Peng, Ames, & Knowles, 2000).

Measures of culture type or congruence are built off of either value or 'philosophy' scales. Value scales measure whether people perceive their own values to be more or less like the organization, whether they appreciate working for the organization, and whether they feel pride in the organization. Philosophy scales measure the degree to which individuals believe there are recognizable beliefs embodying the wisdom or the organization (Bates, Amundson, Schroeder, & Morris, 1995).

Some organizational culture researchers claim "values typically act as the defining elements of a culture" (Chatman & Jehn, 1994, p. 524). Values and beliefs are the basis for several influential organizational culture studies such as the CVF, and those focused on person–organization fit, such as the Organizational Culture Profile (OCP; O'Reilly, Chatman, & Caldwell, 1991). I suspect this is the case because of their long research tradition and, despite the difficulties cited below, because values are attractive as objects of normative control; by substituting one set of values for another, managers believe they can gain normative leverage over their organizations.

But values-based studies of culture suffer from several issues. For one, the concept is polysemous (D'Andrade, 2008). It can mean "goodness," "preference," "price," "worth," or "moral right" (D'Andrade, 2008, pp. 8–11). In some languages like Japanese or Vietnamese, there are no adequate translations of the term (Maltseva & D'Andrade, 2011).[15] And different cultures ascribe meaning to values in different ways. For example, an African American man might construe the notion of equality in terms of race, whereas a Chinese person might think of equality as social equality (Peng et al., 1997). The values literature itself is characterized by a divergence between definitions that ascribe no causal relationship between values and behavior, and those that do (Koopman et al., 1999; Peng et al., 1997).

Another concern is ideational: value scales measure idealized notions about how the world *should* be, rather than how it is actually perceived (D'Andrade, 2008). Values are essentializations, beliefs about the essential character of humans, Differences in values rest on differences in institutionalized values, the values one is *expected* to hold as a member of that institution or society rather than personal and subjective responses (D'Andrade & Maltseva, 2011). Other researchers see values as relational: that is, judgments about one's own values are construed in relation to beliefs about the values of others important to them, such as a woman who values the respect of elders because she believes, in comparison to others, that she cares more about this concept (Peng et al., 1997). Thus, scales such as individual–collectivism or altruism–self interest are measures of complex schemas and "life ways," ways one should live (Maltseva & D'Andrade, 2011).[16] Similarly, research by Schwartz (1994), using his own definition of values as "trans-situational goals, varying in importance, that serve as guiding principles in the life," found that "respondents fail to discriminate sharply among value types that share similar motivational concerns, those located in adjacent regions in the value structure" (p. 32).

Then there are cross-cultural reliability issues. For example, several authors surveying American values report high reliability based on Rokeach's (1973) test–retest reliability method.[17] But research with Chinese participants using this measure showed relatively low reliability (Peng et al., 1997). Studies of differences in assessment methods between importance ratings or rankings of attitudes across groups of Chinese, Singaporean Chinese, and Americans also showed low agreement (Penget al., 1997). As Peng and colleagues state, "the method of asking participants to rate or rank the importance of a set of values and then aggregating these ratings or rankings for comparison cross-culturally may not provide a good picture of values differences" (p. 340). While such reliability studies have not been conducted across all cultures, similar to the difficulties in replicating Hofstede's scales across cultures the implication is that generalized or non-context specific, etic values or attitude measures are not replicable across cultures and therefore not predictive of behavior.[18]

For values to function as normative 'shoulds', as is the wish of all who espouse organizational culture as a normative force, the values need to be internalized by everyone in the organization. One study in health care showed that organizational values congruent with employees' values did increase employee satisfaction, commitment, and performance outcomes (Fitzgerald & Desjardins, 2010). The key word is 'congruent', which is one reason why common values appear to be more easily instilled in small companies. It is hard to conceive of any medium-sized or larger global enterprise with employees all sharing similar values. And the internalization of values is itself fraught with issues.

Structural-functionalists like Durkheim believed social values and beliefs were transmitted unproblematically through a society via its socialization mechanisms such as symbols, rituals or practices (such as child rearing; Strauss, 1992). This idea has been unproblematically adopted by organizational culture theorists. Surely societies do inculcate dominant values in its members, for such acts are critical to its survival, but their transmission is hardly straightforward. As every parent knows, imparting values or beliefs onto a child is not simply a matter of communicating and reinforcing them. Strauss (1992) illustrates this beautifully with an extended fax machine metaphor:

> Transmission is more complicated than this because the social order is more complicated than this. If our culture-ideological milieu were unchanging, unambiguous, and internally consistent, there would be no need to study how social messages are appropriated by individual minds. Early childhood experience would be consistent with adult

experience, explicit messages consistent with each other and implicit messages, and the meaning of a society's messages would be clear to anyone who learned them.

(p. 8)

Organizational culture theorists and leaders who espouse values-based culture change make the error of assuming culture *is* the transmission, rather than the receiving, of cultural messages. How individuals interpret and act on the basis of such messages, not to mention how they make sense of the social order in which they occur, is lost.

Thus, values and norms tend not be internalized unless they are already well socialized (D'Andrade, 2006). Which suggests the more heterogeneous an organization is in terms of professional orientation, technology, ethnic composition, or regions of the world in which it operates, the likelihood of values being universally shared and socialized will be quite low.

Yet another issue with values is that they may be so accepted and routine within a cultural community that they may be enacted without conscious awareness, let alone discussion or debate. Strauss (2012) illustrates with an example from Fredrik Barth: "the Baktaman of western New Guinea have strong norms of sharing that lead to equal living standards but do not have a stated cultural value commending generosity, whereas the Balinese, who have large differences in wealth, do have an explicit value of generosity" (p. 31). Characterizing a culture based on the values a community ostensibly holds is to assume culture is based on norms, whereas in fact these may be reactions or compensations for deeper, more pervasive structures. Societies may have dominant ideologies, but rarely does the visible realm of a culture present a "single, clearly defined, well-integrated reality" (p. 11). And some cultural values are so vague, especially those typically espoused such as at IMCO (e.g. curiosity, courage, collaboration), it is unclear how to translate these into behavior.

Southwest Airlines: Values, or Differentiated Core Purpose?

As a possible counterpoint, there is some evidence that some organizations *do* appear to have a pervasive set of well-socialized values that prescribe social behavior. This is the phenomenon in oft-cited cases like Southwest Airlines, ING, Nucor (for an excellent example, see Heskett, 2011), and more recently and problematically, Amazon (Kantor & Streitfeld, 2015). I suggest the attribution of values as the *cause* of organizational and business success may be misplaced; what is being observed may be better explained by what I call an organization's *differentiated core purpose*.

For example, Southwest's highly differentiated purpose as 'the airline for the common man' and the low cost strategy it has adhered to over the years has served to closely align all of its 'activity systems' such as its low fares; its choice of 737s as the only aircraft type in its fleet; its single class of service; its fast aircraft turnaround times; its point-to-point route structure; its managers helping to clean planes; its hiring practices, and on (Heskett, 2011; Porter, 1996, p. 66). That values of 'teamwork' and 'family' are also to be found at the airline therefore should come as no surprise; Southwest's values *reinforce* its core purpose. I suggest they also arise from shared schemas induced by the tightly coupled tasks, routines and processes aligned to its clearly articulated and differentiated (from other airlines) mission and purpose, and its discipline in maintaining and adhering to these over the years (for example, see Raynor, 2011). While some researchers ascribe values as the cause of Southwest's success, I suggest the values arise out of and are sustained by its tightly coupled and highly congruent practices, many of which have been kept in place for years. These practices induce shared schemas. The values themselves are not the culture, nor the cause of it. One might be tempted into a chicken and egg argument by suggesting Southwest's values were what enabled it to conceive of its differentiated mission to begin with, but the airline itself seems to owe its origins to its unique mission (Heskett, 2011).

What values research tends to show is simply what is espoused by management (Schein, 1992). This will often only bear faint resemblance to a deeper and more pervasive underlying culture or cultures. And yet values-based culture change programs, such as those at IMCO, continue unabated, most likely because they are relatively easy to conceptualize and carry out. Managers are attracted to what on the surface appear to be straightforward and simple solutions to a culture 'problem'.

Ethical Issues: Whose Values?

When values tend to be the imposition of top management's values and beliefs, ethical questions must be raised (for example, see Deal & Kennedy, 1982; Kotter & Heskett, 1992; for a critique, see Alvesson & Sveningsson, 2008; Helms Mills, 2003; Wilmott, 1993). What are these values, and to what end is management attempting to impose them? Some researchers suggest such attempts are both totalitarian as well as contradictory: individual autonomy, creativity and self-realization cannot be normatively achieved by the paradoxical imposition of monoculture (Wilmott, 1993).

My experience suggests, with a few notable exceptions (such as Amazon), management may be less interested in hegemony and more in harmony. As seen in the IMCO case, positing common values is seen as a way to assure organizational harmony and positive employee self-identity. If the organization supplies the 'right' values, people will be happier, and by extension, more productive. If the organization is more productive, good things will follow for all. This was the message at IMCO's Leadership Summit.[19]

Even objectivist researchers such as Heskett (2011) admit that to try and implement a single company culture in a global company it is better to not stress common values and assumptions, but to stress behavior instead. This is tantamount to waving a white flag: one cannot on the one hand argue great companies can be shaped by instilling commonly held values and then on the other admit that to do so in a global company is problematic. This is another example of how current theory and practice falls short.

The evidence presented here raises doubts about objectivist ontology, methods, and ethical motives. This is not to say all objectivist culture studies are flawed, but that ontologized, bounded, reduced, simplified, and conflated approaches simply cannot account for the full range of cultural behavior and experience in organizations, let alone change. That these kinds of approaches to culture are the most common makes the need for an alternative all the more pressing.

Subjectivist Approaches

Subjectivist work on culture is much less prolific than objectivist work. It tends to be characterized by problematic suppositions related to *subjectivity, text,* and *power*.[20]

Problems with the Supposition of Subjectivity

As the famous saying in baseball goes, pitches are not balls or strikes until the umpire calls them. The challenge facing subjectivist approaches to culture is the denial of the presupposition that the pitches are already there to be called (Csordas, 1990). Or in the words of John Searle (1993):

> Whenever we use a language that purports to have public objects of reference, we commit ourselves to realism. The commitment is not a specific theory as to how the world is, but rather *that* there is a way that it is.
>
> (As cited in Spiro, 1996, p. 770)

Melford Spiro (1996, quoting Marcelo Suarez-Orozco) in a similar vein notes:

> As cultural anthropology continues its affair with 'subjectivity' . . . and righteously renounces any scientific' pretensions, it is becoming a storyteller's craft . . . [But] how can such an anthropology be of use to our understanding—and dismantling—of ethnic cleansing, rape camps, and torture camps?
>
> (p. 776)

The association of culture research with ethnic cleansings, rape and torture is not overly melodramatic. To assume all cultural realities, including language, are subjective is to deny the existence of any mind-independent reality, cultural or otherwise. As put by Latour (1993), "when we are dealing with science and technology, it is hard to imagine for long that we are a text that is writing itself, a discourse that is speaking all by itself, a play of signifiers without signifieds" (p. 64).

Modern organizations are built on rationalist principles, themselves a product of science and technology. If the postmodern position is that "science is a particular kind of "storytelling" (Spiro, 1996, p. 771) and "reality is a series of fictions and illusions" (Martin & Frost, 2011, p. 611; Geertz, 1973), then subjectivism, in essence, has little to offer organizational culture praxis, for there can be no common intersubjective, *shared* experience called 'culture'. If organizations have no objective reality (for example, see Evered, 1983), then this position is fundamentally and experientially at odds with anyone who has ever been hired, fired or received a paycheck. Which is perhaps why subjectivist treatment of organizational culture tends to ignore pragmatic concerns and instead focus on critiques of objectivism (Martin & Frost, 2011).

The most significant challenge with subjectivism is ontological: with its fixations on discourse and text, that actors exist in the world and generate texts to begin with is irrelevant. When all texts, stories, and practices are only "truth claims" (Martin & Frost, 2011, p. 611) the only question a manager is left with is one of relevance: 'how does any of this add up to something I can take action on?' And without prescriptions for action, the important contributions of subjectivism in the areas of methodology and interpretation go unheeded in practice.

Problems with the Separation of Text from Context

Subjectivists, in particular poststructuralists such as Foucault (1977), argue social life and discourse is inherently ambiguous, multiplex, and contested, thus emphasize moving discourse away from the individual. To Ricoeur, social action is like a text, and texts are best analyzed without positing the psychological state of the author (Strauss, 1992). The emphasis on text and on a decentered subject has the effect of removing from consideration individual cognition. This renders it, ironically, much like objectivist research.

Truth claims to subjectivists are available by deconstructing texts to uncover the strategies used to represent truth (Martin & Frost, 2011). By uncovering the 'rules' inherent in texts, the rules governing social life can be inferred. Many poststructuralists assume the subject is "absorbed by discourse," and in fact, is only discourse and text (Vike, 2011, p. 385). To Geertz (1973) culture was essentially a semiotic phenomenon, a "web of significance," and signification an act of "construing social expressions on their surface enigmatic" (p. 5). Thus, when it comes to organizational phenomena there is nothing but discourse and text—and one's own subjective, under-determined interpretations (Ainsworth & Hardy, 2004; Alvesson & Sveningsson, 2008; Martin & Frost, 2011; Townley, 1993; Van Dijk, 1993).[21]

But in the interpretation of texts, whose interpretation counts? No amount of analytic reflexivity counterbalances the fact an analyst's particular interpretation of cultural phenomena may not be one shared by anyone else within the community from which such phenomena emanates. And if only subjective interpretation matters, then surely anthropology and social sciences are no different than fiction (Herzfeld, 2001). Self-reference becomes the product, and infinite regression the result: to admit 'where I stand on such and such phenomena' would "itself be fiction" (p. 44). The problem of meaning is sidestepped altogether: 'meaning' is in the text, not in the 'minds' of humans.

But what if culture is not only to be found in texts, but in systems of meaning that manifest through structures, practices, and semiotic codes dependent on context? Martin and Powers (1983), for example, showed how organizational narratives were interpreted differently by different groups within the same organization. Barley (1983), Kunda (1992), and Stewart (2002) have shown how occupational subgroups form their own interpretations of organizational symbols and related phenomena. The focus on text detached from context omits the notion that culture exists in both social and psychological realms, in social artefacts *and* cognitive representations (Shore, 1996). Schemas, for example, might be visible in public phenomena such as the discourse of IMCO executives or their organizational practices, but they may also underwrite how these executives think and feel. They may exist antecedent to the texts through which they are actualized. Subjectivists are correct in outlining the inherent interpretive challenges in this stance. But a subjectivist anthropology that retreats from some form of empiricism does its clients, the practitioners, managers and employees in organizations a great disservice. When what is *cultural* is only symbols, artefact, and language, normative control through culture shaping can be imposed without any epistemological self-doubt, and the ability to confront "unwelcome factual truths" is lost (Spiro, 1996, p. 776).

Problems with the Supposition of Power

One could perhaps dismiss all postmodernist discourse on organizational culture by citing its fundamental rejection of corporate market capitalism. Management control in some form is necessary for capitalist enterprise. The perpetuation of managerial and shareholder goals toward profit and shareholder value, argues the capitalist, is *the* role of management. But dismissing subjectivist concerns with power by citing their opposition to market capitalism and therefore managerial control misses the important contributions such theory makes to our understanding of power and control in organizations.

Subjectivists assume there is only one 'real' system: the power system (D'Andrade, 1995, p. 251). Subjectivist approaches to organizational culture thus begin with the assumption that corporate culture is hegemony

(Ogbor, 2001; Wilmott, 1993). Such positions make the claim culture is a tool for repression and for the perpetuation of management's hegemonic goals (Ogbor, 2001). These approaches rightfully criticize objectivists for lacking a critical perspective on the cultural phenomena under scrutiny. As such, culture shaping is the proverbial lipstick on the pig, lending "a dignified complexion to managerial control." If uncritically examined culture shaping is pure "ideology" (p. 591).

In my experience this is often regrettably the case. Too many executives, in attempting to change their organization's culture will lead with metaphors such as 'drive the culture' and 'change hearts and minds' and 'we need to win'. Participation in organizational culture, according to strong-form subjectivism, requires supplanting one's own identity with the corporate identity (Ogbor, 2001). Similar approaches posit culture as "psychic prisons" constructed by members to ameliorate internal tension or anxiety (Ogbor, 2001). Alvesson and Berg (1992) characterize attempts by organizations to impose values and ideologies as a kind of "third order control" which results in a certain amount of employee disempowerment (as cited in Ogbor, 2001, p. 603).

Viewing culture through the narrow lens of power is not much different than the objectivist tendency to reduce culture to values or personality: the reduction obliterates the inherent complexity of cultural meaning and behavior while obscuring its origins. Conceiving of culture as a tool of oppression is a blunt, value-laden explanation for behavior that is subtler and more ecologically contingent than subjectivist theorist acknowledge. Power relations themselves are grounded in social processes used to maintain power. Power in organizations may be the appropriation of resources by actors as a way to address threats and discontinuities based on how actors make sense of their own worlds (Vike, 2011).

Then there is the issue of pragmatics. Few actors in any society have precise knowledge of the result of their actions taken at scale (Vike, 2011). The idea of power legitimized through cultural hegemony is too often a supposition. The 'oppressed' and 'dominated' embrace, or seem to at least, the values that legitimize their oppression. This is not evidence of hegemony. Conforming to norms is a pragmatic reality of institutional life. People in organizations do seem to be aware of alternative strategies (Vike, 2011).

Subjectivist discourse on organizational power also ignores the fact work is a potential source of meaning, psychic unity and object-gratification, as much for organizational actors at Google or IMCO as it is for cognitive anthropologists. This notion is supported by a diverse literature (for example, see Abbott, 1998; Bucher & Stelling, 1977; Kegan, 1982; Morse & Weiss, 1955; Rosso, Dekas, & Wrzesniewski, 2010). In their review of the extant literature on work and meaning, Rosso et al. (2010) point out that organizations are "very strong contexts that carry unique systems of meaning which likely exert a powerful influence on how individuals interpret the meaning and meaningfulness of their work" (p. 120). People can and do find existential and psychological meaning through work, which to greater or lesser degree may align with the organization's mission and focus. Cultural tension thus may be more a matter of alignment and psychological "truces," in the words of Robert Kegan (1982), with a prevailing culture than of replacing or denying identities.

2. Culture Practice and the Implications of the Objectivist–Subjectivist Divide

The objectivist–subjectivist divide, and the various ontological and epistemic difficulties within these literatures, lead to a lack of consensus on what culture is, and how to measure and change it. This in turn allows executives and practitioners to adopt approaches to culture and culture change that suit their own agendas and worldviews unencumbered by theory.[22]

Intellectual dominance, in part, is a matter of winning the war of definition, and there is a long tradition of definitional warring in culture research: Kroeber and Kluckhorn (1952) identified over 100 definitions of culture. Table 1.2 below, culled from Martin's (2002) and my own review, shows

Table 1.2 Formal definitions of organizational culture

Culture Is . . .	Proponent
Values	O'Reilly et al., 1991; Quinn & Rorhbaugh, 1983
Values, symbols and behavior	Sergiovanni & Corbally, 1984; Berg, 1985
Values, "know how" and assumptions	Heskett, 2011
Leadership traits and personality	Bass & Aviolo, 1993; Gordon & Tomasio, 1992; Denison, 1990; Peters & Waterman, 1982
Shared understandings	Sathe, 1983
Shared meaning	Louis; 1985; Sergiovanni & Corbally, 1984; Berg, 1985
Shared purpose and experience	Meyerson, 1991
Root metaphor	Morgan, 2006
Social rules	Mills, 1988; Schall, 1983
Practices and behavior	Martin, 2002; Swidler, 1986, 2001
Frames of reference	Feldman, 1991
Underlying assumptions	Schein, 1984, 1992
Ideologies	Ogbor, 2001; Wilmott, 1993
Knowledge structures	Bates et al., 1995

a small sample of the diversity of definitions offered by some of the better-known organizational culture theorists:

The diversity in these definitions is in part explained by the different traditions from which culture research emanates. These include management, economics, sociology, social psychology, and industrial-organizational psychology. Notably absent are cognitive and cultural anthropologists, the only discipline that places culture at the center of its intellectual agenda (Stewart & Aldrich, 2015). And while all of these definitions have aspects in common, the only universally shared construct among them is sharedness, and even here there are differences with respect to degrees of sharedness and boundaries (Martin, 2002).

Such diversity untethers practice from theory and evidence. In the absence of academic consensus managers and practitioners selectively draw from research and methods in line with their own interests. Or they choose expediency over efficacy for reasons of time, cost, or perceived complexity. The results are unsurprising, and uninspiring. Culture practice tends to be characterized by *oversimplification, value engineering* and quests for *self-enhancement* (Martin & Frost, 2011).

Oversimplification

As managers and practitioners interpret and selectively adapt theory from a Balkanized field of research, or ignore it altogether, they tend to oversimplify what culture is or privilege already reductionist and simplified work. Such simplifications produce "a high probability of failed adaptation . . . especially those related to improving productivity and performance" (Martin & Frost, 2011, p. 614).

Construct oversimplification or reduction could be considered a reaction to the difficulties in defining and measuring culture, as discussed. But it is also a product of the need to *make use* of it. Often culture in the mainstream is a metonym for speaking about a complex of behavioral habits, norms and values. Gary Smith, the chief executive of Ciena, a telecommunications company, exemplifies this idea in a recent *Corner Office* interview:

> Culture takes an awful lot of time and effort, and it can be destroyed very quickly, because it is built on trust and respect. You're respecting the individual and what they do, and you're trusting them, and they're doing the same for you. That doesn't happen overnight. It's like personal relationships.
>
> (Bryant, *The New York Times*, October 4, 2015)

This passage typifies the popular conception of culture as ontologized, built through willful agency (it takes 'time and effort'), as boundary-less (trust is not problematized as manifesting differently across cultural boundaries), and as value-laden projections (individual and reciprocal respect and trust are important life ways).

Value Engineering & Self Enhancement

Culture as a tool for normative control and positive change is deeply engrained in modern management consciousness and practice. In my 30 years of organizational development (OD) practice with both large multinationals and smaller enterprises, most executives I have observed, including my informants at IMCO, believe they have inordinate influence over their organization's culture. This is not surprising—executives generally tend to overestimate their own influence on their organizations (Ormerod, 2005). Consequently they are continually drawn to the prospect of shaping and controlling it to improve their organizations and profit margins. *Value engineering* is the label Martin and Frost (2011) attach to this phenomenon. It is similar to what Smircich (1983) and her colleagues identified decades ago as the 'independent variable versus root metaphor' issue: is culture something an organization *has*, or is it something an organization *is*? 'Making use' of culture, as such, is a prescription for achieving competitive advantage. This explains the faddism of culture-change programs in the late 1980s and 1990s that continues to this day (Helms-Mills, 2003).[23]

Culture engineering is fueled by the tendency of leaders to try to project or manipulate culture based on their own values, ideologies and preferences (for a good example, see Martin, Sitkin, & Boehm, 1985). Carr (2000) makes the case that culture is another expression of leader narcissism.[24] This view is epitomized in the words of ING founder Arkadi Kuhlmann: "With the right culture, the problems of commitment, alignment, and motivation go away and hierarchy becomes irrelevant" (from Heskett, 2011, p. 42). When culture is so endowed, how can it not be the most compelling domain for executive intervention and manipulation?

Kuhlmann's ethos is hardly the naïve zeal of an overly-enthusiastic CEO. The Corporate Leadership Council, an influential management research organization, extends the logic of normative control by describing culture as capable of "offering scale and impact across thousand of employees" (2004).[25] Kuhlman's idea is shared in companies as diverse as Pizza Hut, Sapient (now part of Publicis), Home Depot, General Motors, and hundreds of others, and effectively is legitimized in numerous business school case studies.[26] A small sample of it is on display every Sunday in the *New York Times Corner Office* column, which publicizes interviews with executives on their conceptions of culture and leadership. In culling a random sample of 25 interviews, without controlling for industry, firm size or gender I found all executives but one (Tae Hea Nahm) believed he or she could directly or indirectly impact the culture of their firms. All that varied was the degree of causality of their own actions (some leaders believed their role was to create an environment rather than directly engineer culture).

One explanation for the prevalence of this conceit among North American business leaders may reside in dominant schemas of individualism and self-development historically prevalent in the United States that have

Table 1.3 Definitions of culture from business leaders

Name	Company	Industry	Culture Is
Andrew Thompson	Proteus	Biomedical	Structure, stories and 'built' value systems
Ann Mulcahy	Xerox	Hardware	How we do things
Byron Lewis	UniWorld Group	Advertising	History—what we've created
Caryl Stern	US Fund for UNICEF	Non Profit	Values
Chris Barbin	Appirio	Internet (Cloud)	Values
David Barger	Jet Blue	Airline	Leadership and HR practices
David Sacks	Yammer	Internet	Environment—letting people voice their opinions
Deborah Farrington	Starvest Partners	Venture Capital	Values
Dennis Crowley	Evernote	Software technology	Practices and behaviors
Dominic Orr	Aruba Networks	Software technology	Behavior, how we do things
Doreen Lorenzo	Frog Design	Consulting	Environment instilled by leader, and rituals
Irwin Simon	Hain Celestial Group	Retail (Food)	Environment and communication by leaders
Jonathan Klein	Getty Images	Media	Leadership principles
Kyle Zimmer	FirstBook	Non profit	Environment created by the collective, helped by the leader
Linda Lausell Bryant	Inwood House	Non profit	Values
Marjorie Kaplan	Discovery Networks	Media	Organizational structure and environment
Mike Sheehan	Hill Holiday	Advertising	Environment instilled by leader
Ori Hadomi	Mazor Robotics	Medical devices (Israel)	How we do things
Romil Bahl	PRXG	Software and Services	Environment instilled by leader
David Novak	Yum Brands	Retail (Food)	Built by reinforcing behaviors that drive results
Peter Loscher	Siemens	Industrial Conglomerate	Practices and behaviors
Tae Hea Nahm	Storm Ventures	Venture Capital	Unspoken norms and practices related to success (vs. espoused)

(Continued)

Table 1.3 (Continued)

Name	Company	Industry	Culture Is
Linda Zecher	Houghton Mifflin Harcourt	Publishing	Norms, practices and physical affordances (e.g. office layouts)
Mark Toro	North American Properties	Real Estate Development	Behavioral norms
Greg Schott	MuleSoft	Software technology	Values, habits and behavioral norms

evolved into a robust cultural model of leadership agency. Individual self enhancement is fused with an idealized (and popularly reinforced) belief in great leadership as one that maximizes profits through the overt creation of an organization molded in one's benevolent and striving self-image. This provides a compelling logic that reinforces the CEO and top management's creativity, humanism and technical brilliance while perpetuating the exultation of leadership that dominates U.S. business and popular culture. Oversimplified or diluted definitions of culture allow this narrative to persist unchecked by contrary evidence or unclouded by epistemic doubt.

My point here is not to contest the salience of sound leadership. It is to suggest the interaction between leadership and culture is much more complex than granted by the folk narrative.[27]

The Self Evidence of Culture

The culture-shaping narrative can become self-fulfilling prophesy in practice. The brilliance of the CEO and the executive team in 'getting the culture right' leads to business success. Therefore any espoused behavioral norm, habit, preference or value can be operationalized as culture on the basis of its apparent effect. The more broadly framed and generalized the construct ('appreciate others', 'work-life balance', 'don't make assumptions', 'be accountable'), the better. Like any folk belief, culture shaping can take on near-mythological status when unabated by empirical evidence.

The few serious studies on culture change effectiveness suggest ambiguous results, anecdotal evidence, or no major effects on anything other than espoused values (Alvesson & Sveningsson, 2008; Ogbonna & Wilkinson, 1993; Siehl, 1985), which typically leads to failed change efforts (Balogun & Johnson, 2005).

For example, a longitudinal study at an electronics manufacturer in Silicon Valley found many of the concerns and interpretations of leaders were not shared over time by employees. Those that were could be explained by other contingent factors such as choice-constraints due to business life cycle or salience and attribution bias by employees in giving retrospective accounts of leader impact (Martin et al., 1985. For similar studies, see Gregory, 1983; Van

Maanen & Kunda, 1989).[28] Smith (2003) summarized 59 change efforts where culture was the objective, either as sole focus or in combination with other types of change. His summary finding was that the success rate for culture change was low. In reviewing the culture–performance relationship in the health care industry, Scott, Mannion, Marshall, and Davies (2003) found simplistic relationships such as 'good performance is the result of strong culture' were not supported.[29] Ogbonna and Harris (2002) concluded staff lower in the organization is "unlikely to be either able or willing to conform to deeper-rooted management-espoused value systems" (p. 50). More damningly, Ogbonna and Wilkinson (2003), in their in-depth study of culture change in United Kingdom grocery retailing found "instrumental compliance" and "skillful parodying" by middle managers and employees was evident in culture-change programs, the result of surveillance, direct control, and the threat of sanction rather than any "transformation of managerial values" (p. 1151).

Meanwhile, a recent Gallup survey finds 70% of U.S. workers do not feel engaged at work, and the problem is most pronounced in larger companies—in other words, those more likely to undertake culture change (Gallup, 2016). As with IMCO, employee engagement is one of the goals of many culture-change programs (for example, see Corporate Leadership Council, 2004; Lockwood, 2007). Considered at scale, these data suggest current culture-change approaches, at a minimum, are not achieving what they are purportedly trying to achieve.

Culture & M&A

One might expect to see evidence of successful culture change or deliberate architecting in the literature on culture in mergers and acquisitions (M&A). However, as with other studies involving organizational culture, this literature is inconclusive at best.

'Culture' is generally considered a critical factor in M&A. In a 2011 survey by Aon Hewitt, a human resources consulting firm, 87% of organizations reported that cultural integration was important or critical to transaction success, and yet cited cultural integration as one of the top three reasons for transaction failure (Fealy, Oshima, Sullivan, & Arian, 2011). The definitiveness of this finding is ironic given the M&A literature's treatment of variables such as culture, integration and performance is inconsistent, and contested. For example, according to Dauber (2012), M&A scholars tend to mix different levels of analysis in studying cultural constructs, such as conflating national versus organizational culture. Organizational culture is typically construed as a unitary monolith, which sidelines a more complex and complete understandings of all of the cultural variables involved. As put by Teerikangas and Very (2006):

> Most studies on the culture-performance relationship in M&A omit the question of levels of analysis within and beyond the organization itself,

(thus) how can we expect them to reach reliable results? Are researchers aware of the cultural reality in the organizations they are surveying?

(p. S36)

Such studies sidestep the epistemic difficulties in studying culture, in essence succumbing to the same issues enumerated for those studying culture and business performance (Cartwright & Cooper, 1993; Mottola, Bachman, Gaertner, & Dovidio, 1997). More broadly, several studies suggest this is due to the lack of a comprehensive framework for defining and measuring culture to begin with (for example, see Detert, Schroeder, & Mauriel, 2000).

Yet, despite the lack of compelling evidence that culture improves business performance or can be profitably leveraged for successful merger integration, and despite the many issues in organizational culture theory and research discussed above, value engineering programs proceed unabashedly unconcerned or oblivious to the lack of evidence in support of such endeavors. The culture consultant at IMCO only needed to reference a single culture study published by an influential management consulting firm to establish legitimacy for the undertaking, even though the basis of that study is subject to all of the issues problematized here.[30] Clearly, managers favor functional criteria over logical tests (Spender, 1989). Appeals to authority, usually in the form of the ever-elusive 'best practice', demand little in the way of rigor. For all of these reasons the valance of culture work is taken by most managers and practitioners as self-evident.

Looking for Culture in All the Wrong Places

Ironically, culture's popularity as an explanatory and normative tool may be due to the fact it is *pervasive* in social systems. Managers seek cultural explanations and interventions *because* culture is intuitively experienced as ubiquitous in behavior and practice. This intuition is not misplaced. It is in fact entirely consistent with an embodied and cognitive theory of culture. But in seeking to shape culture, managers and practitioners are focusing on cultural syndromes rather than what generates culture to begin with. In so doing they inevitably end up with failed interventions and adaptations because the locus of intervention is limited to culture's effects rather than causes. Culture is more complex and systemic than accepted in the folk conception, a complexity we are only beginning to apprehend. The cynical view would suggest the short-term business orientation of most U.S. companies and consequent 'quick fix' mentality it engenders precludes understanding culture as a more complex phenomenon. My view is more nuanced. The current state of the field is showing us that theory and praxis has yet to catch up to intuition. While singular, homogenizing organizational cultures are likely rare and limited to small enterprises, cultures *necessarily* do manifest in all organizations as a product of shared cognition. Whether these regularities manifest as cultural consistencies and organization-wide clarity, as a collection distinct coexisting subcultures, or as characterized by fragmentation, paradox, irony, or ambiguity—the *integration, differentiation* and *fragmentation* perspectives offered by Martin (2002)—is secondary. Cultural communities have discernible root logics that, while hard to detect given the nascence of our instrumentation, nonetheless are discernible amid the din of complex and recursive practices, structures and discourses making up institutional life. As Descola (2013) states, "people appear to regulate their actions as if these were dictated by cultural imperatives that they are nevertheless not able to express" (p. 101). Thus, the task of an anthropology that seeks to be relevant in this sphere is to

> gain an understanding of the logic of this work of composition, by lending an ear to the themes and harmonies that stand out from the great hum of the world and concentrating on emerging orders whose regularity is detectable behind the proliferation of different customs.
>
> (p. 111)

Without consensus in the scientific community on what culture is or how it can be measured, without explanatory frameworks that fully account for the range of cultural behavior and practice in organizations, and without empirical evidence to support such a framework—for a compelling body of evidence will be necessary to persuade pragmatic managers with short attention spans and strong desires to help their own organizations—actors vested in culture work have no incentive to behave or think differently. I know of no CEO today who would willingly ignore his or her own organization's culture. It is naive to suggest management consultancies abandon their lucrative culture change practices on the grounds of academic turbulence and muddle. There is a growing awareness of the inadequacies of the current state of organizational culture research and praxis, IMCO's efforts notwithstanding. Yet no compelling alternative has emerged, at least until now. The only choice for practitioners, thus, is to muddle on.

The consequences of muddling are significant. A lack of efficacy in research combined with naïve practice allows the prevailing values and beliefs of those in power to be unwittingly reified (Strauss, 2012). False agency is granted to those who believe they are doing something by 'changing' culture when they may not be doing anything at all, while false hope may be granted to those suffering in toxic organizational environments. The aspirations of stakeholders to provide better means for managing organizations and enacting positive change are jeopardized (Alvesson & Sveningsson, 2008; Kunda, 1992; Martin & Frost, 2011; Martin, 2002; Smircich, 1985). Enormous physical, financial and human resources are wasted while the opportunity to improve organizations continues to lie in wait.

Culture is a socially normative phenomenon; managers are right to pay attention to it. But the concept breaks down in how it is espoused and how it is conceptualized, measured and operationalized in practice, and as a consequence loses its efficacy, especially when conceived as a dependent variable. If this were *not* the case, the evidence for culture shaping and change would be indisputably clear given the many thousands of organizations who have been trying to engineer their own cultures since the 1980s. At some point this will result in the concept's abandonment altogether. This will be a loss for any of us whose sense of purpose is dedicated to the improved functioning of institutions and organizations in which so many spend so much of their waking lives.

3. Organizational Culture Reconsidered as Functionally Embodied Schemas

Humans exist, think, act and make meaning within a physical, material and cultural world. The alternative formulation offered here begins with the idea cultural meaning is a largely cognitive phenomenon, cognitive not only in the sense of knowledge but also, and perhaps largely, based on situated and embodied *tacit* knowledge.[31] This locates actors within a world not separate from them in the Cartesian sense, but rather one that is physically embodied and represented *within* them. Or in the words of Csordas (1990):

> It is equally in error to seek the objectivist "view from nowhere" and to inordinately privilege subjectivist "inner experience." Objectivity is not a view from nowhere, but a view from everywhere that the body can take up its position, and in relation to the perspectives of "other myselves." This perspective does not deny that objects are given; . . . the body is in the world from the start.
>
> (p. 38)

This embodied view represents a significant departure from prevailing theory. An embodied and situated locus for culture means culture is rooted in the shared cognitive experience as well as the task and technological milieu of the people making up a given cultural community. This means culture cannot simply be engineered towards a normative goal or arbitrarily imposed by actors in ways inconsistent with their own ecology. On the other hand, culture constituted on cognitive universals arising out of kinesthetic, social and cultural experience means culture is capable of underwriting the full range of cultural experience and expression in organizations, from symbols and artefacts to language to social relations to values, practices and routines. In this way the embodied approach *fully* accounts for culture's motive force, from strategic choice to what constitutes innovation to organizational design to branding to conceptions of success, and beyond. Cultural cognition explains the comprehensiveness of cultural experience in all its structural and behavioral affordances, while at the same time offering pragmatic tools for action.

Elaborating Existing Theory: Schein's Model

Edgar Schein (1984, 1992) is one of the few theorists to develop a model for organizational culture incorporating the concept of cultural schemas. First published in 1984, his model established the idea of tacit, preconscious "basic" assumptions underpinning all forms of visible and conscious culture (Figure 1.2).

Schein described these assumptions as tacit, learned knowledge about how "things really are" (p. 4). But he characterized assumptions in part as emanating from espoused values, whereas the functionally embodied framework conceives of values as the result of schemas induced from salient task, social, and cultural experience. Nonetheless, his model speaks to the pervasive nature of shared assumptions as grounding for culture. He was prescient—his model predates or was concurrent with theories of embodiment and more recent cognitive anthropological work. A cultural schemas approach elaborates and explains much of his framework (Figure 1.3):

While Schein's model and theory is well known, the fact it remains one among equals underscores what is being stressed. A few other theorists suggest a connection between mental representation and culture, notably Alvesson and Sveningsson (2008), Harris (1994) and Senge (1992), but by no means can these views be considered the mainstream of organizational culture praxis.

Schemas are basic assumptions employed in sensemaking. Task, technology, routines and other social forms in organizations and professions induce schemas, leading to the delimited character of cultures. Cultures in this way are not coherent wholes, but nonetheless display a patterned "thin" coherence

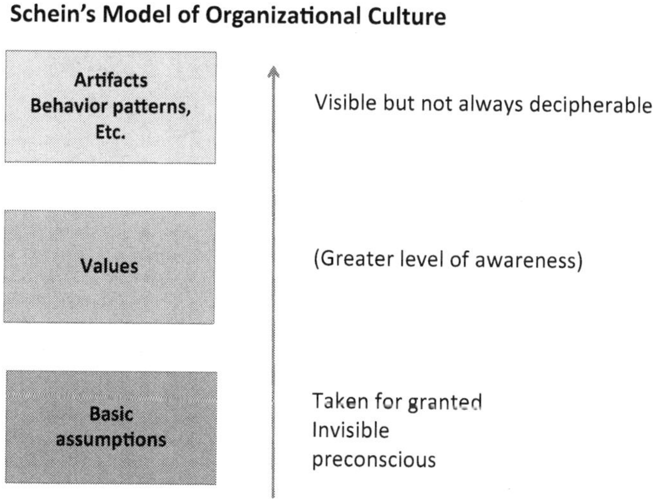

Schein's Model of Organizational Culture

Figure 1.2 Schein's model.

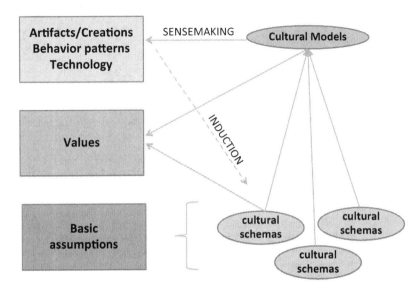

Figure 1.3 Schein's model elaborated by cultural schemas and models.

(Sewell, 2005) indelibly related to and grounded in the cognitions of its members. How this occurs, of course, is what the rest of this book is about.

The functionally embodied framework will not wave away all ontological, epistemological and hermeneutic concerns about organizational culture. There is still much work to be done to bring forward empirical evidence of schemas and cultural models and their affordances across industries and organizational systems beyond IMCO, while acknowledging the hermeneutic difficulties of 'reading' schemas. But a framework that unifies subjective experience with material reality allows us to make an important shift in how we study and intervene in culture. That shift is from thinking of systems and bureaucracies as either wholly autonomous or wholly intersubjective to thinking of these structures as embedded in a social, historical, technological and cultural context in which the actors within them may only *partially* have agency.

Notes

1 Not the company's real name.
2 Most of the senior executives were promoted from roles in the 'old' IMCO. The CEO, for example, was the former chief financial officer.
3 For an example of how culture is conceptualized in mainstream organizational development (OD) education, see Robbins (1998).
4 I use the terms "subjectivist and "objectivist" presented by Csordas (1990), Lakoff and Johnson (1980) and others to characterize the opposing theoretical poles of positivism on the one hand, and postmodern constructivism and

hermeneutics and their variants on the other. I recognize these distinctions are somewhat crude: multiple variations cluster within these labels. But for simplicity, unless making explicit reference to a particular school, I standardize on these two terms throughout.

5 I omit this tradition in my treatment, however, because anthropology has had relatively little influence in management (Stewart & Aldrich, 2015).

6 Many HR consulting firms offer 'culture' assessments. Among them are Towers Watson, Human Synergistics, Denison, and others. For a good example of one such model and approach, see Schneider's *Reengineering Alternative* (1999).

7 Helfrich and his associates (2007) provide the following description the CVF: Organizations with an internal focus and emphasis on control, labeled *hierarchical cultures* (also sometimes referred to as 'bureaucratic' cultures), adopt centralized authority over organizational processes; respect formal hierarchy; and adhere to rules. They place a premium on stability and predictability. Organizations with an internal focus and emphasis on flexibility, labeled *team cultures*, encourage broad participation by employees, emphasize teamwork and empowerment, and make human resource development a priority. Organizations with an external focus and emphasis on flexibility, labeled *entrepreneurial cultures*, exhibit creativity and innovativeness; they place a premium on growth and expanding resources. Organizations with an external focus and an emphasis on control, labeled *rational cultures*, are characterized by clarity of tasks and goals. They place a premium on efficiency and measurable outcomes. These four cultures are proposed as archetypes. In reality, organizations are expected to reflect all four cultures to some degree.

8 This example is taken from Gertler's (2004) contribution to the *untraded interdependencies* thesis, which suggests market exchanges are supplemented, if not eclipsed, by so-called untraded interdependencies—the shared social attributes, conventions, routines, habits, customs and understandings that facilitate interfirm learning. As people within a region move to different employers within the same sector, these interdependencies are strengthened.

9 Hofstede's himself later addressed this question by creating a fifth index (the "Confucian Dynamism" index; Baskerville, 2003).

10 From Van Herk and associates (2004): "Evidence for response style effects was not only found in response distributions on rating scales, but also in discrepancies of these distributions with national consumer statistics and self-reported actual behavior" (Van Herk et al., 2004, p. 346).

11 Chun et al. (1974) studied the tendency to choose extreme ratings on response scales between Korean and American subjects, and these findings were confirmed by Hui and Triandis (1989).

12 For a good example of person–culture fit research, see O'Reilly et al. (1991).

13 The 'Big 5' personality factors, in addition to the three mentioned, are *Emotional Stability* and *Culture*.

14 To evaluate 'co-occurrence' of meaning for each of the big 5 factors, Hakel asked respondents questions of the form "suppose a person is ____—how likely is that he also is ____?" (1974; D'Andrade, 1995, p. 82).

15 The solution in these societies is to ask about an item's importance as principle the respondent's life.

16 The better alternative for Maltseva and D'Andrade (2011) is to use multi-item scales that measure "evaluation frames"—the degrees of agreement or support with an established norm.

17 This is a measure of convergence between two sets of results of the same measurement for the same sample participants. A weaker measure is the convergence of the same measurement for two different sets of participants (Peng et al., 1997).

18 Interestingly, 'scenario' assessment methods where a situation with a behavioral option is presented for each assessed value proved to be more reliable across cultures. This lends support to schema-based assessment methods that require interpretation of case scenarios with at least some context supplied. See Chapter 5.

19 The research on employee engagement supports this view: more engaged employees lead to better financial performance, at least according to some studies (for example, see The Corporate Leadership Council, 2004).

20 This section is not an exhaustive review of postmodernism, hermeneutics or critical theory (etc.), but a more narrow focus on the issues inherent in culture.

21 Hermeneutics itself may be of the more 'objectivist' or 'alethic' variety, the former emphasizing the understanding of meaning, the latter characterized by the dissolution of boundaries between self and object (Alvesson & Skoldberg, 2009).

22 Were this not the case, I submit, influential management consultancies such as Booz & Company and McKinsey would not offer the reductionist, leader and values-centric approaches to culture change that they do (for example, see Aguirre, von Post & Alpern, 2013; McKinsey & Company, 2014).

23 329 companies engaged in culture change programs of some kind between 1980 and 1997 (from a review of North American textbooks on business; Helms-Mills, 2003).

24 Incidentally, narcissism among high-technology CEOs *positively* predicts both their salary and their job tenure. Other research shows behaviors such as displaying overconfidence and self-promotion are positively related to being chosen for leadership positions (Pfeffer, 2015)

25 This study actually is a comprehensive review of employee engagement practices. Culture is operationalized as both an input and output measure.

26 For example, Yale School of Management's case on Sapient (Nagy, Elias, & Podolny, 2007).

27 See Chapters 4 and 8 for how culture and leadership interact under the cultural schemas and models perspective.

28 Salience causes leaders to "figure prominently in people's memories of events," and attribution bias research suggests "people may have only minimal awareness of the situational determinants in decision-making" (Martin, Sitkin, & Boehm, 1985, p. 101).

29 Their evidence suggests this relationship is contingent. Aspects of performance valued within different cultures may be enhanced within firms exhibiting such cultural traits.

30 See earlier reference to the Booz & Company culture survey (Aguirre et al., 2013).

31 This separates this work from that of Bates et al. (1995) and others who conceive of culture as knowledge structures.

Bibliography

Abbott, A. (1998). *The system of professions: An essay on the division of expert labor.* Chicago: University of Chicago Press.

Aguirre, D., von Post, R., & Alpern, M. (2013). Culture's role in enabling organizational change: Survey ties transformation success to deft handling of cultural issues. *Booz & Company Survey.* Retrieved from http://www.booz.com/global/home/what-we-think/reports-white-papers/article-display/cultures-role-organizational-changehttp://linkinghub.elsevier.com/retrieve/pii/S088394170400022.

Ainsworth, S., & Hardy, C. (2004). Critical discourse analysis and identity: Why bother? *Cultural Discourse Studies, 1*, 225–229. doi: 10.1080/1740590042000302085.

Alvesson, M., & Berg, P. O. (1992). *Corporate culture and organizational symbolism: An overview* (No. 34). Berlin: Walter de Gruyter.

Alvesson, M., & Skoldberg, K. (2009). *Reflexive methodology: New vistas for qualitative research.* Los Angeles: Sage.

Alvesson, M., & Sveningsson, S. (2008). *Changing organizational culture: Cultural change work in progress.* Abingdon: Routledge.

Balogun, J., & Johnson, G. (2005). From intended strategies to unintended outcomes: The impact of change recipient sensemaking. *Organization Studies, 26*(11), 1573–1601.

Barley, S. (1983). Semiotics and the study of occupational and organizational cultures. *Administrative Sciences Quarterly, 28*, 393–413. Retrieved from http://scholar.google.com/.

Barnier, A. J., Sutton, J., Harris, C. B., & Wilson, R. A. (2008). A conceptual and empirical framework for the social distribution of cognition: The case of memory. *Cognitive Systems Research, 9*(1), 33–51.

Baskerville, R. F. (2003). Hofstede never studied culture. *Accounting, Organizations and Society, 28*(1), 1–14.

Bass, B. M., & Avolio, B. J. (1993). Transformational leadership and organizational culture. *Public Administration Quarterly,*17(1), 112–121.

Bates, K. A., Amundson, S. D., Schroeder, R. G., & Morris, W. T. (1995). The crucial interrelationship between manufacturing strategy and organizational culture. *Management Science, 41*(10), 1565–1580.

Berg, P. O. (1985). Organization change as symbolic transformation process. In P. Frost, L. Moore, M. R. Louis, C. Lundberg, & J. Martin (Eds.), *Organizational culture* (pp. 281–300). Newbury Park, CA: Sage.

Bernard, H. R., Kilworth, P., Kronenfeld, D., & Salier, L. (1984). The problem of informant accuracy: The validity of retrospective data. *Annual Review of Anthropology, 13*, 495–517. Retrieved from http://social.cs.uiuc.edu/class/cs598kgk-04/papers/informant_accuracy.pdf.

Beuckelaer, A., Lievens, F., & Swinnen, G. (2007). Measurement equivalence in the conduct of a global organizational survey across countries in six cultural regions. *Journal of Occupational and Organizational Psychology, 80*(4), 575–600.

Bryant, A. (2009–2015). The Corner Office. *The New York Times.* Retrieved from http://projects.nytimes.com/corner-office

Bucher, R., & Stelling, J. G. (1977). *Becoming professional* (Vol. 46). Beverly Hills, CA: Sage Library of Social Research.

Carr, A. (2000). Critical theory and the psychodynamics of change: A note about organizations as therapeutic settings. *Journal of Organizational Change Management, 13*(3), 289–299.

Cartwright, S., & Cooper, C. L. (1993). The role of culture compatibility in successful organizational marriage. *The Academy of Management Executive, 7*(2), 57–70.

Chan, L. L., Shaffer, M. A., & Snape, E. (2004). In search of sustained competitive advantage: The impact of organizational culture, competitive strategy and human resource management practices on firm performance. *The International Journal of Human Resource Management, 15*(1), 17–35.

Chanchani, S. (1998). *An empirical validation of Hofstede's dimensions of value.* Working Paper, School of Accounting and Commercial Law, Victoria University, Wellington, New Zealand.

Chatman, J., & Jehn, K. (1994). Assessing the relationship between industry characteristics and organizational culture. How different can you be? *Academy of Management Journal, 37*, 522–553. Retrieved from http://scholar.google.com/.

Chun, K. T., Campbell, J. B., & Yoo, J. H. (1974). Extreme response style in cross-cultural research: A reminder. *Journal of Cross-Cultural Psychology, 5*(4), 465–480.

Corporate Leadership Council. (2004). *Driving performance and retention through employee engagement.* Washington, DC: Corporate Executive Board.

Csordas, T. (1990). Embodiment as a paradigm in anthropology. *Ethos, 18*, 5–47. Retrieved from http://www.openwetware.org/images/5/54/Csordas.pdf.

D'Andrade, R. G. (1965). Trait psychology and componential analysis. *American Anthropologist, 67*(5), 215–228.

D'Andrade, R. (1995). *The development of cognitive anthropology.* Cambridge: Cambridge University Press.

D'Andrade, R. (2006). Commentary on Searle's 'social ontology': Some basic principles. *Anthropological Theory, 6*(1), 30–39.

D'Andrade, R. (2008). *A study of personal and cultural values: American, Japanese, and Vietnamese.* New York: Palgrave Macmillan.

Dauber, D. (2012). Opposing positions in M&A research: Culture, integration and performance. *Cross Cultural Management: An International Journal, 19*(3), 375–398.

Deal, T., & Kennedy, A. (1982). *Corporate cultures: The rites and rituals of corporate life.* Cambridge, MA: Perseus Publishing.

Denison, D. (1990). *Corporate culture and organizational effectiveness.* New York: John Wiley & Sons.

Descola, P. (2013). *Beyond nature and culture.* Chicago: University of Chicago Press.

Detert, J. R., Schroeder, R. G., & Mauriel, J. J. (2000). A framework for linking culture and improvement initiatives in organizations. *Academy of Management Review, 25*(4), 850–863.

Evered, R. (1983). The language of organizations: The case of the Navy. In L. Pondy, G. Morgan, P. Frost, & T. Dandridge (Eds.), *Organizational symbolism* (pp. 157–166). Greenwich, CT: JAI Press.

Fealy, E., Oshima, M., Sullivan, M., & Arian, M. (2011). *Culture integration in M&A (Aon Hewitt).* Retrieved from http://www.aon.com/human-capital-consulting/thought-leadership/m-and-a/reports-pubs_culture_integration_m_a.jsp.

Feldman, M. S. (1991). The meanings of ambiguity: Learning from stories and metaphors. In P. Frost (Ed.), *Reframing organizational culture* (pp. 145–156). Newbury Park, CA: Sage.

Fitzgerald, G. A., & Desjardins, N. M. (2010). Organizational values and their relation to organizational performance outcomes. *Atlantic Journal of Communication, 12*(3), 121–145.

Foucault, M. (1977). *Discipline and punish: The birth of the prison.* New York: Pantheon.

Freeman, L. C., Romney, A. K., & Freeman, S. C. (1987). Cognitive structure and informant accuracy. *American Anthropologist, 89*(2), 310–325.

Gallup. (2016). State of the American workplace. Retrieved from http://www.gallup.com/services/178514/state-american-workplace.aspx?g_source=EMPLOYEE_ENGAGEMENT&g_medium=topic&g_campaign=tiles.

Geertz, C. (1973). *The Interpretation of cultures.* New York: Basic Books.

Gelfand, M. J., Erez, M., & Aycan, Z. (2007). Cross-cultural organizational behavior. *Annual Review of Psychology, 58,* 479–514.

Gertler, M. (2004). *Manufacturing culture: The institutional geography of industrial practice.* Oxford: Oxford University Press.

Gordon, G. G., & DiTomaso, N. (1992). Predicting corporate performance from organizational culture. *Journal of Management Studies, 29*(6), 783–798.

Gregory, K. (1983). Native-view paradigms: Multiple cultures and culture conflicts in organizations. *Administrative Science Quarterly, 28,* 359–376. Retrieved from http://scholar.google.com/.

Guldenmund, F. W. (2007). The use of questionnaires in safety culture research—an evaluation. *Safety Science, 45*(6), 723–743.

Hakel, M. (1974). Normative personality factors recovered from rater's descriptor: The beholder's eye. *Personal Psychology, 27,* 409–421.

Hallowell, I. (1976). *Selected papers of Irving Hallowell.* Chicago: University of Chicago Press. (Originally published in 1954.)

Handwerker, W. P. (2002). The construct validity of cultures: Cultural diversity, culture theory, and a method for ethnography. *American Anthropologist, 104*(1), 106–122.

Harris, S. (1994). Organizational culture and individual sensemaking: A schema-based perspective. *Organization Science, 1,* 309–321. Retrieved from http://scholar.google.com/.

Hartnell, C., Ou, A., & Kinicki, A. (2011). Organizational culture and organizational effectiveness: A meta-analytic investigation of the competing values framework's theoretical suppositions. *Journal of Applied Psychology, 96,* 677–694. Retrieved from http://scholar.google.com/.

Helfrich, C. D., Li, Y. F., Mohr, D. C., Meterko, M., & Sales, A. E. (2007). Assessing an organizational culture instrument based on the competing values framework: Exploratory and confirmatory factor analyses. *Implementation Science, 2*(1), 13.

Helms Mills, J. (2003). *Making sense of organizational change.* New York: Routledge.

Herzfeld, M. (2001). *Anthropology: Theoretical practice in culture and society.* Malden, MA: Wiley-Blackwell.

Heskett, J. (2011). *The culture cycle: How to shape the unseen force that transforms performance.* Upper Saddle River, NJ: FT Press.

Hofstede, G. (1998). Attitudes, values and organizational culture: Disentangling the concepts. *Organization Studies, 19*(3), 477–493.

Hui, C. H., & Triandis, H. C. (1986). Measurement in cross-cultural psychology: A review and comparison of strategies. *Journal of Cross-Cultural Psychology, 16,* 131–152. doi: 10.1177/0022002185016002001.

Hui, C. H., & Triandis, H. C. (1989). Effects of culture and response format on extreme response style. *Journal of Cross-Cultural Psychology, 20*(3), 296–309.

Hutchins, E. (1987). Myth and experience in the Trobriand Islands. In D. Holland & N. Quinn (Eds.), *Cultural models in language and thought* (pp. 269–289). Cambridge: Cambridge University Press.

Hutchins, E. (1995). *Cognition in the wild*. Cambridge, MA: MIT Press.

Jorgensen, J. G. (1979). (8) 309–331.

Kantor, J., & Streitfeld, D. (2015, August 15). Inside Amazon: Wrestling big ideas in a bruising world. *The New York Times*. Retrieved from http://www.nytimes.com/2015/08/16/technology/inside-amazon-wrestling-big-ideas-in-a-bruising-workplace.html?_r=0.

Kegan, R. (1982). *The evolving self: Problem and process in human development.* Cambridge, MA: Harvard University Press.

Koller, V. (2005). Critical discourse analysis and social cognition: Evidence from business media discourse. *Discourse & Society*, 16(2), 199–224.

Koopman, P. L., Den Hartog, D. N., Konrad, E., et al. (1999). National culture and leadership profiles in Europe: Some results from the GLOBE study. *European Journal of Work and Organizational Psychology*, 8(4), 503–520.

Kotter, J. P., & Heskett, J. L. (1992). *Corporate culture and performance*. New York: The Free Press.

Kroeber, A. L., & Kluckhohn, C. (1952). Culture: A critical review of concepts and definitions. *Papers: Peabody Museum of Archaeology & Ethnology*, 47(1), Cambridge, MA: Harvard University.

Kunda, G. (1992). *Engineering culture: Control and communication in a high-tech corporation*. Philadelphia: Temple University Press.

Lakoff, G. (1987). *Women, fire, and dangerous things*. Chicago: University of Chicago Press.

Lakoff, G., & Johnson, M. (1980. Reprinted 2003). Metaphors *we live by*. Chicago: University of Chicago Press.

Lakoff, G., & Johnson, M. (1999). *Philosophy in the flesh*. New York: Basic Books.

Latour, B. (1993). *We have never been modern*. Cambridge, MA: Harvard University Press.

Learning the lingo (2014, January 11). *The Economist*, p. 72.

Levitt, P., & Schiller, N. G. (2004). Conceptualizing simultaneity: A transnational social field perspective on society. *International Immigration Review*, 38(3), 1002–1039.

Lindholm, C. (2007). *Culture and identity: The history, theory, and practice of psychological anthropology*. Oxford: Oneworld Books.

Liu, C., Borg, I., & Spector, P. E. (2004). Measurement equivalence of the German job satisfaction survey used in a multinational organization: Implications of Schwartz's culture model. *Journal of Applied Psychology*, 89(6), 1070.

Lockwood, N. R. (2007). Leveraging employee engagement for competitive advantage. *Society for Human Resource Management Research Quarterly*, 1, 1–12.

Louis, M. R. (1985). An investigator's guide to workplace culture. In P. Frost, L. Moore, M. R. Louis, C. Lundberg, & J. Martin (Eds.), *Organizational culture* (pp. 73–94). Newbury Park, CA: Sage.

Mallak, L. A., Lyth, D. M., Olson, S. D., Ulshafer, S. M., & Sardone, F. J. (2003). Diagnosing culture in health-care organizations using critical incidents. *International Journal of Health Care Quality Assurance*, 16(4), 180–190.

Maltseva, K., & D'Andrade, R. (2011). Multi-item scales and cognitive ethnography. In D. Kronenfeld, G. Bennardo, V. de Munck, & M. Fischer (Eds.), *A companion to cognitive anthropology* (pp. 153–170). Malden, MA: Wiley-Blackwell.

Martin, J. (2002). *Organizational culture: Mapping the terrain*. Thousand Oaks, CA: Sage.

Martin, J., & Frost, P. (2011). The organizational culture war games: A struggle for intellectual dominance. In M. Godwin & J. Hoffer Gittell (Eds.), *Sociology of organizations: Structures and relationships* (pp. 559–621). Thousand Oaks, CA: Sage. Retrieved from http://scholar.google.com/.

Martin, J., & Powers, M. (1983). Truth or corporate propaganda: The value of a good war story. In L. Pondy, P. Frost, G. Morgan, & T. Dandridge (Eds.), *Organizational symbolism* (pp. 145–156). Greenwich, CT: JAI Press.

Martin, J., Sitkin, S., & Boehm, M. (1985). Founders and the elusiveness of a cultural legacy. In P. Frost, L. Moore, M. R. Louis, C. Lundberg, & J. Martin (Eds.), *Organizational culture* (pp. 99–124). Newbury Park, CA: Sage.

McGregor, D. (1960). *The human side of enterprise.* New York: McGraw-Hill.

McKinsey & Company. (2014). *Culture.* Retrieved from http://www.mckinsey.com/locations/midwest/work/valuesandculture/.

Merritt, A. (2000). Culture in the cockpit: Do Hofstede's dimensions replicate? *Journal of Cross-Cultural Psychology, 31,* 283–301. Retrieved from http://scholar.google.com/.

Meyerson, D. (1991). Normal ambiguity? A glimpse of an occupational culture. In P. Frost, L. Moore, M. Louis, C. Lundberg & J. Martin (Eds). *Reframing organizational culture* (pp. 131–144). Newbury Park, CA: Sage.

Miller, D., & Dröge, C. (1986). Psychological and traditional determinants of structure. *Administrative Science Quarterly 31*(4),539–560.

Mills, A. J. (1988). Organization, gender and culture. *Organization Studies, 9*(3), 351–369.

Morgan, G. (2006). *Images of organization.* Thousand Oaks, CA: Sage.

Morse, N. C., & Weiss, R. S. (1955). The function and meaning of work and the job. *American Sociological Review, 20*(2), 191–198.

Mottola, G. R., Bachman, B. A., Gaertner, S. L., & Dovidio, J. F. (1997). How groups merge: The effects of merger integration patterns on anticipated commitment to the merged organization. *Journal of Applied Social Psychology, 27*(15), 1335–1358.

Nagy, A., Elias, J., & Podolny, J. (2007). *Sapient: Defining success was both the challenge and the opportunity.* Retrieved from http://sk.sagepub.com/cases/sapient-defining-success-was-both-the-challenge-and-the-opportunity.

Norman, W. T. (1963). Toward an adequate taxonomy of personality attributes: Replicated factor structure in peer nomination personality ratings. *The Journal of Abnormal and Social Psychology, 66*(6), 574.

Ogbonna, E., & Harris, L. C. (2000). Leadership style, organizational culture, and performance: Empirical evidence from UK companies. *International Journal of Human Resource Management, 11*(4), 766–788.

Ogbonna, E., & Harris, L. C. (2002). Managing organisational culture: Insights from the hospitality industry. *Human Resource Management Journal, 12*(1), 33–53.

Ogbonna, E., & Wilkinson, B. (2003). The false promise of organizational culture change: A case study of middle managers in grocery retailing. *Journal of Management Studies, 40*(5), 1151 1178.

Ogbor, J. O. (2001). Critical theory and the hegemony of corporate culture. *Journal of Organizational Change Management, 14*(6), 590–608.

O'Reilly, C., Chatman, J., & Caldwell, J. (1991). People and organizational culture: A profile comparison approach to assessing person-organization fit. *Academy of Management Journal, 34,* 407–516. Retrieved from http://scholar.google.com/.

Ormerod, P. (2005). *Why most things fail: Evolution, extinction, and economics.* Hoboken, NJ: John Wiley Sons.

Peng, K., Ames, D., & Knowles, E. (2000). Culture and human inference: Perspectives from three traditions. In D. Matsumoto (Ed.), *The handbook of culture and psychology* (pp. 245–264). Oxford: Oxford University Press.

Peng, K., Nisbett, R. E., & Wong, N. Y. (1997). Validity problems comparing values across cultures and possible solutions. *Psychological Methods*, 2(4), 329.

Peters, T. J., & Waterman, R. H. (1982). *In search of excellence: Lessons from America's best-run companies.* New York: Harper Collins.

Pfeffer, J. (2015). *Leadership BS: Fixing workplaces and careers one truth at a time.* New York: HarperCollins.

Porter, M. (2001). Strategy and the Internet. *Harvard Business School Working Knowledge.* Retrieved from http://hbswk.hbs.edu/item/2165.html.

Porter, M. (1996). What is strategy? *Harvard Business Review*, 74(6), 61–80.

Quinn, N. (2011). The history of the cultural models school reconsidered: A paradigm shift in cognitive anthropology. In D. Kronenfeld, G. Bennardo, V. de Munck, & M. Fischer (Eds.), *A companion to cognitive anthropology* (pp. 30–46). Malden, MA: Wiley-Blackwell.

Quinn, R. E., & Rohrbaugh, J. (1983). A spatial model of effectiveness criteria: Towards a competing values approach to organizational analysis. *Management Science*, 29(3), 363–377.

Raynor, M. (2011). *Disruptive innovation: The Southwest Airlines case revisited.* Retrieved from http://www2.deloitte.com/content/dam/Deloitte/us/Documents/strategy/us-consulting-disruptive-innovation-southwest-airlines-09062011.pdf.

Riordan, C. M., & Vandenberg, R. J. (1994). A central question in cross-cultural research: Do employees of different cultures interpret work-related measures in an equivalent manner? *Journal of Management*, 20(3), 643–671.

Robbins, S. (1998). *Organizational behavior: Concepts, controversies, applications.* Upper Saddle River, NJ: Prentice Hall.

Rogoff, B. (1990). *Apprenticeship in thinking: Cognitive development in social context.* New York: Oxford University Press.

Rokeach, M. (1973). *The nature of human values* (Vol. 438). New York: The Free Press.

Rosso, B. D., Dekas, K. H., & Wrzesniewski, A. (2010). On the meaning of work: A theoretical integration and review. *Research in Organizational Behavior*, 30, 91–127.

Ryan, A., Chan, D., Ployhart, R. E., & Slade, L. A. (1999). Employee attitude surveys in a multinational organization: Considering language and culture in assessing measurement equivalence. *Personnel Psychology*, 52(1), 37–58.

Sathe, V. (1983). Implications of corporate culture: A manager's guide to action. *Organizational dynamics*, 12(2), 5–23.

Sayer, A. (1992). Radical geography and Marxist political economy: Towards a reevaluation. *Progress in Human Geography*, 16(3), 343–360.

Schall, M. S. (1983). A communication-rules approach to organizational culture. *Administrative Science Quarterly*, 28(4), 557–581.

Schein, E. H. (1984). Coming to a new awareness of organizational culture. *Sloan Management Review*, 25(2), 3–16.

Schein, E. H. (1992). *Organizational culture and leadership* (2nd ed.). San Francisco: Jossey-Bass.

Schneider, B., & Smith, D. B. (2004). Personality and organizational culture. In B. Schneider and D.B. Smith (Eds.), *Personality and Organizations*, (pp. 347–370). Mawah, NJ: Lawrence Erlbaum Associates.

Schneider, W. (1999). *The reengineering alternative: A plan for making your current culture work.* New York: McGraw-Hill.

Schwartz, S. H. (1994). Are there universal aspects in the structure and contents of human values? *Journal of Social Issues, 50*(4), 19–45.

Scott, T., Mannion, R., Marshall, M., & Davies, H. (2003). Does organisational culture influence health care performance? A review of the evidence. *Journal of Health Services Research & Policy, 8*(2), 105–117.

Searle, J. R. (1993). Is there a crisis in American Higher Education? *Bulletin of the American Academy of Arts and Sciences, 46*(4)24–47.

Senge, P. (1992). Mental models. *Planning Review, 20*(2), 4–44.

Sergiovanni, T. J., & Corbally, J. E. (1984). *Leadership and organizational culture: New perspectives on administrative theory and practice.* Urbana, IL: University of Illinois Press.

Sewell, W. H. (1999). Concepts of culture. In V. Bonnell, L. Hunt, & R. Biernacki (Eds.), *Beyond the cultural turn: New directions in the study of society and culture* (Vol. 34). (pp.35–61). Berkeley: University of California Press.

Sewell, W. H. (2005). *Logics of history: Social theory and social transformation.* Chicago: University of Chicago Press.

Shore, B. (1996). *Culture in mind: Cognition, culture and the problem of meaning.* Oxford: Oxford University Press.

Shweder, R. (1977). Illusory correlation and the MMPI controversy. *Journal of Consulting and Clinical Psychology, 45*(5), 917.

Shweder, R. (1991). *Thinking through cultures: Expeditions in cultural psychology.* Cambridge, MA: Harvard University Press.

Sidanius, J., Feshbach, S., Levin, S., & Pratto, F. (1997). The interface between ethnic and national attachment: Ethnic pluralism or ethnic dominance? *Public Opinion Quarterly, 61*(1), 102–133.

Siehl, C. (1985). After the founder: An opportunity to manage culture. In P. Frost, L. Moore, M. R. Louis, C. Lundberg, & J. Martin (Eds.), *Organizational culture* (pp. 125–140). Newbury Park, CA: Sage.

Smircich, L. (1983). Concepts of culture and organizational analysis. *Administrative Science Quarterly, 28*, 339–358.

Smircich, L. (1985). Is the concept of culture a paradigm for understanding organizations and ourselves? In P. Frost, L. Moore, M. R. Louis, C. Lundberg, & J. Martin (Eds.). *Organizational culture* (pp. 55–72). Newbury Park, CA: Sage.

Smith, K. V., & Schreiner, J. C. (1969). A portfolio analysis of conglomerate diversification. *The Journal of Finance, 24*(3), 413–427.

Smith, M. E. (2003). Changing an organisation's culture: Correlates of success and failure. *Leadership & Organization Development Journal, 24*(5), 249–261.

Smith, P., & Dugan, S. (1996). National culture and the values of organizational employees. *Journal of Cross-Cultural Psychology, 27*(2), 231.

Spender, J. C. (1989). *Industry recipes: An enquiry into the nature and sources of managerial judgment.* Oxford: Basil Blackwell.

Spiro, M. (1996). Postmodernist anthropology, subjectivity, and science: A modernist critique. *Comparative Studies in Society and History, 38*, 759–780.

Stening, B. W., & Everett, J. E. (1984). Response styles in a cross-cultural managerial study. *The Journal of Social Psychology, 122*(2), 151–156.

Stewart, A., & Aldrich, H. (2015). Collaboration between management and anthropology researchers: Obstacles and opportunities. *The Academy of Management Perspectives, 29*(2), 173–192.

Stewart, G. (2002). Uncovering implicit leadership beliefs: Variation between information technology (IT) executives and business executives in a public service agency. *International Journal of Organisational Behaviour*, 5(4), 163–179.

Strauss, C. (1992). What makes Tony run? Schemas as motives reconsidered. In R. D'Andrade & C. Strauss (Eds.), *Human motives and cultural models* (pp. 191–224). Cambridge: Cambridge University Press.

Strauss, C. (2012). *Making sense of public opinion: American discourses about immigration and social programs*. New York: Cambridge University Press.

Strauss, C., & Quinn, N. (1997). *A cognitive theory of cultural meaning*. Cambridge: Cambridge University Press.

Swidler, A. (1986). Culture in action: Symbols and strategies. *American Sociological Review*, 51, 273–286.

Swidler, A. (2001). What anchors cultural practices. In T. Schatzki, K. Knorr-Cetina, & E. Von Savigny (Eds.), *The practice turn in contemporary theory* (pp. 74–92). London: Routledge.

Taylor, F. W. (1916). The principles of scientific management. In J. Shafritz & J. S. Ott (Eds.), *Classics of organization theory* (pp. 69–80). Pacific Grove: Brooks/Cole Publishing.

Teerikangas, S., & Very, P. (2006). The culture–performance relationship in M&A: From yes/no to how. *British Journal of Management*, 17(S1), S31–S48.

Testa, M. R., & Sipe, L. J. (2011). *The organizational culture audit: A model for hospitality executives*. International CHRIE Conference Referred Track, Paper 8. University of Massuchesetts. Retreived from: http://scholarworks.umass.edu/refereed/ICHRIE_2011/Friday/8

Townley, B. (1993). Foucault, power/knowledge, and its relevance for human resource management. *Academy of Management Review*, 18(3), 518–545.

Triandis, H. (1996). The psychological measurement of cultural syndromes. *American Psychologist*, 51(4), 407–415.

Van den Steen, E. (2009). *Culture clash: the costs and benefits of homogeneity*. Harvard Business School Working Paper. Retrieved from http://hbswk.hbs.edu/item/6254.html.

Van Dijk, T. (1993). Principles of critical discourse analysis. *Discourse and Society*, 4(2), 249–283

Van Herk, H., Poortinga, Y. H., & Verhallen, T. M. (2004). Response styles in rating scales evidence of method bias in data from six EU countries. *Journal of Cross-Cultural Psychology*, 35(3), 346–360.

Van Maanen, J., & Kunda, G. (1989). "Real feelings": Emotional expression and organizational culture. In L. Cummings & B. Staw (Eds.), *Research in organizational behavior* (Vol. 11, pp. 43–103). Greenwich, CT: JAI Press.

Vike, H. (2011). Cultural models, power and hegemony. In D. Kronenfeld, G. Bennardo, V. de Munck, & M. Fischer (Eds.), *A companion to cognitive anthropology* (pp. 376–392). Malden, MA: Wiley-Blackwell.

Willmott, H. (1993). Strength is ignorance; slavery is freedom: Managing culture in modern organizations. *Journal of Management Studies*, 30(4), 515–552.

Wood, J., & Vilkinas, T. (2004). Characteristics of chief executive officers views of their staff. *Journal of Management Development*, 23(5), 469–478.

2 The Nature of Grounding
Embodied Cognition, Schemas, and Analogical Transfer

The central idea of this book is that organizational culture is grounded in the professional experience and task focus of its members as they operate in and make sense of their environment. In other words, organizational culture, like any culture, is underpinned and dynamically determined by the human organism in relation its biological, environmental, task, and social context. This is not a strict determinism. Other variables intercede rendering no two cultures exactly alike. These factors nonetheless bound and constrain cultural possibility.

Culture as ecologically determined poses a direct challenge to popular as well as most objectivists and subjectivist conceptions of organizational culture, including notions of culture as causally engineered. To admit some amount of ecological determinism is to suggest culture defined as a dependent variable willfully shaped by the agency of leaders, or made up of etic constructs, *or* as purely decontextualized subjective experience, is a caricature, or wishful thinking.

A 'grounded' culture implies interaction between the human organism and its environment. In the words of the psychological anthropologist Thomas Csordas (1990), the body is the "existential ground" for culture (p. 5). Csordas' is following the pragmatism of John Dewey and the phenomenology of Merleau-Ponty and Bourdieu's *habitus*, a "system of perduring dispositions which is the unconscious, collectively inculcated principle for the generation of structuring practices and representations" (1990, p. 72). A culture, thus, that is 'functionally grounded' requires a theory that accounts for social and task-based cognitive patterning, processes that are accounted for by embodied cognition and its corollaries. This chapter begins with the theory and evidence for embodied cognition, and proceeds with a discussion of cognitive representation and analogical transfer, mechanisms central to the framework offered in this book. I end the chapter with a review of some critiques of embodiment.[1]

1. Embodied Cognition

So called 'embodied cognition' is an umbrella term encompassing a range of related frameworks conceptualized as 'embedded', 'distributed', 'situated', 'meditated' and 'enacted' cognition stemming from the theory of *enactivism* as originally posited by Varela, Thompson, and Rosch (1991), the work on metaphor and embodiment by Lakoff and Johnson (1980, 1999), and Rosch's work on prototypes (2002). While diverse, these theories share the idea that human cognition does not occur only in the brain and central nervous system encased within our bodies, but operates in dynamic interaction with the environment, including the technological and social environment. The degree of dynamism is a source of divergence among paradigms and has to do with the amount of 'offline', or environmentally decoupled, cognitive representation occurring within the mind, as elaborated below (Barnier, Sutton, Harris, & Wilson, 2008; de Bruin & Kastner, 2012). Offline cognition refers to cognitive activities whose referents are distant in time and space or are altogether imaginary and therefore have to be internally represented in some way (Wilson, 2002). But generally theories of embodiment range from relatively modest notions of low-level cognition as a function of sensorimotor experience (our bodies subject to the forces of gravity, etc.), to fully 'enacted' cognition as a reactive interconnectedness between an autonomous actor and the environment (de Bruin & Kastner, 2012; Stewart, 2010; see also Varela et al., 1991). Differences aside, embodied cognition broadly stated, posits the bodies we have, along with the experiences we have inhabiting and moving them through space and gravity as well as in social and cultural environments, circumscribes how we reason and understand the world (Hutchins, 2010; 1987; Johnson, 2007, 1987; Kimmel, 2008; Kitayama & Park, 2010).

This idea is a near universal rejection of Cartesian dualism and stands in contrast with classical view of cognition in cognitive science, which uses the metaphor of the computer to explain cognitive processes; cognition *is* mental computation. The mind is a processing system that manipulates pre- (or sub-) symbolic representations, and the processing capacity of the brain is thought of as modular and impervious to context (de Bruin & Kastner, 2012; Engel, 2010; Fodor, 1975).[2] Thus, according to the 'disembodied' cognition hypothesis, abstract and symbolic conceptual knowledge is all that matters for knowledge. The sensorimotor system is ancillary to or inconsequential in tasks that do not require it (Mahon & Caramazza, 2008). In the last 30 years this view has come under criticism on the grounds neural systems do not operate in isolation from the environment (Barnier et al., 2008); for lacking a phenomenological or experiential basis; and for sidelining social and cultural experience in shaping how we think and reason (de Bruin & Kastner, 2012; Johnson, 1987; Lakoff & Johnson, 1999). The embodied view, thus, takes as axiomatic the totality of human experience, from the biological through the neurological to higher order reasoning and imagining, is scaffolded and mediated by kinesthetic, technological, task, social and cultural experience.

Evidence for Embodiment

The risk with theories of embodied cognition is to succumb to the same reductionist tendencies that beset classic cognitivists. Instead of reducing everything to disembodied computation or modules, the reduction is to neurons, or to holistic self-organizing (Gallagher, 2005). This tendency is seen in the correlation versus causality error often made in considering neurological phenomena. Human behavior is attributed to neuronal configuration, whereas mere correlation is present. The antidote is to not stray too far from the evidence.

There is a growing body of evidence from a wide range of disciplines, from cognitive and developmental psychology, cognitive sociology, psycholinguistics, environmental science, and even management science that substantiates embodied cognition.

From neuroscientific research we know the brain is actively involved in processing physical, abstract, as well as culturally patterned action and emotion, as a growing body of data obtained through fMRI and ERP (event-related potentials) shows (Kitayama & Park, 2010; Lakoff, 2008; Lieberman & Eisenberger, 2010; Lieberman, Eisenberger, Crockett, Tom, Pfeifer, & Way, 2007).[3] Through the concept of 'mirror neurons' neuroscience shows when people think about a physical activity or see someone else perform the activity, the same set of neurons fire as when they physically engage in that activity (Lakoff, 2008). The areas of the brain associated with visual processing are active when people see pictures depicting both actual and implied motion (Kourtzi & Kanwisher, 2000). Neuronal 'spreading activation' along a network of related neurons occurs when two neurons fire at the same time, such as when learning something (Lakoff, 2008, p. 19). The more two neurons fire together, the stronger the link that is formed. This is the basis by which experience shapes the brain (Lakoff, 2008). New experiences and learning leads to chemical changes among neural networks through which spreading activation occurs (Lakoff, 2008).

The body is intimately involved in shaping cognition from birth. Bodily movement in the womb is organized by our own human shape in "ways that provide a capacity for experiencing a basic distinction between our own embodied existence and everything else" (Gallagher, 2005, p. 1). The fact our bodies move through space and are subject to the laws of gravity "anticipates and sets the stage" for the structuring of consciousness (p. 2), and for its central role in cognitive development:

> Movement and the registration of that movement in a developing proprioceptive system (that is, a system that registers its own self-movement) contributes to the self-organizing development of neuronal structures responsible not only for motor action, but for the way we come to be conscious of ourselves, to communicate with others, and to live in the surrounding world . . . movement prefigures the lines of intentionality, gesture formulates the contours of social cognition, and, in both the most general and most specific ways, embodiment shapes the mind.
>
> (Gallagher, 2005, p. 1)

A significant amount of empirical work on the relationship between the body and one's perception of one's own body supports Gallagher's position. For example, an absence of early crawling experience in the infant has a negative impact on the development of spatial perception, and crawling and locomotor experiences effect the perception and ability to estimate height (Campos, Bertenthal, and Kermoian, 1992). Changing posture, such as by experimentally tilting the body, lead to changes in the perception of external space (Bauermeister, 1964; Wapner & Werner, 1965). Similarly, the degeneration of bodily function and the ability to move through disease or injury lead to changes in awareness of body boundaries and bodily integrity (Halligan & Reznikoff, 1985).

Our perceptual system is also intimately tied and attuned to our own bodies in spatial relation to our environment. The human eye continually moves even while it fixes on an object even though this activity remains well below our level of awareness. If these eye movements are counteracted, visual perception fades completely as a result of neural adaptation. Thus, the brain, in active concert with the visual system, is what makes the environment visible (Martinez-Conde, Macknik, & Hubel, 2004). Complementary work on animal mental processes suggests animal cognition has evolved to be compatible with the structure of the physical world (Bregman, 2002). For example, the animal mind must have a mechanism for rotating shape without physically moving an object in order to envision shape change. In a similar vein, the human perceptual ability to hold differing but contiguous perspectives of an object allows us to maintain intact perceptual images while we move in space, as in how we can hold the image of a car constant as we walk around it (Palmer, 1996).

Higher order conceptual thinking is also formed and shaped in part through the experience of physical movement (Hutchins, 2010). Psycholinguistic studies show movement does not activate a specific word but rather a mental simulation of action, suggesting that conceptions of abstractions like time are in part structured by the experience of our own bodies in space and time (Gibbs, 2003). In what is by now a famous experiment in imagined action at San Francisco airport conducted by Boroditsky and Ramscar (2002), people were asked the question *Next Wednesday's meeting has been moved forward two days* and then asked, *What day is the meeting that has been rescheduled?* Passengers getting off a flight were more likely to answer Friday significantly more than passengers waiting to depart, who answered Monday. In other words, people seem to simulate the abstract concept of time in relation to their own bodies or movement of their bodies.

Bodily action also seems to play an important role in facilitating short-term recall. In a series of experiments conducted by Mandler (1983), subjects were presented with descriptions of short action sequences like *living on a farm* or *going to the woods* or *going to the lake*, with each event described in phrases typifying expected behavior for that event (*living on a farm* was described in terms of wearing overalls, milking a cow, growing corn, driving a tractor, etc.). Event recall was compared to groupings of the same events based on abstract categories like *outdoor places* or *animals*. It was easier for subjects to recall the action sequences than the abstract ones, even when subjects were allowed to create their own scenes from the phrases. When subjects classify objects based on abstract features rather than features based on movement or action, their memories do not exhibit the same kind of structuring (Mandler, 1983).

Bodily action does not simply reflect mental concepts; bodily practices, such as gesture, are closely tied to how concepts are formed (Gibbs, 2003). Concepts are created and organized from the experience of bodily movement. Studies of infant gesture by Meltzoff and Moore (1983) showed that newborns from as young as 42 minutes old are able to systematically imitate the gestures of an adult (such as tongue protrusion, mouth opening and closing, and lip protrusion). At six weeks, infants are able to remember and imitate gesture even with a 24-hour delay between testing. In later studies, Brooks and Meltzoff (2008) found that infant gaze following and pointing predicted language development. In a longitudinal study of infants from 10 months through two years of age showed that infants who followed a gaze and looked longer at a target object had significantly more rapid vocabulary growth than infants with shorter looks, even when controlling for factors such as maternal education. When infant pointing to the target was added, these correlations were strengthened.

Vygotsky (1980) considered the convergence of speech with physical activity to be the most significant moment in childhood intellectual development, based on the idea this is the first instance of sensorimotor experience being lexically reinforced. External activities are reconstructed as internal thoughts, and interpersonal processes are transformed into intrapersonal ones via a series of developmental events eventually leading to the internalization, interpretation, and reification of signs and symbols.

Psycholinguistic studies show similar results. For example, Ozcaliskan and Goldin-Meadow (2006) observed that children learning the 'like' construction, as in *x is like y*, precede learning the term through gesture alone. They suggest gesture precedes and provides a supporting context for learning how to speak. Myers (2008) describes biochemists making sense of molecular structure by imaging stresses among the parts of a complex molecule through their bodies. Or consider the various English expressions for valence (*I am right, do it the right way*, etc.). Casasanto (2009) found these metonymies cannot be attributed to linguistic figures of speech alone, because idioms in English associate *good* with right but not with left. He found that right- and left-handers associate positive valence more strongly with the side related to their dominant hands: "Right-handers tended to associate rightward space with positive ideas and leftward space with negative ideas, but left-handers showed the opposite pattern, associating rightward space with negative ideas and leftward with positive ideas" (p. 351). These results, he concludes, provide evidence for the sensorimotor basis of abstract ideas (Casasanto, 2009).

Psycholinguistic research suggests people create mental simulations of real-world actions when they communicate, hear stories, or solve problems (Gibbs & Matlock, 2008). For example, reading sentences that contain visual words and phrases such as *the ant climbed* while performing other tasks can selectively interfere with processing visual information in a visual categorization task. Or when asked to perform a physical action like forming a fist or moving a lever, people's ability to do so while at the same time verifying as meaningful sentences describing unrelated actions, such as *aim the dart* or *close the drawer*, are significantly slower (Gibbs & Matlock, 2008).

In studying comprehension of expressions such as *grasp the concept* or *stomp out racism*, Wilson and Gibbs (2007) showed people responded more quickly when the motor action of *grasping* or *stomping* was followed by the metaphor (as cited in Gibbs & Matlock, 2008). People easily and quickly seem to make sense of *stomp out racism* based on connecting the physical activity of stomping with the abstract concept of racism. Such simulations are not abstract but imagined 'as if' bodily action were involved (Gibbs & Matlock, 2008, p. 167).[4] Complementary physical performance seems to facilitate metaphor understanding; people appear to create a "relevant embodied simulation" to understand a metaphor (Gibbs & Matlock, 2008, p. 167).

Other cognitive linguistic work on metaphor, such as Gibbs' (2003) work on idioms, shows how understanding expressions such as *blow your stack* and *flip your lid* are not 'dead' metaphors but live expressions that derive their semantic power from the fact people's intuition of anger or mind are based on their own bodily experiences. For example, in comprehending anger idioms, people infer causes of anger to be "internal pressure," and that the expression of anger is "unintentional," "abrupt," and "violent" (Gibbs, 2003, p. 12). While this may seem obvious and perhaps explained through linguistic knowledge alone, people also find it easier to comprehend an idiomatic phrase such as *blow your stack* when it is read in a context that describes the cause of anger as internal pressure, rather than in a context that is contradictory, even though the idiom itself is well understood (Gibbs, 2003). People also make decisions much faster in lexical decision tasks— such as associating letter strings with an underlying conceptual metaphor such as ANGER IS HEATED FLUID IN A CONTAINER after having read stories with idioms (*John blew his stack*) rather than those with literal language (*John got very angry*).

There is also extensive evidence that supports the idea that cognition and emotion are neurologically intertwined (Pessoa, 2008). Brain regions involved in cognition have been shown to be involved in processing emotion. The neural processes underlying emotion and cognition are not modular, as thought by classic cognitivists, but integrated in complex and dynamic interactions of different brain areas, none of which are considered to be specifically affective or cognitive (Thompson & Stapleton, 2009). With respect to meaning and sensemaking, thus, embodied cognition considers emotion and cognition as intertwined at biological, psychological, and phenomenological levels (Thompson & Stapleton, 2009).

The neuroscientific research has been extended into domains such as socio-environmental science and business. In studies of dishonest behavior, researchers found the ergonomic design of human environments effects thought, feeling, and action. For example, studies by Yap (2013) and his colleagues tested whether incidental bodily postures imposed by the environment led to increases in dishonest behavior. Individuals who consciously or inadvertently assumed expansive 'power' postures either were more likely to steal money, cheat on a test, and commit traffic and parking violations in a driving simulation. The suggestion was environments that expand the body can inadvertently lead people to feel more powerful, and these feelings can cause dishonest behavior (Yap, Wazlawek, Lucas, Cuddy, & Carney, 2013). In a similar vein, work on posture in human and non-human primates shows posture not only reflects power, it can also produce the feelings associated with it. In contrast to low power poses, adopting high power poses has been shown to increase explicit and implicit feelings of power and dominance, risk-taking behavior, action orientation, pain tolerance, and testosterone (the dominance hormone), while reducing stress, anxiety, and cortisol (the stress hormone; Bohns & Wiltermuth, 2012; Carney, Cuddy, & Yap, 2010; Huang, Galinsky, Gruenfeld, & Guillory, 2010). In addition, adopting high-power poses leads to stronger effects on thought abstraction and action orientation (Huang et al., 2010)

Drawing from neural theory, "connectionist" or "parallel distributed processing" (PDP) artificial intelligence models show how knowledge is comprised of such networks of links and simple "processing units" (Strauss & Quinn, 1997, p. 51).[5] Such models have shown, for example, how secondary neural structures can bind to primary visual or motor structures in the primary cortex, emulating how meanings are first perceived as abstractions without specific details (Regier, 1996). These models suggest thinking does not happen in words but rather via a pattern of interaction among connected units. Cognitive tasks such as learning spatial relationships and word meanings occur through patterns of neural activation. The strength of such interaction varies by the density of the interconnections of the (neuronal) units and the strength of each connection (Regier, 1996; Strauss & Quinn, 1997).

In short, the evidence from these diverse literatures points to the active and foundational role of kinesthetic bodily experience in shaping thought, including abstract thought, and emotion. This becomes especially evident when sociocultural experience is considered.

Sociocultural Grounding

The social, cultural, and cognitive are deeply intertwined (Hutchins, 1995; Rogoff, 1990). We learn about the physical world in part through the social and cultural world. Or in the words of Fleck (1979), "cognition is the most socially conditioned activity of man" (p. 42). To Hutchins (2010), high level cognition comes about as a result of lower level cultural processes "applied to culturally organized worlds of action" (p. 446). In this way, the sociocultural world and the phenomenological world of the actor make each other up.

This constitution is replicated neurologically. The discovery of perception–action links in the brain, like the mirror-neuron research described above, provides a basis for understanding how social behavior may manifest in the brain. Functionally equivalent representations for self and other in the brain provide a platform for integrating the actions of self and other during social interaction (Böckler, Knoblich, & Sebanz, 2010). Neuroscientific evidence also shows how repeated performance of cultural routines result in differences in brain pathways across cultural groups (Kitayama & Park, 2010). Culture influences neural activity via the "specific tools, practices and tasks that are integrated into a more or less coherent, interconnected network" and repeated over time (p. 117). Similarly, emotion, including affect induced from social stimuli, impacts neurotransmitter levels and other neurological processes (Lieberman & Eisenberger, 2010; Lieberman et al., 2007).

As discussed above with Meltzoff's (2007) work, infants represent the acts of others and their own by recognizing equivalences between what they see others do and their own bodily movements. This gives rise to interpreting others as having similar psychological states, such as perceptions and emotions, and is thus considered to be the starting point for social cognition.

Rogoff (1990) believed all learning was culturally and socially situated. Through everyday involvement in social life children come to participate in culture and learn its ways. Parents and adults structure situations that allow children to observe, engage, participate in, and develop culturally and socially valued skills. Collective activity over successive generations constitutes how cultural practices are learned and situated in a cultural and social context (Rogoff, 1990).

Cultural and social practices also influence cognitive performance (Rogoff, 1990). For example, in one study of how children memorize spatial arrays, Mayan nine-year-olds were significantly better than their U.S. counterparts at reconstructing culturally appropriate panoramic scenes, such as a diorama with site-appropriate objects. This contrasted sharply with their much worse performance on list-memory tasks. American children seemed to master mnemonic strategies for remembering lists, likely because of their teaching socialization, whereas Mayan children relied more on spatial relationships, especially when the spatial relationships concerned culturally familiar objects (Rogoff, 1990). Classification based on taxonomy, as is typical in most industrialized societies, versus classification based on functional utility has historically been afforded higher value by researchers. But it may simply be that schooling in industrialized societies emphasizes defining, organizing, and classifying, whereas in societies like the Kpelle, objects are classified based on functional utility (e.g., knife with orange, hoe with potato; Rogoff, 1990). Numerous studies of Piagetian conservation have been criticized on a similar basis, where subjects' interpretation of what was being asked was dependent on local cultural norms of testing and learning. In certain societies, for example, it is uncommon for people when not in formal classroom environments to ask one another questions to which they already know the answer. In these societies, when conservation tasks were modified so as to present the task as informal language with questions such as, "what is the meaning of 'more' and 'the same'?" conservation of quantity was understood quite well (Rogoff, 1990).

Psycholinguistic cross-cultural studies examining interpretation of metaphorical expressions for *hunger* and *desire* conducted by Gibbs (2003) showed how knowing something about how people experience these states predicts what metaphors they use to describe them.[6] The intuition people have about their own embodied experience predicts their use and understanding of metaphor, including idioms (Gibbs, 2003). Kovecses (2008) found that cultural preference overrides what is thought to be common universal schematizations for metaphors for FEAR. Some metaphors, like FEAR IS HEAT (*too hot to handle, don't get burned by him*) are experientially incongruous, because fear is physiologically experienced as cold. Alternative metaphors closer to cultural experience may take precedence over other metaphors applicable to the same target domain. In other words, sociocultural experience may override kinesthetic experience, a finding that helps explain the salience of professionalization and task on cognitive structure (to which we will return in Chapter 4).

Cross-cultural linguistic studies of abstract domains such as space are another source of evidence for sociocultural grounding (for example, see Johnson, 1987; Lakoff & Johnson, 1999; Lakoff, 1987; Levinson, 1996; Regier, 1995). In the last decade the original cognitive linguistic conception of space and time as concepts universally grounded in bodily experience has been challenged by cross-cultural evidence. Most languages conceptualize space in terms of object-centric, egocentric, or absolute terms based on "visio-motor conceptions and actions" (Keller, 2011, p. 63; Levinson, 1996). *North–south* or *up–down* are spatial configurations or culturally determined "styles" (Levinson, p. 199; Regier, 1995). But some languages, like Mayan Tzeltal abstract a north–south orientation from the mountainous incline of the local environment, and this axis remains constant no matter where a Tzeltal speaker travels (Levinson, 1996), indicating the possibility at least that spatial orientation for some cultures is grounded in environmental experience.[7]

Similarly, in two different experiments on spatial relations, Sinha and Jensen de Lopez (2000) found marked differences in response patterns on language comprehension and action imitation tasks between Danish and Zapotec (Mayan) children. They focused on a Zapotec sample because in Zapotec language spatial relations of containment are lexicalized by *stomach*, not by *in* or *on*. In experiments with children between 15 and 30 months, testing Piaget's notion of object permanence that required children to put an object in, on, or under an upright or inverted cup, they found a strong Zapotec bias for canonical containment. Zapotec children consistently showed a preference for putting the object in the cup, even when the cup was inverted. When presented with choices consistent with their cognitive sense of containment, normative orientation (i.e., putting objects in the cup no matter the cup's orientation) overrode their notion of spatial relations. They concluded, very much in line with Vygotsky, that Zapotec children integrate social normative knowledge with their biologically based capacity for schematization,

In another experiment, Zapotec children showed no 'in bias' in language comprehension or imitation tasks as compared to the Danish sample. Sinha and Jensen de Lopez (2000) suggest the differences are cultural, not just linguistic. In Zapotec culture, baskets are not used as containers. In the village where the study was conducted, baskets are commonly inverted for use as covers for tortillas and other food items, and used inverted in children's games such as catching chickens. In addition, cups are quite uncommon. They concluded non-linguistic sociocultural differences are embodied in the material cultures and reified by non-linguistic cultural practice. As they state, "language-acquiring children are 'predisposed' through their experiences of interacting with the material world as . . . is culturally presented . . . to employ comprehension strategies that are consistent with the specific semantics of the languages they are acquiring." (p. 36). Cultural norms and practices may take precedence over sensorimotor preference, which may be indexed and reified by language. Reification can also involve material culture via the anchoring and stabilizing effects of culturally salient artefacts, a discussion I take up below.

Thus, to summarize this tour through the literature, viewing cognition as an embodied and sociocultural process means brain states, motor movements, environmental context and sociocultural primes function as an integrated continuity. To reduce the role of any implies cognition is an undetermined process, which clearly it is not (Kondor, 2013). The evidence suggests the kinesthetic and experiential as well as the social and cultural play a fundamental role in how we think, speak and act. To accept this, then, is to acknowledge that work and professional experience, to some degree, must also play a role in structuring cognition. We continue to examine this question as we turn to the role that schemas—or some form of representational structure—play in cognition and meaning.

2. *Representing Experience*: Image Schemas and Schemas

Humans are structure-seeking creatures (D'Andrade, 1995). All else equal, we seek maximum utility and efficiency in organizing and making sense of sensory information (Rosch, 2002). However, 'making sense' implies a cognitive substrate to mediate between the phenomenal world and the sensemaking agent. Or as provocatively put by Arthur Reber (1989), "sooner or later every discourse on mental process and structure must come to grips with the problem of the form of the representation of knowledge" (p. 226).

The issue of representation is central to the functionally embodied culture framework. The transposability of cognitive representations from kinesthetic bodily and sociocultural experience, rendered through analogical transfer (discussed below), relies on some amount of decoupled processing in order to apply 'knowledge', in whatever form it is constituted from context to another.

Traditional cognitivists hold that representation is either symbolic, that is, there is a one-to-one mapping between the external environment and mental representation, or 'sub-symbolic', whereby there is a one-to-many relation and any external object can figure within one or many internal representations (de Bruin & Kastner, 2012, p. 552). Embodied theories differ in the degree to which they admit offline processing to account for abstract reasoning, creative and moral imagination, false beliefs, and the like (de Bruin & Kastner, 2012; Johnson, 1993). But these are matters of degree; most post-cognitive ecological, enacted and situated theories of cognition generally endorse some form of representation of base-level concepts upon which abstract reasoning can develop (Steiner, 2014).

In general, representation is the cognitive ability of a plastic mind in interaction with the external environment to construct abstract "selective correspondence" with that environment (Ziemke, 1999).[8] These are "contentful physical structures playing a role in cognitive processing" (Steiner, 2014, p. 46). While these are minimal definitions, traditional cognitivists, and most embodied cognitivists, agree representation has ontological status that enables reference to real objects, properties, or states of affairs in the world (Steiner, 2014; but see below).[9]

The Schematic Substrate

Representational structure is at the core of many, but not all, cognitive processes. For example, artificial grammar acquisition and rote learning, under some theories, are based on non-schematic representation (Halford, Bain, Mayberry, & Andrews, 1998). Nonetheless, traditional computational cognitivism and most forms of embodied cognitivism typically account for representation through the concept of schemas.

Traced to Immanuel Kant and the work of Bartlett, Piaget, schema theory accounts for how humans organize sensory and kinesthetic input, mediating between perception and action (Johnson, 1987; Strauss & Quinn, 1997).[10] Schemas are "cognitive representations that include elements and relations between elements, and represent the structure of a situation or activity in the environment" (Halford et al., 1998, p. 204; see also Schank & Abelson, 1977). They encode and represent incoming perceptual information efficiently and guide perception and inference.

As with organizational culture, the schema literature is characterized by a diversity of positions, including those subsumed under computational cognitivism, embodied cognitivism, and those well beyond such as management.[11] Johnson-Laird's (1983) mental models, for example, are tacit processes and models of the world without syntactic structure. Talmy (2000) sees a foundational substrate of conceptual structure common across cognitive domains, including language, with multiple related schematic systems structuring language. He ascribes a related "understanding system" comprised of mental models that underwrite common sense and reason (p. 455). Gallagher (2001), in writing about the body schema, is careful to characterize schemas as "prenoetic systems of processes that regulate posture and movement" existing below the level of "self-referential intentionality" (p. 148). A body perception or image could be thought of as a conscious image of the body; a body schema can be thought of as something in the realm of "habit versus conscious choice" (p. 148). High-level representations appear to play an important mediating role in skilled movement, which does not diminish with practice (Gopher, Karis, & Koenig, 1985). In this way schemas support, or underwrite, intentional activity.

For our purposes, it is useful to organize the various orientations to schemas as either those characterized by conscious procedural or propositional knowledge; as preconscious, non-propositional and tacit modes of representation; or both. While schemas likely play a role in all of these activities, the lack of consensus and precision underscores the challenges in adopting schema theory in the management literature, as I discuss in Chapter 3. Johnson (1987) encompasses all of these positions by stating "schemata are typically thought of as a general knowledge structures, ranging from conceptual networks to scripted activities to narrative structures and even to theoretical frameworks" (p. 19).

Non-Propositional Schemas

Image schemas are the interface between kinesthetic sensory experience and the central nervous system (1999; Lakoff & Johnson,1980). They organize and represent perceptual and sensorimotor inputs as patterns upon which higher order cognition draws from to structure abstract thought (St. Amant et al., 2006). Johnson (1987) defines image schemas as "primitive gestalts that emerge from brain, body and world interaction and provide the essential structure for both constraining meaning and enabling abstract thought" (p. 20). The notion of constraint and enablement are important ideas to the theory of analogical transfer and metaphor, taken up below. Image schemas encode perceptual and sensorimotor experience such as UP–DOWN, BALANCE, CYCLE, PATH–GOAL, FORCE, and so forth. Perceptual input, as spatial structure, is mapped to conceptual structure where the input no longer has any original spatial, auditory, and kinesthetic information (Mandler, 1992; Piaget, 1962). As put by Lakoff and Johnson (1999):

A container schema has the following structure: an inside, a boundary, and an outside. This is a gestalt structure, in the sense that the parts make no sense without the whole. There is no inside without a boundary and an outside, no outside without a boundary and an inside, and no boundary without sides.

(p. 32)

In this way images are not mirrors of the world, nor do they require interpretation, as some arguments against image schemas have suggested (for example, Fodor, 1975; Paivio, 1978) but instead are indirect analogs of the environment. An image schema of PATH, for example, does not have speed or direction information as part of it. Yet PATH can easily be comprehended as an image. Image schemas, thus, have no inherent propositional format for representing meaning (Mandler, 2005).

A great deal of perceptual information is implicit in this way, and image schemas are thought to be part of procedural memory (Mandler, 1992). For example, people learn faces but cannot state explicit features about the faces they have in memory (Mandler, 1992). Yet procedural memory has a kind of schematic visual 'syntax' that can give rise to many cognitive entailments, but it lacks predicate-argument structure that specifies truth conditions. Instead, the structure is preverbal and, in a sense, precognitive (Mandler, 1992).

As perceptually uncommitted forms, image schemas serve as the basis for abstract reasoning. This base structure is replicated in higher order propositional schemas and cultural models. Take, for example, Lakoff and Johnson's (1999) example of the CONTAINER schema:

We can impose a conceptual container schema on a visual scene. We can impose a container schema on something we hear, as when we conceptually separate out one part of a piece of music from another. We can also impose container schema on our motor movements, as when a baseball coach breaks down a batter's swing into component parts.

(p. 32)

The gestalt of CONTAINER is preserved across domains. Interestingly, my research at IMCO suggests something similar. For example, IMCO executives use a number of MACHINE schemas to structure their discourse and organize particular cultural models. Examples include schemas such as *ORGANIZATIONS ARE MACHINES, PEOPLE NEED TO BE TREATED IN THE RIGHT WAY IN ORDER TO PERFORM*, and *STANDARD OPERATING SYSTEMS MITIGATE UNCERTAINTY* (see Chapter 6). The MACHINE schema also appears to structure certain decision-making and project management practices, in the sense of imbuing these practices with mechanistic qualities and properties. The effect of these schemas, while subtle, endows such practices with a particular structure and explanatory character much in the same way that CONTAINER can tacitly and perhaps visually organize teaching a novice baseball player how to swing a bat.

Propositional Schemas

Propositional schemas are *explicit* acts of cognitive processing (Arbuckle, Cooney, Milne, & Melchior, 1994; Crocker, Fiske, & Taylor, 1984; italics mine). Propositional schemas organize recurring "conceptual and propositional knowledge" about typical events and situations (Johnson, 1987, p. 20). They extend to beliefs, guide understanding, and structure the relationship between parts and wholes (Rousseau, 2001). Over time, they can be fine-tuned as environmental feedback improves their accuracy, with more stable schemas lending a sense of order and predictability to the world (Rousseau, 2001). Schemas complete missing or incomplete information (Crocker et al., 1984; Mandler, 1983; Shore, 1996). In essence, they make predictions about the world and "trigger a particular plan of action" (Gick & Holyoak, 1983, p. 10; Halford et al., 1998). A propositional schema, for example, might organize expectations about what happens when one walks into a restaurant or goes on a job interview. One's behavior may be modulated based on the schema, by, say, not walking into the interviewer's office without invitation. As such, schemas are highly *sensitive to activity in particular context* (Strauss & Quinn, 1997, pp. 49–50. Italics mine). There are scene schemas, story schemas, event schemas, and relational schemas—all abstractions about how things within a particular context will go (Crocker et al., 1984; Mandler, 1983; Shore, 1996). Some view schemas as "theories of reality," representational worlds, or cognitive maps (Baldwin, 1992, p. 468). Schemas can also be thought of as 'interrelated wholes'. Anything that triggers a part of a schema will activate the rest of the schema, encoding assumptions about what usually goes with what (Strauss, 2012, p. 10).

With respect to whether schemas are conscious or preconscious, these distinctions are matters of degree, not kind. Schemas will often, but not always, be activated in a context as explicit content of thought. Stereotypes are a good example. Even though a stereotype may have negative connotations and consequences, it is a knowledge structure made up of "learned expectations regarding the way things usually go" (Strauss & Quinn, 1997, p. 49–50). But many stereotypes reside outside the level of conscious awareness until brought into awareness by an outside agent, a triggering event, or through extensive learning. In this way, they are implicit or explicit depending on the individual and his or her experience and self-awareness. Purely non-propositional schemas, on the other hand, generally remain tacit as background features of cognition, "generally accepted that they form the shared presuppositions underlying different opinions about a topic" (Strauss, 2012, p. 11). When brought into awareness, such as a CON-TAINER schema, they may be thought of as so obvious or basic as to resist further analysis.

I suspect propositional and non-propositional schemas exist on a continuum, with basic image schemas and domain-specific non-propositional schemas structuring propositional schemas and more complex mental and cultural models. While theoretical, my research seems to suggest just such a relationship (see next chapter, and Section II). For the organizational scholar, these distinctions are not just academic. They have material implications for how one studies and intervenes in practice using the construct, a discussion explored in the next chapter.

Evidence for Schemas

Explicit research on schemas is limited (Bingham & Kahl, 2013), in part because generating empirical evidence of them represents challenges (see Chapter 5). But a significant amount of indirect evidence supports the idea of schemas, a sample of which is provided here.

Mental imagery shares common brain areas with other major cognitive functions, such as language, memory, and movement, depending on the imagery task. There is no unique mental imagery cortical network; rather, there is a high degree of interaction between mental imagery and other cognitive functions, including language (Mellet, Petit, Mazoyer, Denis, & Tzourio, 1998). How this interaction works remains an area of speculation, however, as Rohrer (2006) points out: "the current state of cognitive neuroscience stops short of specifying neural maps embodying the exact sets of perceptual contour patterns" (p. 130). Nonetheless, he acknowledges the "proposal" for image schemas is "highly consistent with the known facts of neurophysiology"(p. 130).

Schema theory accounts for the organization of sensory information in memory, as is borne out by neuroimaging studies. There is no one location in the brain where memories are stored (Guenther, 2002). Memory consists of lasting patterns captured by neuronal connections, and memory reflects changes to those connections relating to perception, feeling, language, and movement (Guenther, 2002). New or successive experience tends to strengthen these connections. The cognitive system extracts the invariants of an experience and uses them to form reasonable and plausible reconstructions, which is perhaps one reason why recall for general patterns is better than for details of an event (Guenther, 2002).

Medical studies with amputees where missing limbs manifest as feeling in phantom parts of the body are thought to involve a body schema (Gallagher, 2001). From virtual reality studies of anorexic and bulimic patients, manipulations of motor performance have (positive) effect on body perception, and, together with other therapies, have been shown to effect these patients' own body image (Gallagher, 2001). And medical research with stroke victims with hemispheric damage has shown that proprioception (a system that registers its own self-movement, and in this case relates to stimuli concerning position, posture, equilibrium, etc.; Gallagher, 2005) can be recalibrated through the use of wedge-prism glasses that shift the visual field and thereby change the patient's body schema so that he or she is able to reassert motor control (Gallagher, 2001). And as cited above, developmental studies of infant gesture show infants can imitate gestures such as tongue protrusion and mouth opening after a period of delay, suggesting some process of representation operative in memory from an early age.

Compelling evidence for schemas comes from cognitive linguistic studies of language acquisition and metaphor comprehension. For example, learning transitive verb forms (*John throws the ball*) and prepositions like *in* and *on* are considered early linguistic achievements (Mandler, 1992). The prepositions *in* and *on* are usually the first ones learned by English-speaking children, theoretically because the image schema for CONTAINMENT has been developed in the first year. Korean, however, has different verb forms depending on whether the verb is transitive or intransitive. Yet Korean children are aware of this distinction as soon as they use these words (Choi & Bowerman, 1991). Although transitive verbs and prepositions are abstract concepts, they depend on concepts of animacy and causality. Studies with deaf infants and their learning sign language point to the same conclusion. Children seem to rely on spatial relation concepts like AGENT, PATH, GOAL, FORCE, COMPLETED ACTION, POSSESSION, CONTAINMENT, and other concepts from the earliest point at which they learn language (Mandler, 1992). Without schemas, or if, say, learning transitivity was solely based on having to first learn grammatical rules, linguistic transitivity and prepositional phrasing would occur much later (Mandler, 1992). Language acquisition, thus, relies on preverbal concepts in order for meaning to be 'mapped' onto verbal concepts.

The cross-cultural cognitive linguistics work on metaphor done by Kovecses (2005) asserts that basic image schemas, such as those for time and space, are based on body schemas found in hundreds of languages. Indeed, although contested by some cross-cultural research (discussed below), much of cognitive linguistics considers schemas to be a universal notion as the basis for much of how we learn language and reason (Palmer, 1996). The existence of polysemy across many languages suggests language is structured and learned through preverbal imagery encoded in schematic form. For example, in the Tarascan (Michoacan) language, the suffix 'mari' can refer to facial parts or to more abstract flat surfaces, or to vertical surfaces, or a flat part of the body (Palmer, 1996). In Japanese, the expression 'hon' can refer to long thin things as well as trajectories, like the flight of a baseball (Lakoff, 1987).

Studies of narrative and recall suggest an active role for schematic structuring in working memory. Mandler's (1983) narrative comprehension experiments demonstrated how story "schemas" are activated when "criteria features" match descriptors of new perceptual data (Mandler, 1983, p. 35). For example, leaving out expected "story units" in narratives adversely affects story recall (Mandler, 1983, p. 42). In experiments that replicated Bartlett's findings, subjects were given two stories that described episodes connected in time. The episodes were either presented in temporal form or 'interleaved' with one unit of one story interspersed with another. Recall was found to be idealized over time. The more time elapsed between the experiment and the recall, the more dependent on the idealized story recall became, even when subjects were told to tell the interleaved story exactly as they had heard it. What is consciously noted and stored in memory seems to be only what deviates from the expected, strongly suggestive that working memory is influenced by schematic, pre-linguistic construals as well as by linguistic description (Mandler, 1983). This finding is corroborated by the studies on memory bias described in the previous chapter. Biases tend to be in the direction of a norm, such as the system of rules or an underlying pattern in the data. Such distortion effects appear in any memory-based assessment, including in person events such as interviews (D'Andrade, 1995; Freeman, Romney, & Freeman, 1987).

Recall is also much better for visual and spatial objects when scenes are presented in an organized and expected way, such as in Mandler's farmscape experiments with objects like a farmhouse placed with the sky and clouds above (etc.) rather than in a jumbled, disorganized way (house above the clouds, etc.). Even the unordered pictures were recalled as having more order than they actually did (Mandler, 1983). Our brains seem to impose schematic order where none exists in the stimuli (Mandler, 1983).

Lastly, neuro-computational models have shown how cognitive tasks such as learning spatial relationships and word meanings *only* occur through patterns of neural activation based on basic schematic structure. Secondary neural structures bind to primary visual or motor structures in the primary cortex, which suggests meanings, such as understanding a spatial location on a map, must first be perceived as an abstraction that omits specific details (Regier, 1996). Image schemas have also been represented computationally in image schema language (ISL), providing preliminary support to the idea of how the symbolic representation of objects and relationships functions across complex domains such as chess and robotics (St. Amant et al., 2006).

In light of the considerable amount of research and evidence supporting embodied cognition, the case for representational structure mediating between the physical world and cognition is strong. Most theories of cognition converge on the fact it is difficult to consider cognition as embodied without a mediating substrate of representation to account for how low-level cognition structures higher-level thinking. The evidence for schemas, thus, is promising.

3. Schema Induction and Analogical Transfer

Analogical processing is arguably *the* major contributor to the cognitive capacities of humans (Gentner & Colhoun, 2008; Hummel & Holyoak, 1997).[12] Our minds create analogies in order to solve a problem or make sense of our environment. We identify patterns and thereby seek causal connections through analogs (Hummel & Holyoak, 1997).

A schema is created through a process of encoding environmental information via the organism's dynamic and situated experience, including social context. This process generates an abstraction that eliminates most of the spatial information and detail processed during original perception (Johnson, 1987; Mandler, 1992). What is left is a set of correspondences where the underlying structure of the representation is what is highlighted. In forming an analogy we retrieve the analog source structure in order to map elements of the source to a target (Hummel & Holyoak, 1997; Mandler, 1992). This "structure mapping," that is, the process of transferring general schematic structure to new target domains, result in schema "induction" (Hummel & Holyoak, 1997, p. 427; Gentner & Colhoun, 2008; Gick & Holyoak, 1983).[13] In this way abstract thinking consists of chains of progressively more abstract concepts built up from basic-level schemas.[14]

Image schemas play an important role in analogical processing by providing both the spatial-cognitive and structural foundation for more abstract reasoning (Johnson, 1987; Lakoff & Johnson, 1999; Lakoff, 1987). For example, we can project the CONTAINMENT image schema onto the domain of psychological depression. Just as an object can be deep in a container and hard to get out, someone can be deep in a depression and hard to get out (Rohrer, 2006). This is what gives analogy and, by extension, cognitive models, their "inferential power" (Gentner & Colhoun, 2008, p. 7). Thus, in comparing an office to a jail, learners will reference a schema that utilizes the common structure—in this case *forced confinement*—of both cases but eliminate much of the detail (Gentner, Lowenstein, & Thompson, 2003).

Multi-modal interactions among different kinds of experience affect one another; the more congruent the modes of experience the greater the likelihood of schema induction (Hutchins, 2010). Thus, a "base domain" of experience with many "rich linked systems" of schematic relationships (such as those conferred by years of professional experience and accumulated expertise) will yield many potential analogical inferences by providing the corresponding structure for the target problem (Gentner & Colhoun, 2008, p. 4). Schemas learned early and from many different contexts will be more generalizable and tend to resemble a wider variety of new contexts (Strauss & Quinn, 1997). Thus, analogical projection from a basic schematic structure to an abstract concept is not just a structural phenomenon; it is also a developmental one. We learn projection early on as infants, and analogical projections remains a core feature of adult cognition (Rohrer, 2006).[15]

Evidence for Analogical Transfer

Considerable experimental evidence for induction and analogical transfer comes from developmental and experimental cognitive psychology as well as from cognitive linguistics. Piaget influenced research on the conceptual life of infants to such degree that until recently it was assumed infants had no conceptual life and all learning was purely based on sensorimotor activity, largely through imitation (Mandler, 1992). Piaget saw no evidence that infants conceptualize *about* objects, but conceptualization is now thought to occur much earlier, from at least three months of age (Mandler, 1992). Infants appear to have a number of higher order cognitive functions, such as recall, deductive inference, and problem solving. For example, infants show evidence of memory from at least 10 months of age, as discussed in the Meltzoff studies. Infants appear to create primitive schematic construals of what they see, such as SMOOTH, JAGGED, OBJECT STARTS SELF, or OBJECT GOES INTO OTHER OBJECT (Mandler, 2005). This is not hypothesis forming and testing, as some researchers have suggested (Fodor, 1981). Instead, what is believed to be happening is that spatial information is being encoded as schematic representations (Mandler, 1992). In one study, 9–13-month-olds were observed to match auditory and visual patterns. Infants were more likely to look at broken lines or a jagged circle when listening to a pulsing tone, and were more likely to look at a continuous line or smooth circle when listening to a continuous tone. Similarly, they were more likely to look at an arrow pointing up when listening to an ascending tone, and to a downward arrow with a descending tone. Other experiments have shown infants can learn to recognize regularities in simple verbal stimuli, such as noticing the shift from a repeated ABA pattern to an ABB pattern (Marcus, Vijayan, Rao, & Vishton, 1999), or are responsive to the difference between an object beginning to move without anything else coming in contact with it and an object moving when touched by another. Infants as young as four months notice the difference between a ball hitting and launching another ball and the same action interrupted by a short spatial or temporary gap between the balls touching (Leslie, 1982). These studies suggest concepts of projection and analogical transfer are resident from a very early age.

Studies of attention also suggest infants are aware of the concept of goals. As early as five months infants attend to the object of their own reach. By nine months they distinguish between a grasp and apparently unintentional resting of a hand on an object, and by 11 months can distinguish between opening a lid and grasping a toy in a box versus grasping a toy sitting outside a box. Attentiveness to goals is not simply limited to animate objects, but to inanimate objects like lines and circles as well. Infants appear to assume that any object, animate or inanimate, when taking a direct route from a starting point to a destination is following a goal-path, and they may be doing so by creating generalizations across different kinds of displays. Concepts do not generalize to other displays organized by a different concept. Mandler goes on:

> Infants see people get up and take a direct route to the telephone when it rings and they see balls rolling and knocking over other balls. Experience with both animate and inanimate objects following direct paths may lead infants to powerful expectations that at first apply to both kinds of objects.

> (1992, pp. 144–145)

Of course, these studies could be measuring something altogether different, such as stimulus novelty. But the sheer number of studies and the consistency of results suggest learning is inherently analogical, based on the preservation of some kind of schematic structure between one situation and another.

Other studies, such as those on performance on problem solving and memory also show the maintenance of schematic structure across domains (Gentner & Colhoun, 2008; Halford et al., 1998). Studies of perception find that ongoing exposure to specific social configurations and relationships, such as that in groups, can result in the formation of a single image-like representation (Bingham & Kahl, 2013).[16]

In selecting possible interpretations for an analogy, a system of "higher order" relations (such as causal relations) will be preferred over an equal number of independent matches (Gentner & Colhoun, 2008, p. 4). Increasing experience in a problem or task—such as when a child compares two apparently dissimilar objects, will enable the schema used as the basis of comparison to become more and more abstract, provided the common structure forming the basis of the comparison is observed and maintained in the target. For example, a child will not recognize the analogy between descending heights of dolls in a family with a 'Daddy, Mommy and Baby' set and a set of bowls of decreasing diameter. But give the child a closer match, such as of a set of bowls of descending height, and the analogy is made. Once learned, the schema can be applied to progressively more abstract analogs, providing the basis for the creation of relational categories and abstract rules (p. 9). Schema induction, thus, appears to be a function of the number of base analogs used and the content of the base analog itself (Reeves & Weisberg, 1994), furthering the possibility that schema induction is dependent on experience and expertise in a particular domain. This is the theory of progressive alignment thought to play a major role in the development of abstract thinking (Gentner & Colhoun, 2008).[17] It is also central to the theory of functional grounding, discussed in Chapter 4.

Studies on conventional metaphor evolution also provide evidence for how analogical transfer functions in reasoning. Take the phrase *gold mine*. Most native English speakers can guess what the phrase means when used as a metaphor: *something of value*. When paired with another term like *World Wide Web*, the metaphor does not lose its meaning. In fact, it gives rise to new meanings such as *the Web is a gold mine of information*. Our cognitive and linguistic capacity to generate new meanings by extending and blending metaphors is evidence of analogical transfer (Gentner & Bowdle, 2008). Other theoretical and experimental work describes the process by which metaphors structure categories of thought when they progress from novel utterances to conventional stability (Gentner & Bowdle, 2008; Turner, 1991):

> Novel metaphors are processed as comparisons in which the target concept is structurally aligned with the given base concept. But each such

alignment makes the abstraction more salient, so if a given base is used *repeatedly* in a parallel way it accrues a metaphorical abstraction as a secondary sense of the base term. When a base term reaches a level of conventionality such that it is associated abstract schema becomes sufficiently accessible, the term can function as a category name.

(Gentner & Bowdle, 2008, p. 116; italics mine)

This is consistent with how metaphor is considered in neural terms. To Lakoff (2008), a metaphor is a "mapping" (p. 30). As he states, "the overall use of metaphor involves some bindings and inferences in the source domain, bindings and inferences in the target domain, activation of metaphoric maps, and the activation of other related nodes" (p. 30).

To Lakoff and other experiential cognitive linguists, schemas are necessary for metaphor. However, an important distinction needs to be made on how metaphor works in the analogical transfer process. To Lakoff and Kovecses and others, metaphors *create* mental models and structure abstract thought. To Strauss and Quinn (1997), metaphors *reflect* models and schemas. This is an important distinction that has direct bearing on the research in Section II. In the former, metaphor *is* the structuring mechanism. Metaphors provide the basis *for* the analogical transfer from primary embodied experience to abstract thought. In the latter, metaphor is *one* manifestation of the underlying primary embodied experience but not, necessarily, the *only* structuring role in abstract cognition. No metaphor is needed in order to think abstractly, just a metaphorical process. To illustrate, consider Kovecses' (2005) own example of the *building* metaphor, as in ABSTRACT COMPLEX SYSTEMS ARE BUILDINGS. Kovecses seems to insist the core of the schema underlying this metaphor is the BUILDING metaphor (noun form). But if the noun *structure* is substituted, the core meaning of ABSTRACT COMPLEX SYSTEMS ARE STRUCTURES would not be lost. In fact, the concept may be enriched by its semantic indeterminacy because BUILDING is obviously restrictive as a referent. The question would need to be asked whether the speaker really intends BUILDINGS as the source domain, or something more abstract.[18] Strauss and Quinn (1997) and others make a similar point in arguing against the ARGUMENT IS WAR metaphor. From their review of Lakoff and Johnson's own work, they suggest ARGUMENT could be equally thought of as insanity, or as a wild animal, and so on.[19]

The human capacity to analogically extend embodied experience into abstract thought may occur in many different ways, with language, including metaphor, playing a role but by no means *the* definitive role. As Strauss and Quinn (1997) state in their research on conceptions of marriage, "metaphors . . . reflect an underlying schema that people share for thinking about marriage, and that guides their selection of metaphors for it" (p. 144). But their subjects' understanding of marriage exists independently of the metaphors used to talk about marriage.[20]

The evidence presented in the next section, following Strauss and Quinn, shows that metaphor *reflects* something of the way people think but it does not account for it. There may be, however, one exception: idioms. The extensive use of conventional metaphors and idioms may play an important role in anchoring reasoning, as I discuss below and elaborate in Section II.

4. *Beyond the Body*: Cognition as Situated, Mediated and Symbolically Enacted

What privileges the body as the basis of embodiment? Why is CONTAIN-MENT, for example, based on in–out bodily orientation and not, say, a cup? (Sinha & Jensen de Lopez, 2000). Are there material, linguistic, or symbolic grounds for cognition in addition to bodily and kinesthetic experience? The answer to this question has important implications for understanding how task and technology influence how people think and act in organizational and institutional settings.

With regard to spatial orientation, there is evidence that objects and events, as much as bodily experience, provide a foundation for schema induction. As discussed, pre-linguistic infants as young as nine months understand the notion of containment in its canonical sense. From Sinha and Jensen de Lopez' (2000) review of cross-cultural linguistic evidence, they state, "we could conclude that the human body schema is a privileged, but not unique, source domain for the linguistic conceptualization of spatial relations . . . other source domains (e.g. geophysical features) also occur with high frequency . . . [which] reflects their high experiential saliency"(Sinha & Jensen de Lopez, 2000, p. 24). The key here is "experiential." Physical experience, but not necessarily the human body, seems to be the pervasive source for grounded cognition.

Tool use provides a good example. When people use a tool the neural representation of the body schema changes as they move their body in relation to the tool (Kirsh, 2013). The represented shape of an object may be affected by physical interaction with it, particularly if the action is repeated and habitual, as shown experimentally in young children (Smith, 2005). As tool or instrument mastery develops, the tool reshapes perception, altering how one sees and acts, revising concepts and changing how the tool user thinks and interacts with the world (Kirsh, 2013). To illustrate, a guitar cannot naturally achieve the glissando effects of a trumpet. A trumpet cannot achieve the staccato effects of a guitar. The physical contours and material of the instrument constrain the sound—timbre, attack, decay, and so on. In turn, the sound of the instrument, in its actuality and potentiality, affects what the musician attempts to play and even what she 'hears' as possible music. In this way, cognition and material culture make each other up. The actor's interaction with material culture—the tools, instruments and artefacts of that culture—bring forth and shape the cognitive processes of the actor (Malafouris, 2004).[21] How does this occur?

Thompson and Stapleton (2009) suggest that tools when used over time gain a measure of cognitive transparency such that they are no longer experienced as discrete objects but rather the world is experienced *through* them. A classic case comes from the Merleau-Ponty (1962) example of the blind man and his cane. Once skilled at using the cane, he does not experience the cane as an object; instead, the world is experienced at the end of the cane and the cane is transparent to him (in Thompson & Stapleton, 2009). This transparency also occurs for prosthetic limb wearers who report feeling objects coming into contact with their limbs (Thompson & Stapleton, 2009). The non-conscious body schema and the conscious awareness of the body can include inanimate objects (Berlucchi & Aglioti, 1997). The so-called 'rubber hand illusion' suggests the feeling of one's own body can extend to prostheses (Tsakiris, Prabhu, & Haggard, 2006). Thompson and Stapleton propose tools and physical aids are, in fact, incorporated into the body schema. To do so within the cognitive system they must function "transparently in the body's sense-making interactions with the environment" (p. 23).

Social processes as well as cultural practices involving tools in the enactment of routines and tasks, such as coordinating the activities involved in navigating a large ship or flying a commercial airliner, are also shown to anchor abstract thinking (Hutchins, 2005, 2010; Nomura, Hutchins, & Holder, 2006). The ability to do product development work in complex global organizations appears to be grounded in everyday practices and routines of its members (Orlikowski, 2002). One way in which material and cultural practices and tools situate cognition is via the process of offloading. People 'offload' everyday thinking tasks to physical actions and objects (Gibbs & Matlock, 2008). For example, physical simulations about abstract or imagined activities, such as determining whether water will pour first from a wide or narrow glass, will yield incorrect answers unless one physically simulates the action involved. In so doing one is more likely to provide the correct answer (the wide glass) than when one simply tries to answer without physically simulating it (Gibbs & Matlock, 2008).

To Hutchins (2005) the association of material structure with conceptual structure is "very old" and stabilizes conceptual representation (p. 1556). Think of a compass, or an altimeter. These mechanisms orient navigators and pilots not simply because they provide information about direction or altitude but because they employ a basic human cognitive ability to project meaning onto tangible, linguistic, or cultural conventions in order to solve complex problems or reason more efficiently. Such reasoning would be impossible without the use of these artefacts (Hutchins, 2005). Sinha and colleagues (2011b) label such tools "symbolic cognitive artifacts." These are tools that "support symbolic and conceptual processes in abstract conceptual domains, such as time and number" (p. 11). Examples include writing, numeric notational systems, dials, calendars, compasses, and so forth, artefacts that are "external representations of cultural and symbolic practices" (Sinha, Sinha, Zinken, & Sampaio, 2011b, p. 11). Thus, how concepts are cognitively organized and represented may by directly related to how they are not only learned, but how they are put to use, and the context in which this takes place (Mahon & Caramazza, 2008). In other words, cognitive structuring, or schema induction and transfer is directly related to the sensorimotor and kinesthetic experience of task performance and tool use within a specific context. As put by Mahon and Caramazza (2008): "the activation of specific sensory and motor representations complements the generality and flexibility of 'abstract' and 'symbolic' conceptual representations" (p. 68). They go on:

> Another way to state this is that sensory and motor information constitutes, in part, the 'mental stuff' over which specific instantiations of a concept are realized. Of course, the specific sensory and motor information that is activated may change depending on the situation in which the 'abstract' and 'symbolic' conceptual representation is instantiated.
>
> (p. 68)

One of the best examples of how abstract thought is anchored and stabilized by material and symbolic artefacts is in the domain of time. Classic cognitive linguistics considers time to be mapped to space, which Lakoff and Johnson (1980) and others have said is a universal conceptual metaphor. Along with event-based schematizations (e.g., sunrise, winter), time does seem to have experiential grounding, as seen by the TIME IS SPACE metaphor. While not denying the prevalence of time schematicized as SPACE in many cultures, nor denying it to be motivated by experiential events, Sinha and colleagues (2011b) maintain:

> There is no natural prelinguistic, preconceptual schema of Time that, as it were, passively invites and receives (by way of image-schematic structural correspondence) mappings from spatial relational concepts, words and constructions. Rather, in many cases and in many cultures it is the constructed temporal schemas of linearity and cyclicity that permit the conceptualization of temporal relationships as existing in a domain *abstracted from the events themselves*.
>
> (p. 141; italics mine)

In such cases cognitive structuring occurs not on the basis of direct, phenomenological embodied experience, but on the construction of symbols, either in the form of schemas alone and expressed through abstract entities such as numbering systems, or in the form of physical artefacts that "anchor" the symbolic information in material structures (Sinha et al., 2011b p. 142). A time-based interval system such as a calendar allows framing of events within an abstract notion of months and years. Such systems are based on socially constructed counting practices, or on a cultural schema of a linear number line or a cycle. The interaction of these symbolic processes with language and physical artefacts reify as well as enable time reckoning. The important notion here is that the concept of time occurs independently of events occurring "in time" (p. 140). Time conceptualized in this way permits expressions such as *January is before February* and *the party is on Friday* (p. 141). Symbolic cognitive artefacts permit 'socio-cognitive' and cultural practices to be reproduced within cultures (p. 142).[22]

When the stability of the conceptual representation increases, such as those anchored in symbolic and material artefacts like clocks and calendars, the range of complex "manipulations" also increases (Hutchins, 2005, p. 1557). Examples abound: fictive motion, methods of locating oneself on a map, slide rules, tidal charts, and so forth. The concept of a line or cycle itself may have embodied grounding, although this is a notion that Sinha and colleagues reject. To Johnson (1987), however, the grounding of a linear event sequence or a cycle is first experienced in relation to the body. But symbolic cognitive artefacts can also be grounded in abstract representations alone, such as in cultural models supported by metaphor (Sinha et al., 2011b; Strauss & Quinn, 1997). Hutchins (2005) suggests language is the "weakest" form of grounding, especially when the symbols have "arbitrary relations to their referents" (p. 1572) but accords metaphor and conceptual blends special status. In the same way that time is construed on the basis of a line or cycle and materially anchored by artefacts like clocks and calendars, concepts like *capability* or *standard* might be similarly grounded in schemas like *THE RIGHT PEOPLE* and aided by conventional metaphors like *right*, as in 'correct' or 'best'.[23] In fact, Sinha and colleagues (2011b) maintain a key property of symbolic cognitive artefacts is their conventionality. They find expression in symbols and artefacts that a culture takes entirely for granted, such as in conventional metaphor.

The Sinha hypothesis is compelling in that it explains how language, and in particular metaphor, grounds schemas within a cultural domain. This is one reason why metaphors are useful for uncovering schemas. Accordingly, in my data symbolic cognitive artefacts expressed as conventional metaphors without an obvious experiential basis play a key role in structuring several cultural models at IMCO.

5. Some Challenges

The challenges to embodied cognition come in two forms. The first is an evidentiary challenge to strong-form embodiment based on enaction. The second is a more general ontological challenge to representation. The first is more easily bridged.[24]

The enaction framework (Stewart, 2010; Varela et al., 1991) referenced at the outset of this chapter holds that all cognition is grounded in ongoing dynamic interaction with the environment, and that cognition arises out of these 'dynamic couplings' with little, if any consideration for representation. Thus, dynamic interactionism is capable of accounting for all forms of abstract cognition, including abstract reasoning and language. This theory is influenced, in part, by O'Regan and Noe's (2001) concept of sensorimotor contingencies, where the rules and structures of sensorimotor action, such as seeing, are constitutive of cognitive processes. Thus 'seeing' is not based on an image in the retina and then deriving a representation of that image, but rather based on the brain exercising and mastering the contingencies involved in the act of seeing (Engel, 2010). This idea has been extended metaphorically to account for all cognition. That is, "neural states support the capacity of structuring situations through action" (Engel, 2010, p. 226). Along this view, neurons do not carry images of external states. The functional and dynamic interaction with the material world is what provides the grounding for cognition.

The appeal of the enacted view, in part, is phenomenological. Our direct knowledge of our own human experience forms the basis for how we understand others, and for our own theories of cognition, rather than inferring the states of others or simulating them in some way (known as the 'theory theory' and 'simulation' theories of mind; de Bruin & Kastner, 2012; Jacob, 2006).

Left open in this framework is the question of how abstract thinking, or language, comes about or is built up from primary sensorimotor experience (not to mention false beliefs, hallucinations, and similar non-situated events). One enactivist account for abstraction is put forth by Nunez (2010), who argues we can understand concepts such as *infinity* by appealing through metaphor to our embodied understanding of *space* (Nunez, 2010). Such metaphors, however, are based experientially on image schemas—and so we are back at representation.

Thus, despite claims to the contrary, the enactivists version of embodied cognition currently cannot adequately account for offline cognition, that is, cognition that takes place independent of the agent's environment or where agents do not have direct access to another's mental states, beliefs or desires (de Bruin & Kastner, 2012). Evidence to this effect is offered by Mahon and Caramazza (2008), who cite the numerous studies in which patients with motor impairments for using objects are able to nonetheless name the same objects, or with apraxia studies where the subject cannot speak or name the object even though he or she is able to identify it through gesture.

In short, strong-form embodiment cannot offer a satisfactory account of offline, non-embodied or symbolic cognition. There is ample neurological, developmental, psycholinguistic, and cognitive linguistic evidence to suggest offline processing, through the dynamics of schema induction and transfer, must be resident in some way to produce abstract thinking, imagination, moral judgment, and even language. The available evidence does not falsify a more modest version of dynamic embodiment that admits an offline representation that is dynamically situated and highly context sensitive (Mahon and Caramazza, 2008). I would like to think this more modest form leaves us with the capabilities Wilson (2002) frames when she says "the concomitant ability to mentally represent what is distant in time or space, may have been one of the driving forces behind the runaway train of human intelligence that separated us from other hominids" (p. 635).

The more serious challenge to embodied cognition is ontological, and involves reductionism. In essence, this charge is the same as that against phenomenology. That is, phenomenology cannot defend itself from alternative theories or viewpoints except by "reference to its own assumptions" (Lindholm, 2007, p. 193). As pointed out by Vervaeke and Kennedy (2004), image schemas, cannot in any way be invalidated or falsified except through language (metaphor), which is one of the same mechanisms used to identify them in the first place. This echoes Shore's (1996) point that the only way to study schemas is to first invent the notion of them.

The argument against reductionism, ultimately, is empirical (Rohrer, 2006). As I have shown above, there is converging evidence of schematic structuring in cognition. The evidence, however, must go beyond *apparent* embodiment—the claim because thinking has its basis in neural processes it therefore occurs in the body (Lakoff & Johnson, 1999). Correlation is not evidence: "One more fMRI experiment demonstrating that the motor cortex is activated during action observation or sentence processing does not make the embodied cognition hypothesis more likely to be correct" (Mahon & Caramazza, 2008, p. 69). Claims for embodied cognition must go beyond correlation to demonstrate *how* the mechanisms and affordances of cognitive structuring occur on the basis of bodily and environmental experience, including social and cultural experience. Studies, such as the one in this book, need to rely on observed phenomena verifiable through multiple means in order to mitigate coding and related hermeneutic challenges. The evidence tilts strongly in the direction of cognition grounded in all forms of human experience, from the kinesthetic to the social to the cultural, but it may not yet be sufficient to dissuade the hardened positivist or Cartesian dualist. For others, however, the data suggest a compelling foundation exists on which to locate a functionally grounded theory of culture.

Summary

In this chapter I attempted to lay the theoretical and empirical foundation for the functional grounding of organizational culture. This foundation is based on theory and research supporting embodied cognition; that is, that thinking is dynamically embodied, situated and mediated through and through by our experience in a material, social, and cultural world. Abstract reasoning and other forms of offline cognition, including cultural thinking are not possible without a representational substrate explained by schema theory. Schemas are learned (induced) and extended to other domains by the mechanisms of analogical transfer. In the following chapter I elaborate on how 'cultural' schemas make up culture, and, following that, how they are induced based on sustained experience in professional and task-based domains.

Notes

1 It should be noted here that criticisms of embodiment quickly return to the so-called 'hard' problem, that is, the mind–body problem. In the interest of focus, my treatment of this issue will be cursory. I invite the reader to review two important philosophical treatments of this issue, that from Gallagher (2005) or Lakoff and Johnson (1999).

2 A complete treatment of the challenges to computational theories of cognition is beyond our scope. For those interested, I suggest Gallagher (2005).

3 The recent work by Anders Eklund and his associates (for example, see Eklund, Nichols, & Knutsson, 2016) investigating false positives and errors in the software used by much fMRI research raises concerns about the reliability of many fMRI studies, including those cited here. Eklund's critiques have implications especially for weak neuroimaging results. Much of the work cited here is based on significantly strong results replicated by others. Nonetheless, while neuroimaging data forms only a portion of the evidence for functional embodiment, these data are of some concern. As of this writing those researchers cited here have not yet responded to these concerns or published errata concerning their own studies.

4 An alternative explanation, of course, could be the action primed study participants to respond more quickly to the actual verb in the comprehension phrase. But studies with a control group showed no correlation between priming for the verb and comprehension time.

5 It should be noted some enactivists associate distributed processing or connectionist models with computational cognitivism. However, much of the artificial intelligence work on how knowledge is stored and built up through connectionist networks is highly useful and relevant to our understanding of schemas.

6 Gibbs' subjects were from the United States and Brazil.

7 One might argue what is being witnessed has nothing to do with ecology or environment and is instead the effect of language. The direction of causality—does language structure cognition, or is language an effect of cognition—is the linguistic relativity problem outlined by the Sapir-Whorf hypothesis, the proposition (in its 'strong' form) that grammatical categories enable as well as limit worldviews. See Section II.

8 Representation has also been characterized as patterns that can generate behavior without a stable relation to environmental entities, as well as the notion of 'indexical-functional' structures, that is representations of entities in terms of the their functional or spatial relation to the agent, as well as experiential accounts (Ziemke, 1999).

9 A good review of these positions can be found in Steiner (2014). As he states: "Strategically, the rejection of representationalism continues to mark an important difference not only between enactivism and cognitivism (i.e. the computo-representational theory of mind), but also between (some forms of) enactivism and other more recent theories that criticize, amend or even reject the intellectualist, internalist or formalist dimensions of the computo-representational theory of mind . . . by often retaining representationalism. . . More fundamentally, the permanent rejection of representationalism should not be taken as an *easy* task: representationalism is a polymorphous and plastic thesis" (p. 44).

10 Schemas are closely related to prototype theory in the work of Charles Fillmore and Eleanor Rosch (Lakoff, 1987). Prototype theory is based on the notion of class inclusion. "Basic-level" categories, that is, categories containing objects directly perceived such as *cat, tree, animal,* and so forth are generally designated by category names (Rosch, 2002, p. 254). Categories relate to one another through a taxonomy: The greater the inclusivity of a category within a

taxonomy, the "higher the level of abstraction" (p. 254). What locates a thing in a particular category are its common attributes. Thus, *sparrows* are in the *bird* category by virtue of common attributes (wings, feathers, the ability to fly, etc.). Category admittance is based on a diversity of elements: motor movements, shape similarity, averaged shape, and so forth (Rosch, 2002). Rosch further defined basic-level categories as those "for which it was possible to form a mental image isomorphic to the appearance of the class as a whole" (p. 258). Accordingly, Quinn (2005) considers prototype "worlds" to be subsumed in the notion of schema (p. 38).

11 These positions, as to be expected, reflect the various disciplines of their proponents —from philosophy (i.e. Gallagher, Johnson) to cognitive semantics (i.e. Talmy, Lakoff) to cognitive psychology. Here are a few definitions: schemas are action repertoires (Vike, 2011); knowledge structures containing categories of information and relationships among them (Elsbach, Barr, & Hargadon, 2005); structures that interpret stimuli (Narvaez & Bock, 2002); objects of memory in cognitive fields and mental models (Derry, 1996); symbolic units defining grammatical classes, such as for nouns (Langacker, 2002); abstractions mediating between stimuli and response (Casson, 1983); or a systematic selection of aspects of a scene representing the whole (Talmy, 2005); "data reduction devices enabling individuals to negotiate a complex and confusing world" (Balogun & Johnson, 2004, as cited in Rerup & Feldman, 2011, p. 579) and "stable cognitive templates" (Elsbach et al., 2005, p. 422).

12 But not the only process involved. We learn and reason in other ways too. As Gentner states, we learn also "by association, by reinforcement, by automatization, and by statistical learning of sequences. But these capabilities are shared with other animals. My claim is that the positive feedback system between language and structure-mapping processes is what makes humans uniquely powerful learners" (Gentner & Colhoun, 2010, p. 2).

13 Also called schema 'encoding'.

14 This is the same process that Piaget's described in his theory of assimilation, whereby schemas develop through experience with instances. Schemas change with exposure to inconsistencies or the need to accommodate new realities (Ginsburg & Opper, 1979).

15 A complementary view of analogical transfer was proposed by Langacker (1987), who suggested analogical thinking is based on similarities or differences to a prototype, and by schematic extension from a prototype to other cases. This explains why some members of a category may appear to be taxonomic, whereas others appear to be variants.

16 It may be that this single image representation scales to organizations and perhaps accounts for, or aids, in conceptualizing organizations as a single monolithic culture.

17 This matching is age-sensitive, but generally thought to occur at a much younger age than originally conceived by Piaget (Mandler, 1992).

18 The Lakoff position may be thought of as neo-Whorfian. It privileges language as deterministic for structuring how humans think.

19 Vervaeke and Kennedy (2004) argue that most of us do not have any direct experience of WAR, therefore WAR cannot be an adequate experiential source domain for ARGUMENT.

20 Another argument away from Lakoff and Johnson's (1980, 1999) formulation is that not all foundational metaphors occur across all languages. That said, if a particular metaphor such as UNDERSTANDING IS SEEING (or SEEING IS KNOWING; Rakova, 2002) does not appear, say, in Finnish, is not an argument against embodied cognition. It is an argument against the universality of conceptual metaphor.

21 To a radical materialist like Malafouris (2004), there is no individual 'mind', only a mind that exists in the world, situated and enacted in social and cultural ways. In this way schemas and mental models are always temporally emergent and always changing as they interact with other schemas and schema enactments.

22 Sinha's and associates' study of Amondawa (Amazon) conceptions of time found that the Amondawa have no word for 'time,' leading them to assert space–time mapping is not a universal, as thought by Lakoff and Johnson. They state: "The schematization of the domain of time as motion through an imaginary and metaphorical 'space', either cyclical or linear, a schematization that appears to us natural and self- evident, is absent from the Amondawa repertoire of cultural schemas. In short, the conceptual domain of abstract and reified 'Time' is not a human cognitive universal, but a cultural and historical construction, constituted by schematized time-based time interval systems, reflection upon which is language and culture dependent" (Sinha, Sinha, Zinken, & Sampaio, 2011, p. 11).

Sinha and colleagues suggest symbolic cognitive artefacts enable the so-called 'ratchet effect' in culture. This is the theory that cultural transmission is characterized by modifications and improvements which stay within the population readily until further changes 'ratchet things' up again. This process relies on innovation of cultural 'novelties' and on faithful re-transmission (such as through symbolic cognitive artefacts) across generations to keep such cultural novelties in place until new ones come along (Tennie, Call, & Tomasello, 2009, p. 2406).

23 See Section II.

24 In the interest of scope I am omitting a more general discussion of the challenges to phenomenology that also accompany critiques of embodiment. For those interested I would refer you to Dennett (2007, 1991) who states "phenomenology is fiction" (2007, p. 254). For a vigorous and thorough defense of phenomenology, I suggest Gallagher (2005).

Bibliography

Arbuckle, T., Cooney, R., Milne, J., & Melchior, A. (1994). Memory for spatial layouts in relation to age and schema typicality. *Psychology and Aging, 9*(3), 467–480.

Baldwin, M. W. (1992). Relational schemas and the processing of social information. *Psychological bulletin, 112*(3), 461–484.

Balogun, J., & Johnson, G. (2005). From intended strategies to unintended outcomes: The impact of change recipient sensemaking. *Organization Studies, 26*(11), 1573–1601.

Barnier, A. J., Sutton, J., Harris, C. B., & Wilson, R. A. (2008). A conceptual and empirical framework for the social distribution of cognition: The case of memory. *Cognitive Systems Research, 9*(1), 33–51.

Bauermeister, M. (1964). Effect of body tilt on apparent verticality, apparent body position, and their relation. *Journal of Experimental Psychology, 67*(2), 142.

Berlucchi, G., & Aglioti, S. (1997). The body in the brain: Neural bases of corporeal awareness. *Trends in Neurosciences, 20*(12), 560–564.

Bingham, C., & Kahl, S. (2013). The process of schema emergence: Assimilation, deconstruction, utilization, and the plurality of analogies. *Academy of Management Journal, 56*, 14–34. Retrieved from http://dx.doi.org.10.5465/amj.2010.0723.

Böckler, A., Knoblich, G., & Sebanz, N. (2010). Socializing cognition. In E. Pöppel (Ed.), *On thinking: Towards a theory of thinking, Part 4* (pp. 233–250). Munich: Parmenides Foundation.

Bohns, V. K., & Wiltermuth, S. S. (2012). It hurts when I do this (or you do that): Posture and pain tolerance. *Journal of Experimental Social Psychology, 48*(1), 341–345.

Boroditsky, L., & Ramscar, M. (2002). The roles of body and mind in abstract thought. *Psychological Science, 13*(2), 185–189.

Bregman, A. (2002). The auditory scene. In D. Levitin (Ed.), *Foundations of cognitive psychology: Core readings* (pp. 213–248). Cambridge, MA: MIT Press.

Brooks, R., & Meltzoff, A. N. (2008). Infant gaze following and pointing predict accelerated vocabulary growth through two years of age: A longitudinal, growth curve modeling study. *Journal of Child Language, 35*(1), 207–220.

Campos, J. J., Bertenthal, B. I., & Kermoian, R. (1992). Early experience and emotional development: The emergence of wariness of heights. *Psychological Science, 3*(1), 61–64.

Carney, D. R., Cuddy, A. J., & Yap, A. J. (2010). Power posing brief nonverbal displays affect neuroendocrine levels and risk tolerance. *Psychological Science, 21*(10), 1363–1368.

Casasanto, D. (2009). Embodiment of abstract concepts: Good and bad in right-and left-handers. *Journal of Experimental Psychology: General, 138*(3), 351.

Casson, R. W. (1983). Schemata in cognitive anthropology. In B. Siegel, A. Beals, & S. Tyler (Eds.), *Annual review of anthropology* (pp. 429–462). Palo Alto: Annual Reviews.

Choi, S., & Bowerman, M. (1991). Learning to express motion events in English and Korean: The influence of language-specific lexicalization patterns. *Cognition, 41*(1), 83–121.

Crocker, J., Fiske, S. T., & Taylor, S. E. (1984). Schematic bases of belief change. In J. R. Eiser (Ed.), *Attitudinal judgment* (pp. 197–226). New York: Springer.

Csordas, T. (1990). Embodiment as a paradigm in anthropology. *Ethos, 18,* 5–47. Retrieved from http://www.openwetware.org/images/5/54/Csordas.pdf.

D'Andrade, R. (1995). *The development of cognitive anthropology.* Cambridge: Cambridge University Press.

de Bruin, L. C., & Kästner, L. (2012). Dynamic embodied cognition. *Phenomenology and the Cognitive Sciences, 11*(4), 541–563.

Dennett, D. (1991). *Consciousness explained.* Boston: Little Brown.

Derry, S. J. (1996). Cognitive schema theory in the constructivist debate. *Educational Psychologist, 31*(3–4), 163–174.

Eklund, A., Nichols, T. E., & Knutsson, H. (2016). Cluster failure: Why fMRI inferences for spatial extent have inflated false-positive rates. *Proceedings of the National Academy of Sciences, 113*(28), 7900–7905, doi: 10.1073/pnas.1602413113.

Elsbach, K., Barr, P., & Hargadon, A. (2005, July–August). Identifying situated cognition in organizations. *Organization Science, 16*(4), 422–433.

Engel, A. (2010). Directive minds: How dynamics affects cognition. In J. Stewart, O. Gapenne, & A. Di Paolo (Eds.), *Enaction: Toward a new paradigm for cognitive science* (pp. 219–244). Cambridge, MA: MIT Press.

Fleck, L. (1979). *Genesis and development of a scientific fact* (Fred Bradley and Thaddeus Trenn, Trans.). Chicago: University of Chicago Press. (Original work published 1935).

Fodor, J. (1975). *The language of thought.* New York: Crowell.

Fodor, J. (1981). The current status of the innatenes controversy. In J. Fodor (Ed.), *Representations* (pp. 257–316). Cambridge, MA: MIT Press.

Freeman, L. C., Romney, A. K., & Freeman, S. C. (1987). Cognitive structure and informant accuracy. *American Anthropologist, 89*(2), 310–325.

Gallagher, S. (2001). Dimensions of embodiment: Body image and body schema in medical contexts. In S. Kay Toombs (Ed.), *Phenomenology and medicine* (pp. 147–175). Dordrecht, NL: Kluwer Academic Publishers.

Gallagher, S. (2005). *How the body shapes the mind.* New York: Oxford University Press.

Gentner, D., & Bowdle, B. (2008). Metaphor as structure mapping. In R. Gibbs (Ed.), *The Cambridge handbook of metaphor and thought* (pp. 109–128). Cambridge: Cambridge University Press.

Gentner, D., & Colhoun, J. (2008). *Analogical processes in human thinking and learning.* Retrieved from http://scholar.google.com/scholar?q=analogical+processes+in&hl=en&btnG=Search&as_sdt=1%2C5&as_sdtp=on.

Gentner, D., & Colhoun, J. (2010). Bootstrapping the mind: Analogical processes and symbol systems. *Cognitive Science, 34*, 752–775. doi: 10.1111/j.1551-6709.2010.01114.x.

Gentner, D., Lowenstein, J., & Thompson, L. (2003). Learning and transfer: A general role for analogical encoding. *Journal of Educational Psychology, 95*, 393–408. Retrieved from http://scholar.google.com/.

Gibbs, R. (2003). Embodied experience and linguistic meaning. *Brain and Language, 84*(1), 1–15.

Gibbs, R., & Matlock, T. (2008). Metaphor, imagination, and assimilation: Psycholinguistic evidence. In R. Gibbs (Ed.), *The Cambridge handbook of metaphor and thought* (pp. 161–176). Cambridge: Cambridge University Press.

Gick, M., & Holyoak, K. (1983). Schema induction and analogical transfer. *Cognitive Psychology, 15*, 1–38. Retrieved from http://scholar.google.com/.

Ginsburg, H., & Opper, S. (1979). *Piaget's theory of intellectual development.* Englewood Cliffs, NJ: Prentice Hall.

Gopher, D., Karis, D., & Koenig, W. (1985). The representation of movement schemas in long-term memory: Lessons from the acquisition of a transcription skill. *Acta Psychologica, 60*(2), 105–134.

Guenther, K. (2002). Memory. In D. Levitin (Ed.), *Foundations of cognitive psychology: Core readings* (pp. 311–360). Cambridge, MA: MIT Press.

Halford, G., Bain, J., Mayberry, M., & Andrews, G. (1998). Induction of relational schemas: Common processes in reasoning and complex learning. *Cognitive Psychology, 35*, 201–245. Retrieved from http://scholar.google.com/.

Halligan, F. R., & Reznikoff, M. (1985). Personality factors and change with multiple sclerosis. *Journal of Consulting and Clinical Psychology, 53*(4), 547.

Huang, L., Galinsky, A. D., Gruenfeld, D. H., & Guillory, L. E. (2010). Powerful postures versus powerful roles which is the proximate correlate of thought and behavior? *Psychological Science, 22*(1), 95–102. doi: 10.1177/0956797610391912.

Hummel, J., & Holyoak, K. (1997). Distributed representations of structure: A theory of analogical access and mapping. *Psychological Review, 104*, 427–466. Retrieved from http://scholar.google.com/.

Hutchins, E. (1995). *Cognition in the wild.* Cambridge, MA: MIT Press.

Hutchins, E. (2005). Material anchors for conceptual blends. *Journal of Pragmatics, 37*, 1555–1577. Retrieved from http://scholar.google.com/.

Hutchins, E. (2010). Enaction, imagination, and insight. In J. Stewart, O. Gapenne, & A. Di Paolo (Eds.), *Enaction: Toward a new paradigm for cognitive science* (pp. 425–450). Cambridge, MA: MIT Press.

Jacob, P. (2006). Why visual experience is likely to resist being enacted. *Psyche*, *12*(1), 1–12.

Johnson, M. (1987). *The body in the mind*. Chicago: University of Chicago Press.

Johnson, M. (1993). *Moral Imagination: The implications of cognitive science for ethics*. Chicago: University of Chicago Press.

Johnson, M. (2007). *The meaning of the body*. Chicago: University of Chicago Press.

Johnson-Laird, P. N. (1983). *Mental models: Towards a cognitive science of language, inference, and consciousness* (No. 6). Cambridge, MA: Harvard University Press.

Keller, J. (2011). The limits of the habitual: Shifting paradigms for language and thought. In D. Kronenfeld, G. Bennardo, V. de Munck, & M. Fisher (Eds.), *A companion to cognitive anthropology* (pp. 61–81). Chichester: Wiley-Blackwell.

Kimmel, M. (2008). Properties of cultural embodiment: Lessons from the anthropology of the body. In R. Frank, R. Dirven, & T. Ziemke (Eds.), *Cognitive linguistics research: Sociocultural situatedness* (Vol. 2, pp. 77–108). Berlin: Mouton de Gruyter.

Kirsh, D. (2013). Embodied cognition and the magical future of interaction design. *ACM Transactions on Computer-Human Interaction (TOCHI)*, *20*(1), 3.

Kitayama, S., & Park, J. (2010). Cultural neuroscience of the self: Understanding the social grounding of the brain. *Social Cognitive and Affective Neuroscience*, *5*, 111–129. doi: 10.1093/scan/nsq052.

Kondor, Z. (2013). Computation vs. embodied cognition. In A. Coliva, V. A. Munz, & D. Moyal-Sharrock (Eds.), *Mind, language and action* (pp. 206–208). Kirchberg am Wechsel: Austrian Ludwig Wittgenstein Society.

Kourtzi, Z., & Kanwisher, N. (2000). Activation in human MT/MST by static images with implied motion. *Journal of Cognitive Neuroscience*, *12*(1), 48–55.

Kovecses, Z. W. (2005). *Metaphor in culture: Universality and variation*. Cambridge: Cambridge University Press.

Kovecses, Z. W. (2008). Metaphor and emotion. In R. Gibbs (Ed.), *The Cambridge handbook of metaphor and thought* (pp. 380–398). Cambridge: Cambridge University Press.

Lakoff, G. (1987). *Women, fire, and dangerous things*. Chicago: University of Chicago Press.

Lakoff, G. (2008). The Neural theory of metaphor. In R. Gibbs (Ed.), *The Cambridge handbook of metaphor and thought* (pp. 1–35). Cambridge: Cambridge University Press.

Lakoff, G., & Johnson, M. (1980. Reprinted 2003). *Metaphors we live by*. Chicago: University of Chicago Press.

Lakoff, G., & Johnson, M. (1999). *Philosophy in the flesh*. New York: Basic Books.

Langacker, R. (1987). *Foundations of cognitive grammar, vol. 1, theoretical prerequisites*. Stanford. Stanford University Press.

Langacker, R. (2002). *Concept, image and symbol: The cognitive basis of grammar*. Berlin: Mouton de Gruyter.

Leslie, A. M. (1982). The perception of causality in infants. *Perception*, *11*(2), 173–186.

Levinson, S. (1996). Language and space. *Annual Review of Anthropology*, *25*, 353–382. Retrieved from http://scholar.google.com/.

Lieberman, M., & Eisenberger, N. (2010). *The pains and pleasures of social life: A social cognitive neuroscience approach.* Retrieved from http://web.mac.com/naomieisenberger/san/Naomi_Eisenberger_SAN_Papers_files/Lieberman%20%26%20Eisenberger%20(2008)%20Neuroleadership.pdf.

Lieberman, M., Eisenberger, N., Crockett, M., Tom, S., Pfeifer, J., & Way, B. (2007). Putting feelings into words: Affect labeling disrupts amygdala activity in response to affective stimuli. *Psychological Science, 18,* 421–428. doi: 10.1111/j.1467-9280.2007.01916.x.

Lindholm, C. (2007). *Culture and identity: The history, theory, and practice of psychological anthropology.* Oxford: Oneworld Books.

Mahon, B. Z., & Caramazza, A. (2008). A critical look at the embodied cognition hypothesis and a new proposal for grounding conceptual content. *Journal of Physiology-Paris, 102*(1), 59–70.

Malafouris, L. (2004). The cognitive basis of material engagement: Where brain, body and culture conflate. In C. Gosden (Ed.), *Rethinking materiality: The engagement of mind with the material world.* McDonald institute for Archaeological Research (pp. 53–61).

Mandler, J. (1983). *Stories, scripts, and scenes: Aspects of schema theory.* New York: Psychology Press.

Mandler, J. (1992). How to build a baby: II. Conceptual primitives. *Psychological Review, 99,* 587–604. Retrieved from http://scholar.google.com/.

Mandler, J. (2005). How to build a baby: III. Image schemas and the transition to verbal thought. In B. Hampe & J. Grady (Eds.), *From perception to meaning: Image schemas in cognitive linguistics* (pp. 137–163). Berlin: Mouton de Gruyter.

Marcus, G. F., Vijayan, S., Rao, S. B., & Vishton, P. M. (1999). Rule learning by seven-month-old infants. *Science, 283*(5398), 77–80.

Martinez-Conde, S., Macknik, S. L., & Hubel, D. H. (2004). The role of fixational eye movements in visual perception. *Nature Reviews Neuroscience, 5*(3), 229–240.

Mellet, E., Petit, L., Mazoyer, B., Denis, M., & Tzourio, N. (1998). Reopening the mental imagery debate: Lessons from functional anatomy. *NeuroImage, 8*(2), 129–139. doi: org/10.1006/nimg.1998.0355.

Meltzoff, A. N. (1988). Imitation of televised models by infants. *Child Development, 59*(5), 1221.

Meltzoff, A. N. (2007). 'Like me': A foundation for social cognition. *Developmental Science, 10*(1), 126–134.

Meltzoff, A. N., & Moore, M. K. (1983). *54*(3), *Child Development,* 702–709.

Merleau-Ponty, M. (1962). *Phenomenology of perception* [*Phénoménologie de la Perception*]. Abigndon: Routledge.

Myers, N. (2008). Molecular embodiments and the body-work of modeling in protein crystallography. *Social Studies of Science, 38*(2), 163–199.

Narvaez, D., & Bock, T. (2002). Moral schemas and tacit judgment or how the defining issues test is supported by cognitive science. *Journal of Moral Education, 31,* 297–314.

Nomura, S., Hutchins, E., & Holder, B. (2006). The uses of paper in commercial airline flight operations. In *Proceedings of the 2006 20th anniversary conference on computer supported cooperative work,* (pp. 249–258). New York: ACM. doi: 10.1145/1180875.1180914.

Nunez, R. (2010). Enacting infinity: Bringing transfinite cardinals into being. In J. Stewart, O. Gapenne, & A. Di Paolo (Eds.), *Enaction: Toward a new paradigm for cognitive science* (pp. 307–334). Cambridge, MA: MIT Press.

O'Regan, J. K., & Noë, A. (2001). A sensorimotor account of vision and visual consciousness. *Behavioral and Brain Sciences, 24*(5), 939–973.

Orlikowski, W. (2002). Knowing in practice: Enacting a collective capability in distributed organizing. *Organization Science, 13*(3), 249–273.

Ozcaliskan, S., & Goldin-Meadow, S. (2006). X is like Y: The emergence of similarity mappings in children's early speech and gesture. In G. Kristiansen, M. Archard, R. Dirven, & F. Ruiz de Mendoza Ibanez (Eds.), *Cognitive linguistics: Current applications and future perspectives* (Vol. 1, pp. 229–262). Berlin: Walter de Gruyter.

Paivio, A. (1978). The relationship between verbal and perceptual codes. In E. Carterette & M. Friedman (Eds.), *Handbook of perception* (Vol. 8, pp. 375–397). New York: Academic Press.

Palmer, G. (1996). *Toward a theory of cultural linguistics*. Austin: University of Texas Press.

Pessoa, L. (2008). On the relationship between emotion and cognition. *Nature Reviews Neuroscience, 9*(2), 148–158.

Piaget, J. (1962). *Play, dreams and imitation in childhood*. New York: W.W. Norton.

Quinn, N. (2005). How to reconstruct schemas people share, from what they say. In N. Quinn (Ed.), *Finding culture in talk* (pp. 35–84). New York: Palgrave Macmillan.

Rakova, M. (2002). The philosophy of embodied realism: A high price to pay? *Cognitive Linguistics, 13*(3), 215–244.

Reber, A. S. (1989). Implicit learning and tacit knowledge. *Journal of Experimental Psychology: General, 118*(3), 219.

Reeves, L., & Weisberg, R. W. (1994, May). The role of content and abstract information in analogical transfer. *Psychological Bulletin, 115*(3), 381–400. doi: 10.1037/0033-2909.115.3.381.

Regier, T. (1995). A model of the human capacity for categorizing spatial relations. In E. Dabrowska (Ed.), *Cognitive linguistics* (Vol. 6, No. 1, pp. 63–88). doi: 10.1515/cogl.1995.6.1.63, October 2009.

Regier, T. (1996). *The human semantic potential: Spatial language and constrained connectionism*. Cambridge, MA: MIT Press.

Rerup, C., & Feldman, M. (2011). Routines as a source of change in organizational schemata: The role of trial and error learning. *Academy of Management Journal, 54*, 577–610.

Rogoff, B. (1990). *Apprenticeship in thinking: Cognitive development in social context*. New York: Oxford University Press.

Rohrer, T. (2006). Three dogmas of embodiment: Cognitive linguistics as a cognitive science. In G. Kristiansen, M. Archard, R. Dirven, & F. Ruiz de Mendoza Ibanez (Eds.), *Cognitive linguistics: Current applications and future perspectives* (Vol. 1, pp. 119–1468). Berlin: Walter de Gruyter.

Rosch, E. (2002). Principles of categorization. In D. Levitin (Ed.), *Foundations of cognitive psychology: Core readings* (pp. 251–270). Cambridge, MA: MIT Press. (Reprinted from *Concepts: Core Readings*, pp. 189–206, by E. Margolis and S. Laurence, Eds., 1978, Cambridge, MA: MIT Press.)

Rousseau, D. (2001). Schema, promise, and mutuality: The building blocks of the psychological contract. *Journal of Occupational and Organizational Psychology, 74*, 511–541.

Schank, R., & Abelson, R. (1977). *Scripts plans goals and understanding.* Hillsdale, NJ: Lawrence Erlbaum.

Shore, B. (1996). *Culture in mind: Cognition, culture and the problem of meaning.* Oxford: Oxford University Press.

Sinha, C., & Jensen de Lopez, K. (2000). Language, culture and the embodiment of spatial cognition. *Cognitive Linguistics, 11–1/2,* 17–41.

Sinha, C., Sinha, V., Zinken, J., & Sampaio, W. (2011b). When time is not space: The social and linguistic construction of time intervals and temporal event relations in an Amazonian culture. *Language and Cognition, 3–1,* 137–169.

Smith, L. B. (2005). Action alters shape categories. *Cognitive Science, 29*(4), 665–679.

St Amant, R., Morrison, C. T., Chang, Y. H., Mu, W., Cohen, P. R., & Beal, C. (2006). *An image schema language.* Department of Computer Science, North Carolina State University at Raleigh. Retrieved from http://oai.dtic.mil/oai/oai?ve rb=getRecord&metadataPrefix=html&identifier=ADA458943.

Steiner, P. (2014). Enacting anti-representationalism: The scope and the limits of enactive critiques of representationalism. *AVANT, 5*(2), 43–86.

Stewart, J. (2010). Introduction. In J. Stewart, O. Gapenne, & A. Di Paolo (Eds.), *Enaction: Toward a new paradigm for cognitive science* (pp. vii–xvi). Cambridge, MA: MIT Press.

Strauss, C. (2012). *Making sense of public opinion: American discourses about immigration and social programs.* New York: Cambridge University Press.

Strauss, C., & Quinn, N. (1997). *A cognitive theory of cultural meaning.* Cambridge: Cambridge University Press.

Talmy, L. (2000). *Toward a cognitive semantics* (Vol. 1). Cambridge, MA: MIT Press.

Talmy, L. (2005). The fundamental system of spatial schemas in language. In: Hampe, B. (Ed.). *From Perception to Meaning.*(pp. 199–234). Berlin: Mouton de Gruyter.

Tennie, C., Call, J., & Tomasello, M. (2009). Ratcheting up the ratchet: On the evolution of cumulative culture. *Philosophical Transactions of the Royal Society B: Biological Sciences, 364*(1528), 2405–2415.

Thompson, E., & Stapleton, M. (2009). Making sense of sense-making: Reflections on enactive and extended mind theories. *Topoi, 28*(1), 23–30.

Tsakiris, M., Prabhu, G., & Haggard, P. (2006). Having a body versus moving your body: How agency structures body-ownership. *Consciousness and Cognition, 15*(2), 423–432.

Turner, M. (1991). *Reading minds: The study of English in the age of cognitive science.* Princeton: Princeton University Press.

Varela, F. J., Thompson, E., & Rosch, E. (1991). *The embodied mind.* Cambridge, MA: MIT Press.

Vervaeke, J., & Kennedy, J. (2004). Conceptual metaphor and abstract thought. *Metaphor and Symbol, 19*(3), 213–231.

Vike, H. (2011). Cultural models, power and hegemony. In D. Kronenfeld, G. Bennardo, V. de Munck, & M. Fischer (Eds.), *A companion to cognitive anthropology* (pp. 376–392). Malden, MA: Wiley-Blackwell.

Vygotsky, L. S. (1980). *Mind in society: The development of higher psychological processes*. Cambridge, MA: Harvard University Press.

Wapner, S., & Werner, H. (1965). An experimental approach to body perception from the organismic-developmental point of view. In S. Wapner & H. Werner (Eds.), *The body percept*. (pp.9–25) New York: Random House.

Wilson, M. (2002). Six views of embodied cognition. *Psychonomic Bulletin & Review*, *9*(4), 625–636.

Wilson, N. L., & Gibbs, R. W. (2007). Real and imagined body movement primes metaphor comprehension. *Cognitive Science*, *31*(4), 721–731.

Yap, A. J., Wazlawek, A. S., Lucas, B. J., Cuddy, A. J., & Carney, D. R. (2013). The ergonomics of dishonesty: The effect of incidental posture on stealing, cheating, and traffic violations. *Psychological Science*, *24*(11), 2281–2289.

Ziemke, T. (1999). Rethinking grounding. In A. Riegler, A. vom Stein, & M. Peschl (Eds.), *Understanding Representation*. (pp. 177–190) New York: Plenum Press.

3   Motivated Meaning
Cultural Schemas and Hierarchies

From routines to social norms to the use of material artefacts for problem solving and abstract thinking, culture shapes cognitive processes as cognitive processes shape culture. And yet one of the main assertions of the framework put forward in this book is that cognition, through cultural schemas and models, *constitutes* culture. How do schemas and cultural models make up culture? And what is the difference between cultural schemas and models?

In this chapter I take up both questions, starting with the second one first. I explore the nature of cultural schemas and models by describing the relationship between them and why the distinction matters, and outline a schema-model hierarchy that is analytically and pragmatically important for research and practice. I then present the literature on schemas in organizations, including that which relates to functional grounding, and show how schemas constitute culture by providing an underlying 'logic' or core frame of reference for meaning and sensemaking. I provide only the beginnings of that discussion here; the following chapter on socio-functional and task grounding takes this further.

A clarification before I proceed. Throughout I draw from the work of Strauss and Quinn and others from the cultural models school of cognitive anthropology. Their work provides much of the backbone for the functionally embodied framework presented here. However, it should also be mentioned that cognitive anthropologists differ on their approaches to cultural knowledge and understanding. These differences cleave on those who study cognition in practice, that is, the process of thinking and its manifestations in the material world, and those who study the content, form, and organization of cultural knowledge (Strauss, 2012). For those focused on cognition in practice, the material and social context and the processes of thinking as manifested in shared activity, task, and material artefacts matter rather more than shared cultural understandings.[1] In contrast, the cultural models school focuses on the content of shared understanding, whether tacit or explicit (Quinn, 2011; Strauss, 2012). No definitive study of culture in organizations can be considered complete without an understanding of cognitive activity in the context of task and social process. That is why the functionally embodied framework draws from both of these orientations.

1. Cultural Schemas, Cultural Models

Anthropologists have been concerned with the relationship between the mind and culture for generations. Margaret Mead and Ruth Benedict conceptualized culture in terms of basic principles of personality (Lindholm, 2007).[2] Anthony Wallace in the 1960s foreshadowed much of cognitive anthropology today by claiming the mind capable of creating "cultural schemata" (Lindholm, 2007, p. 157). Echoing Sapir and foreshadowing Erikson, Wallace believed the individual was not a product of culture, but rather that culture could be understood as reflecting core psychological processes such as domination and submission, antagonism, and a desire for meaning (Lindholm, 2007). Sapir believed culture was analogous to personality, a kind of "personality writ large" (Lindholm, 2007). And Hallowell (1976), perhaps the first cognitive anthropologist (though credit often goes to Goodenough), viewed the environment as classified and conceptualized in terms of culturally constituted self-attributes. He believed actions, not just language, constituted one's "worldview" (1976, p. 359). Echoing Rosch, his studies of fundamental categories in Ojibwa metaphysics conceptualized cognition in terms of prototypes (Lindholm, 2007).

Levi-Strauss, while not normally credited as such, could be considered another of the early cognitive anthropologists. He was concerned with cultural structures he saw replicated in the brain (Sewell, 1992) and viewed the essential need for a "compromise between history, ecology and mental requirements," a compromise rooted first and foremost in human perception and cognition (Levi-Strauss, 1985, p. 104).

The credit for establishing the agenda for modern cognitive anthropology however goes to Goodenough, who located culture "in the minds of men" (1981, p. 51). Goodenough conceptualized "recipes, precepts, and concepts" as conveyances of cultural knowledge (p. 50).[3] Goodenough, Hallowell and Wallace are the direct link to the work of Shore, Quinn, Strauss, Hutchins, D'Andrade, and other contemporary cognitive anthropologists.

The cognitivist position stands in contrast to Geertz (1973), who rejected the idea that culture exists in human minds (Geertz, 1973; Goodenough, 1981). Geertz's position, which has had some influence on organizational culture theorists,[4] located culture exclusively in public forms, as texts to be read and interpreted, as symbols, as utterances (semiotic forms), artefacts, and other "public phenomena" (Shore, 1996, p. 51). The focus on the symbolic put anthropology into empirical realms. However epistemologically attractive, this limits the range of focus by making culture solely a public phenomenon accessed through whatever is meaningful within a cultural community (D'Andrade, 1995). What is missed is that culture exists in both social and psychological realms, and in their interaction (Shore,

1996). Conceiving of culture as symbols and artefacts sidesteps the question of how cultural phenomena become constituted in the mind and practices of people, and what environmental or social dynamics might account for their existence in the first place.

From the perspective of cognitive anthropology, the individual is the product *of* culture and the essential dynamic *for* culture. The self is always in dynamic relationship to culture, and vice versa (D'Andrade, 1995; Shore, 1996). What mediates between culture and the way people think, learn, act and make sense of the world are cognitive structures and social dialectics residing within and between humans. Bourdieu (1990) described this with his *habitus*, an "acquired system of generative schemes" that produce "transposable . . . schemes of perception, thought and action" that underlies the unity of the "life style of a group or class" (p. 55). This process, in essence, is the "internalization of externality" and the "externalization of internality" (p. 72). As put by D'Andrade (1995): "if culture is placed in the mind . . . this makes possible a *particulate* theory of culture; that is, a theory about the 'pieces' of culture, their composition and relations to other things" (p. 247).

Within organizational settings, this concept allows for the interplay between individual cognition, meaning and public forms, including professional epistemologies and practices, routines, tasks, and technologies. This has broad implications for the study and practice of OD. Schematic structure is the link between all forms of social practice, routine, ritual, and cultural representation and meaning (Kimmel, 2008; Shore, 1996; Sperber & Hirschfeld, 1999; Swidler, 2001).

What then, is a *cultural* schema? To Quinn (2011) it is a generic representation of *shared* experience, or to Strauss (2012), shared "simplified understandings" akin to a stereotype but without negative connotations. As Quinn (2011) states, "of course experience is never perfectly shared . . . but to the extent that it overlaps, these people will come to share cultural schemas" (p. 36).[5] Shared schemas, thus, constitute culture for a community by organizing into a coherent collection of units its shared system of meaning. Or, as put by Shore (2002):

> The most useful unit of culture . . . was the schema . . . an organized framework for making sense of the world that exists in two basic forms: mental models in the mind, and instituted models in the world. A cultural community shared in a vast stock of conventional models of and for experience, and these models came in many forms. They were also distributed socially and personally in complex ways.
>
> (p. 5)[6]

"Cognitive elements," however, is still vague. Strauss and Quinn (1997) add more detail. Cultural *schemas* operate as a "collection of elements that work together to process information at a given time . . . [and are] 'learned expectations' of how things 'usually go'" (p. 49). Schemas fill in incomplete or ambiguous information, and aid cognitive utility and efficiency in social interaction and meaning making. As Strauss and Quinn state: "Just think of everything that can be left unsaid in any conversation because speakers assume their interlocutors share the same schemas" (p. 149).

Cultural models, then, are shared cultural schemas of size and complexity (Quinn, 2011). They contain interrelated schemas used to "present something, to reason with or to calculate from by mentally manipulating parts of the model to solve some problem" (D'Andrade, 1995, p. 180). One schema may serve as a model, or several related schemas may be used to construct a model (D'Andrade, 1995; Strauss & Quinn, 1997). For example, the Ifaluk (Micronesia) cultural model of anger appears to emerge from a social obligation schema (Kovecses, 2005); *social obligation*, in this case, can be seen as a subset of a broader cultural model for *anger*.

2. *Structuring Hierarchies*: From Schema to Model

The definitions offered by D'Andrade, and Strauss and Quinn suggest a hierarchy, an idea consistent with the cognitive linguistic view of schemas built up from more basic sensorimotor image schemas. I suggest hierarchical structuring is a feature of *all* schemas and models. The same kinesthetic, ecological and sociocultural experience affecting image schemas is evident in more complex, domain-specific schemas and models. Vike (2011) makes this point when he claims culture is "a hierarchical system of models" (p. 387). According to D'Andrade (1995), such hierarchy consists of "passing on an interpretation from a lower level schema to a higher schema, until the more or less final, top level interpretation of what is happening is created" (p. 232). In my IMCO research, for example, schemas organize, or *scaffold* cultural models for broad and complex social domains such as leadership and business success (see Chapter 6 for examples).

Schemas are organized according to how useful they are as interpretive devices, and how motivating they are (D'Andrade, 1992, 1995). At the lower end of the hierarchy are what he calls "master motives" or what I consider primitives such as *love, security*, or *play* (D'Andrade, 1995, p. 232).[7] A middle level includes goal schemas about important domains like *marriage, or career* that is structured by the lower-level schemas. For example, the *marriage* schema might be motivated and structured by a *love* or security *schema*. At the highest level are schemas dictating procedural knowledge like *going to the bank* or *finding a birthday present*. This class is entirely dependent on antecedent and more abstract schemas. In this example, one does not simply go to the bank; one goes to withdraw money to buy one's spouse a birthday present in order to fulfill a broader need for love or security, and so forth (D'Andrade, 1995, p. 232; examples his). Hierarchy provides an inheritance structure ranging from basic gestalt-like schemas to procedural and propositional ones to broader and more complex models pertaining to entire domains. This position is consistent with the ontogenic view of image schemas as structures learned early in life while other, domain-specific schemas are learned later (Lakoff, 2008; Lakoff & Johnson, 1999). Thus, cultural models pertain to broad domains such as marriage, or buying a house, or what constitutes good management, and are made up of collections of more primary schemas (Sieck, Rasmussen, & Smart, 2010; Steiger & Steiger, 2008; Stone-Jovicich, Lynam, Leitch, & Jones, 2011; also see Section II). Multiple schemas comprise a cultural model, and many interrelated models make up a culture (see Figure 3.4).

At IMCO, the most basic schemas are image schemas such as *FORCE*. Some are domain-specific but pervasive schemas such as those pertaining to *MACHINE or BUILT STRUCTURE*. The *MACHINE* category, for example, contains schemas such as *ORGANIZATIONS ARE MACHINES* but inherit logic and structure from the generalized *MACHINE* category. Along with other kinds of schemas, such as those pertaining to *BUILT STRUCTURE*, they make up a shared cultural model of business success. The cultural model is delimited and constrained by the structure of the underlying schemas. Thus, business success derives, in part, from operating a well-run machine, or from having all the component parts work well together, which in turns means you treat your people and your machines well, and so forth. These schemas are not discernible as metaphors; many different metaphors might be used within a narrative in which such a schema is expressed. But if one were to use a machine metaphor at IMCO such as *we need to tune up our talent*, its meaning would be well understood. As with other primary schemas, the general *MACHINE* schema provides an organizing frame for structuring and linking together concepts, discourse, as well as practice.

Hierarchy has implications for practice. For example, it is unlikely that image schemas such as *FORCE* or *CONTAINMENT*, were they to be

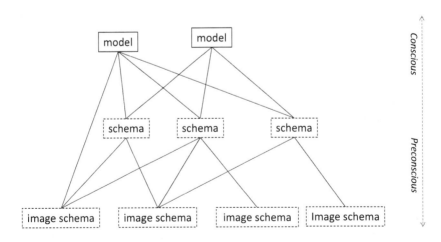

Figure 3.4 Schema-model hierarchies.

brought to a group's attention, would be particularly motivating or useful as objects of inquiry or intervention. These are basic structures of cognition that, when surfaced, appear obvious. It is rather more likely that an instantiation of a domain-specific schema such as *INTELLEGENCE IS FORCE*, when brought to group awareness would be considered more prescriptive and motivating because, so conceptualized, would orient a group to the many ways in which different realms of activity are meaningful, such as *making decisions in a decisive way*, or having *penetrating insight into complex issues*, or in *pushing through ambiguity to achieve clarity*. The schema provides a structuring logic that endows such activities with distinct attributes and character that are highly meaningful to that group.

The Unthought Known

That schemas exist on a continuum from image schemas to functional, domain-specific ones to cultural models varying in the size or complexity based on the domain in which they are applied may be one reason why some scholars have trouble with precise definitions of them. Palmer (1996) characterizes this challenge in observing and cataloging schemas in cultural contexts:

> [Understanding schemas and models] . . . would be easier if [they] were innate or emergent, embodied in some simple way . . . but in fact most are woven into the web of cultural patterns. Image schemas become enmeshed in elaborate cultural models and take meaning from their cultural loci. Life may be a journey in many or all cultures, but a path schema is one thing in an urban shopping mall and another in a furrowed field. In Polynesia, elemental schemas such as UP/DOWN, MALE/FEMALE, and LIGHT/DARK become enmeshed with more obviously cultural notions, such as SEAWARD/INWARD, SACRED/PROFANE, and CLEAN/DIRTY.
>
> (p. 265)

This is because many schemas tend to stay outside of awareness (Descola, 2013; Strauss & Quinn, 1997), which is one reason why schemas are difficult to deal with in applied fields such as organizational development (OD; for example, see Sieck et al., 2010). Language evokes preconscious schemas in much the way same as psychoanalytic process can bring out repressed material or evoke object relations. For this reason I borrow the term *"the unthought known"* from the psychoanalyst Christopher Bollas (1987, p. 4). The unthought known for an individual can cast a shadow on all aspects of that individual's existence without the individual being aware of the shadow until it is brought into consciousness. In a similar vein, schemas operate as Hutchins characterizes them. Once recorded or learned they become what one sees with, but, seldom, "what one sees" (Hutchins, 1980, as cited in

Strauss & Quinn, 1997, p. 154). This transparency allows schemas to constitute reality for a community of group (Strauss & Quinn, 1997).

This is a key point—schemas manifest as tacit tendencies to organize meaning. They reflect cognitive patterns "unconsciously extracted from repeated experience" (Strauss & Quinn, 1997, p. 11). Their implicitness is what renders them pervasive as meaning-making agents; much of the 'knowledge' embedded with them is simply taken for granted. And they remain that way unless evoked or brought into consciousness by an outside agent, or by unforeseen events.

3. The Logic of Practice

The foregoing implies certain schemas are more primary or foundational than others. A foundational schema is an underlying schema that provides a template or pattern constraint on other schemas or models, whereas a primary schema is one of a few schemas that *together* form a network of schemas that serve the same function.[8] Primary schemas organize, constrain, and provide the structuring logic for a community's entire system of cultural practice and meaning.

Bennardo (2011) thinks of such structures as "uniformities" visible across structures and that generate other more complex models, manifesting as "pervasive forms replicated in other domains" (p. 94).[9] He showed, for example, how a foundational model of "radiality" underlies a wide range of Tongan cultural modalities such as time, kinship, religious beliefs, navigational practices, and social relations (p. 496). In acknowledging their salience, he calls such schemas "cognitive molecules" (p. 496). Shore (1996) suggests foundational schemas link related schemas and organize meaning across contexts, serving as a kind of cognitive template. He uses the example of a hub and spoke schema in airline route planning or urban planning (traffic patterns) to illustrate how a foundational schema might manifest across contexts. Examples abound. A candidate today in the Unites States might be the foundational schema of making money, which underlies American conceptions of success across societal and cultural domains well beyond the province of business, such as in the visual arts or music. While one might be tempted to think of foundational schemas as an ethos or a prevailing value, the main difference between schemas and values is that schemas govern how the value or ethos is expressed and what is privileged or delimited within it (Descola, 2013). Schemas manifest across practices as a structuring logic or template that circumscribes and constrains meaning within those practices, the "original matrix" that organizes practice and meaning and through which traces are "discernible in each of their occurrences"(Descola, 2013, p. 94). Values or beliefs, on the other hand, may be espoused reactions or compensations for deeper, unspoken schemas.

Primary schemas are important conceptual anchors for a functionally grounded theory of organizational culture. Bennardo's radial structure, for example, might be visible across discourses, values, beliefs, symbols, practices, behaviors, and so forth, as logic that unifies all of these elements into a coherent cultural framework. Similarly, the logic of how organizational practices are enacted, such as budgeting, financial reporting, procurement, performance review, development, or hiring (etc.) become visible by tracing how primary schemas structure these processes, as I show in Chapter 7. The schemas are typically not the processes themselves, but manifest in how they are interpreted and actualized. Schemas, for example, may emphasize what gets privileged in a management reporting process, such as whether centralized or distributed control is highlighted, or what constitutes "good" reporting, or a "good" report. These points of emphases remain mostly implicit, structured by the resident logic of the schema, in the same way CONTAINMENT helps structure how to teach swinging a baseball bat.[10] Once visible, these practices become candidates for intervention on the basis of their pervasive logic, which by definition would mean the interventions are systemic, carried out at all 'levels of system', to borrow a phrase from Gestalt OD practice. Because of their essential pervasiveness, interventions based on primary schemas are capable of far more powerful and sustained impact.

Schemas in Management

Even the casual traveler in the management cognition literature in search of the concept of schemas will stumble upon a diversity of perspectives and definitions. There are over a hundred different but closely related views of schemas or related constructs in this literature. Walsh (1995) provides an illuminating review of the polysemous ways in which the concept is used. To wit: *Knowledge structures, interpretive schemes, frames, strategic archetypes, industry recipes, dominant logic, interpersonal schemes, organizational paradigms,* and *theories in use* are but some synonyms (Bingham & Kahl, 2013; Johnson, 1990; Steiger & Steiger, 2008; Walsh, 1995).[11]

Schema theory has mainly been used within the management cognition literature to advance theories of the firm and to uncover the "situational" or "dispositional" antecedents to organizational knowledge and behavior (Walsh, 1995, p. 280). What does a firm 'know'? It is implied in Drucker's (1994) *theory of the business* and in theories of knowledge transfer between firms (Gertler, 2004). Schemas are thought to exert influence on firms primarily because they rely on explicit knowledge in the form of standards, roles, practices, skilled practice, as well as hunches, axioms, and intuitions to survive and thrive (Spender, 1996).

Schema theory has been extended to theories of strategy through the so-called "resource view" of the firm, the idea that strategy requires specific resources and competencies to be enacted (Spender, 1996). Work on schemas has also been used in branding with the idea companies endow brands with the cognitive-affective concepts stakeholders hold about a product or service (or company), and that these concepts transcend what executives and employees consciously share (Koller, 2008).

A point of departure between the cognitive anthropological literature on schemas and the management cognition literature is on the question of implicitness. Cognitive anthropology treats schemas mainly as tacit and non-propositional structures of cognition, whereas the management cognition literature treats schemas as something akin to conscious attitudes and propositional logic. Not surprisingly, with few exceptions, the prevailing assumption in the management literature is objectivist—schemas and mental models "mirror the true state of the world" (for example, see Mohammed, Ferzandi, & Hamilton, 2010, p. 879). Barr and colleagues state, "incorrect mental models can lead to correct action" (Barr, Stimpert, & Huff, 1992, p. 17), which suggests schemas have appropriateness given some objective standard for a particular context.[12]

Despite the abundance of schema-oriented theory and research in the management literature, little of it pertains to culture or cultural constructs, such as language (for example, see Mohammed et al., 2010). Culture and the knowledge of the collective "reside in the background, more like a trust and an outcome" (Spender, 1996, p. 22). An exception is Cornelissen (2012), who found evidence of foundational schemas in corporate communications professionals' use of metaphor to explain critical incidents, locating central metaphors such as CHANGES IN PUBLIC OPINION AS PHYSICAL MOVEMENTS (IN SPACE) and COMMUNICATION AS PHYSICAL PRESSURE.[13] Considering this literature through a broader lens, however, there is some evidence of interest in primary structuring phenomena, notably in Steele's (1972) neglected work on organizational overlearning, and in the work on industry archetypes, recipes and industry culture.

Overlearning, Archetypes, and Recipes

Steele's (1972) main thesis was that external business and financial success can blunt internal organizational effectiveness. The success of a particular organizational strategy or business model enacted through its main production tasks, or the primary ways in which an organization realizes its strategy, could lead to the overuse of those same tasks inside the organization. This would lead to preferred styles within those organizations. He called this phenomenon "organizational overlearning" (p. 128).

The cause of overlearning is either the tendency to apply what is familiar and successful in one domain, such as how to sell machinery, to another, such as how to motivate a potential leader, or to try and mitigate anxiety (Steele, 1972). Steele uses several cases across different industries to illustrate. For example, in the airline industry, the primary task is moving people and bags efficiently, quickly, and safely from point A to point B. The "overlearning" of this task is applying excessive time pressure to an organizational change process. The premium on speed and efficiency (or an efficiency schema) is extended to organization restructuring and change efforts to the detriment of those efforts, leading to failed change or adaptation. This tendency is common in airline mergers, as seen recently in the merger of United and Continental (Mouawad, 2012).

Another example is in consumer products. Consumer product companies have deep competence in market research and altering strategies on short notice in order to bring out new products quickly, thereby undermining the competition and operating as if to "keep people guessing" (pp. 129–130). This style when overlearned and applied to inter-departmental functioning manifests as low disclosure across groups about management changes, promotions, resources, and the like because of a fear of leaks. The overlearned *keep them guessing* style applied internally breeds a "war room" (for example, of secrecy and combativeness) atmosphere with little problem disclosure or sense of shared problem solving (p. 130). Another example is with the U.S. Internal Revenue Service (IRS). A climate of "surveillance" and "assumed malfeasance" among taxpayers translates into internal relationships characterized by the same (p. 130). Or in religious institutions where "ideals rather than reality" create the overlearned result that members cannot disclose or discuss problems for fear of causing one another anxiety. Or in law firms who use an adversarial style in litigation or briefs but fear dropping or adjusting that style internally for fear of "unprofessional shifts of opinion" (p. 132).

One could go too far, of course, suggesting overlearning is the manifestation of foundational schema; clearly, we do not know enough about Steele's data to make that claim. One could also go too far with claims of causality. Not all airlines botch restructuring by moving too quickly; not all consumer products companies traffic in secrecy in inter-departmental relations. That said, what is interesting about Steele's work is the phenomenon of overlearning is entirely consistent with a functionally grounded theory of culture. Transposing strategies successful in one domain to another is consistent with analogical transfer. And although Steele did not use the term 'schema', overlearning is consistent with primary schemas unconsciously motivating and patterning behavior and practice across multiple domains, such as inter-department relations or how problems are collectively construed.

Writing from a different tradition and 20 years later, Greenwood and Hinings' (1993) work on strategic archetypes is also suggestive of functional grounding. An "archetype" is constituted by "ideas, beliefs and values that underpin and are embodied in organizational structures and systems" (Greenwood & Hinings, 1993, p. 1052). Although their conception differs in important ways from schemas, they do share the idea that organizational patterns and structures can be pervasive across domains well beyond those for which they were originally intended. These patterns are a function of beliefs, ideas, and values, the components of which are embedded within organizational structures and systems. Thus, firms will move to align strategies and processes to conform to their predominant archetype. This thinking echoes strategy scholars who suggest firms evolve towards forms of internal consistency for economic benefit (Greenwood & Hinings, 1993), as well as institutional logic scholars who observe how broader cultural rules and beliefs structure cognition and practice within particular fields (Lounsbury, 2007).

Greenwood and Hinings' (1993) study of the bureaucratic structure of British municipalities in the 1970s and 1980s suggests two dominant archetypes were in evidence at that time: a *corporate* archetype governed by practices and values adopted from the business world, and a *professional* archetype governed by values and practices emanating from professional and functional work. The corporate type conceived of municipal organizations as an "instrument of community governance" where services were construed as part of an integrated strategy for "managing and influencing the geographic community" (p. 1064). In these organizations they found, for example, that performance appraisals were conducted by senior management based on clear statements of purpose and objective performance targets and measures, with particular attention paid to the effects of services on clients. Recruitment, career development, and rewards based on professional competence were deemed paramount. Conversely, the professional type conceived of municipal organizations as "administrative vehicles for the delivery of essentially disparate services such as education, social welfare, highway construction," and the like (p. 1064). These organizations were characterized by local administration and professional differentiation. In these organizations they found no concept of general management. Appraisal practices were defined by intraprofessional judgment, and recruitment, career development, with rewards emphasizing professional qualifications and experience above all else. Importantly, they state, "the two sets of values are each translated into structures and systems, thus constituting archetypes" (p. 1064).

The challenge with studying archetypes, as with schemas, is that these ideas are so generalized claims for their existence could be read into a myriad of cases and data, perhaps to the point of irrelevance. Hub and spoke, radiality or corporateness recognized as underlying patterns, are still generalized patterns, and generalized patterns by definition omit detail. The detail, however, is necessary for enacting useful organizational culture practice. The important contribution of such studies is not the identification of a general schema or archetype per se, but how underlying common structure manifests across domains. A skeptic might consider organizational practices such as management by objectives not a function of an overarching archetype or schema but simply the product of managerial rational choice. On the other hand, one needs to ask how such a choice might come to be adopted and sustained within an organization if there was not a pre-existing set of cognitive orientations available for managers to adopt to begin with?

The concept or archetypes is echoed in the literature on industry recipes. Managers within the same industry share similar values and beliefs more than those across industries. Industry recipes, to Spender (1989), are a "shared pattern of belief that the individual can choose to apply to his own experience in order to make sense of it and also deal with uncertainty" (p. 61). Spender references Schank and Abelson's (1977) work on scripts, and makes clear these structures are essentially conscious and propositional. In a less restrictive way Huff (1982) argued that an industry "is defined by shared or interlocking metaphors or world views" (p. 125). And in a study of environmental scanning in three industries, Hambrick (1982) notes, "a common body of knowledge appears to exist within an industry . . . which is disseminated through media equally available to and used by executives within the industry" (p. 167). This idea is also echoed convincingly in Gordon's (1991) study of the industry determinants of organizational culture.

Spender's (1989) study of the forklift, foundry, and dairy industries in Great Britain found a high degree of homogeneity amongst the constructs applied by managers in each industry with respect to making sense of uncertainty, business forecasting, and understanding the "contexts of activity" (p. 61). Hodgkinson and Johnson (1994) described how managers within the same industry categorized competitive strategies and competition based on commonly held assumptions ascribed to shared mental models. And in perhaps the best-known study of industry effects on cognition making use of the mental model construct, Porac, Thomas, and Baden-Fuller (1989) found executives in the Scottish knitwear industry shared mental models and made similar strategic choices. Managers shared themes about the boundaries of the competitive domain, with wide (partly implied) agreement about what constituted legitimate competitive process within that domain (Osborne, Stubbart, & Ramaprasad, 2001).

All of these studies are in-depth cases without explicit reference to culture. With culture as a direct object of study, Chatman and Jehn (1994) conducted a comprehensive survey of professionals across industries studying the relationship between industry characteristics and organizational culture. They operationalized culture as values and used standardized etic dimensions administered through surveys of the kind problematized in Chapter 1. In looking at 15 firms representing four industries in the service sector (accounting, consulting, household goods, and the U.S. Post Office), they found less cultural variation between firms "working on the same tasks, using similar procedures, and experiencing similar opportunities to grow" than across industries (p. 522). Industry differences accounted for more variation in culture than differences between individual firms. While values are only the tip of the cultural iceberg, their study nonetheless suggests much less inter-firm cultural variation than most managers and practitioners would care to admit.

Of course, what these studies may be outlining is simply that organizations within the same industry orient their activities toward each other with degrees of interdependence and common interests that shape their cognitions (Weber, 2005). This would appear to most managers and practitioners as face-valid.

But what these studies show is within-industry similarities in cognition are common, which raises the question of agent rationality and ecological constraint. The management cognition literature presumes managers to be rational actors. This is likely because much of it is based on work in cognitive psychology and economics (Walsh, 1995). My sense is the actual state of affairs is murkier. Managers no doubt *intend* to make rational and conscious choices, but what is the basis of that intent? How constrained is it? Is managerial choice bound to cognitive predispositions beyond the conscious awareness of the actor? Descola (2013) characterizes the issue of agency in this way:

> The driving force of conscious agency is hardly supported by ethnological and sociological data; monograph after monograph, they show us that the customs and behavior observable in a collective do not proceed from deliberate agreement but display a consistency and a degree of automatism which its members are generally unable to relate back to a cultural model or a system of explicit rules.
>
> (p. 76)

The "system of explicit rules," such that it exists, would reveal itself to an investigator as pervasive structure organizing cultural practices in subtle and particular forms meaningful to actors in those systems (Sewell, 1992). Conversely, the lack of such an organizing scheme would manifest as an empirical dead end.

Indeed, not all cultural models are made up of foundational or primary schemas (Shore, 1996). What differentiates those that do is a "family resemblance" to other models, which suggests an underlying organizing logic (p. 53). Their manifestations underwrite diverse domains, such as when software engineers impose engineering 'logic' on people management activities, evidenced by the abundance of metaphors like *deep thinking, people platform, future proofing* or *model* (e.g., *legacy model, research model, hiring model*).[14]

The functionally grounded theory of organizational culture suggests all cultures are underpinned not necessarily by a single foundational schema, but by pervasive 'primary' schemas (see Chapter 6). That said, it is important to not over-index this concept. Cultures also exhibit what Strauss and Quinn (1997) label "centrifugal" effects, dynamics that impede and diminish cultural sharing and understanding. Common external values, beliefs, and discourses also undoubtedly shape how organizations function. Organizations may need to conform to significant sector or institutional forces (Gertler, 2004; Greenwood & Hinings, 1993), or regulatory pressures, forces that dilute, impede, or perhaps revise the formation of schemas and cause instability in what I call the *sense-making boundary*, a discussion I take up in the next chapter.

4. Motivated Meaning

Humans seek meaning in what they do in order to make sense of what goes on around them (Rogoff, 1990). Bartlett was among the first to acknowledge culture is an "effort after meaning" (Garro, 2000).[15] To Herzfeld (2001), culture "gains meaning" with its social deployment (p. 25). Cultural inquiry is not just thick description a la Geertz, but requires understanding what the culture under inquiry means to the people in that culture (and also to the researcher; Herzfeld, 2001).[16]

How do schemas and models motivate meaning? First, it is important to distinguish between schemas and meaning. Meanings are not schemas. To Strauss and Quinn (1997), meaning is an "interpretation evoked in a person" (p. 6). A schema is a learned pattern of associations; meaning is what is elicited at a given moment (Strauss & Quinn, 1997). Situations will change, activating different combinations of associations, but the underlying structure of the associations or expectations may not change (Strauss & Quinn, 1997). Cultural meanings arise out of the interaction between events occurring in a material world and an actor's filtered learning and interpretation of those events, a dynamic that is in itself a product of similar previous interactions (Strauss & Quinn, 1997).

Cultural schemas and models motivate meaning in multiple ways. First, humans actively 'model' the world they live in. They are actively and purposefully engaged in making sense of their environment, and do so in culturally relevant and embedded ways. Second, cultural understandings are motivating, in part, because the schemas that make up that understanding are formed through experiences that are emotionally evocative (Strauss & Quinn, 1997). Descola (2013) states schemas organize and structure social relations and emotional responses in standardized scenarios so that "they can be conveyed within a community in a way that is regarded as normal" (p. 103). An example of this is the myriad ways in which the process of becoming a professional exposes one to emotionally important norms for how to act in the community of which one is becoming a part. Third, schemas and cultural models can function as goals. For example, Strauss (1992), in her research with working-class men in Rhode Island, found that a "breadwinner" cultural model (providing for family) characterizing her informants' notions of success was strongly motivating (p. 199). This stood in contrast to the expected and culturally pervasive American Dream cultural model of striving for ever-greater success, of which they were also aware. Within the socio-economic constraints of her informants' lives and their interpretive frameworks, providing for family was construed as the *only* choice. As goals, schemas and models can direct how people behave. Fourth, schemas have psychodynamic resonance. For example, Strauss' (1992) informants' reactions to the American Dream cultural model led to "defensive rationalizations" about their own lives. Similarly, Hutchins (1987) found Trobriand Island myths about relations between living beings and dead spirits to be a cultural defense mechanism.

In a similar fashion Bollas (1987) argues that the search for idealized objects ("the perfect woman," "the perfect job") is a search to transform the self by repairing ego deficits or by splitting off bad self-experience. The object-ideal becomes transformational by holding for the subject the motivating potential of self-transformation. The object-relation itself, construed as a schema, or in Bollas' (1987) terms, the "complex rules for being and relating" (p. 9), becomes the idealized means, ends, and motive force for transformation.[17] Thus, schemas hold deep motive force as both defensive and transformational objects. The process of professionalization, as well as working in organizations with highly motivating missions tend to yield experiences of similar significance in terms of emotional intensity or psychodynamic resonance conducive for inducing cultural schemas.

Precisely how schemas underwrite culture is very complex, but the intent here is to outline some of the dynamics involved. What is hopefully clear is cultural schemas provide an extensive, multi-layered, and pervasive foundation for sense and meaning-making that underwrites all forms of practice, including socially normative behavior and power relations. In other words, the totality of what is taken to be culture.

Notes

1 As put by Nardi (1996), "it is not possible to fully understand how people learn or work if the unit of study is the unaided individual with no access to other people or to artifacts for accomplishing the task at hand" (p. 35).

2 Mead and Benedict saw the unconscious as a repository of cultural symbols, but they both mostly rejected Freud, though they "scavenged Freud for concepts they found useful" (Lindholm, 2007, p. 114).

3 Interestingly, Goodenough (1981) does not mention Rumelhart, Schank, Abelson, and other cognitive psychologists who were studying memory and cognition in this same general period. He was inspired by linguists more than psychologists (Strauss, August 23, 2014, personal communication).

4 Theorists like Alvesson carry the Geertzian torch into organizational culture theory and practice while also finding contemporary cognitive linguistics, such as metaphor theory, useful (for example, see Alvesson & Spicer, 2011).

5 A cultural *schema* to D'Andrade (1995) is "an organization of cognitive elements into an abstract mental object capable of being held in working memory. . . which can be variously filled with appropriate specifics" (p. 179).

6 Shore and other theorists use the terms "schema" and "model" somewhat interchangeably, which is a bit confusing. Shore prefers the term "model" but implies "model" and "schema" are synonyms. I make a distinction between the two.

7 D'Andrade's (1995) conception is inverted from mine, whereby he refers to "master motives" as the "top end" of the hierarchy. This contradicts his earlier characterization in the same text. For simplicity I have chosen to keep with his conception of "master motives" as the low, or foundational, end of the hierarchy.

8 Foundational schemas are similar to the notion of an underlying 'logics' for culture in economic sociology. This view holds that a diffusion of a small number of competing logics underlie culture (for example, see Fiss & Zajac, 2004, as cited in Weber, 2005).

9 Although he terms these foundational structures "models."

10 This is one reason why competency models, especially those developed natively for an organization become excellent ways to trigger or uncover schemas.

11 "Theories in use" (Argyris & Schon, 1996), in particular, are very much like cultural models. But the proliferation of terms in general is a weakness in the literature and one that I do not want to replicate, and thus use the term 'schema' throughout.

12 One notable exception is Rentsch and Klimoski's (2001) work on team schemas. While there are differences, methodologically their work is close to mine with respect to using emic data to systematically analyze shared team mental constructs.
13 The PHYSICAL MOVEMENTS metaphor was central in 10 out of the 26 metaphors listed and a primary structuring agent for the narratives, functioning in much the same way as Shore and Bennardo suggest in linking up related schemas.
14 Drawn from my own research on the metaphors of two occupational groups, software engineers and human resources (HR).
15 Bartlett (1932) was one of the earliest theorists to show how subjects used cultural models to make sense of other cultures. For example, North American subjects used Western culture to make sense of stories from Native American culture. Recalling the native story was made possible by transforming it to make it more consistent with Western culture (as cited in Guenther, 2002). In addition, Bartlett viewed the schema as both a principle of "cognitive organizing" and a unit of analysis relevant to understanding cultural differences (Sinha & Jensen de Lopez, 2000, p. 28)
16 Instead of cataloging cultural elements in ethnography, better to ask to what "uses" are these elements put (Herzfeld, 2001, p. 25)?
17 And which only comes into consciousness through transference and counter-transference in the psychoanalytic process. Schemas are also commonly used in certain cognitive—developmental psychotherapies. For example, see Young, Klosko, and Weishaar (2003).

Bibliography

Alvesson, M., & Spicer, A. (2011). Introduction. In M. Alvesson & A. Spicer (Eds.), *Metaphors we lead by.*(pp. 1–7). Abingdon: Routledge.

Argyris, C. S., & Schön, D. (1996). *Organizational learning II: Theory, method and practice.* Reading, MA: Addison-Wesley.

Barr, P. S., Stimpert, J. L., & Huff, A. S. (1992). Cognitive change, strategic action, and organizational renewal. *Strategic Management Journal, 13*(S1), 15–36.

Bartlett, F. C. (1932). *Remembering: An experimental and social study.* Cambridge: Cambridge University Press.

Bennardo, G. (2011). A foundational cultural model in Polynesia: Monarchy, democracy, and the architecture of the mind. In D. Kronenfeld, G. Bennardo, V. de Munck, & M. Fischer (Eds.), *A companion to cognitive anthropology* (pp. 471–488). Malden, MA: Wiley-Blackwell.

Bingham, C., & Kahl, S. (2013). The process of schema emergence: Assimilation, deconstruction, utilization, and the plurality of analogies. *Academy of Management Journal, 56,* 14–34. Retrieved from http://dx.doi.org.10.5465/amj.2010.0723.

Bollas, C. (1987). *The shadow of the object: Psychoanalysis of the unthought known.* New York: Columbia University Press.

Bourdieu, P. (1990). *The logic of practice.* Stanford: Stanford University Press.

Chatman, J., & Jehn, K. (1994). Assessing the relationship between industry characteristics and organizational culture. How different can you be? *Academy of Management Journal, 37,* 522–553. Retrieved from http://scholar.google.com/.

Cornelissen, J. P. (2012). Sensemaking under pressure: The influence of professional roles and social accountability on the creation of sense. *Organization Science, 23*(1), 118–137.

D'Andrade, R. (1992). Schemas and motivation. In R. D'Andrade & C. Strauss (Eds.), *Human motives and cultural models* (pp. 23–44). Cambridge: Cambridge University Press.

D'Andrade, R. (1995). *The development of cognitive anthropology*. Cambridge: Cambridge University Press.

Descola, P. (2013). *Beyond nature and culture*. Chicago: University of Chicago Press.

Drucker, P. F. (1994). The theory of the business. *Harvard Business Review*, 72(5), 95–104.

Fiss, P. C., & Zajac, E. J. (2004). The diffusion of ideas over contested terrain: The (non) adoption of a shareholder value orientation among German firms. *Administrative Science Quarterly*, 49(4), 501–534.

Garro, L. (2000). Remembering what one knows and the construction of the past: A comparison of cultural consensus theory and cultural schema theory. *Ethos*, 28(3), 275–319.

Geertz, C. (1973). *The interpretation of cultures*. New York: Basic Books.

Gertler, M. (2004). *Manufacturing culture: The institutional geography of industrial practice*. Oxford: Oxford University Press.

Goodenough, W. (1981). *Culture, language and society* (2nd ed.). Menlo Park: Benjamin/Cummings.

Gordon, G. G. (1991). Industry determinants of organizational culture. *Academy of Management Review*, 16(2), 396–415.

Greenwood, R., & Hinings, C. R. (1993). Understanding strategic change: The contribution of archetypes. *Academy of Management Journal*, 36(5), 1052–1081.

Guenther, K. (2002). Memory. In D. Levitin (Ed.), *Foundations of cognitive psychology: Core readings* (pp. 311–360). Cambridge, MA: MIT Press.

Hallowell, I. (1976). *Selected papers of Irving Hallowell*. Chicago: University of Chicago Press. (Originally published in 1954.)

Hambrick, D. C. (1982). Environmental scanning and organizational strategy. *Strategic Management Journal*, 3(2), 159–174.

Herzfeld, M. (2001). *Anthropology: Theoretical practice in culture and society*. Malden, MA: Blackwell.

Hodgkinson, G., & Johnson, G. (1994). Exploring the mental models of competitive strategists: The case for a processual approach. *Journal of Management Studies*, 31, 526–543.

Huff, A. S. (1982). Industry influences on strategy reformulation. *Strategic Management Journal*, 3(2), 119–131.

Hutchins, E. (1980). *Culture and inference: A Trobriand case study* (Vol. 2). Cambridge, MA: Harvard University Press.

Hutchins, E. (1987). Myth and experience in the Trobriand Islands. In D. Holland & N. Quinn (Eds.), *Cultural models in language and thought* (pp. 269–289). Cambridge: Cambridge University Press.

Johnson, G. (1990). Managing strategic change: The role of symbolic action. *British Journal of Management*, 1, 183–200.

Kimmel, M. (2008).Properties of cultural embodiment: Lessons from the anthropology of the body. In R. Frank, R. Dirven, & T. Ziemke (Eds.), *Cognitive linguistics research: sociocultural situatedness, Vol. 2*. (pp. 77–108). Berlin: Mouton de Gruyter.

Koller, V. (2008). Corporate brands as socio-cognitive representations. In G. Kristiansen & R. Dirven (Eds.), *Cognitive sociolinguistics: Language variation, cultural models, social systems* (pp. 389–418). Berlin: Mouton de Gruyer.

Kovecses, Z. W. (2005). *Metaphor in culture: Universality and variation*. Cambridge: Cambridge University Press.

Lakoff, G. (2008). The Neural theory of metaphor. In R. Gibbs (Ed.), *The Cambridge handbook of metaphor and thought* (pp. 1–35). Cambridge: Cambridge University Press.

Lakoff, G., & Johnson, M. (1999). *Philosophy in the flesh*. New York: Basic Books.

Levi-Strauss, C. (1985). *The view from afar*. New York: Basic Books.

Lindholm, C. (2007). *Culture and identity: The history, theory, and practice of psychological anthropology*. Oxford: Oneworld Books.

Lounsbury, M. (2007). A tale of two cities: Competing logics and practice variation in the professionalizing of mutual funds. *Academy of Management Journal, 50*(2), 289–307.

Mohammed, S., Ferzandi, L., & Hamilton, K. (2010). Metaphor no more: A 15-year review of the team mental model construct. *Journal of Management, 36*(4), 876–910.

Mouawad, J. (2012, November 29). For united, big problems at biggest airline. *The New York Times*. Retrieved from http://www.nytimes.com/2012/11/29/business/united-is-struggling-two-years-after-its-merger-with-continental.html?_r=0.

Nardi, B. A. (1996). Studying context: A comparison of activity theory, situated action models, and distributed cognition. In B. Nardi (Ed.), *Context and consciousness: Activity theory and human-computer interaction* (pp. 69–102). Cambridge, MA: MIT Press.

Osborne, J. D., Stubbart, C. I., & Ramaprasad, A. (2001). Strategic groups and competitive enactment: A study of dynamic relationships between mental models and performance. *Strategic Management Journal, 22*(5), 435–454.

Palmer, G. (1996). *Toward a theory of cultural linguistics*. Austin: University of Texas Press.

Porac, J. F., Thomas, H., & Baden-Fuller, C. (1989). Competitive groups as cognitive communities: The case of Scottish knitwear manufacturers. *Journal of Management Studies, 26*(4), 397–416.

Quinn, N. (2011). The history of the cultural models school reconsidered: A paradigm shift in cognitive anthropology. In D. Kronenfeld, G. Bennardo, V. de Munck, & M. Fischer (Eds.), *A companion to cognitive anthropology* (pp. 30–46). Malden, MA: Wiley-Blackwell.

Rentsch, J. R., & Klimoski, R. J. (2001). Why do 'great minds' think alike? Antecedents of team member schema agreement. *Journal of Organizational Behavior, 22*(2), 107–120.

Rogoff, B. (1990). *Apprenticeship in thinking: Cognitive development in social context*. New York: Oxford University Press.

Schank, R., & Abelson, R. (1977). *Scripts plans goals and understanding*. Hillsdale, NJ: Lawrence Erlbaum.

Sewell, W. H. (1992). A theory of structure: Duality, agency, and transformation. *American Journal of Sociology, 98*, 1–29. doi: 0002–9602/93/9801–001.

Shore, B. (1996). *Culture in mind: Cognition, culture and the problem of meaning*. Oxford: Oxford University Press.

Shore, B. (2002). *Globalization, the nation states and the question of "culture": The unnatural history of nations and cultures*. Retrieved from http://www.semioticon.com/frontline/pdf/brad_shore.pdf.

Sieck, W., Rasmussen, L., & Smart, P. R. (2010). Cultural network analysis: A cognitive approach to cultural modeling. In V. Dinesh (Ed.), *Network science for military coalition operations: Information extraction and interaction* (pp. 237–255). Hershey, PA: ICI Global.

Sinha, C., & Jensen de Lopez, K. (2000). Language, culture and the embodiment of spatial cognition. *Cognitive Linguistics, 11–1/2,* 17–41.

Spender, J. C. (1989). *Industry recipes: An enquiry into the nature and sources of managerial judgment.* Oxford: Basil Blackwell.

Spender, J. C. (1996). Making knowledge the basis of a dynamic theory of the firm. *Strategic Management Journal, 17,* 45–62.

Sperber, D., & Hirschfeld, L. (1999). Culture, cognition, and evolution. In R. Wilson & F. Keil (Eds.), *MIT encyclopedia of the cognitive sciences* (pp. cxi–cxxxii). Cambridge, MA: MIT Press.

Steele, F. I. (1972). Organizational overlearning. *Journal of Management Studies, 9*(3), 303–313.

Steiger, D., & Steiger, N. (2008). Instance-based cognitive mapping: A process for discovering a knowledge worker's tacit mental model. *Knowledge Management Research & Practice, 6,* 312–321.

Stone-Jovicich, S., Lynam, T., Leitch, A., & Jones, N. (2011). Using consensus analysis to assess mental models about water use and management in the Crocodile River Catchment, South Africa. *Ecology and Society, 16,* 45. Retrieved from http://www.ecologyandsociety.org/vol16/iss1/art45/.

Strauss, C. (1992). What makes Tony run? Schemas as motives reconsidered. In R. D'Andrade & C. Strauss (Eds.), *Human motives and cultural models* (pp. 191–224). Cambridge: Cambridge University Press.

Strauss, C. (2012). *Making sense of public opinion: American discourses about immigration and social programs.* New York: Cambridge University Press.

Strauss, C., & Quinn, N. (1997). *A cognitive theory of cultural meaning.* Cambridge: Cambridge University Press.

Swidler, A.(2001). What anchors cultural practices. In T. Schatzki, K. Knorr-Cetina, and E. Von Savigny (Eds.). *The Practice turn in contemporary theory.* (pp. 74–92). London: Routledge

Vike, H. (2011). Cultural models, power and hegemony. In D. Kronenfeld, G. Bennardo, V. de Munck, & M. Fischer (Eds.), *A companion to cognitive anthropology* (pp. 376–392). Malden, MA: Wiley-Blackwell.

Walsh, J. P. (1995). Managerial and organizational cognition: Notes from a trip down memory lane. *Organization Science, 6*(3), 280–321.

Weber, K. (2005). A toolkit for analyzing corporate cultural toolkits. *Poetics, 33*(3), 227–252.

Young, J. E., Klosko, J. S., & Weishaar, M. E. (2003). *Schema therapy: A practitioner's guide.* New York: Guilford Press.

4   Functionally Embodied Culture
The Professional and Strategic Grounding of Organizational Culture

The theory of embodied cognition suggests cognition is dynamically embedded and interdependent with the physical, material, social and cultural environment. If this is the case then environments associated with professional work and learning must also be capable of shaping professional and managerial cognition. Schemas induced through sustained experience in social and task contexts are analogically transposed to new contexts, making them salient as resources for sense and meaning making. More primary or dominant cultural schemas organize and structure domain-specific ones, which in turn make up complex cultural models that communities use to make sense of entire domains of activity and life. Viewed this way, cultural schemas and models constitute culture by underwriting shared meaning and practice in all its manifestations, from norms to values to symbols to language (metaphors, tropes, jargon), and extending to complex affordances such as routines, behavioral repertoires, structures, processes, and the like. This is the functionally embodied theory of organizational culture.

That schemas underwrite culture helps explain organizations as "culture bearing milieus" (Frost et al., 1985, p. 19), but it does not give us a more fine-grained understanding of cultural paradox and variation in large, complex human systems like the modern industrial-technological enterprise. Why do some organizations seem to evidence palpable organizational cultures while others do not? Why do certain schemas, and not others, become pervasive within a particular system at a certain time? What dynamics account for how schemas and models function in sensemaking? How are prevailing schemas revised, and what role do leaders play in this, if any? And foremost, what does it mean for culture to be 'grounded' in a professional or strategic task? Addressing these questions bring us to a full understanding of the functionally embodied culture framework, the focus of this chapter.

Doing Things: The Ground of Culture

In its most basic terms the idea is simple: organizations develop cultures by doing things. Cultures form based either on their *dominant professional orientations*, or their *strategic task context*, or both. To the extent strategic tasks manifest as a differentiated organizational purpose—a dominant reason for existence and an evocative and highly motivating mission, the more fertile the experiential context will be for schema induction. Thus, the experience involved in becoming a professional, as well as (or) the tasks, technologies, practices, and routines people interact with and enact in accomplishing work, provide the experiential grounding for cultural cognition. While these may seem like different kinds of environments, they share an important feature. Both are highly meaningful to their members. Thus, 'functional grounding' refers to the sustained experience of working and solving meaningful problems in particular task, technology, sociocultural, and (or) thematically and existentially relevant contexts, and the cognitive imprinting that results. 'Functional' here is in relation to task and work, that is, in the enactment of *things* material and socially meaningful, and in solving problems in particular ways over time.[1] This imprinting, or schema induction, occurs at what Gallagher (2005) calls a *prenoetic* stage, below phenomenal or conscious experience. What is being claimed is not simply that embodied and situated experience shapes mental content, but that it structures *how* people think and behave, what they find meaningful, and therefore what is 'cultural'.

Professionalization and strategic task are necessary for schema induction, but may not be sufficient to manifest a distinct organizational culture.[2] More is needed. Even though Google and Microsoft employ thousands of software engineers, they do not have identical cultures. Even though hospital systems have dominant professional orientations (doctors, saving lives), and perhaps unique missions, each system is culturally distinct. Cultures have, as it were, their own signatures. These signatures reside in the schemas that make up the pool of cognitive resources underwriting the culture or cultures. As resources, they bear the mark of other grounding contexts (national, regional, ethnic, popular culture, and so forth), and some are more indelible than others. They are hardly, if ever, monoliths, except perhaps in smaller enterprises; most organizations evidence multiple cultures in all their diffusionist or fragmentary character (Martin, 2002). And like all resources, schemas can be appropriated and revised. Appropriation happens through discourse, and by exercising power at a so-called *sensemaking boundary* between internal cognitive resources and external contingencies. These dynamics are complex and account for the cultural variation found in organizations. They must also be accounted for in our theory of culture, a discussion I take at the end of this chapter.

1. Professionalization

'Professionalization' encompasses the developmental, social, and cultural acts involved in becoming a member of an occupational group, and the tools, practices, and social contexts that sustain professional/occupational development and communities. The complex cognitive, affective, social and cultural experiences that go into becoming and sustaining the work of an occupation or profession are engines for schema induction and transfer.

I am using the term 'professional' more broadly than in the narrow conception of doctor, lawyer, engineer, and so forth. I favor the frame put forth by Bucher and Stelling (1977) who think of profession as a matter of identity, consisting, in part, of a formal definition of a bounded field of inquiry with a specific range of problems under purview; the use and mastery of specific tools and techniques; personal beliefs about the sense of mission and social value provided by the field; and the concept of a career that is possible to be obtained within it. I would add to this either formal education, apprenticeship or on-the-job exposure where the craft of the field is learned, practised, mastered and socialized, both formally and informally, over time. Thus, construction work as an occupation, for example, qualifies under this definition, as Applebaum's (1981) occupational ethnography convincingly shows.[3] Fast food work, on the other hand, does not. Professions and occupations possess unique schemas that can be imparted to the organizations, or where the work of the profession is closely associated with the core task and mission of the organization.

How does this occur? I suggest there are four key dynamics associated with schema induction and transfer that manifest with professionalization: *Progressive alignment, expertise, social learning*, and *historical legacy*. Each is explored below.

Progressive Alignment

The theory of progressive alignment presented in Chapter 2 holds that once induced, schematic structure will be applied progressively to more abstract analogs through a process of comparison and alignment. Humans are pattern-seeking creatures. In selecting possible interpretations for an analogy, a system of higher-order or causal relations will always be preferred over an equal number of independent matches (Gentner & Colhoun, 2010). Over time this process provides the basis for the creation of relational categories and abstract rules (Gentner & Colhoun, 2010). The idea proposed here is that the process of professionalization, as well as the experience of working within strategic task contexts, described later, induce schemas in just this way.

Arthur Reber's (1989) work on tacit knowledge adds insight into this process. As he states, "failure to explain how complex knowledge is acquired invites the supposition that it was there all the time" (p. 219). When a stimulus environment is highly structured, such as occupational settings like labs, cockpit simulators, court rooms, surgical theaters, classrooms, as well as production task environments such as manufacturing lines, software coding languages, or any routinized work process or set of heuristics sustained over time, people induce an abstract representation of that environment in order to learn and behave in a manner appropriate to that environment (Gertler, 2004; Reber, 1989). This idea extends to the learning of category structure and tacit knowledge in general (Reber, 1989). A rich stimulus domain, such as that experienced through years of learning within a profession, or working in any structured and routinized environment, provides a system of "deep rules" a learner implicitly acquires and retains (Reber, 1989, p. 220).[4] The human processing system appears to have an initial flexibility in selecting a mode of representation, but a commitment to that mode is made early in training and tends to persist (Gopher et al., 1985). The longer and more sustained the exposure to a stimulus environment that is rich, consistently structured, and reinforced through multiple modes, the stronger the induced schemas will tend to be (Gentner & Colhoun, 2010). Even weaker analogical links will become stronger with progressive exposure to new domains (Walsh, 1995).

Progressive alignment occurs through perceptual as well as verbal domains (Gentner & Colhoun, 2010). Pervasive conceptual metaphor usage, for example, is evidence of progressive alignment; over time, the use of analogs creates better and better conceptual matches between source and target. Lakoff and Johnson (1999) make the case based on neural modeling that all metaphorical (analogical) inferences happen in the metaphor's source domain. When source domains are rich with experiential exemplars from which an abundance of schemas can be drawn, stronger or more pervasive schemas are created.

Consider the following example from my own research on software engineers at Microsoft. Following the idea of domain-influenced structure, software engineers presumably should conceive of domains outside of software in ways structured by software engineering task and practice. This is the case, I believe, with how software engineers use STACK as a frequently invoked metaphor across experiential domains, such as to explain career progression (*go up the career stack*) or to describe calibrating the performance of other people (*stack rank*).[5] The STACK metaphor, evoked by a *stack* schema would not 'work' if the structure of the target domain (performance calibration or career progression) did not exhibit at least some features of the source, such as VERTICALITY, in the sense of vertical partitioning of discs in computer hardware architectures. When professionals use metaphors drawn from their own occupational domains to conceptualize about other domains, this is evidence not only of occupationally induced schemas, but also of progressive alignment in action.

Expertise and Knowledge Acquisition

To be a professional by definition implies expertise (Abbott, 1998). The literature on expertise and knowledge acquisition and generation, and more generally on occupational systems of meaning, suggests these experiences are productive ones for schema grounding. A small sample of it is presented here.

Expertise provides a base domain for schemas with a built-in and extensive system of relations (Gentner & Colhoun, 2010; Gick & Holyoak, 1983). Experts tend to have more elements in their schemas and are better able to apply schemas to new circumstances than non-experts because they are better able to integrate contradictory information (Rousseau, 2001). Experts are better at schema abstraction, carrying over salient features from one domain to a novel domain. They also tend to be less influenced by new information, suggesting that schemas learned in professional practice may be harder to change (Rousseau, 2001).

Expertise is acquired, of course, through experience. The literature on expertise is quite clear on what attainment of expertise entails: 50,000 examples (Simon & Chase, 1973, as cited in Gentner, Loewenstein, & Thompson, 2003), thousands of hours (Ericsson, Krampe, & Tesch-Roemer, 1993), or 10 years of dedicated study (Hayes, 1989). Schema induction in this way comes about through repetition, experience, and practice over time. Evidence for this is seen in the greater use of metaphor observed when technical specialists talk to non-technical specialists (Cameron, 2008).

The cognitive effect of expertise has been shown experimentally. For example, when physics students were asked to sort physics problems into categories (such as problems about inclined planes or problems about springs), novices tended to sort on the basis of surface features whereas experts grouped on the basis of major principles governing those problems (Chi, Feltovich, & Glaser, 1981). Experts appear to extract the rules and principles from relevant stimuli in domains in which they have expertise more readily than novices, suggesting that professionals are more likely to encode schemas that reflect the structural characteristics of that domain. This effect has been shown across different domains such as math and language (Blanchette & Dunbar, 2001). Conversely, schema encoding for novices tend to be based on obvious features of the stimulus environment (Gentner, Loewenstein, & Thompson, 2003).

Memory is closely tied to expertise, as shown by a variety of experimental work (for example, see Bellezza & Buck, 1988; in Guenther, 2002). Experience and expertise in a domain facilitates categorization and representation of problems so that storage and retrieval of information is fast and efficient. Greater expertise in a domain results in faster categorization, and the process of categorization is thought to activate a schema (Chi, Feltovich, & Glaser, 1981). One study with domain experts in activities such as chess, bartending, and American football showed that more experience in the domain facilitated recall. Football experts remembered details of fictitious football games better than novices. Chess experts remembered details of chess pieces on a chessboard better than novices, as long as the pieces were arranged consistent with the rules of chess (Guenther, 2002).

Problem solving is also specific in its range of applicability (Rogoff, 1990). Japanese abacus experts can mentally calculate problems with many digits without an abacus, often faster than non-experts, because of the use of 'interiorized representations' of the abacus. Yet at the same time, their memory for the Roman alphabet or the names of fruits is no different than other adults in memory-span tasks (Rogoff, 1990, pp. 51–52).

The way experts and professionals learn to index and code data may be two of the driving mechanisms behind schema induction (Chi, Feltovich, & Glaser, 1981; Goodwin, 1994). Problem solving is a broad concept made up of "the recognition of what counts as a problem as well as the strategies available for solving the problem and the requirements a solution has to meet" (p. 168). What constitutes a problem, even what constitutes seeing a problem as a problem, structures discourse and practice within a community (Abbott, 1998; Fleck, 1979; Knorr-Cetina, 1999; Leonardi, 2011).[6] Bijker (1989) acknowledges as much by stating technological frames are a combination of "current theories, tacit knowledge, engineering practice . . . specialized testing procedures, goals and handling and using practice" (1989, p. 168). He uses an example from the development of plastics in the 1880s and 1890s to describe how chemists at the time did not "see" the applicability of certain resins to the process of chemical synthesis, even though these techniques were being applied in other related domains such as Celluloid and rubber: "The technological frame of synthetic plastics was not yet in existence . . . it simply did not fit in the technological frame of their community" (pp. 168–169). One of the main reasons why was because scientists had another goal at the time: producing dyes (Bijker, 1989). In other words, the goal was motivated by other schemas. Technological frames, thus, are closely linked to underlying schemas. Recognizing a problem and specifying the term of a solution are mediated by goal schemas and cultural models, many of them tacit. How problems are framed and indexed leads to schema induction, and may themselves be the result of pre-existing schemas.

Professional knowledge comes into being through epistemic, functional, social and discursive practices. In describing the methods used by archeologists in the field to transform physical objects into knowledge, Charles Goodwin (1994) suggests "highlighting," "coding," and "graphic representation" are techniques by which phenomenological events become part of an analytic framework (p. 607).[7]

For example, in an archeological site, objects and features are often hard to see, thus *highlighting* literally means drawing a line in the dirt with a trowel to mark an artefact of interest, demarcating what objects are under investigation and possessing "persuasive consequences" (p. 607).[8] A *coding scheme* is the systematic process of transforming physical phenomena into relevant categories and events (Goodwin, 1994). In order to determine the color of a particular specimen of dirt, the archeologist squirts the dirt sample with water and holds the sample under holes against a Munsell color chart to classify the color (Goodwin, 1994).[9] In other words, coding artefact or soil color is a process of classification based on prototypes. *Graphic representation* is the practice by which archeologists make maps of a field site (Goodwin, 1994). Rendering such maps is a social process, because archeologists must work together to discuss and agree on their individual perceptions of the dimensions and locations of specific objects at the site. As Goodwin (1994) clarifies:

> the ability to see in the very complex perceptual field provided by the landscape to which they are attending those few events that count as points to be transferred to a map, are central to what it means to see the world as an archeologist and to use that seeing to build the artifacts, such as this map, that are constitutive of archeology as a profession. All competent archeologists are expected to be able to do this; it is an essential part of what it means to *be* an archeologist.
>
> (p. 615; italics his)

A similar prototype-based classification system is evident in medicine. As provided by Abbott (1998) in his analysis of diagnostic classification, the multiple ways in which diseases are labeled leads to labeling the same disease with several names, such as by "location and type of pathology (multiple sclerosis), by leading symptoms (epilepsy), [or] by etiology (amoebic dysentery)" (p. 43). Diagnostic classification therefore is not a "logical hierarchy from the general to the specific, but a probabilistic hierarchy from the common to the esoteric" (p. 42). Diagnostic classification in medicine exhibits prototype effects constrained by expert knowledge and the system of solution and treatment that classifies problems based on how they are to be resolved. In a similar iterative way field geologists in the oil industry use analogs from exploration of potential drilling sites to compare these to the models they have of these sites. Repeated acts of representing physical sites with geologic models shape the schemas the scientists come to have about the nature of the problem being represented (Almklov & Hepso, 2011).

Thus, through framing, highlighting, coding, and analogical representation, professionals learn "where and how to see" (Goodwin, 1994, p. 615). Professional cognition becomes "entrained" in the minute details and the tools, practices, technologies and modes of production of the profession, and produce knowledge "around which the discourse of a profession is organized" (p. 628). In this way professionals not only acquire knowledge, their very way of thinking becomes structured, or entrained, by the parameters and constraints of the knowledge and task domain itself, a process entirely consistent and predicted by theories of embodied cognition. It is highly likely these cognitive mechanisms operate as Hutchins (2005) and Sinha (2011) and others have described, serving to both offload cognitive tasks and anchor cognition in material as well as symbolic and semiotic anchors, which serves to further reinforce the induced schemas.

Professional seeing and knowledge creation influence ideology and identity, which also aids schema induction. Bunderson (2001) for example, showed how differences in the "ideologies" of work between doctors and administrators shaped the conception of each group's psychological contract with their employer. Doctors conceptualized their own work settings as necessary for and conducive to professional autonomy and standard setting. The individual's role obligations consisted of identifying with the broader professional community and providing "excellent client service" (p. 719). Administrators, on the other hand, conceptualized their work setting and organization as an "economic business" with obligation to provide money and support to professionals. They saw employees (the 'professionals') as "productive resources" (p. 719).

In a longitudinal study of how three professional graduate cohorts in psychiatry, medicine, and biochemistry developed awareness of their own professionalism, Bucher and Stelling (1977) found one of the most significant factors was the sense of mastery novice professionals developed when engaged in actual work and solving client problems. Doing work deemed important to others, whether through "role playing" or taking on independent work to solve problems, was the single most important experience conferring a sense of "professional identity," defined as the moment when the novice professional labeled herself a professional (e.g., as a "biochemist" rather than a "student") (p. 265).

The development of expertise, in summary, can be thought of as a constellation of cognitive and sociocultural activities involved in not just acquiring knowledge, but in learning how to see and think in accordance with the standards and conventions of the domain.[10]

Learning and Affect Intensity

Professional learning is, of course, affect laden. The evidence suggests chemical and neuronal activity associated with emotional experience may aid schema formation. Strong emotions aid recall more than neutral ones (Guenther, 2002). Neurochemical processes associated with memory suggest intense emotions triggered by an event help reinforce neuronal connections, thereby aiding the association of perceptions and concepts with inducing events (Guenther, 2002; Squire, 1987). Even emotional stimuli not consciously perceived appear to be processed in subcortical structures, such that non-consciously perceived stimuli induce "distinct neurophysiological changes and influence behavior towards the consciously perceived world" (Tamietto & De Gelder, 2010, p. 697). Passoa (2008) argues that complex cognitive–emotional behaviors involve high degrees of connectivity across brain regions. One needs to be careful, of course, not to make a causal leap from neuronal activity to behavior, but this research, along with what is known about schematic representation based on neuronal processes, is suggestive that learning and affect are deeply intertwined.

Professional learning involves group problem solving, social evaluation, rites of passage, peer recognition, and acceptance into membership in a wider community of practice, all experiences that foster self-confidence and solidify identity and, as such, are laden with emotion. Lave (1988) suggests cognition is a dialectic between individuals acting where they are situated and their contexts: relationships with other people, feelings, motivation, values, and tools. Professional experience is also replete with social evaluation, which often is emotionally charged. Professional communities are, by definition, normative environments. Medical students, for example, receive intensive and lengthy socialization into the beliefs, values, norms, and accepted practices of medicine deemed important prerequisites for practising the profession (Fonne & Myrhe, 1996). Social and discursive practices reinforce professional ideologies and paradigms that further bind groups to coherent systems of belief.[11]

Emotional involvement precedes but also follows and increases from practice and a growing sense of expertise (Holland & Skinner, 1987).[12] For example, Daley (2001) found client interactions among professional groups affected their own meaning making, especially when clients challenged knowledge, beliefs or assumptions. Social evaluation in this way often is emotionally laden and aids in the production of meaning (Strauss & Quinn, 1997).

Fleck (1979) argued that the ability to perceive scientifically is learned socially, over time, and in a complex socially conditioned ways. Ideas emerge and are expanded upon via social interactions. Problem solving involves "an active learner participating in a culturally organized activity" and in a "community that supports, challenges and guides valued sociocultural activity" (Rogoff, 1990, p. 39). Communities of practices as such shape tacit knowledge inside organizations, and extend outside organizations as professional norms and beliefs are shared through inter-organizational exchange (Abrahamson & Fombrun, 1994; Gertler, 2004). Professional communities thus develop their own "slang, style, sense of taste, judgment, and appropriateness" (Gertler, 2004, p. 146). Communities of practice drive schema formation and proliferation in the wider firm context when the community of practice holds power in the organization, as software engineers might in a software company or doctors in an HMO.

The structure and organization of professional training programs also tend to be congruent with the values of and ideologies of the profession. So-called "programming effects" espouse particular perspectives and "delimit" the career options available, rendering certain types of careers and positions "more likely than others" (Bucher & Stelling, 1977, p. 265). Through apprenticeship, professionals learn to interact with the tools of their trade, acquiring both a professional disposition and learning the profession's constraints (Malafouris, 2004; Rogoff, 1990).

And as discussed, schemas themselves can be emotionally motivating (Strauss & Quinn, 1997). Social power, for example, is experienced as a FORCE image schema (Gardenfors, 2007). They are so, in part, because they contain emotional content and in part because such content motivates thought as well as language and behavior (Kovecses, 2008). In this same way schemas within occupational communities may motivate the way peers evaluate each other or think about standards for success. Stewart (2002), for example, found differences in what 'good leadership' meant between senior executives and IT personnel. The latter thought good leadership meant developing teams to be autonomous, while the former thought it meant developing and articulating a vision for the business. Ostensibly similar concepts of success in the same firm can vary significantly by occupational group based on the schemas informing conceptions of leadership. In the same vein, standards for engineers can vary by engineering discipline, company, and industry.

Historicity

We live in a world of rituals, objects and practices intentionally shaped by previous generations (Sinha & Jensen de Lopez, 2000; Strauss & Quinn, 1997). Take the story of the daughter who always cuts off both ends of the ham before cooking it in the oven. When asked why she does this, she says, "I don't know, my mother always did it this way." When the mother is asked, she says the same thing. When the grandmother is asked, she says, "Oh, we did it that way because we did not have a pan that was big enough to fit the entire ham!" (from Strauss & Quinn, 1997). Schemas, in the form of family lore, are transmitted across generations and in this way come to have historical durability through practice, or what Strauss and Quinn label "historicity." They tend to be reproducible across generations (Strauss & Quinn, 1997).

Professional education and training notwithstanding, cultural schemas are generally not transmitted as bodies of rules and precepts but are internalized little by little, without any overt teaching or transmission (Descola, 2013). More precisely, the kinds of induction mechanisms I am describing here often provide the grounding contexts that make their internalization a matter experience. Schemas come to constitute the logic within a particular practice, discourse, or norm a group takes for granted. While the logic often remains implicit, it can be perceptible across generations and through history.

This idea is illustrated by Andre-George Haudricourt's (1962; in Descola, 2013) fascinating contrast of how Eastern and Western societies have historically treated nature and humans. His thesis suggests Asian societies historically favored the cultivation of rice and yams by focusing on improving the environment surrounding the organism as much as possible so as to favor its growth, rather than by establishing direct control over it. Western and near-Eastern societies favored direct intervention, as seen for example in sheep-raising practices in the ancient Mediterranean area that necessitated permanent and controlling action over animals to ensure their safety. These practices extended well beyond animals, for example, to European practices of growing wheat for cereal. Haudricourt maintains these differences manifest in each region's behavior towards humans. The Near

East and Europe are dominated through history by direct interventions, as depicted in the Bible, and in Aristotle where the notion of the leader who commands his subjects—seen as a collective body—is dominant. The indirect action of Eastern societies can be traced through the precepts for good government conveyed by Confucianism favoring conciliation and consensus (in which plant metaphors are used to represent humans), or in Melanesia where the chief does not issue orders but strives to ensure his actions reflect the general will of the community. Of course, these are sweeping claims, and Descola admits these oppositions are not entirely convincing on all points. But what Haudricourt's thesis does is orient us to the possibility that generalized primary schemas, over generations of inducement and progressive alignment, make it possible for humans to adapt to novel situations which are "perceived as particular cases of situations already encountered" (Descola, 2013, p. 107). This is the key feature of schema transposability and reproducibility. Analogical transfer enables the assimilation of novel cases into an existing cognitive sensemaking framework, which in turn are imparted to social and cultural norms and practices. The progression from the particular to the novel undergoes transformation based on environmental contingencies, as I elaborate below. But the logic of the underlying schemas, as Haudricourt suggests, may remain discernible across generations, often traceable in complex sociocultural practices and adaptations.

Restrepo (2015) offers another intriguing case of schema historicity in his study of the settlement of the Canadian prairies. He examined whether differences in violence across regions were in part due to the historical ability of the state to centralize authority and monopolize violence. He compared settlements in the late 1880s that were located near Canadian Mounted Police (Mountie)-created forts with those that were not. He found that in 2014 communities located at least 100 kilometers from former Mountie forts during their settlement period had 45% more homicides and 55% more violent crimes per capita than communities located closer to former forts. He argues these differences may be accounted for by a violent culture of honor that emerged as an adaptation to the lack of a central authority during the settlement period that has persisted over a century. In line with this interpretation, he found those who live in once-lawless areas were more likely to hold conservative political views. The code or practice, as it were, of honor in these communities may have been fueled by schemas that hold violent retribution rather than the rule of law as legitimate redress for offense, and these schemas, embedded in codes and practices, may have been resident for generations.[13] Restrepo does not draw from schema theory to explain his data, but his research illustrates the complex interplay between ecological and social contingencies and cultural phenomena, and is entirely consistent with Strauss and Quinn's notion of the historical persistence and transmission of schemas.

These cases illustrate historicity on a grand scale. They show how historicity shapes knowledge production and identity through the cumulative conduct of practice, and the adaptation of practice to environmental contingencies. One reason for this is that successive generations put special emphasis on imparting the values of that generation to the next (Strauss & Quinn, 1997). Goodwin (1994) puts it this way: "The ability to build structures in the world that organize knowledge, shape perception, and structure future action is one way that human cognition is shaped through ongoing historical practices" (p. 628). Strauss and Quinn (1997), for example, found that Americans' conceptions of marriage are built on a few underlying schemas that transcend generations. In a similar way, professionals absorb the prevailing norms and values of the previous generation of professionals, often through the process of learning in formal graduate programs or apprenticeships, or working with more senior colleagues. In organizational settings, members may be likely to reject new conceptualizations of organizational images they believe are incongruent with organizational history, tradition, and the collective sense of self (Ravasi & Schultz, 2006). The collective self is organized within a historical context in part provided by organizational history, but also by professional identity. Nearly every one of my IMCO informants, for example, mentioned a key formative experience in their career was learning from a highly respected mentor or boss. Not surprisingly, this group also shares a strong schema associated with first-hand knowing (*THE PRIMACY OF PERSONAL EXPERIENCE*; see Section II). This is not to imply that new generations, especially through the appropriation of new technology, do not rewrite 'the rules' (or at least try) of the profession handed down from the previous generation.[14] But to rewrite the rules means the rules have to have been learned or understood implicitly beforehand. Historicity explains how this happens.

Evidence for Professional Grounding

While the occupational culture literature over the last 30 years has not been overtly concerned with schemas, and little within it accounts for the relationship between professional and organizational culture, this literature does provide some interesting opportunities to *infer* schema induction and analogical transfer through an examination of schema entailments, such as through values and preferences, learning, systems of meaning ('interpretive schemes'), metaphor and discourse, and strategy.[15]

One of the few studies that focuses on the relationship between professional communities, schemas, discourse and practice, not surprisingly, provides the most direct evidence for professional grounding. Dougherty (1992) found pronounced differences in the schemas ("interpretive schemes") concerning product innovation among different occupational groups in two large computer and telecommunications companies and three large manufacturers.[16] Her study identified divergent systems of meaning among four occupational groups within these companies: "technical," "field" (sales), "manufacturing," and "planning" (p. 188). For example, with respect to dealing with uncertainties in the future, the "Technical People" approached uncertainty by "finding out what the (product) design parameters are." The "Field People" dealt with the same uncertainty by figuring out how to "get to buyers, discern if they like the product" and adjust the product for the user. The "Manufacturing People" dealt with uncertainty by thinking about whether manufacturing new products is possible, and how to adjust manufacturing volume. The "Planning People" concerned themselves with determining market forecasts and income projections. Similar "systems of meaning" identified these groups' conceptions of critical product development issues and how the task of development was understood (p. 188). Dougherty claims that schemas, along with departmental routines, were barriers to successful product innovation. Left unaddressed was whether these differences were truly interpretive schemes or merely departmental tasks. One could substitute "job responsibilities" for "interpretive scheme" and her findings would still make sense. Nonetheless, it is clear from her work that, at a minimum, different functions interpret their own work and that of others though unique frames suggestive of underlying schemas. That she found pervasive meaning patterns across similar functions within different industries suggests functional and professional effects may be stronger than industry effects, contradicting the claims of some industry-recipe theorists (Chapter 3).

Professional grounding is also in evidence in work on professional values. For example, Merritt (2000) showed pilots perceive their own work environments to be more autocratic and directive than other occupational groups represented in Hofstede's studies. The profession is obviously aware of the fatal consequences of errors, and spends more time on rules, structure, and standard operating procedures, especially emergency procedures, to mitigate risk and manage abnormal situations (Fonne & Myrhe, 1996; Merritt, 2000). Much of the training on emergency procedures, in fact focuses on the systematic enactment of checklists, as well as, in certain situations, developing automatic embodied responses for problem recognition and resolution. The task environment entrains pilots to action that give rise to "professionally instilled values" (Merritt, 2000, p. 7).[17]

In a different context, Elliott and Scacchi (2003) demonstrated a link between values and work in studying software developers working on open source software. They found that assumptions about the nature of cooperative work and community became engrained in work practices of implementing free software. These beliefs and values enhanced and motivated the resolution of conflicts despite physical distance separation and the amorphous nature of the developer community. The authors believe values influenced work style (at least as regards conflict), but left open the question of whether working on free software also influenced values, hinting at the bi-directional relationship between work and professional values.

Studies across other professional groups point to a relationship between professional practice, behavior, discourse, cognition, and values. Information technology (IT) professionals place a high value on technical knowledge, and express a lack of interest in formal rules (Guzman, Stam, & Stanton, 2008). Hodgkinson and Johnson (1994) attributed the diversity in managerial assumptions across industries to mental models based on occupational roles. Engineers value systems, routines, and machines based on the training they receive that emphasize certainty and continuity (Hyland, Gieskes, & Sloan, 2001). Occupational culture, at least for engineers, may play a more significant role in shaping learning values and behaviors than national culture (Hyland et al., 2001).

There also appears to be marked differences in work environment preferences between professionals and non-professionals. Those in professional occupations indicate a much stronger preference than those in vocational occupations for styles of organizational environment and culture reflecting autonomy, creativity, quality, participation, self-management and constructive interpersonal relationships (Bloor & Dawson, 1994).

With respect to professional metaphor and discourse, Caballero (2006) showed how architects put more stock in visual metaphors over others. Nurses frame the concept of change in ways congruent with their professional work and values through three primary discourse frames: *care for patients, not paper*; *have a hand in our own future*; and *no responsibility without pay* (Rousseau & Tijoriwala, 1999). In my own study of occupational metaphors I found HR professionals index service to others and helpfulness rather than business value in construing their own relations with internal clients.[18] And in one of the most comprehensive studies of professional discourse, Daley (2001) found a wide diversity in the frames and metaphors used by social workers, lawyers, adult educators, and nurses. Table 4.4 below captures some of this diversity:

Daley's research clearly indicates a unique pattern of discourse for each profession. It is difficult to conceive, for example, lawyers, as a group likening their work to a "hummingbird" that "drops a little bit here and there" (Daley, 2001, p. 44). To Daley, professional meaning was related directly to the "nature of professional work in which each group engaged" (p. 47).

From all of these examples we can infer professional grounding. The evidence, while indirect, suggests occupational communities exhibit distinct and pervasive cognitive orientations that manifest in values, discourse, and practice.

2. Strategic Task Context

Organizations develop cultures by doing things. 'Doing things' means performing certain tasks in certain ways utilizing specific tools and technologies and employing certain routines over time. All of these activities create indelible cognitive orientations; task *doing* leaves a kind of cognitive residue, 'residue' being the effects of repeatedly conceiving of and solving problems in particular ways with particular tools and techniques in a particular social order and context. As Hutchins (2005) frames it, the main cognitive effect of cultural schemas is achieved by building the constraints of the task into the structure of the schema.

Strategic task context, thus, is the task, technology, and practices, usually in the form of habits and routines that make up and enable the firm's

Table 4.4 Daley's Professional Discourse Metaphors and Frames

	Social Workers	Lawyers	Adult Educators	Nurses
Nature of own work	Stewards of information Client advocates Understand resistance	Boil a case down to bottom line issues The law is a form of logic (law) Requires a very logical and linear thought process Cases rise and fall on details	That of a hummingbird—take new information and drop a little bit here and there into different groups The process of connection makes knowledge	(need to) Delineate between a stressful (situation with a patient) and a normal (situation)
Attitude toward continuing education	Bring new energy Refresh mind and spirit	A road map for practice Law school is where your brain gets rewired and you learn a new language Decision criteria used to decide whether to attend continuing education programs	A spark for a creative process Pull in what we learned . . . so everybody has the ability to learn it (Want to) see action come of it	A web of information to draw on Revitalize You know what is good information Knowledge is meaningful when you take action on it
Role with clients	Support and defend Help clients differentiate from the system	Separate the emotion from their cases	Resource Conduit	Exude confidence Put the patient in a more relaxed state

principal mode of production. The word *strategic* refers to the idea these activities are core to the way firms produce goods or services and derive revenue. Strategic task context is not limited to organizations. Many of these same effects can be found in professional milieus, but I include them in this section because, unlike professionalization, these dynamics are not exclusive to the social dynamics of becoming professional. For example, human resources (HR) work also entails a material practice environment, but unless it is done in an HR consultancy it is not core to a firm's production of goods and services. In this way task constrains structure; manufacturing firms have difficulty behaving and operating like software firms. Non-government organizations (NGOs) have difficulty behaving and operating like airlines. As Barley (1990, 1996) puts it, there is a pattern that exists between everyday action and overarching patterns of social organization. Schema grounding in organizations and occupations occurs through the dynamic patterns of interaction between material "regularities," using Hutchins' (2005, p. 1575) term, the physical environment of how a firm produces goods and services, and the conceptual structure of those doing the producing. Thus, repeated interaction through the processes and properties of work and technology, along with the demands of complex problem solving give rise to or enhance schemas. Strategic contexts are also enabled by success; the more successful a particular task context is perceived to be, the stronger the cognitive imprinting.

Strategic task contexts are comprised of three grounding elements: *shared task solutions, technological grounding*, and *routines*. These elements tend to be *force-sensitive*: when well aligned and reinforced with a unique, purposeful and meaningful (to its members) organizational purpose that is sustained over time, these effects become especially strong and widely shared, underwriting more palpably distinct culture or cultures. The converse is also true—task solutions, technologies or routines orthogonal to purpose, the product of legacy environments, or not strategically conceived, will tend to fragment or diffuse cultures.[19]

Shared Task Solutions

When people and groups find recurring and successful solutions to the challenges and contradictions confronting them, these solutions tend to spread. Members of the same group who share solutions to the same tasks will tend to develop the same schemas (Strauss & Quinn, 1997, p. 125). The more successful these solutions, the more they will induce or reinforce shared schemas. Strauss and Quinn (1997) label this phenomenon *shared task solutions*:[20]

> Among the common experiences with which human sociocultural life presents members of any community are, inevitably, recurrent tasks, problems, challenges, contradictions, and conflicts. As solutions to these

are invented, the most useful practical and appealing of these solutions tend to spread. Even complex tasks are met by creating and widely sharing the correspondingly complex solutions, such as human language . . . (and these) are ubiquitous in everyday life.

(p. 125)

Shared task solutions are often accompanied—or give rise to—artefacts, tools, technologies, procedures, rules-of-thumb, and systems of knowing and seeing, as discussed above (Knorr-Cetina, 1999). These are cognitively useful for repeated problem solving (Hutchins, 1987). Solutions often become features of problems themselves (Hutchins, 1995; Knorr-Cetina, 1999; Leonardi & Jackson, 2009).

Shared task solutions are motivated by goals that are in turn motivated by cognitive linkages to a great variety of "arousing" experiences (D'Andrade, 1995, p. 239). Not all schemas function as goals, but all goals are schemas, because the cognitive structure of schemas activates and guides action (D'Andrade, 1992). Analogical transfer is motivated by goal attainment, or "pragmatic relevance" (Holyoak & Thagard, 1989, as cited in Gentner & Colhoun, 2008, p. 8). People are more likely to make inferences or import a fact into an analogy when it is connected to other predicates in the target (Gentner & Colhoun, 2008).

Strauss and Quinn's (1997) research on marriage shows how this works. For Americans, shared solutions to the problems inherent in forming lasting marriages *create* a shared schema about what marriage is. The schema is about overcoming obstacles. The schema helps make the goal of overcoming difficulty salient and meaningful. It is also a part of a broader schema in American culture, one that colors many domains of life and is encapsulated in the theme of Yankee ingenuity, hard work, lastingness, and pride in one's work (Strauss & Quinn, 1997).

This same phenomenon is visible in professional and organizational settings. Paoline (2003) asserts repeated problem solving is what endows culture with many of its meanings. In his study of police culture, he shows that exposure to and successfully navigating danger and death in the course of everyday work has a unifying effect on the police community; police organizations are culturally affected by these realities. Without referring to schemas, Paoline suggests the experiential context and goals of police work give rise to this system of meaning. Similarly, LeBlanc's (2008) study of mill workers in Fitchburg, Massachusetts shows how mill work is invested with meaning through the realization of livelihood, and the affirmation of craft and creativity. Extending the idea of meaning to whole industries, Gordon (1991) suggests common assumptions develop within an industry in response to specific customer requirements, competition, or societal expectations (including regulatory requirements) that lead to corporate 'value systems' that prevent organizations from developing strategies or structures in conflict with these assumptions.

Barley's (1983) study of funeral home directors showed how goal and task structure semiotic codes. Funeral directors attempt to convey "naturalness" and "smoothness" in the funeral home experience to obfuscate the anxiety and emotional trauma (for loved ones) of death, and to ensure notions of convenience and ease are conveyed to clients (p. 408). These codes manifest in metonymic expressions of "naturalness" and a "smoothly flowing funeral," as well as in physical layouts and furniture choices for funeral homes (for example, to be made to look like living rooms), and in the processes of posing and removal of the corpse (pp. 406–408). Barley suggests these codes arise from the task of mitigating the anxiety of the funeral by "putting people at ease" and conveying the "naturalness of unnaturalness" (p. 401). The pragmatic relevance of conveying a funeral dictates the choice of particular, non-idiosyncratic language, behavior, and action. Task mitigates and circumscribes funeral home culture via the pragmatics of goal attainment, and the cognitive, linguistic and physical entailments of successfully completing the task. The semiotic codes, while not portraying the whole of a culture, "succinctly capture a major aspect of it" (p. 408). Barley's codes are metonymies structured by schemas that themselves are a product of the goals and strategic task of funeral conveyance.

The concept of shared task solutions inducing cultural schemas is brilliantly illustrated in a historical context by Biernacki's (1994) study of labor practices in the textile industry in England and Germany extending from the end of the Middle Ages into the 20th century. In German textile factories employment was viewed as a service in which workers provided "labor capacity" (p. 68). German workers treated labor time as part of what constituted the work day. British managers, in contrast, saw labor time as objectified in the form of worker output. Weavers in Yorkshire could send substitutes to operate looms. These differences in labor practice organized employment contracts, disciplinary rules, and the way in which workers gauged earnings. For example, with respect to wage contracts, German workers argued they had a right to payment for the time spent waiting without doing work. As Biernacki states, "German workers attached a value to the commitment of time with such *precision* that when they formulated strike demands for waiting money, they often requested that managers graduate the pay not only for lost days but for lost hours" (p. 69. Italics mine). In England, however, factory owners did not offer workers "waiting money," and "nor did British workers ask for it" (p. 70).

The conceptualization of labor as capacity versus output had ramifications beyond the textile mills and factory floors. Different concepts of labor between the two countries extended into the design of factories and led workers in the two countries to make different sets of demands of their employers (Biernacki, 1994). This in turn led to differences in the way Marxist discourse was adopted in factories in England in the early 20th century:

The analysis of everyday practices on the shop floor in Germany suggests that the newly introduced Marxist economic discourse could rest on long-established factory customs that treated employment as the sale of disposition over labor time. A substantial body of British intellectuals tried to disseminate Marxist ideas about time, but even workers who sought revolutionary change in the ownership of production did not absorb this thought.

(Biernacki, 1994, p. 79)

Biernacki makes clear labor *practice* accounts for the rise of different conceptions of how to pay for work or the willingness to accept a particular political discourse. As he states, "the schemas encoded in silent practices within the private factory lent workers the concept of labor they used to voice demands in the public sphere . . . the cultural definition of labor as a commodity was communicated and reproduced, not through ideal symbols as such, but through the hallowed form of unobtrusive practices" (Biernacki, 1994, in Swidler, 2001, p. 84). Biernacki here is describing schema transposability; schemas enacted in everyday work organized and circumscribed other schemas, providing an "infrastructure" for repeated interactional patterns (Swidler, 2001, p. 85).

Technological Grounding

Culture is tightly bound to the material technologies of organizations, or what Leonardi and Jackson call *technological grounding* (Leonardi & Jackson, 2009, p. 395). This is the idea that the core technology of an organization, that is, the technology that gives rise to or enables a firm's primary business, along with the "work and communication practices" enacted by members surrounding it, are constitutive of its culture (p. 395).[21]

In their study of the merger of U.S. West and Qwest, Leonardi and Jackson (2009) demonstrate how technological grounding caused post-merger integration issues because "the culture of each organization was closely intertwined with that organization's core technology" (p. 395). This is the story of a much smaller fiber optics company, Qwest, taking over a much larger and older telephone company, U.S. West, one of the original Baby Bells, and within a matter of a few months completely absorbing it such that, for all intents and purposes, the larger company ceased to exist. Qwest offered a diversity of products and served many markets, which served to direct the company toward attributes of speed and service (Leonardi & Jackson, 2009). Qwest's goal was to enable as many data transfers as possible over its fiber optic networks. The company placed emphasis on these features and quickly became an organization characterized by speed, as echoed in the slogan, 'Ride the Light'" (Leonardi & Jackson, 2009, p. 405). U.S. West, meanwhile had outdated technology but a large market and customer base, and offered "stability," with "stable jobs for employees and stable relationships with customers" (p. 409). Qwest's technology and strategic task context imparted values the company directly appropriated in its merger with U.S. West:

> Qwest officials gained cultural control during postmerger integration by returning to the technology itself to frame the future of the organization . . . technological superiority of one company's product over the other translates to its organizational superiority . . . Technological grounding allowed Qwest to situate discursively the merger in technological rather than organizational terms . . . Qwest relied on the characteristics of its technology to suggest that its dominance over U.S. West was inevitable, despite its relatively smaller size and briefer history.
> (Leonardi & Jackson, 2009, p. 410)

Technology provided Qwest with a "normative frame" that enabled the establishment of behavior, practices, and values it deemed advantageous and more favorable than that of its merger partner (Leonardi & Jackson, 2009, p. 411). Qwest's entire entrepreneurial culture was justified on grounds of its technology, as was the perception that U.S. West was old and bureaucratic and slow. This in turn enabled a sense of faster adaptation and better processing of information related to innovation because the espoused desired values were discernible at a level of "common culture" (Leonardi & Jackson, 2009, p. 411).

One could argue Qwest's discursive situating of the merger had little to do with culture and instead was a simple and convenient rationalization to justify its domination and decimation of the older and larger company. Or, perhaps reifying its own culture as an obvious fact was justification enough. The extensive evidence Leonardi and Jackson (2009) cite from public records, news accounts, and interviews, however, strongly suggests Qwest's technological and task focus provided it with a self-evident (to itself) logic on which to make these claims and justify its actions in the public realm.

Technological grounding is likely the product of a cascade of linkages from the technology itself to interactive practices that employ the technology, to artefacts like role definitions, and, eventually, to discourse. The idea of linkages is taken from Osborne and his colleagues (2001), who make the association between schemas ("mental models") and performance in the pharmaceutical industry. They suggest schemas are "one of several links" in a chain that leads to performance (Osborne, Stubbart, & Ramaprasad, 2001, p. 448). Given what is known about cognition as situated in environmental and task context, it is likely that technology and its attendant tasks induce related schemas that in turn are transposed to other contexts, such as values, memes ("Ride the Light"), and entire narratives that justify and reify the technology.[22] This furthers the progressive alignment of schemas to endow the embedding technological context with significant meaning. This is how, again, the structure of the task, enabled by the technology, structures the cognitive orientations of the actors using the technology.

This idea is closely related to Colfer and Baldwin's (2010) mirroring hypothesis, the idea that a correspondence exists between organizational structure and technical architecture, with causality in both directions. Through a literature review spanning 129 studies of product development, they found product developers with few or no organizational linkages were more likely to design independent system components, while developers with strong organizational linkages were more likely to design highly interdependent system components (Colfer & Baldwin, 2010).[23] Similarly, Barley (1990) showed how the introduction of medical imaging technology in the 1980s changed the roles of laboratory technicians from equipment operators to diagnosticians. With the advent of the new technology, technologists routinely spoke of anatomy and disease pathology visible in images, and provided probable prognoses to doctors. This "interpretive knowledge" was partially explained by the new machines, but also was a response by technicians to the information now available in the images (Barley, 1990, p. 82). The new technology changed the roles of lab technicians such that they now had more administrative discretion over their own work, and their behavior changed as a result. The technology, and the response of technologists, challenged the established social order with doctors and staff (Barley, 1990).[24]

Thus, technological and task grounding make available an array of cognitive artefacts—language, symbols, metaphors, discourse frames, logic—in which to situate narratives and practices. Technology activates cultural schemas by drawing "frames around resources that will guide people's problem construction practices" (Leonardi & Jackson, 2009, p. 363). By acting as a frame, technology concepts play an important role in determining what cultural resources will be used to develop subsequent technological artefacts. Technological frames can also inhibit inter-departmental collaboration, which in turn impacts innovation (Leonardi, 2011).[25] Technology, especially when central to an organization's history and strategic focus, as it was at Qwest, comes to be "endowed with symbolic value" because the technology itself represents solutions that pattern meaning and frame collective action (Leonardi & Jackson, 2009, p. 397). Qwest's technology provided it with a built-in logic for domination. I suspect the logic was pervasive. It provided the material grounding for schemas to be induced, appropriated, and transposed, both through explicit discourse and action and through implicit means, such as the prevailing attitudes of the management team.[26]

While technology and task have the potential to ground the cognitive orientations of organizational members it does not mean it will in every case. *How* organization members perceive the grounding source is key. For example, technology has the potential to induce new shared schemas, but this is a function of how central the technology is to a firm's means of production, how that technology is put to use to solve salient problems, how members interpret the new technology and what meaning they attach to the solutions it provides. It is also a function of what professional predisposition (other schemas) dominant communities bring to the technology to begin with. And obviously this is a recursive relationship. What the research above suggests, however, is that when the technology is closely associated with the firm's core means of production and accounts for its success according to the actors involved, the schemas induced by the technology will tend to spread (much like activation in a neural network) across practices, behaviors, values, and discourse. This is an important dynamic for a firm's culture to be functionally grounded.

Routines

Organizational routines might be thought of as the result of technological grounding. While this is the case at times, routines are also capable of structuring cognition because of the cognitive nature of repetition (Mandler, 1983; Munby, Versnel, Hutchinson, Chin, & Berg, 2003; Rerup & Feldman, 2011; Rousseau & Tijoriwala, 1999; Rousseau, 2001).[27] Professional and organizational routines are a key mechanism in schema induction because they enable progressive alignment. It is also what makes schemas *durable* (Strauss & Quinn, 1997). The process of internalization, following the theory of progressive alignment, occurs through experience garnered over time through the enactment of routines.

Routines both constitute schemas and are capable of structuring them, or in Johnson's (1990) words, "the limited range of capabilities based on an organization's available routines and physical assets are closely linked to the cognitive structure of the paradigm" (p. 186). Routines are linked to organizational capabilities, as well as to its history, social context, and environment. Managers do not reconstruct new ways to solve the same problems (Johnson, 1990); routines guide the gathering and interpreting of evidence to reconstruct the past (Neisser, 1967, 1981, as cited in Guenther, 2002). In these ways, routines contain as well as generate organizational cognition.

Summary: Pervasive Grounding

The claim could be made that strategic task grounding and professionalization are simply alternative, albeit perhaps more elaborate formulations of contingency theory, the idea that organizational characteristics such as structure are made to fit contingent environmental or technological circumstance (for example, Donaldson, 2001). Thus, Qwest's narrative for its absorption of U.S. West was a discursive strategy based on its superior technology to justify its actions, and not the effect of more pervasive, and perhaps tacitly shared, cognition. But contingency theory cannot explain how such a narrative might have come about to begin with, or why it became so widely shared and adopted within Qwest. With respect to technology, contingency theory's main claim is "the more routine the technology, the more formalized the structure" (Barley, 1990). Questions as to why similar technologies may yield different structures, or vice versa, remain unexamined (Barley, 1990). Indeed, task and technological form appear to take shape in many different ways in organizations: through social forms like routines, communication networks, and through structural resources such as span of control and the design of jobs (Barley, 1990; Colfer & Baldwin, 2010; Perrow, 1984).

The key point in functional grounding is that humans in organizations *will* manifest shared schemas. What determines whether these schemas are unique or pervasive, versus conventional or, say, appropriated from stock cultural scripts, is a function of the sustained exposure to and reinforcement within the grounding contexts. The most important contribution of embodied cognition to organizational culture is the idea that the task and material environment, as well as sociocultural experience, indelibly pattern cognition, and that this patterning is pervasive. Returning to Hutchins, the constraint of the task, to which I would add the technology or routine, manifest in the structure of the schema. The manifestation is not literal, in the sense of content, but structural, functioning more like the dried riverbeds and arroyos in a desert landscape shaped by running water. Over time these become features of the landscape and serve as transits for humans and animals. The running water is the dynamic induction environment; the arroyos the schemas left behind. The schemas in evidence at IMCO are not fully articulated strategies, values or behavioral norms. Rather, they are abstractions like *MACHINE* or *BUILT STRUCTURE* or *PHYSICAL OBJECTS*, gestalt analogs of the physical and social environment in which they were induced, lending more concrete propositions or practices their sense of structure, form and coherence.

Taken as a whole, a pattern of practices, discourse, norms, and values congruent with professionalization and strategic task context are evident across a wide range of literature. Whether these entailments are fully convincing in all respects as evidence of pervasive schemas, as I believe they are, is a question left open for more empirical work.

3. Cultural Determinism: *How Schemas Permeate Organizations*

The functional grounding idea put forth here does not yet completely explain how cultures form or are perpetuated in organizations. How do some organizations manifest cohesive cultures, while others appear to have fragmented ones? What accounts for cultural variance? How do macro-environmental factors such as ethnic culture or economic conditions intercede? And what about individual agency? Surely leaders, as the popular narrative would have it, shape culture? The question, in essence, is how do cultural schemas permeate complex organizations made up of multiple professional groups, geographic operating regions, and strategic task contexts, and can this process be in any way shaped or engineered? This section examines each of these questions.

The mechanism of cultural diffusion, I suggest, is *sensemaking*. Actors appropriate schemas as resources in sensemaking, evidenced and aided by discourse and power. Sensemaking, of course, is dynamic and recursive. It occurs in response to environmental and ecological triggers, and relies upon cognitive resources already indelibly shaped by professionalization and the strategic task context.

To Spender (1996), a firm's strategic choices, product designs, modes of production, organizational designs, market engagement strategies, and so forth could all be otherwise and yet still lead to the same result. Firms are "semi-autonomous organic systems" that exist in perpetually "underdetermined" states because their "essential dynamic," in the form of Latour's "quasi-objects," can "never be captured" (pp. 18–19). Spender's biological metaphor evokes the essence of modern organizations situated in ever-shifting economic, social, technological, and political contexts. Yet Spender's conception is only possible when organizations are conceived of as independent of the people, tasks, technologies, and ecologies in which they are situated. His conception fails to take into account the fact organizations are made up of people who daily bring situated cognitive orientations to bear on the milieus in which they work. To the extent the effects of professionalization and strategic task are more or less present and pervasive in the cognitive orientations of actors will determine the range of strategic choices the organization makes and the extent to which it evidences a discernible culture. Groundedness suggests a degree of determinism, and determinism undermines (especially in the United States) the folk belief in individual self-actualization and achievement.[28] It also challenges postmodernist discourse on power, gender and domination.

Determinism, of course, is not the whole story. No two organizations, as no two cultures, are exactly alike. Dominant professional orientation and strategic task context *enculturate* organizations. They endow the organization with its experiential milieu for the inducement and progressive alignment of schemas. But schemas manifest in a myriad of ways that might appear to be underdetermined at any moment in time but, in fact, are not because actors are continually appropriating them as resources in the production of sensemaking in response to their environment (Sewell, 2005). Discourse, power, and the precise nature of what I call the *sensemaking boundary* will serve to shape or revise existing schemas, leading to relatively unified, fragmented or diffuse cultures. In this way organizational cultures take on a degree of ecological determinism bounded by the cognitive predispositions of their actors and the tasks and technologies they enroll in the pursuit of both commerce and existential meaning, but also maintain a veneer of under-determinedness shaped by their own ecological contingencies.

What Makes a Resource?

To understand cultural schemas in the context of sensemaking it is important to understand their function as resources. Resources are human practices and behaviors *generated* by schemas, as well as semiotic forms like money, or physical resources like land or factories (Sewell, 2005). Resources are how social structure manifests and schemas are brought into being through their affordances. Reformulating Giddens' definition, Sewell

(2005) provides an elegant account of this relationship by suggesting social structure itself is the product of schemas *and* resources:[29]

> To take perhaps what is the most obvious case, an immense stack of Hudson Bay blankets would be nothing more than a means of keeping a large number of people warm were it not for the cultural schemas that constituted the Kwakiutl potlatch; but given these schemas, the blankets given away in a potlatch, became the means of demonstrating the power of the chief and, consequently, acquiring prestige, marriage alliances, military power, and labor services.
>
> (p. 135)

Hudson Bay blankets are the physical manifestation of a Kwakiutl chief's power, a resource endowed with meaning by cultural schemas. What makes something a resource is a "consequence of the schemas that inform their use" (Sewell, 2005, p. 135). Importantly, in Sewell's (1992, 2005) conception, schemas are the effects of resources as resources are the effects of schemas:

> A factory is not an inert pile of bricks, wood and metal. It incorporates or actualizes schemas, and this means the schemas can be inferred from the material form of the factory. The factory gate, the punching-in station, the design of the assembly line: all of these features of the factory teach and validate the rules of the capitalist contract.
>
> (2005, p. 136)

In this way resources make schemas causally bidirectional. Schemas not "empowered or regenerated by resources would eventually be abandoned and forgotten, just as resources without cultural schemas to direct their use would eventually dissipate and decay" (Sewell, 2005, p. 13). Swidler (2001) takes Sewell's argument further by acknowledging practices are a kind of resource.[30] Practices are "simultaneously material and enacted, but also patterned and meaningful, both because they enact schemas and because they may be read for the transposable schemas they contain" (2001, p. 79).[31] Cultural practices may be inconsistent, overlapping, and multiple, and certain kinds of practices, like certain schemas, scaffold others.[32] Practices function as the connective tissue between professionalization, strategic task contexts, and sensemaking. This relationship is always dynamic and evolving in a context determined by environmental contingencies and constraints, and shaped by actors involved.

Schemas and Sensemaking

Sensemaking is the collective movement to provide satisfactory accounts of what happens in order to render meaningful the world around us. It is individual meaning-making writ large. To Weick and his colleagues, it is the "retrospective development of plausible images" (Weick, Sutcliffe, & Obstfeld, 2005, p. 409). In organizations, sensemaking occurs when the current state is perceived as being different from the desired. It also applies to the comprehension of practices and processes, such as the innovation process, or in interpreting market events (Bingham & Kahl, 2013; Cornelissen, 2012; Weick et al., 2005). Forms of organizational sensemaking include discourse frames, narratives, institutional codes and conventions, and practices, all of which are structured by cultural schemas (Cornelissen, 2012; Weick et al., 2005). Sensemaking drives most forms of decision making, from portfolio rationalization, budgeting, resource allocation, hiring and promotion, and so forth. Sensemaking extends to strategy, specifically in how a firm construes its core competencies, target markets, and its overall "theory of the business" (Drucker, 1994).[33]

Schemas permeate and are sustained in organizations in part through the production of sensemaking. They are liable to be revised in the context of macro-environmental, institutional, and economic forces as organizations attempt to adjust or make sense of these events. The sections below describe this process.

The paradox of schemas is that they tend to blind choice while making apparent the entire array of choices or, in the language of Bourdieu (1990), "the habitus tends to protect itself from crises and critical challenges by providing itself with a milieu to which it is pre-adapted as possible . . . a relatively constant universe of situations tending to reinforce its dispositions" (p. 61). It is within this apparent paradox that schemas underlie sensemaking. Making sense in organizations is constrained by the milieu to which actors are pre-adapted, an adaptation predisposed by their professional orientation or the strategic task context of the organization. Sensemaking, thus, is context sensitive, both in terms of the range of events possible within an organization given its specific industry, market, task and technology context, and how these events are construed based on the cognitive predispositions of those doing the sensemaking. Cultural schemas become pervasive in organizations in manifold ways, but primarily through their "efficiency in performing the cognitive task, they address" (Strauss & Quinn, 1997, p. 163), which is to say they both facilitate and limit the encoding of information in the production of collective sensemaking (Barr, Stimpert, & Huff, 1992).

For instance, Hodgkinson and Johnson (1994) found managers across different industries drew from many frames of reference to make sense of their own environments, including functionally derived ones. Sensemaking in a medical context was found to be "thinking acted out" and applied knowledge and technique (Weick et al., 2005, p. 412). Management teams understand and take action in ways dependent on the meaning they assign to events, and tend to make sense of change in ways that fit their "schemes" (Gioia & Chittipeddi, 1991, p. 434). Team schemas enable team performance by facilitating anticipation of events, the interpretation of information, and allow a team to develop "shared causal accounts" of events (Mohammed, Ferzandi, and Hamilton (2010).[34] On the other hand, schemas ("interpretive schemes") can inhibit technology and market knowledge and, consequently, innovation (Dougherty, 1992).

Ravasi and Schultz (2006) illustrate this process in their longitudinal study of the Danish audio and video electronics firm Bang & Olufsen (B&O) and the firm's attempt to successively renew their corporate image over three decades. They observed managers drew on the company's cultural heritage as a reservoir of shared legacies, which imparted a sense of "distinctiveness" and provided a well of "shared understandings under environmental pressures" that gave B&O managers a sense of "resilience" (pp. 451–453). The shared understandings could be inferred as a reservoir of schemas that oriented the sensemaking based on shared legacy.

Harris (1994), Leonardi (2011), Ravasi and Schultz (2006), and Sieck and his colleagues (2010) are among a small group of organizational researchers incorporating the concept of schemas into theories of culture and change. Common to these views is that organizational culture provides its members with "cues" for sensemaking—about what their organization is about, and for providing "some sense of it" (Ravasi & Schultz, 2006). But this burdens an ephemeral and magical notion of 'culture'. My claim is that it is not culture writ large that provides these cues but the underlying cultural schemas that make such cues seem relevant and salient to begin with.

Discourse Appropriation and Differentiated Core Purpose

Cultural schemas have what Strauss and Quinn (1997) call *thematicity*; they can be evoked in a wide variety of contexts to become cultural themes (Strauss & Quinn, 1997). As Foucault pointed out, "discourse can spread across boundaries of subcultures" such as law or social science (in Strauss & Quinn, 1997, p. 118). Managers appropriate existing schemas and models in the form of discourses to enable and focus their own sensemaking (Cornelissen, 2012; Weick, 1995). Executives selectively draw upon "socio-cognitive representations" best suited to enhance the system or sustain the power relations within it (Koller, 2008, p. 394). Discourses are used to maintain, extend, or gain power, drawing upon cultural schemas that "normalize" and "homogenize" but also, at times, to "hierarchize," "exclude," and "marginalize" (Sewell, 2005, p. 172).

Left open is the question of which discourses, and why? Although not all schemas become cultural themes, schemas are more likely to be spread when the experiences of actors possessing them bear a thematic resemblance to each other (Strauss & Quinn, 1997). In an organization these likely will come from the dominant professional communities in the organization, or be supplied by actors working on the salient tasks and technologies that best address the issues confronting the organization. The schemas and models that are most plausible are those that best explain what a community is experiencing and provide the most successful solutions to the problems on hand. When they do, they anchor the discourses that become relevant and thematic across the organization.[35]

Differentiated Core Purpose

A unique form of thematicity occurs in organizations that posses a clear *differentiated core purpose*. These firms provide fertile material and experiential contexts for schema induction and transposition, and by extension cultural spreading. I differentiate 'purpose' from strategy or mission to denote the sense of existential meaning a core purpose imparts. A differentiated core purpose is a shared and affect-laden organizational goal considered unique to a majority of its members, whose achievement is deemed essential to the betterment of society, humankind, or the planet, or whose unique purpose in other ways is highly motivating to its members. Differentiated core purpose typically transcends normal capitalist or commercial ambitions. The very meaningfulness and affective content of the core purpose motivates and provides the context for schema induction.

Organizations with differentiated core purpose enact strategic tasks, technologies and routines closely aligned to that purpose, and in so doing provide the greatest number of induction contexts for its members. This is why it is easier to discern a unified and palpable culture in a small start up, or in an organization with a mission that is highly motivating and meaningful *and* that possesses well-aligned structures and processes aligned to their core purpose. The latter, in particular, is critical for schema induction. These firms induce and progressively align shared schemas in all of their material and social contexts, and do so repeatedly over time. These contexts, cognitively speaking, are thematically consistent. It is not enough to simply have motivating goals; were that the case, non-governmental organizations (NGOs) would have highly unified cultures, which clearly they do not. Nor is it enough to have well-aligned structures and practices without particularly motivating or meaningful core purpose. It is the unique combination of the two that provides a sustained and consistent culturally thematic environment for grounding.

Thus, those who attribute values or behavioral norms as the *cause* of culture, and by extension corporate success, I suggest, have it backwards. The values and norms are expressions of the underlying schemas that motivate them, and are perpetuated by discourse and practices that are thematically consistent. Embodied cognition and functional grounding tell us the social and task environment produced by highly meaningful core purpose combined with tightly aligned practice, structure and discourse provide the cognitive substrate for values, norms, and the like to come into being to begin with. I suggest this better accounts for what appear to be distinct cultures at well-known cases such as Southwest Airlines, ING, or Tom's of Maine.[36] While speculative, these so-called strong cultures show the effects of thematic and self-reinforcing schemas, made so by a high number of well-aligned induction contexts.

Power

Power is the control over resources and social context (Vike, 2011).[37] As actors exercise power through decision making, allocation and deployment of resources, establishing problem frames and agendas, and determining rewards, they invoke shared schemas that structure and lend coherence to these activities. Such practices are concentrated around powerful agents who deploy resources and define meanings, as well monitor and control resources and outcomes (Sewell, 2005).

Discourse is appropriated as actors take on the rhetoric of identities sanctioned by powerful others in the organization. They come to speak in a manner aligned with the norms of the intended audience in an effort to present themselves favorably, gain access to resources, or maintain power (Strauss, 2012). Doing so often involves what Strauss calls conventional discourse, defined as shared schemas expressed in "stock ways" (p. 20). Conventional discourses and metaphor make up an important part of the way people affiliate in organizations, especially with those in power, and is one way schemas become widely diffused and shared.[38]

An illustration comes from my Microsoft experience and research.[39] A metaphor frequently heard in the company invoked the term *ship*, referring to the physical task of boxing computer disks and shipping it to distributors. For many years this was the principal ways the company distributed software. The metaphor typically took the form of a question, such as *when is that group shipping their code?* (When will the group's software code be ready?) or *when will HR ship their new policy?* (When will HR publish the new policy?). The discourse invoked from the task context of software distribution, appropriated by those deemed most powerful in the organization—software engineers—provided a kind of linguistic currency for non-technical groups of lower status, such as HR, to be admitted into a kind of pseudo-insider status by speaking in ways acceptable to the broader technical community. The appropriation of technical jargon and discourse by non-technical groups was common and involved several other metaphors derived from software, such as *stress test (we need to stress test that idea), load balance (I want to load balance your work), bandwidth (I don't have bandwidth for that right now), capacity (does that group have capacity to take that on?)* and so on. Speaking this way at Microsoft, or any other software company, would be considered entirely conventional and appropriate.[40]

Sanctioning discourse and ordering meaning is what executives and dominant coalitions do in the process of sensemaking. This involves appropriating pragmatically relevant or convenient discourses, setting the agenda for en-actment, authorizing practices, allocating resources, determining the degree and extent of monitoring and control, selecting and evaluating staff, and so on (Kellogg, 2011). Dominant coalitions are most often top executives who determine the selection, allocation, and tracking of resources (Barr et al., 1992), but may also include professional groups close to the firm's core means of production, such as software engineers in software companies, creative professionals in advertising firms, social workers in NGOs, doctors in HMOs, and so forth. The most powerful groups within organizations tend to be those most closely associated with the organization's core means of production; the power these groups hold comes about because their sche-mas tend to become resources others appropriate and employ for social desirability or power, and therefore 'make the most sense' to the widest number of constituents.

At IMCO, for example, the most powerful groups according to my infor-mants are operations (manufacturing), engineering, and finance.[41] Not sur-prisingly, it is difficult for non-dominant groups, such as marketing or HR, to control or change prevailing narratives or decision-making processes. And as a kind of proof, both of these functions are notoriously understaffed and underfunded. IMCO's HR infrastructure, for example, has long been recognized by members of HR and outsiders as considerably outdated in terms of technology and practice.

The Sensemaking Boundary

The social world is in constant flux, never in more than what Bourdieu (1990) calls a "temporary equilibrium" in the dynamics of reconciliation where "distributions and incorporated or institutionalized classifications is constantly broken and restored" (p. 141). As the cognitive underpinnings of that order, cultural schemas are never static; they are in constant flux as managers draw upon them to makes sense of their worlds or reconcile com-peting frames of reference (Hodgkinson & Johnson, 1994). Resident cul-tural schemas can be muted and subject to the potential of revision by other forces. This is why an organization may appear to be underdetermined at any given moment. Its apparent underdetermined state is the manifestation of forces acting on what I call the sensemaking boundary.

The sensemaking boundary is where collective sensemaking in the face of environmental triggers and stressors is carried out, as depicted in Figure 4.5. This is the boundary between a firm's shared cognitions manifested in re-sources endowed by schemas, and the external environment in which it op-erates. The metaphor 'boundary' is not used here to mean a rigid barrier, but rather in the meteorological sense. A boundary between air masses as repre-sented by the imaginary line drawn on weather maps depicting the location and direction of systems of differing barometric pressure and temperature. Like colliding fronts, it is a locus of dynamism, the place where competing

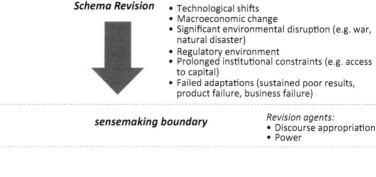

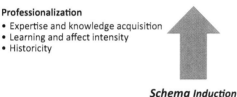

Figure 4.5 The dynamics of schema induction and revision in organizations.

forces borne by internal cultural schemas are re-interpreted, framed, debated, and resolved, at least temporarily. The boundary is always shifting as it is impinged upon by external forces.

Gordon (1991) suggests that between the external environment and the internal manifestations of power and control, culture "intervenes in the form of necessary assumptions and related values" (p. 1991). While there is little research on how schemas are reconciled at the group and organizational level (Bingham & Kahl, 2013), sensemaking at this boundary I suggest is the application, in explicit and implicit ways, of existing schemas to the prevailing external challenges faced by the organization. This sensemaking boundary is also where prevailing schemas are revised.

Schema Revision

Prevailing schemas can be revised in several ways. The first is via the effect of forces residing beyond the direct control or influence of the organization, such as those exerted through macro-economic, institutional, regulatory, technological, regional, or ethnic cultural influences.[12] Gertler (2004) employs a similar notion to explain how institutions shape individual action though the systems of rules and arrangements that shape the values, attitudes, and expectations of actors. While the relationship between any single corporation and the 'ecosystem' in which it operates is porous, institutional constraints, defined as the entities and arrangements within labor markets, education and training, governance structures, and capital markets, tend to shape the organizational premises, plans, expectations, justifications, and traditions (Gertler, 2004; Weick et al., 2005).[43]

An example of this can be seen in the history of deregulation in the U.S. railroads in the 1950s and 1960s, which, in a succession of events triggered changes to the "interpretive schemes" of railroad managers (Barr et al., 1992). The recent economic crises of 2008–2012, the events of September 11, 2011, institutional forces in the form of new regulations such as Sarbanes Oxley, new technology such as social networking, and the effects of regional culture such as that found in Baden-Wurttemberg or 'Route 128', as discussed earlier, are other examples. Gertler (2004), echoes Polanyi's view that social and economic systems are inextricably bound together, and proposes that institutional practices such as education and training, systems of governance, capital market constraints, and other similar factors shape firm culture. I agree, but want to sharpen the focus by suggesting they provide the impetus for schema revision that in turn shapes culture.

Some of these forces act indirectly. For example, industry growth can increase firm risk taking and innovation, which may drive schema revision (Gordon, 1991). Changes in regulatory environments may change capital distribution requirements, such as for banks, which in turn might revise schemas and models related to risk management (Gertler, 2004). With respect to regional influences, Gertler (2004) describes how regional communities of practice, especially within specific industrial-technological regions like Baden-Wurttemberg in Germany, with its long traditions of shared labor practices and information sharing across firms, influence the organizational cultures of firms operating within the region. And some of these effects might be stronger or weaker, depending on the organizational context. For example, a start-up in Silicon Valley might be more affected by institutional dynamics such as access to capital, or by the power motives or mission ideation of its founders, whereas the schemas and models shared in a large manufacturing company such as IMCO might be more affected by task environments such as manufacturing industrial pumps or brake pads. D'Andrade (1995) sums this phenomenon up best by stating "the motor for evolutionary advancement to more complex forms of organizing and society is technology and economy" (p. 6).

Another variable that may have impact on schema revision (or grounding) is the sense of urgency normatively imposed by leaders, or by external triggers such as customer reactions or buying trends. The more urgent the need to respond to the trigger, the stronger the likelihood of schema revision. This is perhaps why culture 'shaping' or, in the parlance of this framework, schema revision, is easier to enact in start-ups or small companies. The sense of urgency is much harder to experience or manufacture in large organizations where the economic impact of decisions is much more diffuse and long term.[44]

Also included here are forces salient to particular organizations but not necessarily a whole industry, such as the 2011 split of IMCO into three smaller companies (described in Section II). A merger of two companies could be another example exerting pressure at the sensemaking boundary. However, as depicted in the Qwest story, a merger in and of itself may not be what triggers schema revision but the perceived power differential between the two merging firms.

Another way in which schemas may be revised at the sensemaking boundary is through the effects of power. However, unless the external or environmental stressor is clearly acknowledged and shared by members of that community, such as an economic crisis or a pending merger, the pure exercise of power to revise prevailing schemas in the absence of external stressors is difficult. Usually this will require a significant appropriation and manipulation of resources, or require extraordinary leadership vision and charisma capable of bringing to bear new shared cognitive orientations, rather than simply nominal compliance or agreement.

4. Leadership & Culture

By now it should be apparent that the relationship between leadership and culture is much more complex than granted in the popular business narrative. Certainly through the appropriation of power and discourse at the sensemaking boundary leaders play a role in shaping culture, but the relationship is not directly causal. It may appear as causal, as discussed in Chapter 1, because of the rugged individualism schema dominant in the United States and parts of Western Europe, in combination with the corporate self-enhancement bias and the tendency of practitioners to reduce highly complex and ambiguous social phenomena to simple and digestible ideas, all contribute to over-privileging leadership in corporate culture. The functionally embodied framework fundamentally recasts this formulation.

This relationship between leadership and culture is not directly causal, but there is a relationship. Successful change in the world of culturally embodied minds requires that leaders possess awareness and understanding of the cultural–cognitive substrate through which their organizations function and make sense of their surroundings, combined with the discursive ability to reorient frames of reference, and the systemic awareness, patience and stamina to change practices to sustain the intervention. Revising or learning new schemas cannot occur through isolated events, such as promulgating new values, or via unsustainable or non-reinforcing strategic task contexts.

Essentially there are two domains of intervention: the *semiotic* and the *structural*, the latter manifesting in the form of practices, including social practice. The rest of this section provides an outline of these activities; Chapter 8 provides more detail and examples.

First, a leader intent on changing culture must understand what can and cannot be changed or leveraged. This requires a deep understanding of the prevalent schemas in the organization to determine how they manifest in semiotic practice, specifically in sensemaking and discourse. This can take the form of what Johnson (1990) calls paradigm reframing, calling into question obsolete schemes and framing new ones in compelling ways to compel the organization to action (Gioia & Chittipeddi, 1991). Leaders can create "cultural coherence" (Sewell, 2005, p. 174) by appropriating schemas that already make sense to followers, and revise schemas via a process of changing discourse frames and metaphors (and similar), purposefully reorienting schemas by introducing compelling novel metaphors from adjacent, but still recognizable and meaningful domains. Blending or appropriating new metaphors into novel constructs shifts attention and energy within a group and aligns action (Bingham & Kahl, 2013; Cornelissen, 2012; and see Chapter 2). To do this, leaders need to have the credibility and competence to be listened to in the first place to authentically and influentially invoke new schemas or revise existing ones. Simply espousing unfamiliar or radically new metaphors, frames and discourses is insufficient; the system will reject the virus. Cultural schemas perceived to be too "out there" will tend not be adopted.[45]

This is not to suggest schema revision must always be undertaken by outsiders. The cultural context will tend to dictate how much outside influence can be tolerated. Strong cultures—or rather, organizations with a few primary and widely shared schemas—will tend to resist outsider influence, labeling it as 'too different' and thereby marginalizing it. At the same time, schema revision requires that leaders and change agents possess enough outsider perspective and presence while sharing in the primary schemas of the system in order to enact successful change.

Second, and more importantly, to revise schemas leaders must influence and necessarily reshape the task context. This is the most difficult and underleveraged aspect of culture change because to do so requires change close to the firm's core means of production. Often leaders do not have the patience or stomach for this magnitude of change. Changing the task context means establishing the critical priorities and agenda for the enterprise, marshaling and allocating resources, and sanctioning or instilling practices, routines or technologies highly aligned with or capable of inducing new schemas. To the extent these actions are successful depends on whether such deployment 'makes sense' within the pre-existing schematic framework, or whether the case for change is compelling based on the forces acting at the sensemaking boundary.

5. Functionally Embodied Culture

As Vike (2011) points out, people are always picking, choosing and adapting their cultural models to make sense in their world. While this process may be more automatic than Vike acknowledges, professional groups and task contexts provide the organization with a set of cognitive resources that through sensemaking come to make up an organization's 'culture'. At the risk of rendering in a static form a fundamentally dynamic system, Figure 4.6 below graphically depicts these relationships.

Networks of primary shared (cultural) schemas make up more complex cultural models that organizational members use to make sense of their environments, and in so doing structure cultural affordances: Discourses (including metaphors, idioms, tropes, conventional discourse, problem frames, stories, myths, standards); artefacts (including symbolic cognitive artefacts); practised values and norms; behaviors; routines, practices and behavior; and material forms such as brands, logos, and office décor and layouts (etc.). If the schemas and models are robust enough in terms of sensemaking utility and motive force in the context of the organization's mission and environmental context, they will come to make up an organization's culture. They will be what the organization's actors are predisposed to use in the production of sensemaking to begin with because they emerge out of the dominant professional community and the strategic task context of the organization of which they are a part.[46]

Of course, there is an inherent circularity to this argument. How can schemas not make sense to an organization in the business of producing these

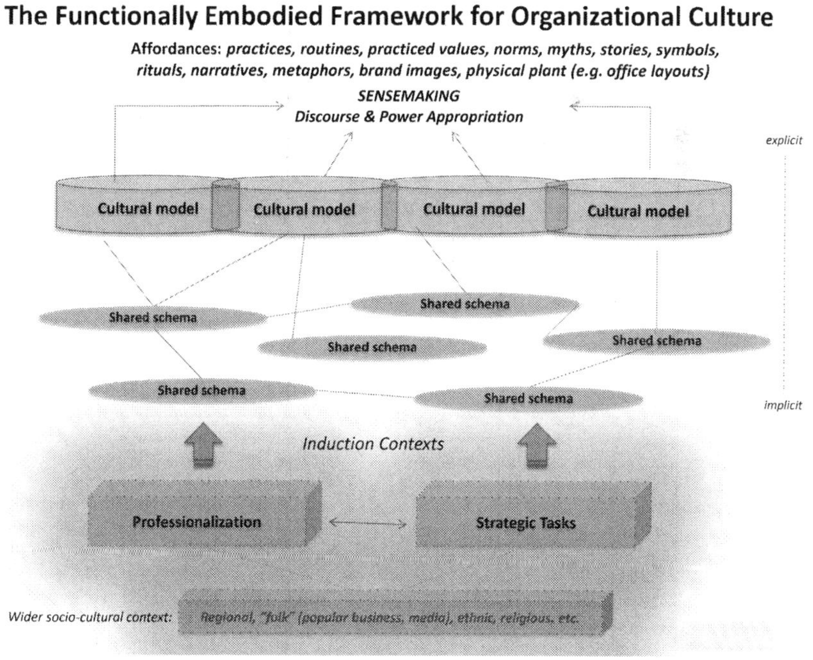

The Functionally Embodied Framework for Organizational Culture

Figure 4.6 Culture anchored in functionally embodied schemas and models.

schemas in the first place? How can professionalization and strategic task contexts give rise to shared schemas if these same tasks and cognitive orientations account for their existence? What comes first, the context or the system of meaning that endows these orientations and tasks with significance?

The way out of the circularity is to return to three basic points. First, a core principle of embodied cognition is *interactionism*: the organism and its environment are in constant interaction. The actor is embedded within a pre-existing kinesthetic, task (material), and sociocultural context while also an agent in that context, and this dynamic occurs in time. A useful metaphor is *scaffolding* (Bolender, 2008; Griffiths & Stotz, 2000): the environment scaffolds individual cognition while at the same time being shaped by shared (cultural) cognitions.

The second is Sewell's reminder that it is only through establishing and appropriating resources that organizations, in the act of collective sensemaking, bring schemas into being. Schemas would remain a product of individual cognition were they not enacted by groups in the production of cultural meaning and sensemaking. Schemas, culturally speaking, are irrelevant until organizations *organize*, that is, until they enact strategic choices and appropriate resources in the pursuit of shared goals. This is also why cultural interventions are most effective and sustainable against schema affordance structures—the manifestations in practice of schemas.

And third is Hutchins' idea that schemas are seldom what are seen but is what one sees *with*. As such they are always antecedent to action while at the same time subject to revision on the basis of that action, the double loop of environmental feedback. Thus, what comes first is *collective agency*. When actors move to sensemake, the lens through which they do so and the resources they appropriate in doing so are structured by the schemas and cultural models grounded in the orientations of those doing the sensemaking.

Without a set of particular schemas underwriting the range of resources organizations use to productively function in the broader environment, organizational life would hold little meaning for its members beyond the basic fulfillment of capitalist goals. Extending the line of reasoning from Bourdieu, Sewell, Strauss, Quinn, and Descola and others, I suggest it is the organization and production of meaning within specific professional and task milieus that endow modern organizations with the power to attract and hold its members, even if such holding is temporary and fragmented. Organizations and bureaucracies are simultaneously in the business of producing "indifference" (Herzfeld, 1992) in order to segment and marginalize non-conforming members and extend a notion of iconic cultural homogeneity to preserve the status quo, as they are in the business of containing and producing cultural meaning. Organizations structure conformity as much as they satisfy existential goals for meaning and psychodynamic goals for the mitigation of anxiety (Hirschhorn, 1992).

To dismiss this argument on the basis of circularity, thus, is to miss the point. Corporations and bureaucratic organizations are constituted for a purpose. Regardless through what lens one might judge that purpose, it is a purpose that draws people to them. That purpose is ultimately the pursuit of goals that are meaningful to its actors beyond the mere production of goods and services or the generation of profit. Returning us to the earlier discussion from Chapter 3, meanings are personal, evoked *interpretations*. Professionals in organizations enact tasks and routines and appropriate tools and technologies in order to find solutions to the problems they and their community interpret as meaningful. Cultural meanings in an organization thus are a combination of what is meaningful to the individual *and* that which the individual cathects within the wider professional and organizational community. What might be most meaningful to our chemical engineer in Houston might be to support his family, but he also finds meaning in the work that he does because it provides a means to support his family *while* allowing him to work on problems of interest professionally, and to do so within a broader professional community. To return to Descola (2013):

> The stabilization in frameworks of thought and action of our practical engagement with the world . . . is based primarily upon our capacity to detect qualities in existing things and to consequently infer links that they are susceptible to maintain and the actions of which they are capable . . . that which exists outside of our body and in interface with it presents itself as a finite ensemble of qualities and relations which can or cannot be actualized by humans according to the circumstances and to the ontological options which guide them.
>
> (pp. 78–79)

The collective human effort toward meaning, implied by Descola in his notion of "qualities," is what accounts for the loose determinism of organizational functioning. Far from underdetermined, if one adopts the idea that cultural schemas are resources to be appropriated, often implicitly, one begins to see how organizational states are, in fact, quite determined. To see this one has to shift the analytical lens from visible forms such as material structures and texts (and imputed natural kinds) to the underlying structures that give rise to these forms to begin with. The habitus cannot create "unpredictable novelty" nor can it reproduce its "original conditions." The limits of habitus are "historical and socially situated conditions" (Bourdieu, 1990, p. 55).

This is not to say it could not be otherwise if the forces of ecological disruption at the sensemaking boundary are sufficiently powerful. Macroenvironmental forces alter schemas, sometimes radically. New technology clearly induces or revises schemas. Power can revise or bend or even subvert schemas by denying or diverting the resources necessary to enact them, or, less often, through the sheer will or extreme narcissism of an oligarch. Ethnic, regional, and wider social influences can firmly scaffold or revise prevailing schemas.[47] Firms are, after all, dynamic social systems. Cultures do not stand still for their portraits. But until such radical disjunction comes along to disturb the sensemaking boundary, organizational cultural life is not in any way underdetermined.

SECTION I: CONCLUDING REMARKS

Cultures are hardly ever neatly coherent wholes. Rather, they are continually at risk of transformation by resources and practices brought under stress at the sensemaking boundary by the demands of the market, institutional constraints, macro-economic or environmental disjunctions, or even by despotic leaders. Actors always "know more culture than they can use" (Weber, 2005, p. 230) and not all grounding effects will manifest in a cultural community at any given time. This is similar to what Strauss and Quinn (1997) see as the "centrifugal" aspects of culture. Cultural schemas can be contradictory, loosely integrated, contested, subject to change, and weakly bounded. They can also be 'centripetal': thematically related, durable, and motivating. In addition to all that, they are mostly invisible, which is what makes them difficult as subjects of study. The schemas and models that make up a culture are always eligible to be altered, *provided* they can be brought into consciousness and made visible for altering. This should not be interpreted as an endorsement of causal culture shaping by the inputs of a self-enhancing leader or the imposition of espoused norms or values. By now it should be evident that organizations, as well as cultures, are far too complex for that. Were this possible we would not be 40 years into our collective fascination with organizational culture with rather little to show for it. Instead, what I have been suggesting is interventions in culture must be targeted at the schemas themselves, or more precisely, their induction contexts. They must also necessarily be multi-modal, systemic, simultaneous, and sustained. In the functionally embodied framework, the better question, thus, is not whether leaders can or cannot shape culture, but whether they have the stamina, courage, wisdom, skill and patience to do so.

In short, what is being proposed through these last chapters is that the embodied, situated and dynamic nature of cognition means that professional sociocultural experience as well the forging of shared task solutions within socio-technical enterprise induce shared schemas readily transposable across experiential contexts. Importantly, such schemas are not just propositional in terms of content; they are *epistemic*. They provide the structuring logic for all forms of organizational practice, from the semiotic to the behavioral to the normative. This logic usually remains implicit, running in the background but as an essential scrim through which actors make sense, organize, structure and justify practice, and take action in highly meaningful ways within their environments. This explains why 'engineering cultures' or 'sales cultures' or 'mission driven cultures' (etc.) become the dominant metaphors people use to describe their own organizations. It explains, perhaps, why Home Depot and Amazon cultures are characterized in part by pervasive metrics and measurement orientations that belie their retail and online task context, or why Google, as the inventor of Internet search, is obsessed with data in virtually all aspects of their business, or why the dewatering division of WaterCo, IMCO's water technology cousin, has a pervasive crisis schema befitting of its primary task of removing unwanted water from any site or application on-demand.[48] It is not that these cultures are monoliths; these metonymies simply characterize what it feels like to live, work, and make sense within these milieus.

At this point it is time to shift from theory to evidence and implication. In Section II I explore how the functional embodiment takes shape within the culture-bearing milieu of IMCO and discuss what this may mean for the theory and practice culture and culture change.

Notes

1 Its important to note here that 'functional' does not refer to *functionalism*. The latter is a strategy that views cognition as reducible to computation and silicon-based processes (Gallagher, 2005).

2 That is also to say the converse: organizations that do not have a dominant professional coalitions or an enrolling set of tasks and technologies, or do not manifest a differentiated purpose, will likely also not provide the kinds of experiential and social contexts to induce distinct schemas (or attract and be able to revise prevailing schemas; more on that below). This is a theoretical position, of course, although the preliminary evidence bears this out. This is not to say such organizations do not have cultures. All do, but their underlying models may not be distinctly identifiable with a profession or mission.

3 Applebaum's detailed ethnography shows construction work to be characterized by skilled trades made up of craftwork and handicraft technology, distinct apprenticeships, strong informal work administration, and a strong social structure. Construction workers tend to actively distance themselves from the corporate entities that employ them, typically through union-based or subcontracting employment practices. Most construction workers think of themselves as independent contractors and trades workers outside of any corporate hierarchy (Applebaum, 1981).

4 Reber bases his assertion on laboratory evidence in studying memory using artificial grammar recall. I am obviously extending his results to the domain of professional learning overall, although I believe the other evidence presented in this chapter makes this leap justified.

5 From my own pilot study of conceptual metaphor in software engineering groups.

6 One of the most complete and absorbing accounts of social construction of knowledge in professional and scientific practice is in Knorr-Cetina (1999). For an incisive account of the production of knowledge of the individual expert, see Mialet's (2003) analysis of Hawking.

7 See also Goodwin's (1994) discussion of how the professional discursive practices of the police shaped the outcome of the Rodney King trial.

8 Other fields make similar distinctions. For example, Gestalt psychologists talk about figure/ground relationships to distinguish what is perceptually salient (Goodwin, 1994).

9 The "Munsell book" is a tool "where the multifaceted complexity of nature is transformed into the phenomenological categories that make up the work environment of a specific discipline" (Goodwin, 1994, p. 608).

10 Omitted is discussion of the role of language in schema induction, or in cognition generally. As Dewell (2005) notes: "Language might influence the organization and further development of (schematic) patterns in any number of subtle ways . . . in other words, some of the universally similar characteristics of a schematic adult concept like CONTAINMENT might reflect the influence of language as well as the influence of nonverbal experience" (p. 385–386). Cross-cultural studies of literacy have shown how literacy and cognitive skills are closely related and embedded through the specific practices involved in the use of literacy promote different cognitive skills (Rogoff, 1990, p. 54).

11 In the interest of space, I have omitted discussion of occupational choice and schemas. There is no doubt in my mind, however, of the relationship between motivation, occupational choice, and schema induction. Holland's (1959) theory of vocational choice holds that people are motivated to seek out occupational environments consistent with their personalities. These factors can be classified into different groups, which can be useful in vocational counseling (Miller & Bass, 2003), including as typologies used by the U.S. Department of Labor (Kwantes & Boglarsky, 2004).

12 While Holland and Skinner studied the motivating force of romance among college-age women, there are parallels to be drawn with other domains of activity that have motivating force, such as work and professional recognition and satisfaction.

13 Restrepo's research shows data from the 1911 census reveal that settlements far from the Mounties' reach had unusually high adult male death rates. He also used data from hockey to reveal the influence of culture on behavior. Though players interact in a common environment, those who were born in areas historically outside the reach of the Mounties are penalized for their violent behavior more often than those who were not (Restrepo, 2015).

14 For an interesting and very contemporary take on this phenomenon, a recent lead story of the *New York Times Magazine* presents a view of what is happening in Silicon Valley between younger and older generations of engineers (Lu, 2014).

15 Although somewhat out of vogue now, occupational culture has been a focus of extensive inquiry over the last 30 years; thus there is an abundance of material to draw from (for example, see Barley, 1983; Fonne & Myrhe, 1996; Gregory, 1983; Helmreich & Merritt, 2001; Hyland et al., 2001; Paoline, 2003; Schein, 1992; Smircich, 1983; Van Maanen & Barley, 1984). A branch of sociology also deals substantively with professional and occupational enculturation and socialization (for example, see Abbott, 1998; Bucher & Stelling, 1977; Bunderson, 2001; Daley, 2001).

16 "Large" was defined as organizations exceeding $1 billion in annual revenue and more than 20,000 employees (Dougherty, 1992).

17 My own experience as a professional pilot provides an example. One of the main tasks to master when learning to fly twin-engine propeller airplanes is how to control the airplane when one engine fails. The asymmetric thrust created by the operating engine and the drag caused by the windmilling propeller causes the airplane to yaw in the direction of the failed engine. Controlling the aircraft under such circumstances requires quick problem recognition and control inputs, especially on takeoff. To teach fast and appropriate reactions instructors often use the mnemonic device *dead-foot-dead-engine* to recognize which engine has failed. The phrase, literally, means the foot 'pushed back' by the force of the rudder pedal deflection corresponding to the failed engine. In other words, you recognize which engine has failed *kinesthetically*, by the position of your foot. You don't have time when low to the ground to assess what the instruments are telling you or to look over your shoulder to verify a failed engine. Since seconds

may mean the difference between life and death, this kind of kinesthetic training is essential to safely fly twins. Cognitive artefacts like checklists are based on this same idea of disciplined repetition. You *always* follow the checklist, and there are checklists for nearly all normal and abnormal procedures (Helmreich & Merritt, 2001).

18 Unpublished dissertation research pilot (2013).

19 We will return to this idea in Chapter 8.

20 Within organizations, Hughes (1987) suggests problems in firms are not actually "solved." They are just treated as solved. This is an overly constructivist view that does not quite track to real life. *Some* problems in firms are *very much* solved, such as when an embezzling or a sexually harassing CEO is fired, or when a business abandons a failing product line or departs a country. But I take their point. In most cases, the schemas underlying the construction of an issue remain intact long after the issue has ostensibly been "solved."

21 Of course, conglomerates and diversified technology companies like General Electric, Siemens, and IMCO, may have several 'core' technologies. And not all firms exhibit technological grounding. There likely is a relationship between the degree of homogeneity or heterogeneity between business mission and technology, although no research to my knowledge has been done on this.

22 This concept does not contravene Latour, Hughes, or Bijker (for example, see Bijker, 1989; Latour, 1996) or other STS researchers who would make the opposite claim: that technology is socially constructed. By now the idea that the relationship of causality is bidirectional, hopefully, is clear.

23 These findings were most strongly supported within firms. Across firms, support for this finding was weaker (Colfer & Baldwin, 2010).

24 This was signaled in part by the name change of these departments from 'radiology' to 'medical imaging.' Name changes such as this signal a change in the social order (Hughes, 1958, as cited Barley, 1990).

25 In a study of the patterns of sharing of technical innovation among departments in a large U.S. auto manufacturer, Leonardi found members of one department were not able to understand the reasons why members of another department did not share their ideas for a new technology. Technology concepts were being used to construct the problems the technological artefact was designed to solve (Leonardi, 2011).

26 As Spender (1996) states, the boundary between the explicit and tacit is porous.

27 Repetition may be closely associated with imitation, of which there is an extensive literature. Semiotic functioning to Piaget was thought to develop partly through imitation (Ginsburg & Opper, 1979). In the same vein, Shore (1996) describes how ritualized postural techniques and walkabout rituals in Samoan and Australian aboriginal culture when learned through mimesis become essential to acquiring and sharing important cultural concepts such as *mana* ("generative potency" or "luck") and *tapu* ("sacred," "bound," "set aside"), as is the case in Samoa (Shore, 1996). Similarly, Bourdieu's study of the Kabyles' postures and movement patterns ("hexis") is further evidence that some schemas are structured through daily activities (Bourdieu, 1990).

28 By 'individual will' I am referring to what is arguably a foundational schema in U.S. history of the rugged individualist as exemplified by Wolfe's *The Right Stuff* (1979) and other texts.

29 As Sewell (2005) points out, 'structure' is one of the most problematic terms in social science.

30 Swidler (2001) offers a metaphor of a *toolkit* but her construct is the same. Actors consciously adopt or subconsciously enact cultural schemas based on the degree to which they help explain and solve prevailing issues.

31 The reference to Geertz in the notion of 'read' is not lost.

32 In Chapter 7 I introduce the term 'affordance structure' to encompass Swidler's conception cultural practice.

33 Drucker sees basic assumptions underlying his theory of the business, and therefore, ostensibly, a connection with schemas. My suggestion of sensemaking is made in light of the fact most firms in my experience construe questions about what business they are in or their core competencies in conscious terms. There may be cultural schemas underwriting these terms, but the act of forging a theory of the business is entirely rational and explicit.

34 The challenge with Mohammed and colleague's definition of "team mental models" is that it is hard to distinguish between their definition from thoughts and types of knowledge.

35 Storytelling is another way in which professional communities transfer localized knowledge to the wider organization (Gertler, 2004).

36 I condition these examples because evidence of these organizational cultures is only available second-hand from the literature, and no study of them employing schema theory exists that I know of.

37 Power is obviously a complex topic with a long and well-covered tradition in the management literature. Zaleznik and Kets de Vries (1975) provide a classic overview, as does Kanter (1979).

38 Conventional discourses might also have symbolic value in a cultural community. By appropriating common discourse, a cultural community might achieve a kind of social unity and familiarity much in the same way early Christianity co-opted the symbolism of its pagan predecessors (Herzfeld, 2001).

39 Pilot study of the schemas of software engineers and HR, 2012–2013.

40 I acknowledge many of these metaphors have become so popular in conventional discourse that their source domains may no longer be attributable to software development. This conventionalization can be linked to the ubiquity of computing and software development within the media and popular culture in 21st century American public life.

41 The only area where HR appears to have significant influence is in managing labor relations and contracts with unions, activities closely related to manufacturing production.

42 As discussed in Chapter 1, I remain somewhat ambivalent about the notion of a monolithic, static national culture, and thus have omitted it here. While clearly there are enduring pervasive national cultural patterns that are likely the manifestations of underlying primary schemas, beyond the issues outlined in Chapter 1, at the organizational level I suspect these schemas are too generic to be appropriated in ways that can discernibly shape culture. This is likely because of the dynamism of national cultures in a globalized and interconnected world economy, and the power of technologies such as social media. Even pervasive common schemas in the United States such as *The Profit Motive* or *individualism* cannot be uniquely attributable to the United States. Thus the link from national culture to firm culture loses much of its explanatory power. For this reason I much prefer to focus the lens on regional cultures.

43 Through industry trade groups, professional organizations, governmental lobbying, political action committees, board memberships, and other mechanisms corporations endeavor to shape the business environments in which they operate. However, even in firms with the political, financial, and human wherewithal, such as Google or Microsoft, I submit its influence on the entire industry is muted, subject to macro-level forces from other similar actors engaged in the same activities in the same system.

44 As a member of two technology and Internet start-ups, and then as a co-founder of my own technology company, I know the pressures of economic uncertainty

permeate every aspect of organizational functioning, from hiring to purchasing office supplies.

45 Microsoft, for example, has historically had difficulty assimilating and enculturating executives from outside the organization, for I suspect just this reason, as the recent naming of Satya Nadella as new CEO attest. As a long-time employee and well-respected engineer with a long track record of success, Nadella's appointment was a tacit recognition of the difficulties of outsiders imparting new cultural models to a system with as many durable models as Microsoft.

46 Bloor and Dawson (1994) submit if the number of employees within a given occupational group is sufficiently large within an organization (for example, an accounting firm, or dot com), the preferences of that group may exert enough pressure on the organizational culture so that the culture as a whole reflects the preferences of the occupational group (Bloor & Dawson, 1994). My sense is that it is more complicated: I suggest it is not so much numbers as schema motive force that account for professional group's influence on a host culture. Banks, despite being filled with bankers and finance professionals, do not have identical cultures. Software companies differ in their cultures despite a large number of software engineers; simply look at the differences between Microsoft, Google, and a start-up in the Mission District of San Francisco (Yu, 2014). These differences are not simply a matter of how many similar professionals reside within the firm or, for that matter, where the epistemic boundary for culture is drawn.

47 As stated earlier, I have purposefully omitted in-depth discussion of the effects of wider societal, regional or ethnic influences on organizational models. One reason is this discussion is well beyond the scope of this study. I suspect there are many ways in which these influences permeate organizational culture. Within the framework I am proposing, one way might be in how routines are constituted. Another might be in how tasks come to be organized and practised. And yet another might be in the particular socialization practices of a particular profession within a national or ethnic culture. In all cases, however, I submit these forces manifest at the sensemaking boundary; members have to reconcile the opposing forces insinuated by these influences.

48 Sources: Home Depot (Charan, 2006); Amazon (Kantor & Streitfeld, 2015). Google (personal informants); WaterCo (personal informants).

Bibliography

Abbott, A. (1998). *The System of professions: An Essay on the division of expert labor*. Chicago: University of Chicago Press.

Abrahamson, E., & Fombrun, C. J. (1994). Macrocultures: Determinants and Consequences. *Academy of Management Review 19*(4), 728–755. doi: 10.5465/AMR.1994.9412190217

Almklov, P. & Hepso (2011). Between and beyond data: How analogue field experience informs the interpretation of remote data sources in petroleum reservoir geology. *Social Studies of Science, 41*(4), 539–561. DOI: 10.1177/0306312711403825

Alvesson, M., & Spicer, A. (2011). Introduction. In M. Alvesson & A. Spicer (Eds.), *Metaphors we lead by*. (pp. 1–7). Abingdon: Routledge.

Applebaum, H. A. (1981). *Royal blue: The culture of construction workers*. New York: Holt Rinehart & Winston.

Argyris, C. S., & Schön, D. (1996). *Organizational learning II: Theory, method and practice*. Reading, PA: Addison-Wesley.Barr, P. S., Stimpert, J. L., & Huff, A. S.

(1992). Cognitive change, strategic action, and organizational renewal. *Strategic Management Journal, 13*(S1), 15–36.

Barley, S. (1983). Semiotics and the study of occupational and organizational cultures. *Administrative Sciences Quarterly, 28*, 393–413.

Barley, S. (1990). The alignment of technology and structure through roles and networks. *Administrative Science Quarterly, 35*(1), 61–103.

Barley, S. (1996). Technicians in the workplace: ethnographic evidence for bringing work into organization studies. *Administrative Science Quarterly, 41*(3), 404–441.

Bartlett, F. C. (1932). *Remembering: An experimental and social study*. Cambridge: Cambridge University Press.

Bennardo, G. (2011). A foundational cultural model in Polynesia: Monarchy, democracy, and the architecture of the mind. In D. Kronenfeld, G. Bennardo, V. de Munck, & M. Fischer (Eds.), *A companion to cognitive anthropology* (pp. 471–488). Malden, MA: Wiley-Blackwell.

Biernacki, R. (1994). Time cents: The monetization of the workday in comparative perspective. In: R. Friedland & D. Boden, (Eds.). *NowHere: space, time, and modernity*. Berkeley: Univ of California Press.

Bijker, W. (1989). The social construction of Bakelite: Toward a theory of invention. In W. Bijker, T. Hughes, & T. Pinch, T (Eds). *The Social construction of technological systems: New directions in the sociology and history of technology*. (pp. 159–187).Cambridge, MA: MIT Press.

Bingham, C., & Kahl, S. (2013). The process of schema emergence: Assimilation, deconstruction, utilization, and the plurality of analogies. *Academy of Management Journal, 56*, 14–34. Retrieved from http://dx.doi.org.10.5465/amj.2010.0723.

Blanchette, I. & Dunbar, K. (2001). Analogy use in naturalistic settings: The influence of audience, emotion, and goals. *Memory and Cognition, 29*, 730–735. doi: 10.3758/BF03200475

Bloor, G., & Dawson, P. (1994). Understanding professional culture in organizational context. *Organization Studies, 15*(2), 275–295.

Bolender, J. (2008). Hints of beauty in social cognition: Broken symmetries in mental dynamics. *New Ideas in Psychology, 26*(1), 1–22.

Bollas, C. (1987). *The shadow of the object: Psychoanalysis of the unthought known*. New York: Columbia University Press.

Bourdieu, P. (1990). *The logic of practice*. Stanford, CA: Stanford University Press.

Bucher, R. & Stelling, J.G. (1977). *Becoming professional*. Beverly Hills, CA: Sage Library of Social Research, Vol. 46.

Bunderson, J.S. (2001). How work ideologies shape the psychological contracts of professional employees: doctor's responses to perceived breach. *Journal of Organizational Behavior, 22*, 717–741. doi: 10.1002/job.112

Caballero, R. (2006). *Re-viewing space: Figurative language in architects' assessment of built space (Vol. 2)*. Berlin: Walter de Gruyter.

Cameron, L. (2008). Metaphor and talk. In R.Gibbs (Ed.). *The Cambridge handbook of metaphor and thought*. (pp. 197–211). Cambridge: Cambridge University Press.

Charan, R. (2006, April). Home Depot's blueprint for culture change. *Harvard Business Review*. Retrieved from: https://hbr.org/2006/04/home-depots-blueprint-for-culture-change

Chatman, J., & Jehn, K. (1994). Assessing the relationship between industry characteristics and organizational culture. How different can you be? *Academy of Management Journal, 37,* 522–553. Retrieved from http://scholar.google.com/.

Chi, M., Feltovich, P. & Glaser, R. (1981). Categorization and representation of physics problems by experts and novices. *Cognitive Science, 5,* 121–152.

Colfer, L. & Baldwin, C. (2010). The mirroring hypothesis: theory, evidence and exceptions. *Harvard Business School Working Paper.* Retrieved from: http://hbswk. hbs.edu/item/6361.html

Cornelissen, J. P. (2012). Sensemaking under pressure: The influence of professional roles and social accountability on the creation of sense. *Organization Science,* 23(1), 118–137.

Daley, B. (2001). Learning and professional practice: A study of four professions. *Adult Education Quarterly, 52,* 39–54. doi: 10.1177/074171360105200104

D'Andrade, R. (1992). Schemas and motivation. In R. D'Andrade & C. Strauss (Eds.), *Human motives and cultural models* (pp. 23–44). Cambridge: Cambridge University Press.

D'Andrade, R. (1995). *The development of cognitive anthropology.* Cambridge: Cambridge University Press.

Descola, P. (2013). *Beyond nature and culture.* Chicago: University of Chicago Press.

Dewell, R. (2005). Dynamic patterns of containment. In B. Hampe, and J. Grady (Eds.). *From perception to meaning: Image schemas in cognitive linguistics.* (pp. 369–394). Berlin: Mouton de Gruyter.

Donaldson, L. (2001). *The contingency theory of organizations.* Thousand Oaks, CA: Sage.

Dougherty, D. (1992). Interpretive barriers to successful product innovation in large firms. *Organization Science, 3*(2), 179–202.

Drucker, P. F. (1994). The theory of the business. *Harvard Business Review, 72*(5), 95–104.

Elliott, M. S., & Scacchi, W. (2003). Free software developers as an occupational community: resolving conflicts and fostering collaboration. *In Proceedings of the 2003 international ACM SIGGROUP conference on supporting group work* (pp. 21–30). New York: ACM

Ericsson, K. A., Krampe, R. T., & Tesch-Römer, C. (1993). The role of deliberate practice in the acquisition of expert performance. *Psychological Review, 100* (3), 363.

Fiss, P. C., & Zajac, E. J. (2004). The diffusion of ideas over contested terrain: The (non) adoption of a shareholder value orientation among German firms. *Administrative Science Quarterly, 49*(4), 501–534.

Fleck, L. (1979). *Genesis and development of a scientific fact* (Fred Bradley and Thaddeus Trenn, Trans.). Chicago: University of Chicago Press. (Original work published 1935).

Fonne, V. & Myrhe, G.(1996). The effect of occupational cultures on coordination of emergency medical service aircrew. *Aviation, Space and Environmental Medicine, 67,* 525–529.

Frost, P. J., Moore, L.F., Louis, M.R., Lundberg, C.C., & Martin, J., (1985).An allegorical view of organizational culture. In P. J. Frost, L.F. Moore, M.R. Louis, C.C. Lundberg, & J. Martin, (Eds.), *Organizational culture* (pp. 13–25). Newbury Park, CA: Sage

Gallagher, S. (2005). *How the body shapes the mind.* New York: Oxford University Press.

Gardenfors, P. (2007). Cognitive semantics and image schemas with embodied forces. In Krois, J.M.,Rosengren, M., Steidele, A., & Westerkamp, D. (Eds.), Embodiment in cognition and culture, (pp. 57–73). Philadelphia, PA: John Benjamins.

Garro, L. (2000). Remembering what one knows and the construction of the past: A comparison of cultural consensus theory and cultural schema theory. *Ethos, 28*(3), 275–319.

Geertz, C. (1973). *The interpretation of cultures.* New York: Basic Books.

Gentner, D., Lowenstein, J. & Thompson, L. (2003). Learning and transfer: a general role for analogical encoding. *Journal of Educational Psychology, 95*, 393–408.

Gentner, D., & Colhoun, J. (2010). Analogical processes in human thinking and learning. In A. von Müller & E. Pöppel (Series Eds.) & B. Glatzeder, V. Goel, & A. von Müller (Vol. Eds.), *On thinking: Vol. 2. Towards a theory of thinking* (pp. 35–48). Berlin: Springer- Verlag.

Gertler, M. (2004). *Manufacturing culture: The institutional geography of industrial practice.* Oxford: Oxford University Press.

Gick, M.& Holyoak, K. (1983).Schema induction and analogical transfer. *Cognitive Psychology, 15*, 1–38.

Ginsburg, H. & Opper, S. (1979). *Piaget's theory of intellectual development.* Englewood Cliffs, NJ: Prentice Hall.

Gioia, D. A., & Chittipeddi, K. (1991). Sensemaking and sensegiving in strategic change initiation. *Strategic Management Journal, 12*(6), 433–448.

Goodenough, W. (1981). *Culture, language and society* (2nd ed.). Menlo Park: Benjamin/Cummings.

Goodwin, C. (1994). Professional vision. *American Anthropologist, New Series, 96*(3), 606–663.

Gopher, D., Karis, D., & Koenig, W. (1985). The representation of movement schemas in long-term memory: Lessons from the acquisition of a transcription skill. *Acta Psychologica, 60*(2), 105–134.

Gordon, G. G. (1991). Industry determinants of organizational culture. *Academy of Management Review, 16*(2), 396–415.

Greenwood, R., & Hinings, C. R. (1993). Understanding strategic change: The contribution of archetypes. *Academy of Management Journal, 36*(5), 1052–1081.

Gregory, K. (1983). Native-view paradigms: multiple cultures and culture conflicts in organizations. *Administrative Science Quarterly, 28*, 359–376.

Griffiths, P. & Stotz, K. (2000). How the mind grows: A developmental perspective on the biology of cognition. *Synthese, 122*, 29–51.

Guenther, K. (2002). Memory. In D. Levitin (Ed.), *Foundations of cognitive psychology: Core readings* (pp. 311–360). Cambridge, MA: MIT Press.

Guzman, I. R., Stam, K. R., & Stanton, J. M. (2008). The occupational culture of IS/IT personnel within organizations. *ACM SIGMIS Database, 39*(1), 33–50.

Hallowell, I. (1976). *Selected papers of Irving Hallowell.* Chicago: University of Chicago Press. (Originally published in 1954.)

Hambrick, D. C. (1982). Environmental scanning and organizational strategy. *Strategic Management Journal, 3*(2), 159–174.

Harris, S. (1994). Organizational culture and individual sensemaking: A schema-based perspective. *Organization Science, 1*, 309–321.

Haudricourt, A. G. (1962). Domestication des animaux, culture des plantes et traitement d'autrui. *L'homme (2)*,40–50.

Hayes, J. R. (1989). Cognitive processes in creativity. In J.A. Glover, R.R. Ronning, & C. Reynolds, C. (Eds.), *Handbook of creativity*. New York: Springer

Helmreich, R. & Merritt, A. (2001). *Culture at work in aviation and medicine: National, Organizational and professional influences.* Hampshire, UK: Ashgate House

Herzfeld, M. (1992). *The social production of indifference.* University of Chicago Press.

Herzfeld, M. (2001). *Anthropology: Theoretical practice in culture and society.* Malden, MA: Blackwell.

Hirschhorn, L. (1992). *The Workplace within: The psychodynamics of organizational life.* Cambridge: MIT Press.

Hodgkinson, G., & Johnson, G. (1994). Exploring the mental models of competitive strategists: The case for a processual approach. *Journal of Management Studies, 31,* 526–543.

Holland, J. L. (1959). A theory of vocational choice. *Journal of Counseling Psychology, 6*(1), 35.

Holland, D. & Skinner, D. (1987). Prestige and intimacy: the cultural models behind American's talk about gender types. In D. Holland and N. Quinn (Eds.) *Cultural models in language and thought.* (pp.78–111). Cambridge: Cambridge University Press.

Huff, A. S. (1982). Industry influences on strategy reformulation. *Strategic Management Journal, 3*(2), 119–131.

Hughes, T. (1987). The Evolution of large technological systems. In W. Bijker, T. Hughes, & T. Pinch, T (Eds), *The social construction of technological systems: New directions in the sociology and history of technology.* (pp. 51–82). Cambridge, MA: MIT Press.

Hutchins, E. (1980). *Culture and inference: A Trobriand case study* (Vol. 2). Cambridge, MA: Harvard University Press.

Hutchins, E. (1987). Myth and experience in the Trobriand Islands. In D. Holland & N. Quinn (Eds.), *Cultural models in language and thought* (pp. 269–289). Cambridge: Cambridge University Press.

Hutchins, E. (1995). *Cognition in the wild.* Cambridge: MIT Press

Hutchins, E. (2005). Material anchors for conceptual blends. *Journal of Pragmatics, 37,* 1555–1577.

Hyland, P., Gieskes, J. & Sloan, T. (2001). Occupational clusters as determinants of organizational learning in the product innovation process. *Journal of Workplace Learning, 13,* 198–208.

Johnson, G. (1990). Managing strategic change: The role of symbolic action. *British Journal of Management, 1,* 183–200.

Kanter, R.M. (1979). Power failure in management circuits. In: J. Shafritz and J.S. Ott (Eds.). *Classics of organization theory.* (pp.449–461). Pacific Grove, CA: Brooks/Cole Publishing.

Kantor, J., & Streitfeld, D. (2015, August 15). Inside Amazon: Wrestling big ideas in a bruising world. The New York Times. Retrieved from:http://www.nytimes.com/2015/08/16/technology/inside-amazon-wrestling-big-ideas-in-a-bruising-workplace.html?_r=0

Kellogg, K. C. (2011). Hot lights and cold steel: Cultural and political toolkits for practice change in surgery. *Organization Science, 22*(2), 482–502.

Knorr-Cetina, K. (1999). *Epistemic cultures: How the sciences make knowledge.* Cambridge, MA : Harvard University Press.

Koller, V. (2008). Corporate brands as socio-cognitive representations. In G. Kristiansen & R. Dirven (Eds.), *Cognitive sociolinguistics: Language variation, cultural models, social systems* (pp. 389–418). Berlin: Mouton de Gruyer.

Kovecses, Z W. (2008). Metaphor and emotion. In: R. Gibbs (Ed.). *The Cambridge handbook of metaphor and thought.* (pp: 380–398). Cambridge: Cambridge University Press.

Kwantes, C. T., & Boglarsky, C. A. (2004). Do occupational groups vary in expressed organizational culture preferences? A study of six occupations in the United States. *International Journal of Cross Cultural Management, 4*(3), 335–354.

Lakoff, G. (2008). The neural theory of metaphor. In R. Gibbs (Ed.), *The Cambridge handbook of metaphor and thought* (pp. 1–35). Cambridge: Cambridge University Press.

Lakoff, G., & Johnson, M. (1999). *Philosophy in the flesh.* New York: Basic Books.

Latour, B. (1996). *Aramis, or the love of technology.* Cambridge, Harvard University Press.

Lave, J. (1988). *Cognition in practice: Mind, mathematics and culture in everyday life.* Cambridge University Press.

LeBlanc, C. J. (2008). Men-of-the-mill, Work, Craft and Meaning: A Qualitative Case Study of Paper Mill Workers in Fitchburg, Massachusetts. *ProQuest.* Retrieved from:https://books.google.com/books?hl=en&lr=&id=CPa W4P6Gq6kC&oi=fnd&pg=PR1&dq=leblanc+%26+mills+1995+competitiv e+advantage+begins+with&ots=qMovQNkz4n&sig=HIYkb855gHdKVT-2p 7UqWislZVM#v=onepage&q&f=false

Leonardi, P. (2011). Innovation blindness: Culture, frames and cross-boundary problem construction in the development of new technology concepts. *Organization Science, 22,* 347–369.

Leonardi, P. & Jackson, M. (2009). Technological grounding: Enrolling technology as a discursive resource to justify cultural change in organizations. *Science, Technology and Human Values, 34,* 393–418. Doi: 10.1177/016224390832877

Levi-Strauss, C. (1985). *The view from afar.* New York: Basic Books.

Lindholm, C. (2007). *Culture and identity: The history, theory, and practice of psychological anthropology.* Oxford: Oneworld Books.

Lu, Y. (2014, March 16).A tale of two valleys. *The New York Times Magazine,* p.28.

Malafouris, L. (2004). The cognitive basis of material engagement: where brain, body and culture conflate. In C. Gosden (Ed.), *Rethinking materiality: The engagement of mind with the material world.* (pp. 53–61). McDonald institute for Archaeological Research.

Mandler, J. (1983). *Stories, scripts, and scenes: Aspects of schema theory.* New York: Psychology Press.

Martin, J. (2002). *Organizational culture: Mapping the terrain.* Thousand Oaks: Sage.

Merritt, A. (2000). Culture in the cockpit: Do Hofstede's dimensions replicate? *Journal of Cross-Cultural Psychology, 31,* 283–301.

Mialet, H. (2003). Reading Hawking's presence: An interview with a self-effacing man. *Critical Inquiry, 29*(4), 571–598.

Miller, M. J., & Bass, C. (2003). Application of holland's theory to a nonprofessional occupation. *Journal of Employment Counseling, 40*(1), 17–23.

Mohammed, S., Ferzandi, L., & Hamilton, K. (2010). Metaphor no more: A 15-year review of the team mental model construct. *Journal of Management, 36*(4), 876–910.

Mouawad, J. (2012, November 29). For united, big problems at biggest airline. *The New York Times*. Retrieved from http://www.nytimes.com/2012/11/29/business/united-is-struggling-two-years-after-its-merger-with-continental.html?_r=0.

Munby, H.,Versnel, J., Hutchinson, N., Chin, P. & Berg, D. (2003). Workplace learning and the metacognitive function of routines. *Journal of Workplace Learning (15)*3, 94–104. DOI:10.1108/13665620310468432

Nardi, B. A. (1996). Studying context: A comparison of activity theory, situated action models, and distributed cognition. In B. Nardi (Ed.), *Context and consciousness: Activity theory and human-computer interaction* (pp. 69–102). Cambridge, MA: MIT Press.

Osborne, J. D., Stubbart, C. I., & Ramaprasad, A. (2001). Strategic groups and competitive enactment: A study of dynamic relationships between mental models and performance. *Strategic Management Journal, 22*(5), 435–454.

Palmer, G. (1996). *Toward a theory of cultural linguistics*. Austin: University of Texas Press.

Paoline, E. (2003). Taking stock: toward a richer understanding of police culture. *Journal of Criminal Justice, 31*, 199–214.

Perrow, C. (1984). *Normal accidents: Living with high risk technologies*. New York: Basic Books

Pessoa, L. (2008). On the relationship between emotion and cognition. *Nature Reviews Neuroscience, 9*(2), 148–158.

Porac, J. F., Thomas, H., & Baden-Fuller, C. (1989). Competitive groups as cognitive communities: The case of Scottish knitwear manufacturers. *Journal of Management Studies, 26*(4), 397–416.

Quinn, N. (2011). The history of the cultural models school reconsidered: A paradigm shift in cognitive anthropology. In D. Kronenfeld, G. Bennardo, V. de Munck, & M. Fischer (Eds.), *A companion to cognitive anthropology* (pp. 30–46). Malden, MA: Wiley-Blackwell.

Ravasi, D., & Schultz, M. (2006). Responding to organizational identity threats: Exploring the role of organizational culture. *Academy of Management Journal, 49*(3), 433–458.

Reber, A. S. (1989). Implicit learning and tacit knowledge. *Journal of Experimental Psychology: General, 118*(3), 219.

Rentsch, J. R., & Klimoski, R. J. (2001). Why do 'great minds' think alike? Antecedents of team member schema agreement. *Journal of Organizational Behavior, 22*(2), 107–120.

Rerup, C. & Feldman, M. (2011). Routines as a source of change in organizational schemata: the role of trial and error learning. *Academy of Management Journal, 54*, 577–610.

Restrepo, P. (2015). The mounties and the origins of peace in the Canadian prairies. *MIT Department of Economics Graduate Student Research Paper No. 15-01*. Available at SSRN: http://ssrn.com/abstract=2671980

Rogoff, B. (1990). *Apprenticeship in thinking: Cognitive development in social context*. New York: Oxford University Press.

Rousseau, D. (2001). Schema, promise, and mutuality: the building blocks of he psychological contract. *Journal of Occupational and Organizational Psychology, 74*, 511–541.

Rousseau, D. & Tijorowala, S. (1999). What's a good reason to change? Motivated reasoning and social accounts in promoting organizational change. *Journal of Applied Psychology, 84,* 514–528.

Schank, R., & Abelson, R. (1977). *Scripts plans goals and understanding.* Hillsdale, NJ: Lawrence Erlbaum.

Schein, E. (1992). *Organizational culture and leadership (2nd Edition).* San Francisco, CA: Jossey-Bass.

Sewell, W. H. (1992). A theory of structure: Duality, agency, and transformation. *American Journal of Sociology, 98,* 1–29. doi: 0002–9602/93/9801–001.

Sewell, W. H. (2005). *Logics of history: Social theory and social transformation.* Chicago, IL: University of Chicago Press.

Shore, B. (1996). *Culture in mind: Cognition, culture and the problem of meaning.* Oxford: Oxford University Press.

Shore, B. (2002). *Globalization, the nation states and the question of "culture": The unnatural history of nations and cultures.* Retrieved from http://www.semioticon. com/frontline/pdf/brad_shore.pdf.

Sieck, W., Rasmussen, L., & Smart, P. R. (2010). Cultural network analysis: A cognitive approach to cultural modeling. In V. Dinesh (Ed.), *Network science for military coalition operations: Information extraction and interaction* (pp. 237–255). Hershey, PA: ICI Global.

Sinha, C. (2011). Living in the model: The cognitive ecology of time—A comparative study. In Lorenzo Magnani (Ed.) *Proceedings of the 12th International Conference on Model-Based Reasoning. Studies in Applied Philosophy, Epistemology, and Ethics.* (pp. 1–19). Berlin: Springer.

Sinha, C., & Jensen de Lopez, K. (2000). Language, culture and the embodiment of spatial cognition. *Cognitive Linguistics, 11–1/2,* 17–41.

Smircich, L. (1983). Concepts of culture and organizational analysis. *Administrative Science Quarterly, 28,* 339–358.

Spender, J. C. (1989). *Industry recipes: An enquiry into the nature and sources of managerial judgment.* Oxford: Basil Blackwell.

Spender, J. C. (1996). Making knowledge the basis of a dynamic theory of the firm. *Strategic Management Journal, 17,* 45–62.

Sperber, D., & Hirschfeld, L. (1999). Culture, cognition, and evolution. In R. Wilson & F. Keil (Eds.), *MIT encyclopedia of the cognitive sciences* (pp. cxi–cxxxii). Cambridge, MA: MIT Press.

Squire, L. R. (1987). *Memory and brain.* New York: Oxford University Press

Steele, F. I. (1972). Organizational overlearning. *Journal of Management Studies, 9*(3), 303–313.

Steiger, D., & Steiger, N. (2008). Instance-based cognitive mapping: A process for discovering a knowledge worker's tacit mental model. *Knowledge Management Research & Practice, 6,* 312–321.

Stewart, G. (2002).Uncovering implicit leadership beliefs: Variation between information technology (IT) executives and business executives in a public service agency. *International Journal of Organisational Behaviour, 5*(4), 163–179

Stone-Jovicich, S., Lynam, T., Leitch, A., & Jones, N. (2011). Using consensus analysis to assess mental models about water use and management in the Crocodile River Catchment, South Africa. *Ecology and Society, 16,* 45. Retrieved from http://www.ecologyandsociety.org/vol16/iss1/art45/.

Strauss, C. (1992). What makes Tony run? Schemas as motives reconsidered. In R. D'Andrade & C. Strauss (Eds.), *Human motives and cultural models* (pp. 191–224). Cambridge: Cambridge University Press.

Strauss, C. (2012). *Making sense of public opinion: American discourses about immigration and social programs.* New York: Cambridge University Press.

Strauss, C., & Quinn, N. (1997). *A cognitive theory of cultural meaning.* Cambridge: Cambridge University Press.

Swidler, A.(2001). What anchors cultural practices. In T. Schatzki, K. Knorr-Cetina, and E. Von Savigny (Eds.). *The Practice turn in contemporary theory.* (pp. 74–92). London: Routledge

Tamietto, M., & De Gelder, B. (2010). Neural bases of the non-conscious perception of emotional signals. *Nature Reviews Neuroscience, 11*(10), 697–709.

Van Maanen, J. & Barley, S. (1984). Occupational communities: Culture and control in organizations (No. TR-ONR-10). Alfred P. Sloan School of Management, Cambridge, MA. Retrieved from https://scholar.google.com/scholar?hl=en&q=Occupational+communities%3A+Culture+and+control+in+organizations&btnG=&as_sdt=1%2C5&as_sdtp=

Vike, H. (2011). Cultural models, power and hegemony. In D. Kronenfeld, G. Bennardo, V. de Munck, & M. Fischer (Eds.), *A companion to cognitive anthropology* (pp. 376–392). Malden, MA: Wiley-Blackwell.

Walsh, J. P. (1995). Managerial and organizational cognition: Notes from a trip down memory lane. *Organization Science, 6*(3), 280–321.

Weber, K. (2005). A toolkit for analyzing corporate cultural toolkits. *Poetics, 33*(3), 227–252.

Weick, K. (1995). *Sensemaking in organizations.* Thousand Oaks, CA: Sage Publications.

Weick, K. E., Sutcliffe, K. M., & Obstfeld, D. (2005). Organizing and the process of sensemaking. *Organization Science, 16*(4), 409–421.

Young, J. E., Klosko, J. S., & Weishaar, M. E. (2003). *Schema therapy: A practitioner's guide.* New York: Guilford Press.

Yu, Yiren. (2014, March 16). Trouble in start-up land. *The New York Times*, 28–34.

Zaleznik, A., & Kets de Vries, M. F. (1975). *Power and the corporate mind.* New York, NY: Houghton Mifflin.

Part II

Cultural Schemas in a Diversified Industrial Manufacturer

5 Investigating Schemas
Contexts, Methods, and Challenges

A point of differentiation between this study and others in the management literature discussed in Chapter 3 is that the latter treats schemas mainly as explicit and propositional features of cognition. Studying what groups explicitly know is not without its own epistemological challenges, but is more straightforward than studying the implicit aspects of cognition. As Descola (2013) puts it, schemas are usually so internalized within a cultural community they "seldom surface in reflexive deliberations" (p. 92). If many cultural schemas are tacit, more *what we use to see with* than what we see, this presents obvious methodological and interpretivist challenges. How to render the tacit explicit, or at least explicit enough for investigation? To trace, say, *radiality* through to its manifestations as expressed in the layout of Tongan towns, how does one keep one's bearing in what can fast become an analytic and interpretivist maze? Is *radiality* a feature of shared Tongan cognition, or the product of Bennardo's analysis, or a bit of both? How do we read into practices endowed with cultural meaning the underlying schemas that motivate them without imposing our own patterns and configurations of meaning?

At issue is circularity. To Alvesson and Skoldberg (2009), all objects of study are social constructions. Not only are problems constitutive features of the questions that frame the problem, the situatedness of the observer and observed are features of the investigation. On the other hand, one can also "oversocialize" research (p. 269), reducing everything to interpretation or social construction, thereby failing to commit oneself, in the words of Searle, to the fact there is a world "out there" to begin with, or, importantly, to practical relevance.

This chapter picks its way through these epistemological thickets. I begin with a proposed resolution to the circularity question, a resolution that treads a middle path between constructivism and positivism.[1] I then turn to a discussion of schema research methods, followed by a short but necessary excursion into linguistic relativity and the role metaphor plays in this research. I end by describing the specific research design at IMCO.

1. Principled Ambivalence

To understand this middle path we must return again to Descola's reconciliation of subjectivism and objectivism:

> It thus hardly makes sense to oppose, as modernist epistemology does, a single and true world, composed of all the objects and phenomena potentially knowable, to the multiple and relative worlds that each one of us creates through our daily subjective experience. It is more plausible to admit that that which exists outside of our body and in interface with it presents itself as a finite ensemble of qualities and relations which can or cannot be actualized by humans according to the circumstances and to the ontological options which guide them, rather than as a complete and autonomous totality awaiting to be represented and explained according to diverse points of view.
>
> (2013, pp. 78–79)

Descola's phenomenology brings the body and its world "interface" into the epistemological picture. Phenomenological grounding, however, carries epistemic risk, requiring the investigator to take an extra step. Noting this, the anthropologist Michael Herzfeld (2001) suggests we must,

> Balance the advantages of both a pragmatic self-distancing and an ethical engagement that is also grounded in direct field experience. Consistent with this perspective of *principled ambivalence*, anthropologists have resisted disembedding the philosophy of the discipline from theoretical reappraisals and from ethnography.
>
> (p. 22; italics mine)

"Principled ambivalence" is a useful frame for a mode of analysis that is neither wholly empiricist nor wholly constructivist, but that still maintains a reflexive stance. The key is a twofold commitment to questioning one's own methodological and cultural assumptions, on the one hand, and to improving the efficacy of the research by progressively improving the analysis, on the other. The former is achieved not by a kind of cultural solipsism or soul searching but by asking what else could explain the results, and what were the assumptions used to achieve these results. The latter is achieved by methodological triangulation; that is, by using multiple modes and levels of analysis to examine the phenomenon in question in order to make more acute the overall analysis.

These steps do not amount to any kind of epistemological guarantee. The mixing of methods creates obvious cross-validity issues. On the other hand, I suggest a multi-modal approach is the only one capable of yielding sufficient amounts of data to make possible an analysis of phenomena as elusive as schemas. This approach also has the benefit of generating data saturation. With more data, patterns are more readily discerned. This serves to increase confidence in the findings, however provisional they might be.

But none of this is possible without analytical reflexivity. This is particularly important with cognitively oriented organizational culture research, for three reasons. First, the praxis is in its infancy. For this approach to have efficacy it must be accompanied by the fine print explicating what was done, why, and how it led to the results. Second, managerial pragmatism forces any new treatment of organizational culture to proceed with the end in mind. For this study not to wind up in the dustbin of interesting but pragmatically useless culture theory it must substantiate its claims with observable and replicable data, whether those data be qualitative or quantitative, and to refine its theoretical edifice based on that data. Little of the framework presented in Section I will prove useful in practice without attempts to draw from the analyses conclusions and refinements to the overall theory that, in turn, might inform future praxis. Third, there is an important distinction to be made between what Herzfeld (2001) calls "language-based" versus "language-derived" models of meaning (p. 53). In the former, all is text, and therefore all decodable, but truth claims are limited to the decoded subject. In the latter, the focus is on linguistic meaning, which by definition is reflexive. We cannot, of course, know what our subjects really mean or find meaningful via the deconstruction of any single utterance. But to assume words are wholly unreliable for accessing knowledge about inner states, or are simply the subjective expression of an underdetermined inner state, sidelines the potential of discourse as an analytic tool in studying cognition. Language-derived methods permit what Herzfeld refers to as a "heuristic deployment" of models into domains beyond language (p. 53). Mitigating the effects of the inherent subjectivity of this approach requires accruing a body of evidence based on what informants say, and then attempting to substantiate any patterns observed through affordances that may be traced through to related domains of practice.

And so the project proceeds in such a manner, picking and threading its way between contrasting epistemologies while reflecting on the methodological and interpretive choices throughout. This describes intent. When studying schemas, additional problems must be confronted, ranging from the ontological to the epistemic to the pragmatic, elaborated below.

Ontological and Epistemic Challenges

One problem with studying schemas is that to study them you have to first invent the idea of them (Shore, 1996). All research on cultural models tends to be itself presented as a cultural model (Koller, 2005). Such circularity makes the study of schemas ontologically problematic (Krasny, Sadosky, & Paivio, 2005). This is one reason, perhaps, why some anthropologists prefer to study cognition in practice (for example, see Lave, 1993).

This is the same critique leveled at social and cultural structural analysis in general. Because common structure can be observed by an outsider for any collection of "texts" within a group does not necessarily mean that structure has any psychological reality for individuals within that group (Shore, 1996). The same argument, of course, can be levied at the majority of etic organizational culture research (see Chapter 1). Nonetheless, to improve on existing theory requires overcoming the challenges that beset it.

Those who contest the existence of schemas also contest their status as agents in embodied cognition. These theorists point to Kant and Bartlett's original conceptions of schemas as, a priori, disembodied abstractions of thought whose main function is to synthesize perceptual information (Krasny et al., 2005). Yet the evidence presented in Section I is a systematic refutation of this view. Kant and Bartlett conceived of schemas before the existence of neurological, linguistic and empirical evidence for embodied cognition. The evidence for cognitive structure that is independent of language, kinesthetically and socioculturally grounded—despite debates on particulars—is strong and well accepted in cognitive neuroscience, linguistics, psychology, and anthropology. History is filled with instances of theoretically posited phenomena before instrumentation and methodology was sufficiently advanced to empirically discern their existence (for example, see Fleck, 1979; Knorr-Cetina, 1999). The fact "evidence conforms to conceptions just as often as conceptions conform to evidence" (Fleck, 1979, p. 28) cannot be the ontological argument against schemas, for that would be to undermine much of the history of science. Nor can the notion that entities like mind and meaning are ultimately unknowable because of their inherently social and constructed nature. The human organism lives in a natural world subject to biological and physical laws. This phenomenological view does not deny that the unreflective generation of knowledge is epistemologically problematic, nor does it deny the need to be well sensitized to the limits and distortions of its investigative modalities. Schema research is characterized by subtlety and nuance and is still evolving. As methods are perfected better knowledge will come about. But "facts" do eventually tend to arrive through "thought constraints" (Fleck, 1979, p. 95). The study of schemas is no different.

Thus, the reply to the circularity argument is this. Once constituted in language or other forms, the schema or cultural model becomes 'real' in the sense it exists as an affordance. As text, utterance, and (or) as practice. In the language of Gestalt, a *figure* now exists. The ontological status of a schema is always contingent upon its manifestation in time and space as constituted by actors. In this way schemas are like echoes. One first has to generate the sound to witness the phenomenon.

Epistemic Stance

And the means by which the sound is generated is critically important. Thus a second reply to the circularity argument is epistemic. To observe common structure across a collection of 'texts' requires such structure to be made manifest, and then verified by establishing its psychological reality for an individual or group. In the case of schemas, this involves progressive identification and coding using multiple modalities until "theoretical saturation" occurs (Alvesson & Skoldberg, 2009, pp. 58–65; Quinn, 2005; Walsh, 1995). As Quinn (2005) points out, one should never rely solely on metaphor or any other single mode of linguistic analysis to study schemas, however abundant and compelling those data may be (see also Gibbs & Perlman, 2006). Bennardo (2011) calls for using both linguistic methods such as word counts, metaphor lists and analyses of whole passages of discourse, as well as cognitive methods such as the quantitative analyses of interview data (as in this study), as well as free lists, pile sorts, and map drawings. In radical discourse-analytic terms, consistency between utterances or texts is no guarantee of validity (Alvesson & Skoldberg, 2009). However, if multiple modes of analysis begin to reveal pervasive patterns, confidence that these patterns have meaning and reality for actors within the community under study can result.

Of course, discerning patterns also implies the patterns have meaning and reality for the researcher, a potentially problematic assumption. Rohrer (2006) suggests that the process of "mapping" metaphors to metaphor classes, a part of my process, can at times appear entirely "ad hoc" (p. 137). Biernacki (2012) provides a fierce challenge to social and ethnographic coding, citing the significant biases imposed by the researcher. His solution is to appeal to an accepted prototype, a so-called "ideal type" (p. 145) from which coding can be derived. This Platonic remedy is difficult to apply in cases such as schema and cultural models research, however, where new research is being conducted and no ideal type yet exists. Various researchers have tried to navigate around this by using dual coding techniques whereby a second, knowledgeable analyst reviews the assignment of schemas or metaphors to broader thematic classes (for example, see Bernard, 2011; Sieck, Rasmussen, & Smart, 2010). While perhaps a useful hedge against bias or data indeterminacy, unless the other coders are truly detached from the social and cultural context from which the data originate, I am not sure separate coding does more than perpetuate a cycle of subjectification. At the same time, in organizational studies knowledge of context is critical. I am not sure the coding of an analyst unfamiliar with the discursive habits of executives in a global manufacturing company, or the jargon of modern business discourse in general, is helpful in advancing our understanding of the cognitive orientations of these groups. Familiarity with IMCO's business and operating environment, and familiarity with manufacturing management and business vernacular in general, was critical to my own understanding of the context of the discourse I analyzed, and to untangling the many threads of possible meaning within it. In this way metaphor and discourse analysis in this tradition shades over into a kind of linguistic ethnography. Biernacki's answer to coding bias in the absence of an ideal type is to use the investigator's own reflexivity to "spawn attention to the type's fragility rather than dogmatism" (p. 145). Which brings us back to where we started.

Ultimately, the effective use of discourse analytic techniques to locate schemas comes down to judgment (Quinn, 2005). Schemas are relatively discrete structures linked to other discrete structures (Rohrer, 2005), thus sensitivity to how each relates to the other, and each to the whole, is important. Quinn's answer in her study of marriage, in addition to reflexivity, was pragmatic. Did the interpretation enrich the overall analysis? Did the metaphor or schema make sense in the context of the broader discourse? This is the stance taken here.

But How Empirical Is it?

From the opposite perspective, one might also question whether the informants in a studied sample in any way represent what people actually think, or that this constitutes the "culture" of the group (Rohrer, 2006)? As put pithily by McGlone (2007), "although metaphors in discourse sometimes seem to stick out like a sore thumb, metaphors in the mind are far harder to find" (p. 123). Barley (1983) counters with a reminder: "If one's informants are representative of the population one wishes to generalize to, then the mapping (of semantic structure) should be informative" (p. 410).

In my case, I can safely say I met Barley's standard by including in my sample the CEO, the top divisional executives, and several other general managers of IMCO. To the extent this community shares schemas and cultural models, a putative claim about IMCO's culture, at least provisionally for top management, can be made. The fact my data was generated in a "naturalistic context" provides some assurance that what I analyzed, in fact, is how people really speak, and presumably think in this particular context (Rohrer, 2006, p. 137; Gibbs & Perlman, 2006).

Another way to inject more empiricism into the analysis is to try and falsify one's hypotheses by acknowledging other reasons why people might say what they say within that context (Gibbs & Perlman, 2006). These are not guarantees of empiricism, but hedges to help render the data in a more empirical light.

Adduction

The primary research method used here is *adduction*, the process of revealing foundational patterns and structure from particular instances (Alvesson & Skoldberg, 2009). I used several kinds of adductive analyses to arrive at an analytically parsimonious set of categories, and then conducted both quantitative analyses based on these data and subjected the data to face validation with a subset of the original informants (including the CEO). The quantitative and face validation methods provided methodological triangulation of the qualitative data, and this iterative approach refined and sharpened the analysis and its implications (see Chapters 7 and 8). With respect to the implications of these data at IMCO and other organizations, I used an extended case method (Burawoy, 1999) based on action research and my own ethnographic observations.

The main challenge with adductive methods is hermeneutic: Who is doing the interviewing and analysis? What are his or her assumptions? What might the interviewee be experiencing in relation to the researcher, such as social desirability bias (Strauss, 2012)? How does the interviewee react to the data generated by the researcher? A hermeneutic stance problematizes the actor and participant mental frames (Alvesson & Skoldberg, 2009). Bennardo (2011), for example, uses informant drawings as partial evidence for his foundational radiality schema. I have no doubt radiality is a dominant schema in Tonga, and yet, in such an analysis, imposed interpretations are inevitable. The question, then, is what can be done to balance the over-imposition of the researcher's own interpretations (or schemas)?

Quinn (2005) achieved a measure of reflexive balance by clarifying at the end of each interview what her informants had said through a checklist that itemized topics that may not have been already covered. This allowed her informants to reflect on their answers, and, if necessary, clarify what they had said. A check on whether informants are telling the researcher what they think the researcher wants to hear (social desirability) is to see whether the interviewee makes conflicting statements (Strauss, 2012). While I did not use a checklist I repeatedly checked for understanding in the interviews by repeating back what I heard to ensure my understanding was consistent with what the speaker intended.

Who Cares?

Adductive methods always run the risk of bringing to light deep structures that ultimately are trivial. Descola (2013) points this out when he states "either (1) the structures that are identified are so general that they cannot explain the specificity of the particular cultural configuration, or (2) else they are so particularized by their historical contexts that they turn out to be unsuited to any comparative endeavor" (p. 92). What he does not readily admit is that the issue lies with the researcher. The challenge with studying schemas is to achieve a balance between, on the one hand, an abstraction that abstracts away all that is interesting and meaningful, and, on the other, a naturalistic reformulation that winds up as a restatement of what the actors are already saying (Alvesson & Skoldberg, 2009). If a schema is a "simplified representation" of cognitive phenomena, how simple does the representation have to be before it is analytically and pragmatically useless (Walsh, 1995)?

The reader might well have this reaction reading the schemas I present from IMCO. At first glance they may appear to be trivial structures related to, for example, thinking concretely or privileging first-hand experience.[2] The control for irrelevance, thus, is to trace the schema through its affordances—the discourse and practices in which the schema manifests. Pervasive schemas will manifest across discourse and practice so as to appear essential or causal, and these are the objects of pursuit here. These schemas may provide the template on which more elaborate cultural models are built much in the same way as software source code enables additional software to be written based on it.

My Work at IMCO

A reflexive stance is vitally important given the nature of schema research; it is all the more so in my case because I have been involved in a long-term consulting relationship with IMCO since 2010.[3] I have visited many IMCO sites around the world and interacted with employees at every level of the organization, from the hourly shop floor worker to executive management. These relationships enabled me to have frequent and often daily access to the firm and resulted in invitations to participate in events like the Leadership Summit. My consulting work enabled me to use IMCO as a research site and extended case study to begin with, and my overall knowledge of the organization enabled me to make productive choices in the research design and analysis. But, as might be expected, my experience also has given me a set of assumptions about the organization and its practices. Where appropriate I point these out and explain how they color the analysis. That said, cultural schema analysis is greatly enhanced by knowing the context in which they are acquired and realized (Bennardo, 2011). Thus, an extended case study comprised of participant observation and action research, in conjunction with the methods described here, was essential for verifying how the schemas adduced manifest in practice (Gioia & Chittipeddi, 1991). My knowledge of and access to IMCO was an ideal opportunity to observe these phenomena and their adaptive structures.

Empirical, Not Empiricist

Any study of cognition "in the wild," to borrow Hutchins' term, requires mixed methods and multiple levels of analysis underpinned by an empirical orientation that privileges what is being observed while reckoning the limitations of the observer. The adductive approach here, thus, is guided by Herzfeld and Descola's modest brand of empiricism, a kind of empirical anthropology that is inherently empirical but not "empiricist" (Herzfeld, 2001, p. 21): "Clearly our ideas our often influenced by the people we study . . . to recognize the contributions that informants make to our theoretical formulations is to engage in a discussion that is not only epistemological but also ethical . . . " (p. 22). While imperfect, this stance allows the voice of the observed and the underlying patterns by which the observed make meaning come to the foreground. It also addresses the inevitable hermeneutic concerns raised by a study of this kind. This is not only pragmatic; it is ethical, especially where organizational culture change is concerned.

2. Linguistic Determinism

So far I have sidestepped another important ontological and epistemic issue, that of linguistic determinism. Originally posed by Edward Sapir and taken up by his student, Benjamin Lee Whorf, linguistic determinism is the idea that language shapes thought, or, more precisely, that linguistic categories delimit conceptual categories (Duranti, 2009). For our purposes, one might claim functional grounding has nothing to do with professionalization or strategic task context and is instead the exclusive effects of language *shaping* the thinking of my informants. This would be a serious claim. As such, the issue merits a few words.

The extreme version of linguistic determinism holds that "specific language constrains thinking and perception in particular directions, which add up to a particular world view" (Gumperz & Levinson, 1991, p. 615). One could argue, for example, that the evidence posed for analogical thinking in Chapter 2 based on studies of conceptualizations of time reflect conceptual systems shaped by language and metaphor. Closer to home, one might argue mainstream conceptions of organizational culture and change assume linguistic determinism. Positing desired norms or values and publishing them on posters and websites and featuring them in training programs is sufficient to change a culture because new language will shape thinking.

The strong form of linguistic determinism, that thought and behavior are *entirely* determined by language, has been largely abandoned in the last 20 years based primarily on evidence that universals do exist in cognitive development, specifically in perceptions of categories such as color, and that multiple modes of thinking exist independent of language (Boroditsky, 2001; Gumperz & Levinson, 1991; Talmy, 2000). Talmy (2000) states our system of understanding and common sense and reason are made up of underlying mental models existing separate from language, while sharing features with it. Nonetheless, some weaker forms of determinism have not been ruled out.

For example, as discussed earlier, spatial categories are almost never encoded in the same way across languages (Keller, 2011; Levinson, 1996). Levinson (1996) argues that language may limit conceptualization of abstract entities like space. He cites cases such as that in Guugu Yimidhirr, an Australian aboriginal language that uses cardinality (*north, south, etc.*) instead of spatial prepositions (*in, on, in front, behind, etc.*) to describe location (*John is north of the building versus John is in front of the building*). However, many studies of this kind are limited by the fact speakers are usually tested in their own language; as such there is no way to ascertain whether the stimuli and instructions mean exactly the same thing in both the speaker and the researcher's language (Boroditsky, 2001).[4] Determinism may be operative in special cases such as in shaping abstract thought when sensory input is minimal or unclear (as with the direction of motion of time). This may be what is being observed with my informant's use of certain conventional metonymies such as *right* (*the right person, the right level*; see Chapter 6).

On the other hand, for some kinds of abstract thinking language may be bypassed altogether. Studies of motion suggest visual processes in most cases are impervious to language (Cardini, 2010).[5] Abstractions such as time, as shown earlier, may be based on schemas of linearity and cyclicity that allow temporal relationships to be conceptualized through socially constructed means such as numbering systems, or via physical artefacts like calendars and clocks.

Linguistic determinism may also be conflated with cultural determinism, as shown by Sinha and Jensen de Lopez' (2000) work on spatial cognition with Danish and Zapotec children. Clark's (1991) work on lexical meaning shows how language *reflects* social and cultural context. Thus, meaning may be the result of localized or culturally patterned referential practices: *murder* has different meaning for a lawyer than an anti-abortion activist; *She's very New York* will have strong cultural referents for some groups, but be meaningless for others (Clark, 1991). Language (especially metaphor and narrative) may be an instrument for social control and order, such as in Samoan village councils or a law court (Duranti, 2009), but this is not evidence of linguistic determinism, only that language circumscribes some forms of cultural and institutional behavior. Systems of cultural meaning may be borne by language (in particular through conventional metonymy and conventional discourse), but likely originate in or are motivated by underlying cultural schemas. Thus, it may be that language is predisposed to sociocultural context as well as play a role in structuring it. The evidence from IMCO, in fact, suggests just this.

In sum, while there is some evidence suggesting language plays a role in shaping thinking, there is no definitive evidence that language is a dominant or even significant influence on conceptual categorization (Keller, 2011). Keller (2011) puts it cogently when she says, "language may play a structuring role in some encounters, may support alternative modes of thought and action in others, or may be sidelined, or even contradicted by other modalities such as imagery, emotion or embodied actions" (p. 75). Duranti (2009) sees language as a "non neutral" medium. When we use language we make an ontological commitment to it as "a tool that plays a role in the ways in which speakers think and act as well as in the ways in which an activity is socially organized" (p. 30).

As we return to considering discourse and metaphor as research modalities, basing a definitive study on culture using language alone is likely to be inconclusive; other methods will be needed to advance definitive claims. However, this does not mean discourse and metaphor are not productive modalities for *initiating* an investigation into cultural meaning and, at a minimum, focusing our attention on what is salient for a community. Language is a necessary, but not sufficient, method for fully explicating culture. And it certainly is not sufficient for changing it.

3. Finding Schemas in Everyday Speech

Naomi Quinn (2005) pioneered a new method for studying cultural meaning based on the analysis of causal reasoning, idealization, and metaphors in ordinary speech. In analyzing patterns of reasoning and idealizing in her informants' discourse and use of metaphor to describe common dilemmas in marriage, she uncovered a robust cultural model of American conceptions of marriage. Quinn's insight was that patterns of reasoning and idealizing reveal the structure of how people think about a domain (Lakoff, 1987; Quinn, 2005; Strauss & Quinn, 1997). Quinn's approach provides the foundation for the primary research method used here. I analyzed patterns of reasoning and idealization in how my informants dealt with common business challenges and so developed an understanding of the cultural schemas that underpin and organize their cultural knowledge.

Quinn's findings departed from the structural linguistics of the 1960s and 1970s, which held that the "meaning of objects and events are equated with the meaning of the words that label them" (Quinn, 2011, p. 35). Indeed, prior to the development of schema theory, the focus in discourse was lexical—single terms (Strauss, August 23, 2014, personal communication; see also D'Andrade, 1995). After schema theory, thought was considered irreducible to symbolic and lexical processing (Rumelhart, 1993; Rumelhart & Ortony, 1977). With this divorce came an increase in interest in metaphor not as a feature of language but as an object of thought and emotion (Quinn, 2011; Strauss & Quinn, 1997). Cognitive linguists now define metaphor as a "*cognitive* mechanism" whereby "one experiential domain" is wholly or partially projected onto another "so that the second domain is partially understood in terms of the first one" (Barcelona, 2003, p. 3; italics mine).

Focusing on everyday speech was a productive choice because a vast majority of everyday expressions contain metaphor or metonymy, and thus offer a potentially valuable trove of data (Lakoff & Johnson, 1980; Palmer, 1996). Among Quinn's most important insights was that the metaphors themselves were not the basis of a shared understanding of marriage but that the underlying schemas signaled by the metaphors were (Strauss & Quinn, 1997; also see Chapter 2). As Strauss and Quinn state, "although language holds the clues to the cultural schema . . . the schema is far from isomorphic with the language, or obvious from it; certainly it is not retrievable from any given metaphors the speakers use" (p. 144). This was a somewhat startling discovery in light of conventional views of metaphor, and also stood in contrast with Lakoff and Johnson's (1980) influential theory of metaphor in cognitive linguistics.

Building off earlier work by Johnson-Laird (1983), Rosch (2002), and Rumelhart and Ortony (1977), Lakoff and Johnson (1980) asserted that abstract reasoning is inherently metaphorical. Image schemas are simplified redescriptions of kinesthetic experience and thus the source for conceptual metaphor, metonymy, blending, and framing, and these form a bridge to complex and abstract thought (Lakoff & Johnson, 1980). Lakoff and Johnson's position on metaphor has been critiqued for being too literal. That is, abstract thinking is impossible without knowledge of concrete concepts (for example, see McGlone, 2007, or Rakova, 2002).[6] I suggest their view is more nuanced. Johnson's (1987) characterization of the relationship between schemas and metaphors is quite clear when he states kinesthetic image schemas provide the structuring basis—the "channels"—for reasoning and understanding by constraining the "choice of source and target domain" (p. 116). Image schemas delimit the range of possible patterns of reasoning, as I suggested in Chapter 2, and is a feature of all schemas, not just image schemas. As Johnson (1987) states:

> To say that image schemata "constrain" our meaning and understanding and that metaphorical systems "constrain" our reasoning is to say that they establish a range of possible patterns of understanding and reasoning. They are like channels in which something can move with a certain limited, relative freedom. Some movements (inferences) are not possible at all. They are ruled out by the image schemata and metaphors.
> (p. 137)

But Johnson obfuscates matters by admitting metaphor into the picture, thereby conflating a property of language with a property of cognition. Cognition may not be as literally metaphorical as Lakoff and Johnson would have it—*thoughts are buildings* may be equally well understood as *thoughts are structures*. In using metaphor to identify schemas but not make metaphors isomorphic with them, Strauss and Quinn restored this separation.

Except in certain cases, schemas are not directly identifiable from metaphor. Close analysis of single words or short phrases alone cannot convey what meaning these words or phrases have for a person or a group. D'Andrade (1995), in his study of American beliefs about illness, showed how analysis of terminology alone was insufficient for understanding what a group's beliefs might actually be about a subject. He asked his research subjects to match 30 illness terms (*chicken pox, strep throat*, etc.) with 30 causal phrases (*you can catch ___ from other people* or *you never really get over___*, etc.) and then rate the resulting belief frame as true or false. This required his subjects to make 900 independent judgments, some based on unlikely combinations such as *you can catch dental cavities in bad weather*. What he realized was that subjects managed to rate all 900 items not from the words in the matching statements alone but by using "other things they already knew" (1995, p. 126). To figure out whether subjects were basing their answers on the logical relationships implied by the terms, he subjected all responses to a program to map out the causal relationships based on the formal definitions of terms in each belief frame. While many causal and taxonomic connections could be drawn based on definitions alone (for example, that *contagious diseases are caused by germs*), this did not explain how his subjects successfully answered novel questions about disease. He states: "To understand American beliefs about colds, measles, polio, etc. requires an understanding of the germ *schema* and this cannot be obtained from an analysis of the properties of diseases alone." (p. 129). The shared germ schema rather than the specific dictionary meaning of the terms or the taxonomic relationship between them was needed to explain beliefs about disease. Even when using an abundance of terms like disease names, it was impossible to fully explicate a group's understanding of that domain based on word meanings alone. Similarly it is impossible to assert the existence of underlying schema from discrete metaphor alone because of the degree of polysemy of many of the metaphors. Polysemy pertains not only to analysis but to usage. I suspect my IMCO informants were using metaphor pre-consciously in phrases such as *drive the project* or *we're looking for experience.*[7]

What Is the Function of Metaphor?

In the traditional view, when people use metaphor they do so for a reason, such as to convey meaning more quickly, simply, or economically, or resolve contradiction (Armenakis & Bedeian, 1992; Pondy, 1983; Schon, 1993; Strauss & Quinn, 1997). I have observed that metaphor may be important to confer legitimacy or to influence, as when a speaker invokes a metaphor from a specialized domain to communicate with someone of perceived importance in that domain. Metaphors may also be "generative" to enable new images, perceptions, and possible worldviews (Morgan, 2006; Schon, 1993; and see Chapter 9). In these ways metaphors are functional, conscious and deliberate speech acts designed to do something—to reframe, to convince, to motivate, and so forth. This perspective is compatible with the "standard pragmatic model" of metaphor comprehension, which holds that metaphors are implied similes; any metaphor can be understood through inclusion of the word *like* (Glucksberg, 2008, p. 68). Thus, *my job is a jail* is understood as my job is *like* a jail. Doing so allows the utterance to be understood as a literal comparison (Glucksberg, 2008; for a critique, see Johnson, 1987). Under this view metaphor has no special linguistic or cognitive status (Glucksberg, 2008).

But metaphor comprehension is not simply a matter of comparing concepts through simile and computing the literal meaning, and this model has been invalidated empirically (Giora, 2008; Glucksberg, 2008; Ortony, 1993; Rumelhart, 1993). When someone says *my job is a jail*, what is meant literally is that one's notion of *job* belongs in the same class of things as *jails* (Glucksberg, 2008). There is no comparison; the two concepts in the analog are blended so as to form a single concept (Fauconnier, 1997; Paivio & Walsh, 1993). Metaphors are class inclusion statements. And prior context matters. When it is reinforcing and salient, people have no difficulty processing metaphors at the same rate as literal language (Giora, 2008). If metaphor were *only* a matter of language, context would not make much difference in comprehension.[8] Metaphor comprehension also looks different neurologically than literal language.[9]

Metaphors, it seems, really are different. But this is not to ignore the obvious. Metaphors *do* inject meaning, resolve paradox, economically communicate, attract power, and help frame new attitudes and actions, among other affordances. But to presuppose metaphor is *only* the product of functional language underestimates the role metaphors play as preconscious features of cognition.

Metaphors in Management

Metaphor has been a popular locus of research in the management literature (for example, see Alvesson & Spicer, 2011; Basten, 2001; Cleary & Packard, 1992; Morgan, 2006; Shue & Lacroix, 1998).[10] The prevailing notion of metaphor in this literature however is quite different than my use of metaphor here, and these differences are worth briefly noting.

Some theorists suggest metaphor defines a group's reality (Cleary & Packard, 1992). Some focus on foundational or "root" metaphors that relate semiotic signs to broader cultural and social domains whereby "notions of what corporations are and how they should be managed . . . organize the cultural repertoire for talking about corporations" (Weber, 2005, p. 232). Morgan (2006) suggests "all theory is metaphor" and that organization's metaphors characterize their "nature" (pp. 4–6).[11] Metaphor, not surprisingly, is also considered a productive way to study organizational culture (Basten, 2001; Martin, 2002).

On the surface this seems like an interesting way for managers and practitioners to conceptualize organizational phenomena. To "see" an organization metaphorically may allow for new ways to construe organizational dilemmas or constraints. These approaches maintain fidelity with the subjectivist tradition of text, rather than what lies behind text or gives rise to it.[12] Studying the metaphors of a cultural community may also be fruitful ways to understand something about that community's culture (D'Andrade, 2005; Quinn, 2005).

But beyond the basic idea that social and cultural realities can be discerned through language, there are two problematic issues with these kinds of studies. First, one cannot help but notice their reductionist and ontologizing tendencies. To try and capture an organization's 'nature' or essence through a root metaphor is not unlike characterizing an organization in terms of personality traits, as discussed in Chapter 1. The reduction conflates a property of language with a property of organization and obscures fruitful analysis and intervention in trivial overgeneralization. Next, the functionalist view that metaphor is *solely* a matter of language, as discussed above, is counter to current cognitive science. Much metaphor use is automatic and preconscious, and as a result presents potentially fruitful avenues for studying the implicit structure and content of collective thought.

Cultural Cognition and Metaphor

Metaphor is included in this study for several reasons. In including it I join a handful of other scholars who see metaphor as a productive way to access cognitive structure (for example, Alvi, 2011; Armenakis & Bedeian, 1992; Caballero, 2006; Cornelissen, 2012; Tsoukas, 1991).[13] First, metaphors may signal cultural "exemplars," which, themselves, are schemas (Strauss & Quinn, 1997, p. 145). Speakers do not randomly select metaphors; they are drawn from "shared exemplars" of the concept such that the speaker conveys "outstanding" and "unambiguous" highlights of the intended point (p. 145). For example, Quinn's subject's cultural model of marriage was partially described by analogy to success, with many of her subject's metaphors drawn from the domain of success (Strauss & Quinn, 1997). Quinn (2005) likens metaphor use in speech to "flags waving," signaling "intersubjectively shared examples of what they stand for" (p. 49).

Second, metaphors not only reflect properties of thinking but also provide clues as to how thought is structured (Vervaeke & Kennedy, 2004). This is not evidence of linguistic determinism as much as how language aids cognitive organization. As shown in Chapter 2, metaphors, especially when conventionalized, may link knowledge from one abstract domain, such as space, to another, such as time (Gentner & Bowdle, 2008). And, as I show in Chapter 6, metaphors help link schemas into more complex cultural models. In reflecting cultural exemplars, metaphors may lend stability to a culture by reifying certain discourses as well as institutional symbols and codes (Cornelissen, 2012). Discourse in general, and metaphor in particular thus become ways to understand the cognitive orientations and cultural knowledge of groups (Garro, 2000; Koller, 2008).[14]

Third, our cognitive and linguistic capacity to generate novel metaphors may be evidence of schema induction and analogical transfer based on functional grounding (Gentner & Bowdle, 2008). One example can be seen in how Americans use precious possession and game metaphors to describe life more often than Hungarians, who use struggle, war, and compromise metaphors more (Kovecses, 2005). While this could be argued as simply a matter of preference, I would submit the schemas underlying these metaphors might be tied to experiences in the cultural ecology and history of each country. Precious possession in the United States might reflect a capitalist, profit-oriented foundational schema underlying many aspects of U.S. cultural and social experience. The fact war has been fought on and near Hungarian soil within the last 100 years may account for the prevalence of war metaphors in Hungarian. At IMCO, the many metaphors in evidence related to manufacturing suggest that task environment's salience as an induction context.

Fourth, sensemaking begins with noticing and highlighting what is significant and meaningful, and metaphors play an important role by providing figurative labels of what is salient (Weick, Sutcliffe, & Obstfeld, 2005). A good example is the conventional metaphor *learning curve*. The term is partly a diagnostic frame for assessing novice performance within a domain (*he is going up the learning curve*), partly an evaluation (*she had a steep learning curve in that role*), and partly prescription (*he can do it but there will be a learning curve for him*). Organizational speech is characterized by hundreds of similar metaphors linking discourse with action: *our strategy is to build skill in that area*; *we are working on the transactional processes*; *he developed the solution*; and so forth.

Metaphors also contain cognitive biases emanating from the projective conceptual structure of schemas reflected in the metaphor that drive behavior. For example, Alvi (2011) showed how pervasive bias expressed through metaphor led to misconceptions in organizational strategy, which in turn led to inappropriate action.[15] In these ways metaphors hold sensemaking together by providing the schematic means to diagnose, evaluate, and prescribe action (Cornelissen, 2012).

In short, metaphor provides important clues and insights into a community's system of cultural meaning, as well its ecological context. At the same time, because schemas can activate and guide action, using metaphors as a way to locate schemas, or validate them as is the case here, is a productive way to understand the implications of culture on action, including the many enactments of organizational sensemaking such as strategy and decision making.

4. *Additional Methods*: Quantitative Validation

Despite the fact quantitative studies of culture based on etic constructs are subject to the many problems described in Chapter 1, cultures can be productively studied through quantitative methods, especially when the items under investigation have been derived through emic means (for example, see Bernard, 2011; Maltseva & D'Andrade, 2011).

One of the most important questions to answer through quantitative analyses concerns the construct validity of the culture—whether what informants say or do correlates highly with what other informants say or do (Handwerker, 2002). Construct validity refers to the observed match between a set of observations and the theoretical construct it purports to measure (Cronbach & Meehl, 1955). Several types of analyses, such as cluster analysis and multidimensional scaling help answer questions about whether there are patterned relationships among cultural variables. But in order to directly test the hypothesis that a specific set of scale items makes up an independent set of measurements of another unseen and underlying variable, as is the case with the validation of schema constructs derived from discourse, only factor (FA) or principal components analysis (PCA) can directly tests this hypothesis (Bernard, 2011; Handwerker, 2002).[16]

The quantitative study was another form of data triangulation. Of specific interest were two questions. First, could quantitative analyses verify the qualitative codings? Second, were there discernible differences between IMCO and non-IMCO respondents? The schemas, identified and coded through qualitative discourse analysis may not have been solely or completely described by language, thus FA and PCA could potentially describe an underlying general orientation, a hypothetical variable behind the language. If differences could be discerned, this could be evidence that the schemas make up at least a part of a distinct IMCO culture.

FA is a technique for identifying and interpreting common underlying variables in a set of data (Bernard, 2011). Factors are identified sequentially to explain the most variance in data not already captured by previous factors. Thus, factor 1 explains the most variance, factor 2 the second most, and so on. Each factor could signal the existence of an unseen variable at the intersection of a given schema item and a given factor. The larger this intersection could signal the relative importance of that factor (Handwerker, 2002). PCA is useful in data-intensive domains such as meteorology, image processing, genomic analysis, and machine learning where coherent patterns in data can be detected more clearly, as was the need here (Ding, & He, 2004). Where PCA is used, K-means is also applied in the subspace (Ding, & He, 2004). K-means clustering is an efficient error minimization method that uses prototypes (centroids) to represent clusters by optimizing the squared error function (Ding, & He, 2004). K-means was used here to visualize the clustering in two dimensions by first projecting the data to a two-dimensional subspace and then applying K-means to the projected data. We also chose K-means because it included all schema items, as compared to FA, which in this case might have retained many unclassified items. We also looked at the p-value for the mean result for each schema—that is, is the probability of getting these results under the assumption that the true mean result for both groups (IMCO and non-IMCO) would be the same. By computing the p-values and choosing a significance level, we could assess which schemas were answered differently by the two groups (IMCO and non-IMCO) to a statistically significant degree. Results are discussed in the next chapter.

Methodologically, the major challenge in this approach lay in the fact the adduced schemas needed to be not only be coded 'correctly', that is, in a way reasonably discerned by others, but also expressed in language identical to or very close to the language of my informants. The risk in not adhering to the inducing language was to discern factors solely on the basis of semantic features (D'Andrade, 1995; Maki, & Buchanan, 2008). For example, there is some debate whether knowledge for meaning (semantic memory) and knowledge for words in context (associative memory) actually measure the same thing (Maki & Buchanan, 2008).[17] In addition, veering from the original language ran the risk of potentially turning the adducing passages into etic constructs, thereby falling into the same epistemological trap as traditional etic culture surveys. The control for this was to use verbatim passages from which the schemas were adduced, only adding words if the phrase was unclear when isolated on the survey, and then only minimally so. For example, a passage denoting a schema such as *"So we have a very good operating system if you will, to look forward . . ."* would not make much sense out of context in a multi-item agreement–disagreement scale. Thus, the passage was changed to *you need standard operating systems to run this business*, a statement more clearly expressing the logic of the adduced schema. In this way FA and PCA, and their accompanying data visualization techniques, were ways to control for coding subjectivity while at the same time helping to determine whether the schemas adduced from IMCO's executive team were in any way characteristic of IMCO as a whole.

5. IMCO Research

Interviews

In the fall of 2013 I conducted 10 interviews with the top executive management team of IMCO. I interviewed the CEO, her four direct reports who are the presidents of IMCO's four business divisions, and several key divisional business leaders within each of the four divisions.

Informants were chosen on two criteria. First, I only selected individuals in general management roles as opposed to functional roles (e.g., the chief financial officer or head of marketing). I defined *general management* as responsibility for an end-to-end business with profit and loss accountability and the mandate of integrating the work of multiple heterogeneous functions. A general manager must bring together the work of operations, sales, engineering, marketing, and so forth, and help orchestrate the output of these functions to achieve business goals. Thus, all informants had the same kind of job.

Second, beyond the four presidents I chose general managers on the basis of geographic diversity, or on the uniqueness of their business relative to other IMCO businesses. By that I mean a sample of individuals whose business portfolio and purview was as distinct as possible from other leaders in my sample. For this reason I chose to interview the leader of the industrial pump division's Asia region, as well as the leader of the railway shock absorption business within the automotive division. This approach was designed to ensure the schemas adduced in totality were more likely the result of factors like professional orientation or strategic task focus rather than on local economic conditions, the market dynamics of a particular segment such as railways, or the effects of a particular national or regional culture.

Demographically, all informants were male except for one (the CEO). Racially all were white except for two (one Asian, one Indian subcontinent).

Table 5.5 List of Interviews

Title	Main Business	Professional Background & Training
President	Industrial pumps	Finance
President	Connectors	Operations, MBA
General Manager, Asia	Industrial pumps	Operations
President	Brake pads, shock absorption	Operations, Engineering, MBA
CEO	IMCO	Finance
General Manager	Connectors	Finance
President	Aerospace components	Operations, Engineering, MBA
General Manager	Aerospace components	Engineering
Senior Vice President, GM	Industrial pumps	Operations
General Manager	Shock absorption	Operations

Four out of 10 were non-native English speakers fluent in English.[18] All had engineering, finance, or manufacturing operations backgrounds, as summarized in Table 5.5.

Interviews

We understand what is unfamiliar by analogy to what is more familiar (Strauss & Quinn, 1997), which is why I chose to interview subjects about their business strategies, the challenges they faced actualizing them, and the mitigations they envisioned or had undertaken to overcome them.[19] Strategic challenges for business leaders are familiar, of course, in the sense they have to formulate, defend, and refine strategy as a core part of their jobs. But strategy barrier mitigation is unfamiliar in the sense it is a view of future or emergent events. In this sense they are idealizations; subjects will tend to draw on what is familiar to identify and make sense of issues, and formulate goals to solve perceived challenges. This is in line with how Quinn's informants talked about marriage, not in the abstract, but as married people. A typical cultural schema takes the form of a prototypical or idealized sequence of events. Capturing reasoning and idealizations, thus, provided excellent clues about shared schemas (Strauss & Quinn, 1997). I theorized subjects would draw from familiar schemas, especially those grounded in or compatible with their own professional experience and the unique strategic task environment of IMCO.

Following Quinn (2005), I used an open-ended interview to elicit spontaneous and everyday discourse as I believed this approach would yield analytically rich material. My intent was to keep the interviews as conversational as possible to allow informants to feel comfortable and familiar so they might be able to express themselves in relatively open and unencumbered ways. I had met six of my 10 informants through prior consulting work. Those I did not personally know had heard of my firm's work at IMCO.

Each subject was asked four questions. The first was to describe their own organization's business strategy at the unit of consideration relevant to them. Thus, the divisional presidents talked about their division's strategy, and the divisional general managers talked about their regional or unit-specific business strategy, and so forth. The second was to describe the top challenges they saw, of any kind in any domain, associated with executing their strategy. The third was to describe what mitigation(s) they advocated or were undertaking for the challenges enumerated. The last question was about culture. I asked each person to describe IMCO's culture, and then describe his or her own divisional culture. This question was not originally part of my plan, but in the course of conducting pilot interviews I realized asking directly about culture was another way to elicit schemas because their answers would trigger conceptualizations outside of everyday experience. This was also a good way to obtain more data about common ways organizational culture is conceived. I asked follow-up questions to clarify answers or allow elaboration when answers seemed incomplete. All informants were asked the same questions. Interviews lasted between 60 and 90 minutes. Half of the interviews were by phone, and half in person. All interviews were recorded and transcribed.

Summary

The two questions in support of the framework for functionally embodied culture proposed in the first section of this book motivate this study. First, *is there evidence of schemas within IMCO anchoring a definitive culture?* If so, do the schemas suggest *functional grounding?* Second, does the evidence support, at least provisionally, *functionally embodied culture?* If primary or pervasive schemas based on professionalization or strategic task context can be shown, this would lend substance to the theory.

Addressing how these questions were to be asked and analyzed required a somewhat careful slog through the river and tributaries of schema-discourse and metaphor research methods. This is the case in part because the methods used are still new. This is the first study I know of that uses Quinn's approach in an organizational setting. This is also the case because the theoretical framework proposed for organizational culture needs to be fully explicated for it to be useful. The next two chapters describe how the data was analyzed as well as the results and their implication for IMCO and beyond.

Notes

1 This middle ground also represents, to my mind, the liberation of the modern anthropological project from the dead-end of sterile, decontextualized positivism or endlessly self-referential postmodernism.
2 Unless a basic image schema such as *FORCE* provided a foundation for more domain-specific schemas and surfaced in multiple places, other than noting it in the data I did not isolate it in the analysis.

3 These projects consisted of building bespoke, emic competency models, or 'career frameworks' to define career progression for major functions (engineering, sales, operations, etc.). The work involved extensive interviewing with functional leaders (usually mid and upper level managers), coding and analysis of interview responses, and working iteratively with functional leadership groups to refine and produce a completed set of competencies and career progression criteria.

4 For example, the concept of *sameness* may be interpreted as *identical* in one language versus *similar to* in another. Boroditsky gets around this in her studies of English and Mandarin conceptions of time by testing native Mandarin speakers who also speak English (Boroditsky, 2001).

5 Cardini (2010) provides experimental evidence against linguistic relativity on the basis of his study of native Italian and English speaker differential attention to motion (i.e., manner of motion versus path of motion) in visual (video) versus verbal recognition tasks. Even though English speakers displayed far greater difference than Italians in their verbal descriptions of motion with many more nouns and adjectives and more information to describe the manner of motion, responses on non-linguistic performances were close to identical: Both groups exhibited the same differential attention for manner vs. path of motion. Cardini acknowledges one possibility for this may have to do with the nature of visual perception. Linguistic influence might affect perception only weakly, so that only "particularly sophisticated stimulus material" can bring differences (i.e. Whorfian effects) to life" (pp. 1455–1456).

6 McGlone (2007) calls Lakoff and Johnson's position "hyper-literal": "Lakoff asserts that our knowledge of abstract concepts is quite literally subsumed by our knowledge of concrete concepts. A conceptual system arranged in this fashion, however, would seem incapable of generating propositions about abstract concepts with figurative intent. For example, a conceptual system whose knowledge of theories was a subset of building knowledge should assume that theories are not merely metaphoric 'buildings,' but literal buildings!"(p. 122).

7 The use of conventional metonymies, in particular, may be less about discourse and more about cognitive anchoring, further discussed in the next chapter.

8 In studies of reading time comprehension of literal versus figurative meanings for paraphrases of ambiguous statements such as *must you open the window*, which can be paraphrased as a direct request (*close the window!*) or a more literal one (*is it necessary that you open the window?*), Rumelhart's student, Ray Gibbs found that comprehension took no longer for indirect paraphrases when the context was known as for direct paraphrases with no known context (Rumelhart, 1993, p. 75). Comprehension cannot be based on first determining literal meaning because in-context indirect and out-of-context direct paraphrases are processed at the same rate (Rumelhart, 1993).

   Rachel Giora's (1997, 2008) graded salience hypothesis builds and modifies Gibbs' work by claiming comprehension is less about whether language is literal or figural but rather on degrees of "salience": the frequency, familiarity, and the nature and amount of context provided (1997). Highly salient words and phrases, whether literal or figurative are easier (quicker, more intelligible) to process than less salient ones, which require additional cognitive resources and are "activated after more salient interpretations" (Diaz, Barrett, & Hogstrom, 2011, p. 320). Thus, idioms (*spill the beans*) take longer to read in less salient but literal contexts (i.e., actually spilling beans) than in a context suggestive of their idiomatic meaning (i.e., divulging a secret), while novel metaphors (*their bone density is not like ours*) take longer to read in non-salient, figurative contexts (i.e., they are not as tough as us) than in contexts that "invite literal interpretations," that is, actually comparing bone density scans at the doctor's office (2008, p. 153).

9 It is well established that the left hemisphere of the brain is critical to language processing (Bookheimer, 2002, as cited in Diaz, Barrett, & Hogstrom, 2011). Recently, it has also been found that the right hemisphere is also involved in language, especially in comprehending figural and metaphorical language (Diaz, Barrett, & Hogstrom, 2011). Studies using fMRI techniques show novel sentences and novel as well as familiar metaphors are actively processed in both hemispheres, with conventional metaphors (e.g. *sweet dreams*) showing more activity in the left hemisphere, while novel metaphors and figurative sentences showing greater activation than literal sentences in the right (Diaz, Barrett, & Hogstrom, 2011). One hypothesis is that novel figurative sentences and metaphor require more bilateral involvement because they pose more integration demands on comprehension (Diaz, Barrett, & Hogstrom, 2011).

10 There is also an abundance of literature in the subjectivist and symbolic tradition on institutional narrative and discourse, including metaphor, such as Wilkins' (1983) discussion of stories that "control" organizations (1983, p. 81), or Evered's (1983) assertion that the "language" of the U.S. Navy "constructs the social world" of the Navy (p. 127).

11 One cannot help but notice the reductionist and ontologizing tendencies in these and similar studies. To try and capture an organization's 'nature' through a root metaphor is not unlike characterizing an organization in terms of personality traits (Chapter 1).

12 Alvesson and Skoldberg (2009), for example, treat organizational metaphor as a kind of poetics.

13 For example, as mentioned earlier, Cornelissen (2012) studied metaphor to research the foundational schemas of communications professionals. He focused on "critical incidents" in his interviews with informants, defined as "an unprecedented event for the professional that required him or her to make an immanent decision about the role and use of communication" (p. 121).

14 Knorr-Cetina (1999) claims narrative and discourse are cultural enactments that "come into view through the definitions of entities, through systems of classification, [and] through the ways in which epistemic strategy, empirical procedure and social collaboration are understood" (p. 10), entailments which often take shape in metaphor. Koller (2005) goes further by claiming "cognitive ideologies" are acquired and reproduced through discursive practices, including metaphor (p. 204).

15 Evered (1983) takes the extreme view of how language constitutes behavior in his study of jargon in the U.S. Navy. He asserts an "organization has no objective reality" (in a positivist sense) but is "created daily by the linguistic enactments of its members" (p. 126). I suspect it takes more than discourse to acquire a cognitive ideology or create a sense of reality within an organization—the role of task and technology, and the effects of physical and social events necessarily impinge upon an actor's unfettered discursive intentions.

16 Multidimensional scaling (MDS) is another quantitative and visual technique for analyzing schemas. MDS provides a spatial representation based on the set of similarities in the data (Bernard, 2011). For example, Rentsch and Klimoski (2001) elicited teamwork schemas through group interviews that asked interviewees to describe prototypical events that occur on a team. Interview data were analyzed for the most frequently occurring descriptors, and high frequency descriptors were identified to develop a teamwork schema questionnaire. In the questionnaire, 15 statements such as "personal preferences were combined to achieve team goals" and "members are concerned with working for their own personal benefit" were developed. Each event statement was paired with another and participants were asked to rate the similarity of each statement on an 11-point scale ranging from *very dissimilar* to *very similar*. Data were then analyzed using MDS (Rentsch & Klimoski, 2001, p. 113).

17 In their study of the relationship between knowledge for meaning (semantic memory) and knowledge for words in context (associative memory), Maki and Buchanan (2008) showed through lexicographic measures that semantic similarity is separable from word association norms, and these in turn are separable from abstract representations derived from computational analyses of large bodies of text.

18 Native languages were Italian (2), Arabic (1), and Hindi (1).

19 My focus on challenges is closely related to the Critical Incident Technique (CIT; Bradley, 1992; Edvardsson & Roos, 2001; Mallak, Lyth, Olson, Ulshafer, & Sardone, 2003). CIT encourages informants to describe critical, context-specific situations and their response to them so that salient evaluation schemas are more likely to be conveyed (Flanagan, 1954, in Mallak et al., 2003). An emic position is stressed whereby the emergence of data from the informant is highlighted without the imposition of structure. CIT in this way is also capable of generating cultural data (Mallak et al., 2003).

Bibliography

Alvesson, M., & Skoldberg, K. (2009). *Reflexive methodology: New vistas for qualitative research*. Los Angeles: Sage.

Alvesson, M., & Spicer, A. (2011). Introduction. In M. Alvesson & A. Spicer (Eds.), *Metaphors we lead by.* (pp. 1–7) Abingdon: Routledge.

Alvi, F. (2011). Rethinking the institutional context of emerging markets through metaphor analysis. *Management International Review, 52,* 519–539. doi: 10.1007/s11575-011-0113-0.

Armenakis, A., & Bedeian, A. (1992). The role of metaphors in organizational change. *Group and Organization Management, 17,* 242–247.

Barcelona, A. (2003). Introduction: The cognitive theory of metaphor and metonymy. In A. Barcelona (Ed.), *Metaphor and metonymy at the crossroads* (pp. 1–30). Berlin: Mouton de Gruyter.

Basten, M. R. C. (2001). The role of metaphors in (re)producing organizational culture. *Advances in Developing Human Resources, 3,* 344–354.

Bennardo, G. (2011). A foundational cultural model in Polynesia: Monarchy, democracy, and the architecture of the mind. In D. Kronenfeld, G. Bennardo, V. de Munck, & M. Fischer (Eds.), *A companion to cognitive anthropology* (pp. 471–488). Malden, MA: Wiley-Blackwell.

Bernard, H. R. (2011). *Research methods in anthropology*. Lanham: Rowman Altamira.

Biernacki, R. (2012). *Reinventing evidence in social inquiry: Decoding facts and variables*. New York: Palgrave Macmillan.

Bookheimer, S. (2002). Functional MRI of language: New approaches to understanding the cortical organization of semantic processing. *Annual Review of Neuroscience, 25*(1), 151–188.

Boroditsky, L. (2001). Does language shape thought? Mandarin and English speakers' conceptions of time. *Cognitive Psychology, 43*(1), 1–22.

Bradley, C. P. (1992). Uncomfortable prescribing decisions: a critical incident study. *BMJ: British Medical Journal, 304*(6822), 294.

Burawoy, M. (1999). The extended case method. *Sociological Theory, 16,* 4–33.

Caballero, R. (2006). *Re-viewing space: Figurative language in architects' assessment of built space* (Vol. 2). Berlin: Walter de Gruyter.

Cardini, F. E. (2010). Evidence against Whorfian effects in motion conceptualisation. *Journal of Pragmatics, 42,* 1442–1459.

Clark, E. V. (1991). Acquisitional principles in lexical development. In S. Gelman & J. P. Byrnes (Eds.), *Perspectives on language and thought: Interrelations in development* (pp. 31–71).Cambridge: Cambridge University Press.

Cleary, C., & Packard, T. (1992). The Use of metaphors in organizational assessment and change. *Group & Organization Management, 17,* 229–241.

Cornelissen, J. P. (2012). Sensemaking under pressure: The influence of professional roles and social accountability on the creation of sense. *Organization Science, 23*(1), 118–137.

Cronbach, L. J., & Meehl, P. E. (1955). Construct validity in psychological tests. *Psychological Bulletin, 52*(4), 281.

D'Andrade, R. (1995). *The development of cognitive anthropology.* Cambridge: Cambridge University Press.

D'Andrade, R. (2005). Some methods for studying cultural cognitive structures. In N. Quinn (Ed.), *Finding culture in talk* (pp. 83–104). New York: Palgrave Macmillan.

Descola, P. (2013). *The ecology of others.* Chicago: Prickly Paradigm Press.

Diaz, M., Barrett, K., & Hogstrom, L. (2011). The influence of sentence novelty and figurativeness on brain activity. *Neuropsychologia, 49*(3), 320–330. doi: 10.1016/j.neuropsychologia.2010.12.004.

Ding, C., & He, X. (2004). K-means clustering via principal component analysis. In *Proceedings of the Twenty-First International Conference on Machine Learning* (p. 29). New York: ACM.

Duranti, A. (2009). Linguistic anthropology: History, ideas and issues. In A. Duranti (Ed.), *Linguistic anthropology: A reader* (2nd ed., pp. 1–60). Malden, MA: Blackwell.

Edvardsson, B., & Roos, I. (2001). Critical incident techniques: Towards a framework for analysing the criticality of critical incidents. *International Journal of Service Industry Management, 12*(3), 251–268.

Evered, R. (1983). The language of organizations: The case of the Navy. In L. Pondy, G. Morgan, P. Frost, & T. Dandridge (Eds.), *Organizational symbolism* (pp. 157–166). Greenwich, CT: JAI Press.

Fauconnier, G. (1997). *Mappings in thought and language.* Cambridge: Cambridge University Press.

Fleck, L. (1979). *Genesis and development of a scientific fact* (Fred Bradley and Thaddeus Trenn, Trans.). Chicago: University of Chicago Press. (Original work published 1935).

Garro, L. (2000). Remembering what one knows and the construction of the past: A comparison of cultural consensus theory and cultural schema theory. *Ethos, 28*(3), 275–319.

Gentner, D., & Bowdle B. (2008). Metaphor as structure mapping. In R. Gibbs (Ed.), *The Cambridge handbook of metaphor and thought* (pp. 109–128). Cambridge: Cambridge University Press.

Gibbs, R., & Perlman, M. (2006). The contested impact of cognitive linguistic research. In G. Kristiansen, M. Archard, R. Dirven, & F. Ruiz de Mendoza Ibanez (Eds.), *Cognitive linguistics: Current applications and future perspectives* (Vol. 1, pp. 211–228). Berlin: Walter de Gruyter.

Gioia, D. A., & Chittipeddi, K. (1991). Sensemaking and sensegiving in strategic change initiation. *Strategic Management Journal, 12*(6), 433–448.

Giora, R. (1997). Understanding figurative and literal language: The graded salience hypothesis. *Cognitive Linguistics, 8,* 183–206.

Giora, R. (2008). Is metaphor unique? In R. Gibbs (Ed.), *The Cambridge handbook of metaphor and thought* (pp. 143–160). Cambridge: Cambridge University Press.

Glucksberg, S. (2008). How metaphors create categories—quicky. In R. Gibbs (Ed.), *The Cambridge handbook of metaphor and thought* (pp. 67–83). Cambridge: Cambridge University Press.

Gumperz, J., & Levinson, S. (1991). Rethinking linguistic relativity. *Current Anthropology, 32*(5), 613–623. Retrieved from http://escholarship.org/uc/item/44w544hc#page-1.

Handwerker, W. P. (2002). The construct validity of cultures: Cultural diversity, culture theory, and a method for ethnography. *American Anthropologist, 104*(1), 106–122.

Herzfeld, M. (2001). *Anthropology: Theoretical practice in culture and society.* Malden, MA: Blackwell.

Johnson, M. (1987). *The body in the mind.* Chicago: University of Chicago Press.

Johnson-Laird, P. N. (1983). *Mental models: Towards a cognitive science of language, inference, and consciousness* (No. 6). Cambridge, MA: Harvard University Press.

Keller, J. (2011). The limits of the habitual: Shifting paradigms for language and thought. In D. Kronenfeld, G. Bennardo, V. de Munck, & M. Fisher (Eds.), *A companion to cognitive anthropology* (pp. 61–81). Chichester: Wiley-Blackwell.

Knorr-Cetina, K. (1999). *Epistemic cultures: How the sciences make knowledge.* Cambridge, MA: Harvard University Press.

Koller, V. (2005). Critical discourse analysis and social cognition: Evidence from business media discourse. *Discourse & Society, 16*(2), 199–224.

Koller, V. (2008). Corporate brands as socio-cognitive representations. In G. Kristiansen & R. Dirven (Eds.), *Cognitive sociolinguistics: Language variation, cultural models, social systems* (pp. 389–418). Berlin: Mouton de Gruyer.

Kovecses, Z. W. (2005). *Metaphor in culture: Universality and variation.* Cambridge: Cambridge University Press.

Krasny, K., Sadosky, M., & Paivio, A. (2005). Unwarranted return: A response to Mcvee, Dunsmore and Gavelek's (2005) "Schema theory revisited." *Review of Educational Research, 77,* 239–243. doi: 10.3102/003465430301958.

Lakoff, G. (1987). *Women, fire, and dangerous things.* Chicago: University of Chicago Press.

Lakoff, G., & Johnson, M. (1980. Reprinted 2003). *Metaphors we live by.* Chicago: University of Chicago Press.

Lave, J. (1993). Introduction: The practice of learning. In S. Chaiken & J. Lave (Eds.). *Understanding practice: Perspectives on activity and context* (pp. 3–34). Cambridge: Cambridge University Press.

Levinson, S. (1996). Language and space. *Annual Review of Anthropology, 25,* 353–382. Retrieved from http://scholar.google.com/.

Maki, W. S., & Buchanan, E. (2008). Latent structure in measures of associative, semantic, and thematic knowledge. *Psychonomic Bulletin & Review, 15*(3), 598–603.

Mallak, L. A., Lyth, D. M., Olson, S. D., Ulshafer, S. M., & Sardone, F. J. (2003). Diagnosing culture in health-care organizations using critical incidents. *International Journal of Health Care Quality Assurance, 16*(4), 180–190.

Maltseva, K., & D'Andrade, R. (2011). Multi-item scales and cognitive ethnography. In D. Kronenfeld, G. Bennardo, V. de Munck, & M. Fischer (Eds.), *A companion to cognitive anthropology* (pp. 153–170). Malden, MA: Wiley-Blackwell.

Martin, J. (2002). *Organizational culture: Mapping the terrain*. Thousand Oaks, CA: Sage.

McGlone, M. S. (2007). What is the explanatory value of a conceptual metaphor? *Language & Communication, 27*(2), 109–126.

Morgan, G. (2006). *Images of organization*. Thousand Oaks, CA: Sage.

Ortony, A. (1993). Metaphor, language and thought. In A. Ortony (Ed.), *Metaphor and thought* (pp. 1–18). Cambridge: Cambridge University Press.

Paivio, A., & Walsh, M. (1993). Psychological processes in metaphor comprehension and memory. In A. Ortony (Ed.), *Metaphor and thought* (pp. 307–328). Cambridge: Cambridge University Press.

Palmer, G. (1996). *Toward a theory of cultural linguistics*. Austin: University of Texas Press.

Pondy, L. (1983). The role of metaphors and myths in organization and in the facilitation of change. In L. Pondy, G. Morgan, P. Frost, & T. Dandridge (Eds.), *Organizational symbolism* (pp. 157–166). Greenwich, CT: JAI Press.

Quinn, N. (2005). How to reconstruct schemas people share, from what they say. In N. Quinn (Ed.), *Finding culture in talk* (pp. 35–84). New York: Palgrave Macmillan.

Quinn, N. (2011). The history of the cultural models school reconsidered: A paradigm shift in cognitive anthropology. In D. Kronenfeld, G. Bennardo, V. de Munck, & M. Fischer (Eds.), *A companion to cognitive anthropology* (pp. 30–46). Malden, MA: Wiley-Blackwell.

Rakova, M. (2002). The philosophy of embodied realism: A high price to pay? *Cognitive Linguistics, 13*(3), 215–244.

Rentsch, J. R., & Klimoski, R. J. (2001). Why do "great minds" think alike? Antecedents of team member schema agreement. *Journal of Organizational Behavior, 22*(2), 107–120.

Rohrer, T. (2005). Image schemata in the brain. In B. Hampe & J. Grady (Eds.), *From perception to meaning: Image schemas in cognitive linguistics* (pp. 165–198). Berlin: Mouton de Gruyter.

Rohrer, T. (2006). Three dogmas of embodiment: Cognitive linguistics as a cognitive science. In G. Kristiansen, M. Archard, R. Dirven, & F. Ruiz de Mendoza Ibanez (Eds.), *Cognitive linguistics: Current applications and future perspectives* (Vol. 1, pp. 119–1468). Berlin: Walter de Gruyter.

Rosch, E. (2002). Principles of categorization. In D. Levitin (Ed.), *Foundations of cognitive psychology: Core readings* (pp. 251–270). Cambridge, MA: MIT Press. (Reprinted from *Concepts: Core Readings*, pp. 189–206, by E. Margolis and S. Laurence, Eds., 1978, Cambridge, MA: MIT Press).

Rumelhart, D. E. (1993). Some problems with the notion of literal meanings. In A. Ortony (Ed.). *Metaphor and thought* (pp. 71–82). Cambridge: Cambridge University Press.

Rumelhart, D. E., & Ortony, A. (1977). Representation of knowledge. In R. Anderson, R. Spiro, & W. Montague (Eds.), *Schooling and the acquisition of knowledge* (pp. 100–132). Hillsdale, NJ: Lawrence Erlbaum Associates.

Schon, D. (1993). Generative metaphor: A perspective on problem-setting in social policy. In A. Ortony (Ed.), *Metaphor and thought* (pp. 137–163). Cambridge: Cambridge University Press.

Shore, B. (1996). *Culture in mind: Cognition, culture and the problem of meaning.* Oxford: Oxford University Press.

Shue, L. L., & Lacroix, C. (1998). Teaching an old system new tricks: Organizational members' use of metaphor to make sense of pedagogical innovation. Unpublished dissertation. ERIC Document Reproduction Service No. ED 426 437.

Sieck, W., Rasmussen, L., & Smart, P. R. (2010). Cultural network analysis: A cognitive approach to cultural modeling. In V. Dinesh (Ed.), *Network science for military coalition operations: Information extraction and interaction* (pp. 237–255). Hershey, PA: ICI Global.

Sinha, C., & Jensen de Lopez, K. (2000). Language, culture and the embodiment of spatial cognition. *Cognitive Linguistics, 11–1/2,* 17–41.

Strauss, C. & Quinn, N. (1997). *A cognitive theory of cultural meaning.* Cambridge: Cambridge University Press.

Strauss, C. (2012). *Making sense of public opinion: American discourses about immigration and social programs.* New York: Cambridge University Press.

Talmy, L. (2000). *Toward a cognitive semantics* (Vol. 2). Cambridge, MA: MIT Press.

Tsoukas, H. (1991). The missing link: A transformational view of metaphors in organizational science. *Academy of Management Review, 16,* 566–585.

Vervaeke, J., & Kennedy, J. (2004). Conceptual metaphor and abstract thought. *Metaphor and Symbol, 19*(3), 213–231.

Walsh, J. P. (1995). Managerial and organizational cognition: Notes from a trip down memory lane. *Organization Science, 6*(3), 280–321.

Weber, K. (2005). A toolkit for analyzing corporate cultural toolkits. *Poetics, 33*(3), 227–252.

Weick, K. E., Sutcliffe, K. M., & Obstfeld, D. (2005). Organizing and the process of sensemaking. *Organization Science, 16*(4), 409–421.

Wilkins, A. (1983). Organizational stories as symbols which control the organization. In L. Pondy, G. Morgan, P. Frost, & T. Dandridge (Eds.), *Organizational symbolism* (pp. 157–166). Greenwich, CT: JAI Press.

6 Seeing Schemas
Research at IMCO

In the religious ritual life of North-West Zambia *kusolola* is the term given to the idea of making visible what has been concealed and resists articulation, what Victor Turner (1975) calls, respectively, divination and revelation. It is tempting to characterize the process of investigating and validating schemas that follows in this chapter as a sort of *kusolola*, revelation without the religious connotations. If we could just locate in our own organizations the one foundational schema that structures all other structures, the secrets of organizational cultural life would surely follow. For the practitioner seeking the 'truth' to unlock the hidden secrets of culture, this is seductive, and I cannot in honesty claim immunity to this attraction. My cultural *kusolola* was initially drawn to Shore and Bennardo's foundational schema concept as a powerful way of explaining organizational culture. What if culture *could* be reduced, in an elegantly and powerfully cognitive-structuralist way, to a single logic?

Perhaps fortunately, I did not find any such singular logic at IMCO. There was no singular dominant schema at IMCO that appeared to underwrite all others. What I did uncover was a constellation of interrelated schemas that together anchored many of the cultural models used by the IMCO executive team. Some of these schemas appear also to be figural for other IMCO informants. They may be thought of as primary, in the sense they structure more elaborate cultural models, and therefore the culture of that system. In and of itself this to me is a more exciting finding. *Networked primary schemas* may account for the diversity, complexity, and interlaced nature of cultural models within a modern corporate enterprise.

This chapter describes the results of the qualitative and quantitative research conducted at IMCO as described in the previous chapter. The qualitative research identified schemas and schema categories, and used metaphor to help substantiate the results; the quantitative research was used as validation of the qualitative work.

1. *Results*: Causal Reasoning Analyses

The interviews with the IMCO CEO and her executive team described in the previous chapter yielded approximately 17 hours of recorded material. Each recording was transcribed and analyzed. Once the content of the interviews were coded, several months were spent in the analysis.

Focusing on schema and metaphor involved close reading and re-reading of each transcript, often replaying specific passages many times to be sure I understood the speaker's point. Using Quinn's (2005) method for uncovering schemas discussed in the previous chapter, my primary analytic technique consisted of isolating causal reasoning contained within short passages of discourse. The supporting techniques consisted of metaphor analysis as well as the quantitative study.

Causal reasoning analysis consisted of locating if–then constructions, idealizations, reasons for, and outcome statements. These were statements containing phrases such as *if you do x, y and z will happen, b happens because of a and c, what I would like to see happen is m,* and so forth. Once attuned to these types of constructions within sentences or whole passages, my ability to discern such patterns became quite honed and I was struck by the quantity of such constructions in my informants' speech.[1]

In this way I adduced 264 schemas, some through a single sentence, some through a long paragraph or one- or two-minute story with several digressions but that nonetheless maintained a clear logic or idealization throughout. Using an iterative process, I labeled each schema with a short phrase or sentence that captured its logic or idealization, such as *STRATEGIES HAVE DIRECTIONS* or *TALENT IS FORCE.*[2] The labels initially were placeholders, but over time as I sifted through my data they were refined to become accurate handles for the schema.

I then grouped individual schemas into categories. This initially was an attempt to organize the vast amount of text I had to work with, but soon became a valuable analytic technique in itself. Categories were groupings based on the common logic contained within each schema, such as schemas whose logic or idealization pertained to *MACHINES* or *STANDARDS.* Categorizing helped to better see how many of the passages were anchored in common logic. It also controlled for coding bias. For example, even if I interpreted the logic of a passage such as *"So as we get along as business leaders, we drive the business forward"* as *GOOD RELATIONSHIPS DRIVE BUSINESS,* and classified the schemas as pertaining to machines based on the verb 'drive' and the conventional metonymy for causal action DRIVE, the *MACHINE* category in which this schemas was placed allowed me over time to see if it made sense in relation to others in the same category. As the category was built up, if a particular schema came to seem inconsistent with others in that category it was reclassified. In this iterative fashion over time I arrived at a picture of informant schemas by analyzing and re-analyzing data at different levels of consideration, zooming in to actual passages and schema labels, zooming out to the categories, continually refining labels and categories in this way while trying to let the data dictate where I looked and how I classified.

In this way I created 11 distinct schema categories (Figure 6.7). Since my focus was cultural schemas, I looked at the degree to which schemas were shared by counting how many were invoked by more than one speaker. Often the same speaker invoked the same schema multiple times, accounting for higher overall frequencies, but this did not mean the schema was shared by anyone else.

As Quinn found with her subjects, causal reasoning tends to be fragmentary. In many cases the logic had to be discerned by identifying several related statements and piecing together bits of intertwined logic. Like searching for clues to a robbery from shards of broken glass, the metaphor analysis (described below) helped confirm or redirect what I was seeing in the causal reasoning analysis by suggesting how a particular narrative passage made sense, or not. And the relationship was bidirectional. Sometimes the causal reasoning informed the metaphor categorizations; sometimes the metaphor categories informed the reasoning analysis. And sometimes the metaphors in a particular passage had nothing to do with the causal reasoning in the same passage but were simply rhetorical flourishes, figures of speech, or, intriguingly, cognitive anchors, as I describe later. All of these analytic techniques were mutually reinforcing and compatible.

Primary Schemas

Out of 264 adduced schemas in 11 categories, six categories—*STANDARDS AND COMPETENCE, BUILT STRUCTURE, THE PRIMACY OF PERSONAL EXPERIENCE, MACHINE, LIVING THINGS*, and *SPATIAL LOCATION*—comprised 84% of all schemas (221 out of 264). Like Quinn's findings about American conceptions of marriage, that just six categories constituted more than three-quarters of all schemas in my sample was the first indication that common ways of thinking underpin much of my informants' discourse (Figure 6.7).

What is obvious at this level of analysis is the overall character of the schemas. The categories are consistent with an organization in the business of making things. One would be surprised to see schemas related to machines or personal experience associated with, say, a financial services firm or, farther afield, a social services non-profit.

Figure 6.7 also shows degrees of sharedness, with the shared percentage in each category. Of 264 schemas, 73 were shared. The most shared category was *SPATIAL LOCATION* at 45% (10/22), followed by *THE PRIMACY OF PERSONAL EXPERIENCE* with 42% (14/34), and *BUILT STRUCTURE* with 25% (10/40). Along with *STANDARDS AND COMPETENCE* (17%; 12/71), these four categories comprised 63% of all shared schemas.

Both the categorization and sharedness analyses suggest relatively few types of schemas structure most of the ways these executives make sense of their collective experience. This claim is based on categories, groupings of

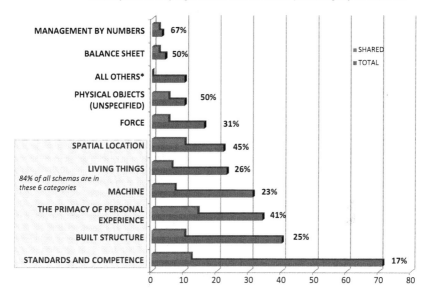

Schemas by Category, with Percentage Shared
Count of schemas by logic theme, with count and percentage of those shared

Figure 6.7 All schemas by schema category with percentage shared.

common logic within individual schemas. While I endeavored to maintain close fidelity to the logic suggested by the passage in which each schema was adduced, arguably these categories could have been the product my own biases. To better understand the significance of these data, we need to look at the underlying schemas in each category.

Schema Networks

What stands out from the analysis of individual schemas is the relationship among categories, depicted graphically in Figure 6.8. The bubbles depict the category name, with individual shared schemas below each. The arrows show the bi-directional nature of the reasoning emphasis between categories.

To assert any one schema or schema category as foundational would be to minimize the explanatory richness of informants' discourse and sensemaking. All are necessary to support, enhance, extend, or further legitimize the discourse. And yet far from being random or accidental, these relationships are logical and reasonable in the IMCO context, grounded in the realities of a global manufacturing business.

Interconnected schemas structure most of the discourse at IMCO

Shared schemas by category (with total number of schemas and percentage shared in each category)

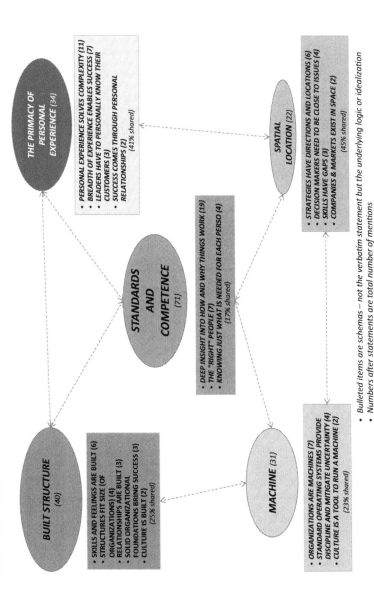

THE PRIMACY OF PERSONAL EXPERIENCE (34)

- *PERSONAL EXPERIENCE SOLVES COMPLEXITY (11)*
- *BREADTH OF EXPERIENCE ENABLES SUCCESS (7)*
- *LEADERS HAVE TO PERSONALLY KNOW THEIR CUSTOMERS (3)*
- *SUCCESS COMES THROUGH PERSONAL RELATIONSHIPS (2)*
  (41% shared)

SPATIAL LOCATION (22)

- *STRATEGIES HAVE DIRECTIONS AND LOCATIONS (6)*
- *DECISION MAKERS NEED TO BE CLOSE TO ISSUES (4)*
- *SKILLS HAVE GAPS (3)*
- *COMPANIES & MARKETS EXIST IN SPACE (3)*
  (45% shared)

STANDARDS AND COMPETENCE (71)

- *DEEP INSIGHT INTO HOW AND WHY THINGS WORK (19)*
- *THE "RIGHT" PEOPLE (7)*
- *KNOWING JUST WHAT IS NEEDED FOR EACH PERSO (4)*
  (17% shared)

BUILT STRUCTURE (40)

- *SKILLS AND FEELINGS ARE BUILT (6)*
- *STRUCTURES FIT SIZE (OF ORGANIZATIONS) (4)*
- *RELATIONSHIPS ARE BUILT (3)*
- *SOLID ORGANIZATIONAL FOUNDATIONS BRING SUCCESS (3)*
- *CULTURE IS BUILT (2)*
  (25% shared)

MACHINE (31)

- *ORGANIZATIONS ARE MACHINES (7)*
- *STANDARD OPERATING SYSTEMS PROVIDE DISCIPLINE AND MITIGATE UNCERTAINTY (4)*
- *CULTURE IS A TOOL TO RUN A MACHINE (2)*
  (23% shared)

- Bulleted items are schemas – not the verbatim statement but the underlying logic or idealization
- Numbers after statements are total number of mentions

Figure 6.8 Shared schemas by category, with relationships between categories.

Tables 6.6 through 6.10 provide detail for these five most prominent categories, showing how many people referenced each schema, and representative verbatim passages. Each table also contains a list of the other schemas mentioned by only a single speaker. *LIVING THINGS*, counted as part of the 84% most prevalent schema categories, is not included in this detail because it is a conventionalized category common across business in North America.[3]

STANDARDS AND COMPETENCE

During the interviews I was struck by the number of times informants referenced the idea of an abstract standard of excellence. So I was not surprised at how frequently schemas about standards and competence—doing things well and in the correct way—manifested in the analysis. *STANDARDS AND COMPETENCE* refers to an idealized standard perceived as necessary to succeed across all domains of management, from manufacturing operations to financial management to people management. This category contained by far the greatest number of schemas (71), and was invoked regardless of the topic under discussion. Thus, schemas such as *CLEAR THINKING SOLVES ISSUES*, or *FOCUS IS KEY TO SUCCESS*, or *GOOD PLANNING LEADS YOU OUT OF ISSUES* were uttered with frequency almost as if rules of thumb, or common wisdoms. One might be tempted to claim the nature of the interview—focusing on challenges and mitigations—begged the answer. Any answer would appeal to a standard of competence. But IMCO executives' idealized standard is much more generalized than other groups I have studied. In the same interview with software engineers and human resources (HR) professionals, for example, software engineers most often referenced a design or coding ideal, and HR people a client satisfaction and service ideal. These executives have a more generalized concept of excellence and apply it more often across a greater number of contexts.

One might also be tempted to subcategorize *STANDARDS AND COMPETENCE* schemas into finer-grained categories, such as schemas about leadership competence, but the evaluative and rule-like aspect apparent in all of them suggested the more inclusive category. Subjects did not simply speak about leadership or teams or other aspect of their business in neutral terms; they characterized these domains with an evaluative and idealized sense of mastery, structured in the form of *one needs to achieve x level of mastery in order to successfully do y in domain z*. This basic logic was evident no matter what the speaker was speaking about.

As seen in Table 6.6 and Figure 6.8, *DEEP INSIGHT INTO WHY AND HOW THINGS WORK* is the most frequently referenced individual shared schema, mentioned 19 times. This schema is about the need to possess incisive knowledge and insight about a domain to understand how and why it functions as it does. The category also contains *THE 'RIGHT' PEOPLE*

Table 6.6 STANDARDS AND COMPETENCE Schemas (71)

Shared schemas150	*Verbatim passage containing the schema (key phrases in bold)*
DEEP INSIGHT INTO HOW AND WHY THINGS WORK *Times referenced: 19* *Number of people referencing: 6*	*But if you are looking to evolve or grow or change an organization like we are, or you're coming in new to an organization,* **you need to be very good with your listening skills and your perception skills, so that you can find those things that are** *said either directly or indirectly.* *you have to be able to have the* **strong degree of ability to do cost, lead-time estimating, and then on top of that you have to be able to manage two or better than the cost of the lead time that you've committed to. Project management is incredibly fundamental to this type of business.** *That's precisely the reason for this structure . . .* **what we did not have was a deep understanding of the market and the segmentation.** *So there was nothing about the chiller that really got changed.* **But it was understanding what the customer's problem is.** *The customer's problem turned out to be that they didn't care about the cheapest chiller [they arrived at the same fifty bucks], but their problem was that when the contractor needed the part it had to be a non-issue. So if they had to pay $500 more, they didn't even notice it.* **So it's an example, how do you look at something, what makes something tick? And then you get to the lever that makes it tick.** **You've got to understand what motivates them, what makes them tick and how they learn. And if you don't then you will fail as a manager. And** *they will fail as your subordinates . . .. (to do that you have to)* **Keep the balance, get to know them all individually.** *(you have to have)* **have the deep knowledge** *of your manufacturing abilities . . . (and) deep knowledge of what other businesses do.* *(the key talent skill is) to enable,* **to gather that fundamental understanding of what's going on in the business,** *understanding where you need to go, what your weaknesses are, and then* **blending that together into what you need to take your organization to the next step.** *Otherwise you get to talent that misses the mark.* *But if you are looking to evolve or grow or change an organization like we are, or you're coming in new to an organization,* **you need to be very good with your listening skills and your perception skills, so that you can find those things that are said either directly or indirectly.**

Shared schemas150	Verbatim passage containing the schema (key phrases in bold)
THE "RIGHT" PEOPLE *Times referenced: 7* *Number of people referencing: 3*	**getting the right people in the right places** *(is key to change) . . . But it (the organizations) didn't have the right people in the right place.* *I'm not averse to any work structure . . . they all work as long as you have the right people.* **So it's all about making sure you have the right people,** *which I also believe is the core competency of what the company can be . . .* **I've been able to hire really strong people to support me.** *If you pretty much focus on any part of your business that is not doing well, you have to be honest with yourself and say,* **do you really have the right people in your organization?** *You gotta look at your strategy too, but if you find the right people, they also help you get the right strategy, especially if they have the right experience and knowledge. So I err on really hiring top talent.*
KNOWING JUST WHAT IS NEEDED FOR EACH PERSON *Times referenced: 4* *Number of people referencing: 3*	**But you have to figure out when your people need structure and when your people need support and you have to give them either structure or support depending on the need,** *and if you give them one and they need the other then they should be asking for a little bit of trouble.*

Unshared schemas (bold = mentioned more than once by same speaker, with number of mentions)
ASPIRE TO SOMETHING LUDICROUS
BALANCE IS FAIRNESS
CAPABILITIES ARE DEVELOPED THROUGH EFFORT
CAPABILITIES NEED TO BE RELIABLE
CLEAR THINKING SOLVES ISSUES
CONSTRUCTIVE CONFLICT LEADS TO BETTER CONTRIBUTIONS
CULTURES HAVE RULES
DEVELOPING OTHERS IS KEY TO SUSTAINABILITY
EXCELLENCE REQUIRES STANDARDS (2)
EXCELLING REQUIRES MASTERY OF HUMAN DYNAMICS
FOCUS IS KEY TO SUCCESS
GOOD LEADERS COMMAND RESPECT
GOOD MATERIALS PREVENT PRODUCT FAILURE
GOOD PLANNING DRIVES GROWTH (2)
GOOD PLANNING LEADS YOU OUT OF ISSUES
GREAT PRODUCTS MAKE MONEY
GROWTH REQUIRES GLOBAL THINKERS
INTERPERSONAL PROBLEMS SHOULD BE SOLVED PROFESSIONALLY AND EFFICIENTLY
JUST ENOUGH KNOWLEDGE
LEADERSHIP IS GENERATING FOLLOWERSHIP (2)
LEADERSHIP IS KNOWING WHAT PEOPLE NEED
MANAGING COMPLEXITY IS BALANCING MANY THINGS AT ONCE (2)
METRICS LEAD TO GOOD OPERATIONS
MODELS ENABLE THE RIGHT DESIGNS
ORGANIZATIONS MUST ALLOW TRACKING, MONITORING AND CONTROL

(Continued)

Table 6.6 (Continued)

PEOPLE CAN PERFORM IF THEY ARE GOOD
PERFECT FORECASTING IS ACCURACY
PERFECTING THE BALANCE BETWEEN EFFICIENCY AND PEOPLE
DEVELOPMENT
PERFECTING WHAT IS TRIVIAL
PROBLEMS HAVE A ROOT CAUSE—AND ARE SOLVED BY FOLLOWING THE
SAME RECIPE
REPITITION YEILDS PROFICIENCY
RESPONSIBILITY REQUIRES AUTHORITY
RULES LEAD TO SUCCESS
SUCCESS IS COMPLETENESS
VERIFICATION BRINGS CERTAINTY
WE NEED AN OWNERSHIP MINDSET (2)

---

schema, a frequently occurring conventional metonymy I discuss in detail in the next chapter. These are good examples of the inclusive process of adducing schemas. Locating the highest level of categorization applicable to the greatest number of schemas while preserving the essence of the logic of the individual passage. Obviously these were judgment calls, but they were based on an extensive and iterative sifting of the data, as well as my familiarity with the speaker's context based on my knowledge of IMCO.

As suggested by Figure 6.8, *STANDARDS AND COMPETENCE* schemas interact with those in other categories, such as *BUILT STRUCTURE* and *MACHINE*, underscoring their function as an interlaced network.

BUILT STRUCTURE

This category contains a prevalence of schemas such as *SKILLS AND FEELINGS ARE BUILT, STRUCTURES FIT SIZE (OF ORGANIZA-TION), RELATIONSHIPS ARE BUILT,* and so on. While many of these are conventional discourses found in mainstream business,[4] all refer specifically to things built. It struck me in considering these passages that the notion of *concretizing the abstract* was dominant, such as in the phrases "*so you recognize that you need to change the structure of the organization to fit the size of the organization,*" and "*that's really a huge challenge to build leadership confidence.*" The insinuation of building things, an obvious connection to manufacturing, is clear.

What is also interesting about *concretizing the abstract* is how it relates to *STANDARDS AND COMPETENCE.* One could say *STANDARDS AND COMPETENCE* 'needs' the *BUILT STRUCTURE* category (and others) to render concepts such as *DEEP INSIGHT INTO HOW AND WHY THINGS WORK* intelligible. One 'sees' into *things. THE 'RIGHT' PEO-PLE* are 'right' for some *thing.* This is clear in a statement from the head of the Asia region: "*I think I'm being successful if I can get this organization's foundation solidified in a solid strategic direction*" (coded as *SOLID OR-GANIZATIONAL FOUNDATIONS BRING SUCCESS*). The standard,

Table 6.7 BUILT STRUCTURE Schemas (40)

Shared schemas	Verbatim passage containing the schema (key phrases in bold)
SKILLS AND FEELINGS ARE BUILT Times referenced: 6 Number of people referencing: 2	what I'm trying to do is . . . **build competencies** where they're not. That's really a huge challenge to **build leadership** confidence.
STRUCTURES FIT SIZE (OF ORGANIZATIONS) Times referenced: 4 Number of people referencing: 2	So you recognize that you **need to change the structure of the organization to fit the size of the organization.** You need to change all of your infrastructure and processes.
RELATIONSHIPS ARE BUILT Times referenced: 3 Number of people referencing: 2	So we want to be creative and take every opportunity into **a relationship-building opportunity,** especially with the customers, and build the growth angle.
SOLID ORGANIZATIONAL FOUNDATIONS BRING SUCCESS Times referenced: 3 Number of people referencing: 2	I think I'm being successful if I can get this organization's foundation solidified in a solid strategic direction to go in.
CULTURE IS BUILT Times referenced: 2 Number of people referencing: 2	And everything that they do is helping in shaping the culture.

Unshared schemas (bold = mentioned more than once by same speaker, with number of mentions)
BUSINESS MODELS FIT CULTURES
EXPERTISE RESIDES IN SEGMENTS
GAPS ARE CONTAINERS
GOOD, RELIABLE AND TRUSTWORTHY TEAMS ARE BUILT
MANAGERS HELP EACH OTHER (AS A PART OF MANAGEMENT)
MODELS NEED TO BE FLEXIBLE
MORALE IS MANUFACTURED
PEOPLE QUALITY IS REINFORCEABLE
PHYSICAL MODELS ENABLE FINE TUNING
PIPELINES DRIVE GROWTH
PLANS ARE BUILT
PROBLEMS CAN BE BROKEN DOWN BY LEVELS
SKILLS HAVE LEVELS
STRATEGIES ARE DESIGNED
STRUCTURE DRIVES DECISION MAKING
STRUCTURE AND SUPPORT IS LEADERSHIP
STRUCTURE NEEDS TO BE APPROPRIATE TO THE MISSION (3)
TEAMS ARE BUILT
TECHNOLOGY IS A MOVEABLE OBJECT
TRUST IS BUILT

implied by *"solid strategic direction,"* and personal competence denoted by *"being successful"* are fused to *"foundation solidified."* The conceptual blend renders the abstract concept as a tangible standard.

Many schemas have just this character, providing a kind of scaffolding in order to make other schemas clear or more complete. Many do not make much sense except in relation to others, which is what led me to embrace the idea that the thinking of these executives is underwritten by *interrelated* logic. While these are conceptual entities adduced by my own categorizations, the many relationships among them are striking.

The next most adduced category is *THE PRIMACY OF PERSONAL EXPERIENCE*. It is also the second most shared at 42%. The concept of personal experience was conferred with unique status among my informants as a kind of prerequisite for knowledge, hence the use of 'primacy'. The vernacular is 'seeing is believing', but more than just believing, these schemas denote that first-hand knowledge is essential for successful management. It is exemplified in this passage from an executive talking about what makes a successful leader: "*They know what's going on, they know their financials, they understand the business of it. It is complex, so therefore I have to stay on top of it*" (*PERSONAL EXPERIENCE SOLVES COMPLEXITY*).

Every business context, of course, places a premium on domain experience. What is significant here is the degree to which *first-hand* knowledge is privileged in lieu of specific domain knowledge. Software engineers, for example, tend to privilege 'elegant' code or 'clean' design. Sales people might privilege sales results or customer satisfaction. IMCO executives significantly emphasize *first-hand* knowledge and experience. One might argue this is the nature of general management. Yet successful general managers in large, complex organizations actually must master an opposing skill. It is impossible in complex and dynamic organizations for general managers to have expertise in all domains under their purview, thus to succeed they must develop and master higher-leverage skills such as delegation, incisive questioning, and the development of trusted subordinates.[5] But tacitly at least, the idea of personal experience for general managers and top executives at IMCO is highly indexed, as referenced by a general manager who openly struggled with this tension:

> *You have to know when to dive in or when to dive out of situations. How close do I get? Among my peers, my peers think I should dive in more—and so I listen to that. And then I will select on that . . . but then I also realize that people need to learn too. So if they have me solve issues and dive in to the issues without explaining it to them, I'm sure not changing them, or I'm not testing them effectively. Sometimes you have to let the fire start, to see if other people figure out that there is a fire and what they do with it.*

The concept of scaffolding again emerges. Consider the schema embedded in the following passage: "*So that you can build realistic time frames*

Table 6.8 THE PRIMACY OF PERSONAL EXPERIENCE Schemas (34)

Shared schemas	Verbatim passage containing the schema (key phrases in bold)
PERSONAL EXPERIENCE SOLVES COMPLEXITY Times referenced: 11 Number of people referencing: 5	I wanted to be **personally close to the effort.** So that you can build realistic time frames and not just regurgitate what people told you; **so that you can see clearly and understand clearly the interaction between the various functions.** **You have to know when to dive in or when to dive out of situations . . . How close do I get?** Among my peers, my peers think I should dive in more—and so I listen to that. For one it's experience. I know this company, like I said, for over 25 years, . . . and I've seen the things that work and the things that didn't work, and I was always in the middle of it, whether it was finance or operations, I was always a part of the strategy and what happened . . . again you see what worked best and what doesn't and you keep that in mind. So there's an expectation **that they know their business, they know what's going on, they know their financials, they understand the business of it. It is complex, so therefore I have to stay on top of it and my team knows that**
BREADTH OF EXPERIENCE ENABLES SUCCESS Times referenced: 7 Number of people referencing: 4	**It's kind of like if you're going to be an operations manager, you have to spend time in manufacturing supervision, warehousing, shipping, then you have to get into the supply chain, do purchasing planning understand all these areas** . . . I think to be an effective GM you have to be able to sit in meetings and talk strategy. And then you have to go to a meeting in HR and talk culture, what is the temperature of our people out there today as we go through change management, and then you have to be able to talk operations specifically. **You really have to go from tactical to strategic and talk across a broad range of functional activities and speak intelligently.** . . . the language to communicate the strategy to the person walking on the shop floor is very different from the language to communicate the same strategy to the CEO. **And you got to be able to play at all levels.**
LEADERS HAVE TO PERSONALLY KNOW THEIR CUSTOMERS Times referenced: 3 Number of people referencing: 3	**So the customer relationship and their endorsement is going to be a key** for you as a new GM. So because without that, you're not going to be able have sustainable growth, it will grow, but it won't be sustainable.

(Continued)

Table 6.8 (Continued)

Shared schemas	Verbatim passage containing the schema (key phrases in bold)
SUCCESS COMES THROUGH PERSONAL RELATIONSHIPS Times referenced: 2 Number of people referencing: 2	*I have a relationship all across corporate. I think* *that's another key is relationships. I have many* *relationships where I can pick up the phone to any* *of those functions and call them and say "what are* *you doing? This doesn't make sense. What do you* *need to understand?" It's just having relationships* *with all of these stakeholders . . . it's all in the* *interest of having a better product in the end.*

Unshared schemas (bold = mentioned more than once by same speaker, with number of mentions)
ADDING VALUE MEANS BEING PHYSICALLY CLOSE TO THE ISSUE
EXPERIENCE ENABLES STABILITY
EXPERIENCE SHAPES THINKING
FOCUS ON THE IMMEDIATE PROBLEM FIRST
INFORMATION MUST BE VERIFIED
PERSONAL COMMUNICATION SOLVES PROBLEMS (2)
PERSONAL EXPERIENCE IS THE BEST TEACHER
SUCCESS COMES THROUGH PERSONAL RELATIONSHIPS (2)
YOU HAVE TO INTERACT WITH ALL MANAGERS
VISION COMES FROM EXPERIENCE
WE NEED TO SEE THE DATA

and not just regurgitate what people told you; so that you can see clearly and understand clearly the interaction between the various functions." One needs *first hand experience* (PRIMACY OF PERSONAL EXPERIENCE) of events in order to determine and create *(BUILT STRUCTURE)* the appropriate *standard (STANDARDS AND COMPETENCE)*. *Personal experience, standard knowledge,* and *structure* interrelate as main concepts rendering the logic of the passage complete. I suggest this is not accidental but an expected and necessary way for IMCO executives to reason. Even if these schemas were coded differently, the relationships among them would still be discernible.

MACHINE

Table 6.9 depicts the fourth largest category, *MACHINE*, with 31 schemas. This category encompasses references to machines as well as operating systems, the tools needed to make machines run better, and the concept of *fixing*.[6]

References to organizations as machines and instruments to operate or improve them were evident in 10 out of the 31 schemas, as in *"we needed a guy who could get inside that business, help fix that business . . . and drive lean . . . the guy we brought in is a very solid operator . . . we identified he was a strong operator."* Another passage exemplifies the idea of culture as a

Table 6.9 MACHINE Schemas (31)

Shared schemas	Verbatim passage containing the schema (key phrases in bold)
ORGANIZATIONS ARE MACHINES Times referenced: 7 Number of people referencing: 2	The CEO and myself **retooled the entire company.** **We needed a guy who could get inside that business, help fix that business . . . and drive lean** . . . the guy we brought in [M], is a very solid operator . . . we identified he was a strong operator. We absolutely have a strong operator. **the organization just took off.**
STANDARD OPERATING SYSTEMS PROVIDE DISCIPLINE AND MITIGATE UNCERTAINTY Times referenced: 4 Number of people referencing: 3	So we build the tools. Every week we look at the outlook of forecasts of orders and sales, and profits and revenue of the business by product, by location. **So we have a very good operating system if you will,** to look forward, especially being in aerospace . . . So the team pretty much uses all the data and tools to be able to manage our business. **If there are performance issues to the customers, obviously we have to jump on it and then we fix it.** **Standard operating systems have rhythm, a standard way of doing things.**
CULTURE IS A TOOL TO RUN A MACHINE Times referenced: 2 Number of people referencing: 2	And I **try to utilize it** (culture) and try to use a business approach to **help me get to the result** without ignoring the entire culture spectrum under which I operate.

Unshared schemas (bold = mentioned more than once by same speaker, with number of mentions)
BUSINESSES HAVE INTERCHANGEABLE PARTS
COMPANIES ARE VEHICLES
CULTURE IS A MACHINE
GOOD MANAGERS GUIDE ORGANIZATIONS
GOOD RELATIONSHIPS DRIVE BUSINESS
MACHINES BREAK DOWN
MARKETS ARE MACHINES
ORGANIZATIONS ARE VESSELS (3)
PEOPLE ARE MACHINES (2)
PEOPLE CAN FIX THEIR PROBLEMS (2)
PERFORMANCE CONNECTS TO SUCCESS (2)
PRESSURE BRINGS OUT TALENT
RELATIONSHIPS NEED TO BE OPTIMIZED FOR SUCCESS

tool that can improve performance, as in "*I modified my style so I can use the Asian culture to motivate the group of people I have in Asia to perform to the best of their ability and achieve the result*" (*CULTURE IS A TOOL TO RUN A MACHINE*). The metaphor flagging the schema concerns performance of the people in Asia. One could, I suppose, think of this logic as pertaining to the performing arts or sports, but in the context of "*modified my style so I can use the Asian culture"* in the context of *achieving a result* suggests a machine that needs modification to its inputs (culture) to achieve an output (the business result).

As with schemas in other categories, *MACHINE* schemas draw from others to flesh out the discourse in which they appear. *MACHINE* schemas are usually elaborated by *STANDARDS AND COMPETENCE* and *THE PRIMACY OF PERSONAL EXPERIENCE* schemas. For instance, operating systems as ways to mitigate business uncertainty, as seen in *STANDARD OPERATING SYSTEMS PROVIDE DISCIPLINE AND MITIGATE UNCERTAINTY* suggest not an abstraction but a machine standard. *THE PRIMACY OF PERSONAL EXPERIENCE* schema seen in the passage *"so he's optimizing—his tendency is to optimize based on what he's used to, and not to optimize based on what the market needs"* connects the idea of *optimizing* to what one is personally *"used to."*

SPATIAL LOCATION

The least mentioned among the top six categories but the one with the highest percentage of sharing is *SPATIAL LOCATION* (10/22, 45%; Table 6.10). Many spatial schemas are common in business, and serve to support or reinforce other schemas, which I believe accounts for their high degree of sharedness. Conventionalized spatial schemas are often contained in conceptualizations about strategy, such as *we need to move into that market, the business is going south,* or *our strategy needs to take us to there.* Also common is the *SKILLS HAVE GAPS* schema, as in *"there might be a little bit of the gap there with some of the team as well."*

A few spatial schemas in this study, however, are less common, such as *DECISION MAKERS NEED TO BE CLOSE TO ISSUES.* This shared schema obviously relates to *PRIMACY OF PERSONAL EXPERIENCE* but differs in that actor proximity or perspective is either not referenced, or is clearly spatial, as when specified in terms of hierarchy against an entrepreneurial ideal: *"(you have to) drive decision making to the lowest level . . . (the reason why is) you own it (the business) cradle to grave, 'versus I have to get 12 people in a room to have a P&L discussion' . . ."* (*DECISION MAKERS NEED TO BE CLOSE TO ISSUES;* Table 6.10). *SPATIAL LOCATION* schemas also interlace with *STANDARDS AND COMPETENCE* typically through the concept of *gaps,* as in *"trouble making that leap,"* the implication being that the gap cannot be crossed due to lack of competence.

The Patterns of Structure

What may be clear from the foregoing is that the coding of schemas could have been otherwise and yet the findings would be similar. Would not more apt category names, better schema labels, or more insight into the logic of

Table 6.10 SPATIAL LOCATION Schemas (22)

Shared schemas	Verbatim passage containing the schema (key phrases in bold)
STRATEGIES HAVE DIRECTIONS AND LOCATIONS *Times referenced: 6 Number of people referencing: 3*	So if you're executing, **you have to have a strategy of where this business is going to go,** and what will it take to get there and what will there be for our shareholders, what's the payoff. **We're moving into the adjacent market.** So what we're doing is **building a strategic map** of where we want to be 5 years from now, **and where the capability gaps are,** whether it's the talent, product, channel, account positions, whatever the key drivers are.
DECISION MAKERS NEED TO BE CLOSE TO ISSUES *Times referenced: 4 Number of people referencing: 3*	My observation is that we move way too slow. And it could be my background in high tech. But I just see that it's a relatively slow organization. And it's because there's so much . . . **the delegation of authority is such that a lot of decisions need to move way up the line, and to people who don't add any value, because they're not close enough to the organization.** I actually had a consultant I was hiring for Africa, that I structured the contract such so we could terminate it with 30 days notice. So **the full exposure was $8 or $9k, or something like that, and it had to go all the way up to (CEO),** because at the time she was acting president, **then it had to go through the legal loop at least 3 times, and then it had to go to (President), and back down.** And this thing took 3 months, it seemed like, it took a long time, for exposure of $7k. **And you can imagine at their levels, they don't have any value to bring to the decision,** understandably.
SKILLS HAVE GAPS *Times referenced: 3 Number of people referencing: 2*	With the change with us to more of a execution operational base culture, you know, some of the people . . . have trouble making that leap to a little more of a discipline, rigor, hitting numbers, executing on commitments, **there might be a little bit of the gap there** with some of the team as well. So I have to **work with them to see who can bridge that gap and who cannot.**
COMPANIES & MARKETS EXIST IN SPACE *Times referenced: 2 Number of people referencing: 2*	So our challenge is formulating a **strategy to access the space** and right now through market survey, we've determined that there's really only one viable company.

Unshared schemas *(bold = mentioned more than once by same speaker, with number of mentions)*
BUSINESS PERFORMANCE IS ON A VERTICAL SCALE
CAPABILITIES NEED TO BE CLOSE TO CUSTOMERS
COMMUNICATION LEADS TO ALIGNMENT
DECISIONS ARE DIRECTIONS
PROBLEMS HAVE VISIBLE LOCATIONS
QUALITY IS A PLACE
RISKS ARE POINTS ON A LINE

each chunk of discourse yield different insights? Levi-Strauss saw schemas (without calling them such) as hidden by simplistic vernacular that served to impoverish them (Descola, 2013). As Quinn found with her study of marriage, individual words often only partially convey a schema. In the search for the products of *mental* content, therefore, how can language bear the brunt of our analyses?

The answer to this resides in the fact we are searching for *patterns*. Causal reasoning analysis revealed distinct patterns characterized primarily (though not exclusively) by notions of *standards, personal experience, structure, machinery* and *spatial relationships*. These patterns represent not only how IMCO executives express themselves, but how they *think*. While the content of thought as captured in these passages is largely explicit, the structure and character of it is implicit, conveyed by the nature of the logic and idealizations. The interrelatedness of the schemas and the way they are used in combination to enrich, support and frame the overall discourse is an expression of this tacitness. Schemas not only provide the foundation for more elaborate cultural models, but also structure many of the practices observed at IMCO, to be discussed later.

All that said, this single mode of analysis is not sufficient for fully illuminating schemas. Which means we must turn to a secondary method, metaphor.

2. *Results:* Metaphor Analysis

The point of the metaphor analysis was not so much to reveal schemas but to validate them, and to support claims of functional grounding. A concentration of metaphors in certain source domain classes, or certain types of metaphors (metonymy, conventional, etc.) would validate that particular schemas are cognitively real for these executives and relate to IMCO's task context and are not simply a function of discourse or coding. Of course, this is a bit like asking the fox to differentiate between turkeys and chickens as he stalks the hen house; my analysis of schemas could have predisposed my sensitivity to the metaphor analysis. While a possibility, I tried to control for this by conducting the metaphor analysis at the same time as the schema analysis so as to not have a finalized set of findings to which I was committed.

As with the schemas analysis, I continually refined the classification of metaphors and categories. This meant classifying, reclassifying, and challenging the analysis to determine whether a given metaphor was plausible given the sentence, and given what the speaker might have been trying to convey.

I classified a metaphor as any non-literal analogical mapping between domains, and metonymy as any mapping within the same domain. Procedurally, I first counted all metaphors and sorted them by topic of conversation (for example, Figure 6.9). Since speakers often digressed or rambled, topics resembled, but did not exactly correspond to, the question asked. Thus, a question about strategy could turn into an answer about culture or organizational challenges, therefore the topic consisted of what the speaker was speaking about, not the content of the question.[7]

I then grouped metaphors by class. This was a subject heading to classify metaphors by source domain. For example, some of the classes concerning challenges included CHALLENGES AS PHYSICAL OBJECTS or CHALLENGES AS SPATIAL LOCATIONS. Metaphor classes were built up inductively from smaller classes. Thus, CHALLENGES AS PHYSICAL OBJECTS contained subclasses such as metaphors about BUILT STRUCTURE or metaphors involving CONTAINERS. Each subclass was comprised of the metaphors themselves. Thus CONTAINERS consisted of metaphors such as "*I looked into the financials*"; "*the right culture in the talent and in the managers*"; and "*we tend to be very inwardly focused*," and so forth. Assignment of a metaphor to a subclass and class was based on the lowest possible category inferred from the context of the sentence. This was one way to try to overcome the effects of polysemy.[8] Class assignment, of course, was a function of intuition, but an intuition honed by months of analysis, the imposition of analytical rules, and a distilled sensitivity to the diction and discourse patterns of my subjects. I was as unparsimonious as possible with class designations in order to resist the temptation to impose too much structure on the data too quickly. This inductive, bottom-up approach preserved an emic position in the research.

The analysis thus produced 2,651 metaphors grouped into 26 source domain classes. By classifying individual metaphors into source domain classes, over time I came to see how the source domains matched the schema categories. This was not a one-to-one correspondence, but as the number of metaphor classes built up, a correspondence with the schemas took shape. As Quinn suggested, each individual metaphor flags the potential existence of an underlying schema. The greater the number of metaphors with the same or similar source domain, the higher the likelihood of a collection of schemas related to that domain. If the results of the metaphor classification on the whole yielded the same or similar results to the causal reasoning analysis, this could mean the schemas adduced were cognitively real and salient for informants. It would be unlikely that informants could share a number of schemas, such as those in the *BUILT STRUCTURE* category, and use metaphors with a similar source domain if these structures were not in some way a feature of their thinking and not simply accidents of speech. And a high prevalence of metaphors related to manufacturing, or metaphors suggestive of the strategic task environment of IMCO, could be taken as provisional evidence of functional grounding.

Another feature of the analysis was to look at whether a metaphor was novel, conventional, or a metonymy. As discussed in Chapter 5, to Barcelona (2003; also see Radden, 2003) metonymies are closer to schemas because they are experientially more primary. So an abundance of particular metonymies would theoretically correspond to prevalent schemas, and a particular class of metonymy could be indicative of that class's overall importance.[9] I classified metaphors as conventional if they were slang, jargon, or common idiomatic expressions in North American business discourse. Speakers used conventional metaphor to such an extent that, in many ways, analyzing them for content alone became almost pointless. The use of idioms or jargon often rendered the point being made *less* clear. Thus, I suspected my informants' use of conventional metaphors was for a different purpose, which led me to the idea of conventional metaphors as cognitive anchors, discussed below. All of these methods enriched the overall analysis and produced a saturation of data that increased overall confidence in the results.

Flags, Linkages, and Grounding

Of 2,651 unique metaphors identified, 72% (1,1912) were concentrated in just four source domain classes (Figure 6.9). The process of sifting and classifying that many metaphors over many months bestowed confidence in my classification scheme given the sheer numbers involved. While there were more metaphor classes than schema categories, the most frequent classes corresponded remarkably well with the schema categories. Many of the patterns seen in the schema analysis were seen in the source domains, with a high degree of alignment between the two modes of analysis. Because a high percentage or metaphors were contained in just four source domains, I considered these classes representative of the whole. Thus the discussion that follows is limited to these four classes.

LIVING THINGS was the most frequently referenced source domain, with 596 metaphors (22.5% of all metaphors). The prevalence of this class was no surprise. LIVING THINGS is a highly conventionalized class of metaphor common in business discourse. I would expect every organization in North America and Western Europe to show similar frequencies.[10] What was more noteworthy was the *near equal* prevalence of the other three classes: PHYSICAL STRUCTURE OR OBJECT, SPATIAL LOCATION and MACHINE together made up nearly half (49%) of the remaining classes (Figure 6.9). The PHYSICAL STRUCTURE OR OBJECTS class with 22% (591) of all metaphors not only showed a high number of metaphors pertaining to unspecified *physical objects*, but also to *structures*, the action of *building* things, and to the notion of a *piece* (Table 6.11).

Unlike the schema analysis, I did not separate a general *physical object* from a *built structure* class. This was due to the polysemy of many metaphors; the effect of such a distinction was of marginal analytic value as it did not impact the results. That said, *built structure* was the most frequent metaphor subclass (Table 6.11) with 95 metaphors, more than twice as frequent as any other subclass. This reinforced the idea that the concept of *built structure* is both discursively and cognitively figural for this group.

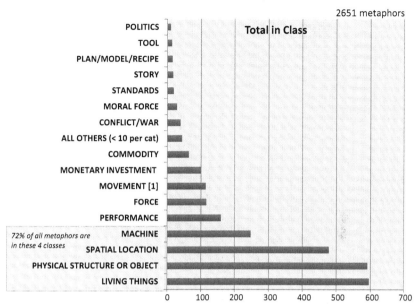

Figure 6.9 Most frequently mentioned metaphor source domains.

The interview topic of Challenges and Mitigations generated 70% of all the metaphors.[11] Tables 6.11–6.13 show a sample of the metaphors for this topic, beginning with PHYSICAL STRUCTURE OR OBJECT and the most frequent subclasses, along with the actual metaphor exemplars within the subclasses.

The metaphors informants used often did more than mark the presence of underlying schemas. They also made the schemas more robust and at times linked different schemas. For example, from the table above one can see how PHYSICAL OBJECT metaphors relate to schemas pertaining to *STANDARDS AND COMPETENCE*: "*our ability to put that (acquisition capability) in place*"; "*And a lot of it frankly is setting the expectations across the board (for better standards)*," etc. In other cases, PHYSICAL OBJECT metaphors linked a *BUILT STRUCTURE* schema with a *PRIMACY OF PERSONAL EXPERIENCE* schema, as in "*such that I could step away from the business and not have it collapse.*" These metaphors not only served to enrich the narrative but also to connect bits of logic into coherent wholes.

Table 6.11 PHYSICAL STRUCTURE OR OBJECT metaphors

CHALLENGES OR MITIGATIONS AS STRUCTURE THAT IS BUILT	PROBLEMS ARE PHSYICAL OBJECTS	CHALLENGES OR MITIGATIONS AS PARTS OR PIECES	CHALLENGES OR MITIGATIONS AS CONTAINER	STRATEGY OR MITIGATION AS STRUCTURAL SUPPORT	INITIATIVES, ROLES, PROCESSES, PLANS ARE OBJECTS
95	37	34	30	29	22
build engineering competency	The internal barriers are oftentimes the way we identify the gaps	its very difficult to put it all together (information, complexity)	and the team believes they can do x amount in volume	the product lines that support those markets	I could fill the role
build global competence	(for the contractor) it should not show up as an issue	it's a 2-piece puzzle	I looked into the financials	I have had tremendous success with it (the structure)	I could fill it professionally
building the idea of a global engineering community	So far it's not a big issue	I was able to do the growth piece as well	One biggest challenge that I see with IMCO as a whole is that we tend to be very inwardly focused	we jump on the business review	especially the technical competency and know-how resides in the US
build a pipeline (of successors)	instead of letting things kind of waffle around.	the HR piece (is going to be . . .)	the right culture in the talent and in the managers	(points of leverage) that we can bring to the table and secure more business	I was always part of the strategy and what happened
build a robust cadence of meetings	try to find the threads of things in the different issues that apply to your business	that's why I've been discussing the growth piece	bringing in the talent,	we've been really focused on getting our foundation solidified	And our ability to put that (acquisition capability) in place

build a talent development program	if you're looking at it (the issues) too finitely, you might not see things you might see otherwise	the other part (of the answer) is . . .	you bring into the organization (an expert)	The interview process at Hewlett Packard, etc. are very structured at how they're executed	you'll have to interface with all the managers and understand how everything goes together to be most effective.
we will address that (the gap) through work structure	there's a bunch of examples where they think they see stuff (issues)	versus just one piece (of the business that you own)	They step into the organization	and it gave me the opportunity to articulate why and set the bar higher (for making better hires)	All of these (processes) are not very smooth so far
that's what the purpose of this structure is		the next piece that is most important is the operational excellence piece	(I'm not the benchmark) in each one of these	And a lot of it frankly is setting the expectations across the board (for better standards)	but we need to weigh actions there
it's a stand-alone (the business)		engineering can be split into two different functions	there are still silos where problems (always fall from somebody else)	I think I'm being successful if I can get this organization's foundation solidified (in a solid strategic direction)	That (plan) was town out the window within 30 days
it's no different than the way you would do a VC		so many things to be on top of	it goes into complexity (talent challenges)	(have in place) morale in such that I could step away from the business and not have it collapse	

(Continued)

Table 6.11 (Continued)

CHALLENGES OR MITIGATIONS AS STRUCTURE THAT IS BUILT	PROBLEMS ARE PHSYICAL OBJECTS	CHALLENGES OR MITIGATIONS AS PARTS OR PIECES	CHALLENGES OR MITIGATIONS AS CONTAINER	STRATEGY OR MITIGATION AS STRUCTURAL SUPPORT	INITIATIVES, ROLES, PROCESSES, PLANS ARE OBJECTS
95	37	34	30	29	22
the talent required to run that structure		so many things to be on top of (2)	(we simply can't) develop internally		
		it's so complex (the business) therefore I have to stay on top of it	I don't have the visibility (into those organizations)		
		Personal challenge for me is to keep on top of all the demands that come from IMCO	(there are still silos where) problems always fall from somebody else		
		And then once you have the parts in order (of the model)	we put these types of account plans in our GDP (planning process)		
		is a particular piece of technology (that is highly leveraged in its application)	They (people who don't work together) all have their own channels and silos		

splitting departments into different areas of focus.

the competitive landscape being very, very fragmented

There's a huge opportunity to consolidate the fragmentation in this marketplace

are from pieces that we simply can't develop (internally)

And the next piece around that strategy

So there's an element here

So I started with the operational piece

(roll it up) into this market segment leader (relationship between PLMs and segment leaders)

because you can look at internal meetings

when you only have a 5 pound bag . . . (i.e. you can only do so much)

SPATIAL LOCATION (Figure 6.9) was the next most frequent source do-main with 478 (18% of the total) metaphors. Spatial metaphors, like spatial schemas, are highly conventionalized. They are also a feature of engineering discourse, so it was not surprising to find it in this group given that 30% of my informants had engineering backgrounds (Table 6.5), and that IMCO's industrial products are highly engineered. But the frequency of SPATIAL LOCATION metaphors at IMCO was noteworthy for several additional reasons. First, the two most prevalent subclasses within this domain were CHALLENGES AND MITIGATIONS AS LOCATIONS, specified and un-specified (Table 6.12), containing a number of metaphors having to do with personal experience, as in (*you have to*) "*stay in front of them*" (*the chal-lenges*); "*I was always in the middle of it*"; "*You're talking aerospace here, I got a medical thing over here, I got rail over here, I got heavy equipment over here*" (describing a factory floor); and "*people who don't add any value, because they're not close enough to the organization.*" These meta-phors are well suited to illuminating *PRIMACY OF PERSONAL EXPERI-ENCE* schemas. It would be difficult to express a schema about personal experience without a location referent.

Second, the next most frequent subclass, CHALLENGES AND MITI-GATION AS HIERARCHY, beautifully illuminates *STANDARDS AND COMPETENCE* schemas, as in "*the first 4 or 5 are going to be somewhere in the top 12*"; "*they had trouble coming up to the new expectations; "he concentrated all his attention at his level*"; and "*decline already so low that we won't be able to support a manufacturing plant for such a business.*" Again, it would be hard to express a schema involving an expectation of competence without thinking spatially in terms of a hierarchy. The high prevalence of complementary (to the schemas) metaphors is an indication of the pervasiveness of such schemas.

Third, spatial metaphors link up different schemas. For example, "*You really have to go from tactical to strategic and talk across a broad range of functional activities*" joins a *PRIMACY OF PHYSICAL EXPERIENCE* schema with a *STANDARDS AND COMPETENCE* schema. The logic of the passage is about the need to be knowledgeable and credible across do-mains. At the heart of the schema is the spatial metaphor *go from . . . and talk across*. Without the concept of *across a range of activities*, the twin ideas of *standard of mastery* and *physical experience* cannot be joined. This example illustrates how metaphors play a central role in linking different schemas. At IMCO, most such linkages are established by relatively few classes of metaphor.

The source domain of MACHINE (247 metaphors, 9% of total) was the next most frequent, containing a high number of metaphors involving *fixing, running, optimizing*, and *functioning*. MACHINE metaphors that relate to *fixing* or *operating* (as in operating a business) are also highly con-ventionalized in business discourse.

MACHINE metaphors relate closely to *PRIMACY OF PERSONAL EXPERIENCE* schemas, such as "*I was an expert at fixing broken*

Table 6.12 SPATIAL LOCATION metaphors

CHALLENGES AND MITIGATION AS LOCATION (SPECIFIED)	CHALLENGES AND MITIGATION AS LOCATION (UNSPECIFIED)	CHALLENGES AND MITIGATION AS HIERARCHY	PROBLEMS ARE PLACES
50	44	43	25
you have to be in front of that	looking around the corner (forecasting and predicting)	is there a really cool technology sitting down there at (position #) 33?	I go there, I know where to start, we studied the productivity of the line, find the root cause and find the actions
(you have to) stay in front of them (the challenges)	move their way around a complex organization	the first 4 or 5 are going to be somewhere in the top 12	he is also doing the same that I'm doing in trying to find better what we can do and identify the actions
I was always in the middle of it	. . . in all areas, from financial to backend (used to rigor)	they (my team) had trouble coming up to the new expectations	its not easy to find the root cause and the corrective action for that
put in place different solutions for noise isolation	we can get back into the innovation and technology area	more of an execution operational base culture	when to dive in and when not to dive in (to issues)
the people gap, the talent gap (gap in skills)	let's start with the position (in the marketplace)	he concentrated all his attention at his level	you have to know when to dive in or when to dive out of situations,
from an operations excellence standpoint	So that works both on the talent identification side as well as the talent development side	And then yeah, then you can get down to the processes themselves (and after you adapt the organization to optimize those)	How close do I get? (to the issue)
shifting my focus from there to India	So the guys and gals that work for me, the guys and gals that work around me, and the guys and gals that work above me	(And you got to be able to) play (communicate) at all levels.	my peers think I should dive in more

(Continued)

Table 6.12 (Continued)

CHALLENGES AND MITIGATION AS LOCATION (SPECIFIED)	CHALLENGES AND MITIGATION AS LOCATION (UNSPECIFIED)	CHALLENGES AND MITIGATION AS HIERARCHY	PROBLEMS ARE PLACES
50	44	43	25
we're going to be totally off the mark (with our forecast)	it could be one organization over and they do an excellent job	Decline already so low that we won't be able to support a manufacturing plant for such a business	So if they have me diving into issues without explaining it to them (my team)
So this is one area where we need to focus on	(some people) have trouble making that leap to a little more of a	it takes time to bring everybody to that level	Because if we make a misguided judgment there
in terms of the execution, I think that on that front I go back to the talent	there might be a little bit of the gap there with some of the team as well	but we need to strive for higher results and we need to have higher expectations of ourselves	So knowing and having the real good sense of competitive map and landscape is very important (to avoid problems in the market)
There are so many places to go making acquisitions	So I have to work with them to see who can bridge that gap and who cannot	(the biggest challenge) . . . will be the talent underneath.	I had someone map out (the value stream . . .)
what is the space, who is in the space	and I was able to go into the front end of the business	(the company to buy) could be a couple levels down out there day to day	Because sometimes the best and fastest way to fill that gap is . . . .
it's a place where we didn't do well	expand our strategic addressable market	they develop people below and around them.	as you dig in you find all kinds of complexities
but throughout the different functions we've been making pretty significant changes	start looking at adjacencies	the delegation of authority is such that a lot of decisions need to move way up the line	We looked at this business and said, ('We're not generating any value with this company')
Look for the areas in the current or adjacent markets	Although on the commercial side it's (business) been very good	(we are aligned) all the way down to the factory to the guy shipping product out the door	and then you have to work your way through all the complexities.

(focus on) the end market segment	people who don't add any value, because they're not close enough to the organization	(I encourage) the layer down	everything you do there is not easy because (they are an emerging market)
they kind of isolated us off in a favorable way,	In the back you have all your factories and they're just make parts and they're not really tied into the end customers.	(we are moving to) multiple GMs across the top	maybe everybody sees around that corner
(a few dollars saved through) back operation synergies	Just the front part of the organization places orders through the factory	with functional expertise down the sides (i.e. describing an organizational chart)	
There are resources around strategy, there are resources around finances, resources around HR	to try to get some market share where we are	they kept elevating it (the issue, to a higher level in the organization)	
I'll speak to it from an engineering point of view	You're talking aerospace here, I got a medical thing over here, I got rail over here, I got heavy equipment over here (describing factory floor)	So I instituted a process cascading from one customer down to just a very low level new technology	
we are very well positioned either on quality and cost	a personal challenge would be (this sounds weird, I wish it wasn't recorded right now) but some recognition for what's going on up here	if you know what you're trying to achieve you put those elements on top of the cascade	
and that (the efficiency) is everywhere	(So we bring all this information or chatter) back to the core		

businesses"; *"I had been fixing the foot track of the business"*; *"so I'd fix it and they'd move me"*; *"My (old) business, I ran it for 4 or 5 years"*; and *"when you start turning that many dials at once to get this pointed in the right direction."* They also help illuminate *STANDARDS AND COMPETENCE* schemas, as in *"people may or may not have all the competencies to function in their new role"*; and *"somewhere in the past that connection (between performance and business viability) has been missed."* Machines require standards in order to be appropriately calibrated and maintained. This class also links related schemas, as in *"obviously we have to jump on it and then we fix it"* (*BUILT STRUCTURE* and *MACHINE*), or *"you can get down to the processes themselves and after you adapt the organization to optimize those"* (*SPATIAL LOCATION* and *STANDARDS AND COMPETENCE*).

Metaphor class analysis illuminated how metaphors help link up schemas in a network of logic and discourse, providing affirmation of the cognitive salience of these schemas for this group of informants. The source domains also corresponded closely to the schema categories, suggestive of functional grounding in a manufacturing environment. These metaphors all 'make sense' in an ecology of machines, structures, and standards.

Language Games?

As put forth in Chapter 5, a major challenge in any research on discourse is to confront the possibility what is being observed has nothing to do with cognition but is simply the result of a "language game" (Martin & Frost, 2011). This is the view that what is being elicited is the effect of rhetoric in popular discourse, not anything related to how people think. For example, Urciuoli (2008) asserts that market and labor discourse shapes the way people talk about employment and skills, evidenced by a preponderance of metaphors concentrated on the market value of one's own skills. This position in its strong form refutes most of the cognitive stance on embodied and culturally situated cognition and instead suggests linguistic determinism. Discourse, and by extension cognition, is based on other discourse and not on language-independent factors that influence cognition.

There is no doubt that popular discourse plays a role in my informants' speech. Conventional metaphors, after all, did comprise 52% of all metaphors (Figure 6.10). Taylor (2006) points out that the difference between what is idiomatic and non-idiomatic is not clear-cut. Meaning-in-context may not be able to be discerned by the word alone. And use-in-context may have many variants. But the data provided earlier suggest the pervasiveness of the particular metaphors concerning physical objects, spatial location and machines is unique to IMCO, if not to manufacturing in general. If what I observed were simply the effects of language games without grounding on the basis of task context, a close correspondence with the schema categories would not be readily observed.

One way to test this is through synonyms. Could one substitute a different label without changing the essential meaning of the underlying text from

Table 6.13 MACHINE metaphors

PERTAINING TO A MACHINE	FIXING MACHINES	PEOPLE ARE MACHINES
27	25	23
mechanism we use in meetings	then it became a matter of not only how do you fix what's broken	people may or may not have all the competencies to function in their new role
the way that we run it (the business)	We all see examples of issues we need to fix and ways that we need to fix them	I understand the way people have to operate
we're going to have to do root lock	we should be able to get this fixed (supply chain issues)	somewhere in the past that connection (between performance and business viability) has been missed
We network with a lot of technical folks	I want to see my team fix this (problem)	people have to perform and deliver results
we've taken a few cycles off (i.e. time off)	these are not easy problems to fix	I recognize that the connection(between performance and business viability) is missed
cranking up the innovation	we can fix it (the business)	Having gone through that process in 2013 I shifted gears
My (old) business, I ran it for 4 or 5 years	I was an expert at fixing broken businesses	I use it (feedback) to bring attention the deficiency and then I work with the individual in a way to fix it
they're taking these technologies and customizing them for specific customer applications	it was really 8 businesses that were broken	or really to help someone fix a deficiency
the mechanics of how we do that (generate profi-)	keep (the parts of the business) what you can fix	there was a general manager, the one that was not performing, that had to be changed, so this was changed 4 or 5 months after I was in the job
when you start turning that many dials at once to get this pointed in the right direction.	I had been fixing the foot track of the business	it's mostly just getting them to the right spots so that they can optimize their contributions
let's look up and see how we want to drive this business	I saw this classic American business that was broken here	if you trust people they can perform very well

(Continued)

Table 6.13 (Continued)

PERTAINING TO A MACHINE	FIXING MACHINES	PEOPLE ARE MACHINES
27	25	23
We had gotten out of synch with corporate headquarters on some of this stuff	so I'd fix it and they'd move me	we identified he was a strong operator
you can get down to the processes themselves and after you adapt the organization to optimize those	and be able to fix it (the change) for them	We absolutely have a strong operator
he was running a $200MM division	I know personally based on my own gauge	what makes (people) them tick
even if it's still up to date in the technology	obviously we have to jump on it and then we fix it	Engage with their event engineering
to make a technical emergency of their (the customer's) request of quote	We are also working obviously on the supply chain	you have to have the engagement of the people of the strategy, the engagement of the people in the execution, so you have to get them to engage
then you flip the switch and it actually comes out	engage in fast engineering for certain solutions	I would advise my successor to also keep the broader IMCO . . . very engaged in the development of the strategy and the execution
you want that back into what you need to do with your (operating stock)	We have to service the customer with . . .	it's around keeping the broader team, if you will, engaged
we are not optimally utilizing our fixed assets	and that (the efficiency) is everywhere	
operating stock		
the (business) channels needs to be switched out		
fast forward another 10 or 12 months		

which the schema or metaphors were adduced? For example, many metaphors about standards were classified as FORCE because they were about exerting purposeful action to achieve a goal, such as *"he's surely smart enough to do that"* or *"he was able to maintain stability in the region."* *"We needed a guy who could get inside that business"* could conceivably be coded as a PHYSICAL OBJECT or STRUCTURE metaphor, or perhaps even a HOUSE metaphor, but I coded it as MACHINE (Table 6.17) because the speaker was talking about fixing things in a manner similar to a mechanic getting under the hood of a car. The discrete metaphor does not convey that; my knowledge of the context of the conversation and the environment is what enabled the coding. Even if other classes or labels were more palatable to a different coder, the overall pattern suggested by the data would likely be the same. This is because the use of synonyms in labeling would not necessarily change the general pattern. The sheer number of metaphors classified (2,651), along with the number of source domains (24), suggests the likelihood of coming up with classes nearly identical to the schema categories is low. I had my own analytical filters, to be sure, many of them based on my experience at IMCO.[12] But despite these constraints, the fact two different analytical techniques yielded similar results lends confidence to these results.

And it provides evidence for the cognitive salience of these schemas for informants. As mentioned, it is not clear how informants could share schemas such as those for *PHYSICAL OBJECT, FORCE, SPATIAL LOCATION,* and *MACHINE,* and also use metaphors with the same or similar source domains if these structures were not in some way features of how they think and make sense of their environment. And the prevalence of specific conventional metaphors and metonymies in fact signals their important structuring role in the cognition of my informants.

Metaphor and Metonymy as Symbolic Cognitive Artefact

Humans have a basic cognitive ability and tendency to project meaning onto tangible, linguistic, or cultural conventions in order to solve complex problems or reason more efficiently. In many cases such reasoning would be impossible without the use of these conventions, as discussed in Chapter 2. To Hutchins, the association of material structure with conceptual structure stabilizes conceptual representation. These so-called *symbolic cognitive artefacts* (Sinha et al., 2011) support and extend conceptual processes within abstract domains.

In order for cognitive artefacts to function as tools and resources they need to be highly conventionalized in the culture to begin with. Language in general is a weaker form of this phenomenon, but metaphor in particular, as pointed out by Hutchins, has special status. A key feature of a symbolic cognitive artefact is *conventionality:* cultural meaning finds expression in symbols and artefacts a culture takes entirely for granted. Conventional metaphors function as symbolic cognitive artefacts by allowing abstract cognitive representations to be grounded in taken-for-granted language. Take the phrase *"there might be a little bit of the gap there with some of the team as well"* (Table 6.12). The speaker is using the spatial metaphor *gap* to refer to skill and capability deficits within his team. *Gap* is an abstraction— a *skill* gap. The manager, of course, lacks a precise measure or physical object of reference to conceptualize how this deficit might manifest, and yet has little trouble reasoning about how to address it. The metaphor is so conventionalized I suspect the speaker hardly realizes he is using it. And yet it functions to cognitively ground the problem in a common frame in order to support and enable reasoning about a solution.

The same is seen with the conventional metonymy *fix* (Table 6.12), as in *"then it became a matter of not only how do you fix what's broken,"* or *"so I'd fix it and they'd move me."* Here *fixing* is a stand in for an elaborate set of ideas about how to address complex organizational or business problems. Or consider the conventional metaphor embedded in the verb *build*, as in (Table 11) *"build engineering competency"*; *"build global competence"*; *"build a pipeline of successors"*; or *"build a robust cadence of meetings."* These are referents to abstract and complex processes, such as developing successors for leadership roles in a structured and sustainable fashion. The simple conventional metonymy reduces reasoning about such complexities to something straightforward and tangible, if not trivial. The reduction is enabled by the metonymy; complex cognition is off-loaded to a common

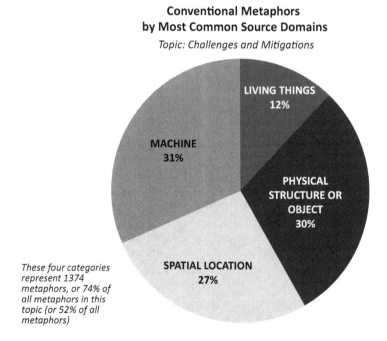

Figure 6.10 Conventional metaphors by most frequently mentioned source domains.

linguistic proxy in order to free up cognitive resources for other tasks. Such highly conventionalized metaphors and metonymies function as cognitive tools, not unlike how an altimeter or a compass enables and extends abstract reasoning and problem solving in the domains of time and space.

Within the topic of Challenges and Mitigations, source domains for conventional metaphors concerning physical structures or objects (such as *build*), machines (such as *fix*), and spatial location (such as *gap*) made up nearly three-quarters of all metaphors, and represented a rather remarkable 52% of all metaphors regardless of topic (Figure 6.10).

'Right'

The most compelling example of a conventional metonymy functioning as a cognitive resource is best seen within the schema *THE RIGHT PEOPLE (STANDARDS AND COMPETENCE*, Table 6.6), anchored by the conventional metonymy *right*. During the interviews and in the analysis I was struck by how frequently this idiom was used, as in *"the right people," "the right talent," "the right skills"* and so forth. Of course, there is nothing particularly idiosyncratic about *right*: the metonymy is highly conventionalized. What is noteworthy here, however, is its prevalence. Not counting uses of 'right' as a figure of speech (as in 'right' for *correct)* or an adjective ('right now'), there were 54 uses of 'right' as a conventional metonymy (Table 6.14) across all source domains. This was by far the most prevalent individual metaphor in the data, alone accounting for over 2% of all metaphors. Its frequency not only validates *THE RIGHT PEOPLE* schema; it highlights the salience of *STANDARDS AND COMPETENCE*.

The metonymy allows IMCO executives to reason and sensemake across domains using the same cognitive shorthand. The metonymy highlights and, I suspect, speeds up reasoning across domains, from strategic planning to materials forecasting to hiring. As with all symbolic cognitive artefacts, *right* stabilizes the schema and allows for other, more abstract cognitive operations to be performed, such as reasoning about strategy. Consider the following passage from one executive:

> *If you pretty much focus on any part of your business that is not doing well, you have to be honest with yourself and say, do you really have the right people in your organization? You gotta look at your strategy too, but if you find the right people, they also help you get the right strategy, especially if they have the right experience and knowledge. So I err on really hiring top talent.*

Clearly this executive is using *right* as linguistic and cognitive shorthand to both stabilize the schema (*THE RIGHT PEOPLE*), in the sense of making it clear, while also conveying an entire chain of reasoning concerning strategy and hiring built on it.

Table 6.14 The Uses of 'Right'

Metaphor Source Domain Class (all topics)	Instances	Examples
GAME	4	*"Playing right"; "the right team"*
INVESTMENT	3	*"Picking the right markets"*
MORAL FORCE	3	*"There is a right way and a wrong way"*
PHYSICAL STRUCTURE OR OBJECT	8	*"The right capacity"; "the right culture in the managers"*
LIVING THINGS	20	*"The right people"*
SPATIAL LOCATION	5	*"Get to the right place"*
PLAN/MODEL/RECIPE	1	*"The right formula"*
MOVEMENT	1	*"on the right path"*
COMMODITY	2	*"The right competencies"*
FORCE	2	*"Sending the right message"*
STANDARDS	3	*"Right or or wrong or indifferent"; "if you get these right"*
MACHINE	1	*"Turning many dials at once to get pointed in the right direction"*
WAR	1	*"the right targets"*

Ironically, as a conventional metonymy *right* may also obscure meaning. Someone's 'right way' or 'right skill' may not be another's. And yet in an environment where the need for standards and high competence are paramount, it is no surprise that a class of schemas should stand out marked and anchored by a widely used and well-understood idiom such as *right*.

Conventional metaphor analyses, along with source domain analysis, lent strong support for the findings accrued through the schema analysis. That more than half the metaphors in my sample (52%, Figure 6.10) were conventionalized metonymies pertaining to source domains concerning physical structures or objects (*build*), machines (*fix*), spatial location (*gap*) and standards (*right*) is evidence of both the valance of the adduced schemas and of functional grounding in manufacturing. These cognitive artefacts could not function as such if they were not common and well understood within the community to begin with. To be sure, these particular metonymies are conventionalized in business in general, but their prevalence at IMCO is not accidental. On the contrary, they are to be entirely expected given a complex global organization in the business of building physical machines and objects where the appeal to standards is of critical importance.

"Thought collectives" are always more "stable" than individuals, and provide a more substantive basis for studying cognition (Fleck, 1979, p. 44). The metaphor frequency analysis and the analysis of sharedness became hedges against idiosyncratic interpretations. Simply put, after the

25th occurrence of the conventional metonymy *right*, for example, I was compelled to seek out what was common across all uses. I could not very well interpret *right* one way in one context and another way in another. And while this may sound obvious, the sheer number of metaphors and schemas compelled me to pay attention to how I was interpreting each one. To control for my own familiarity with IMCO I tried to maintain as emic as possible a stance in relation to the data. Again and again as I sifted through the interview transcripts over the course of several months I tried to return to what the speaker was saying, rather than to my own interpretation of it based on my familiarity with the speaker or my knowledge of IMCO's business context.

3. *Results:* Quantitative Analysis

The purpose of the quantitative analysis, as stated earlier, was for validation of the data adduced through qualitative means. Of interest were two questions: Whether the schemas identified and categorized in the reasoning analysis could be grouped by factors independently determined through the quantitative analysis, thereby lending support to the coding choices; and, to see whether there were discernible differences between IMCO and non-IMCO respondents. With the latter the goal was to classify respondents solely on the basis of their degree of agreement or disagreement with the schema phrases.[13] If such differences were discerned, this could provide further evidence that the constructs comprised a part or whole of a distinct IMCO culture.

We administered a construct validation study using 61 adduced schemas with a group of 55 volunteer IMCO employees (none of whom had been interviewed) and a control group of 24 non-IMCO respondents from different industries and professions (n=79). Each respondent was presented with a short sentence based on the schema, absent additional context, and asked to rate the degree of agreement or disagreement with the statement as applied to their own work setting. All efforts were made to present verbatim phrases from the interviews, pre-coding, to reduce interpretation errors among respondents and to better validate coding efficacy. We analyzed the data using exploratory factor analysis (FA) and principal components analysis (PCA) with k-means clustering.[14] The schemas surveyed were those shared within the six most frequently adduced categories, in addition to those in the *FORCE* and *PHYSICAL OBJECTS* categories (Figure 6.7), as well as a few additional unshared schemas that exemplified their particular categories.[15]

Coding Validation

Factor loadings were set at a threshold of .05. A loading of less than .05 is quite weak; with lower thresholds one would start to see loadings with multiple factors (see DeCoster, 1998). Each schema was assigned a cluster based on the factor with which it loaded most strongly, and each cluster was labeled based on the category name representing the majority of schemas in that cluster. Each cluster was then assigned a percent score based on how many schemas from the original schema category could be grouped into the cluster based on the factor loading. Ideally we would see schemas of a similar type (e.g. *STANDARDS AND COMPETENCE*) clustered together, which would validate the coding. Also included were 'communalities', the square of the loading that shows how much of the variance was explained by the factor. Schemas with higher communalities were more representative of the underlying factor; that is, the factor explained more of the particular schema's variance. Table 6.15 shows this detail along with the survey items and the original schemas.[16]

Of the 61 schemas tested, nearly half (27, or 44%) loaded based on a distinct underlying factor (Table 6.15). These loadings were favorably grouped into seven distinct clusters. The number of clusters was based on the results—the number of factors yielding the best cluster score. An increase in the number of clusters might have resulted in more schemas loading with more factors, but the results would have been less informative because many schemas loaded with more than one factor. Thus, six of seven clusters showed consistency with the adduced categories. Of those six, four showed strong consistency. For example, Cluster 1 (Table 6.15) shows that 75% of the schemas loaded together based on an underlying factor, suggesting a correspondence to *BUILT STRUCTURE*.

Across all the clusters, *BUILT STRUCTUTRE*, *MACHINE*, and *FORCE* corresponded to the categories adduced by the qualitative research. When communalities were considered, two of the three 'mixed' clusters (2 and 7) showed the *PERSONAL EXPERIENCE SOLVES COMPLEXITY* schema explained much of the variance in those clusters. In the mixed cluster (Cluster 4, LIVING THINGS), *LEADERSHIP IS PASSION* best represented the underlying factor. While LIVING THINGS is a common schema category, the individual schema *LEADERSHIP IS PASSION* could also be thought of as related to personal experience *(THE PRIMACY OF PERSONAL EXPERIENCE)*.[17]

While it is the case that 34 schemas did not load with any factor and thus are unclassified, this does not necessarily invalidate the qualitative categorizations. First, the sample is small (55 IMCO respondents). It simply could be the case that this slice of IMCO only shares about half the schemas adduced from senior management, and thus no shared culture exists (although the face validation work and the study of how these schemas manifest in practice, described in the next chapter, suggests otherwise).

Second, some of the schemas could be misclassified. In looking at the schemas within the 'mixed' clusters, several could have been classified under *STANDARDS AND COMPETENCE*. They were not because of the parsimonious nature of the qualitative classifications. If a more precise category could have been inferred, the schema was classified in that category; if not, it was not.

Table 6.15 Factor Analysis of Qualitatively Adduced Schemas, by Resulting Clusters

Cluster Name	Cluster Score	Original Schema Category	Factor Loading	Com- munalities	Survey item (verbatim)	Schema
			Threshold > 0.5			
1: BUILT STRUCTURE	75%					
		BUILT STRUCTURE	0.74	0.55	"relationships are built"	RELATIONSHIPS ARE BUILT
		BUILT STRUCTURE	0.73	0.54	"confidence is built"	SKILLS AND FEELINGS ARE BUILT
		BUILT STRUCTURE	0.72	0.51	"culture is built"	CULTURE IS BUILT
		FORCE	0.71	0.51	"people get you to where you want to go"	TALENT IS FORCE
2: (MIXED: THE PRIMACY OF PERSONAL EXPERIENCE)	33%					
		THE PRIMACY OF PERSONAL EXPERIENCE	0.79	0.62	"the business is so complex you need to stay on top of it"	PERSONAL EXPERIENCE SOLVES COMPLEXITY
		STANDARDS AND COMPETENCE	0.72	0.52	"you need to have fundamental understanding of what's going on in the business"	DEEP INSIGHT INTO HOW AND WHY THINGS WORK
		SPATIAL LOCATION	0.71	0.5	"when you're a leader you have to look behind you to see what's going on"	STRATEGIES HAVE DIRECTIONS AND LOCATIONS
		STANDARDS AND COMPETENCE	0.71	0.5	"good listening helps you find what is said "	DEEP INSIGHT INTO HOW AND WHY THINGS WORK

(Continued)

Table 6.15 (Continued)

Cluster Name	Cluster Score	Original Schema Category	Factor Loading	Com-munalities	Survey item (verbatim)	Schema
		FORCE	0.59	0.34	"leaders need to leverage talent"	TALENT IS FORCE
		THE PRIMACY OF PERSONAL EXPERIENCE	0.5	0.25	"adding value means being physically close to the issue"	ADDING VALUE MEANS BEING PHYSICALLY CLOSE TO THE ISSUE
3: BUILT STRUCTURE	100%					
		BUILT STRUCTURE	0.65	0.42	"structure drives growth and develops talent"	STRUCTURE NEEDS TO BE APPROPRIATE TO THE MISSION
		BUILT STRUCTURE	0.59	0.35	"models solve uncertainties"	MODELS NEED TO BE FLEXIBLE
		BUILT STRUCTURE	0.55	0.31	"plans lead you out of problems"	PLANS ARE BUILT
4: (MIXED: LIVING THINGS)	50%					
		LIVING THINGS	0.75	0.57	"if you don't have conviction you will fail"	LEADERSHIP IS PASSION
		LIVING THINGS	0.69	0.48	"Culture is what makes people act in certain ways"	CULTURES ARE PEOPLE
		BUILT STRUCTURE	0.62	0.38	"competence is built"	SKILLS AND FEELINGS ARE BUILT
		STANDARDS AND COMPETENCE	0.58	0.34	"debates about contrary points of view lead to better contributions"	CONSTRUCTIVE CONFLICT LEADS TO BETTER CONTRIBUTIONS
		BUILT STRUCTURE	0.53	0.28	"skills have levels"	SKILLS HAVE LEVELS
		BUILT STRUCTURE	0.51	0.27	"When you get along with your peers"	RELATIONSHIPS ARE BUILT

Category		Schema			Quote	Label
5: MACHINE	100%	MACHINE	0.82	0.67	"people are machines"	PEOPLE ARE MACHINES
		MACHINE	0.73	0.54	"organizations are machines"	ORGANIZATIONS ARE MACHINES
6: FORCE	75%	FORCE	0.78	0.61	"talent is force"	TALENT IS FORCE
		STANDARDS AND COMPETENCE	0.66	0.43	"leadership is generating followership"	LEADERSHIP IS GENERATING FOLLOWERSHIP
		FORCE	0.6	0.36	"Engagement is a force"	ENGAGEMENT IS A MOTIVATING FORCE
		FORCE	0.51	0.26	"talent and skill get you to new levels"	TALENT IS FORCE
7: (MIXED: THE PRIMACY OF PERSONAL EXPERIENCE)	50%	THE PRIMACY OF PERSONAL EXPERIENCE	0.8	0.64	"personal experience leads to the best insight"	PERSONAL EXPERIENCE SOLVES COMPLEXITY
		STANDARDS AND COMPETENCE	0.51	0.26	"you have to be able to balance a lot of things at once"	MANAGING COMPLEXITY IS BALANCING MANY THINGS AT ONCE
UNCLASSIFIED		(34 schemas)				

In Cluster 2 for example, the *"leaders need to leverage talent"* item (*FORCE*) could have been classified as a *STANDARDS AND COMPETENCE* schema because one could infer the logic pertains to leadership competence. It was not coded as such because the speaker's logic in this case was ambiguous.

The quantitative validation exercise reminds us again that schemas cannot be completely represented by language. The fact some schemas are unclassified is not a failure but rather is to be expected. Schemas are often more complex than what can be conveyed in a single sentence. The fact there are at least seven clusters present suggests there are discernible patterns of shared mental content at IMCO, approximating what was identified in the qualitative study. While this may sound like a modest claim, in light of the framework being proposed—that culture is grounded in shared tacit mental representations—the existence of any shared representations confirmed by FA is not trivial given the limitations of language-derived modes of analysis and rerepresentation. When these data are triangulated with qualitative data and face validation (see next chapter), a distinct and directionally intriguing picture begins to emerge.

IMCO vs. Non-IMCO: A Distinct Culture

The second part of the quantitative validation consisted of attempting to group respondents solely on the basis of how they answered the schema items. We clustered respondents using FA (thresholds of .05) based on the factor on which their responses loaded. We then labeled each group based on whether they were 'IMCO' or 'non-IMCO'. Results were classified and visualized with K-means clustering on PCA-reduced data. We also computed the p-value for the mean result for each schema—the probability of getting these results under the assumption that the true mean result for both groups (IMCO and non-IMCO) was the same (see Chapter 5).

The results were promising. As visualized in Figure 6.11, IMCO respondents did in fact answer a majority of the schema questions differently than their non-IMCO counterparts.[18] The shaded background regions in Figure 6.11 show the clusters. The saturation of the shading of the regions represents the strength of the clustering.

The K-means clustering does not definitively imply there is a subset of unique 'IMCO' schemas. IMCO employees may simply answer differently to all schemas, for example. Thus, a complementary and more statistically correct method for assessing whether schemas were answered differently by the two groups was to look at the significance test. Table 6.16 shows 19 statistically distinct schemas for IMCO versus non-IMCO respondents at the 0.5 significance level. The p-value is the probability of observing these results under the null hypothesis; that is, that IMCO and non-IMCO respondents answered in identical ways on average. The lower the p-value, the more likely the question was answered differently by IMCO respondents (values lower than .05 are statistically significant).

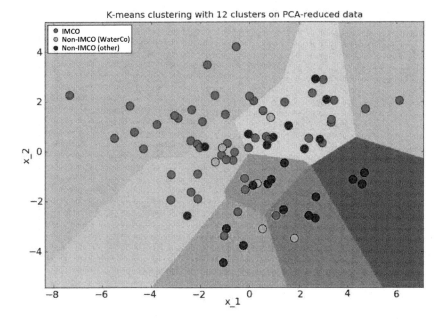

Figure 6.11 Clustering of results by IMCO and non-IMCO.

From Table 6.16 we can see how these 19 schemas were answered differently by the two groups.[19] *PRIMACY OF PERSONAL EXPERIENCE* schemas, in particular, can be seen as unique to IMCO respondents (7 out of 19, or 36%), and most of the frequently adduced schema categories—*STANDARDS AND COMPETENCE, BUILT STRUCTURE, LIVING THINGS, SPATIAL LOCATION*, and *FORCE* are, overall, more figural for IMCO respondents.

One might be tempted to the view that 19 out of 61 unique schemas is not a particularly compelling result. This position should be tempered. In addition to the analytical caveats described above, no large organization can be expected to have a wholly unique or bounded culture, for the reasons already described. Cultures by definition are porous, contested, dynamic, and fragmented. That a unique set of constructs emerges at all at IMCO, supported by two complementary but methodologically distinct modes of analyses, is directionally promising.

Summary

In this chapter I have presented evidence showing the existence of a coherent and pervasive set of schemas at IMCO shared by the executive team and at least some others in the organization. I have used a process of triangulation

Table 6.16 Schemas with Statistically Significant Differences in Response, IMCO vs. Non-IMCO

Schema	Schema Category	Mean IMCO	Difference from non-IMCO	p-value (significance level: 0.05)	Survey item (verbatim)
PERSONAL EXPERIENCE SOLVES COMPLEXITY	THE PRIMACY OF PERSONAL EXPERIENCE	3.93	0.72	0.01	"personal experience leads to the best insight"
PERSONAL EXPERIENCE SOLVES COMPLEXITY	THE PRIMACY OF PERSONAL EXPERIENCE	3.37	0.7	0.01	"to see how things work you need to be in the middle of it"
BREADTH OF EXPERIENCE ENABLES SUCCESS	THE PRIMACY OF PERSONAL EXPERIENCE	3.8	0.64	0.01	"you have to have breadth of experience"
BREADTH OF EXPERIENCE ENABLES SUCCESS	THE PRIMACY OF PERSONAL EXPERIENCE	3.22	0.64	0.01	"you can't go on what people tell you. You need to see for yourself"
DEEP INSIGHT INTO HOW AND WHY THINGS WORK	STANDARDS & COMPETENCE	4.1	0.55	0.01	"you need deep insight into how things work"
CONSTRUCTIVE CONFLICT LEADS TO BETTER CONTRIBUTIONS	FORCE	4.08	−0.38	0.02	"debates about contrary points of view lead to better contributions"
WE NEED AN OWNERSHIP MINDSET	STANDARDS & COMPETENCE	4.19	0.69	0.02	"we need an ownership mindset"
CULTURE IS HOW PEOPLE BEHAVE	LIVING THINGS	4.15	0.44	0.02	"culture is how people behave"
ISSUES ARE PHYSICAL OBJECTS	PHYSICAL OBJECTS	4.51	−0.28	0.02	"challenges come at you from different directions"

Statement	Category				Quote
STRATEGIES HAVE DIRECTIONS AND LOCATIONS	SPATIAL LOCATION	3.95	0.58	0.02	*"when you're a leader you have to look behind you to see what's going on"*
BUSINESS IS A BALANCE OF RISK AND REWARD	BALANCE SHEET	3.3	0.63	0.02	*"managing a business is managing a financial portfolio"*
ADDING VALUE MEANS BEING PHYSICALLY CLOSE TO THE ISSUE	THE PRIMACY OF PERSONAL EXPERIENCE	3.57	0.61	0.03	*"to find the root cause you need to be close to the problem"*
BREADTH OF EXPERIENCE ENABLES SUCCESS	THE PRIMACY OF PERSONAL EXPERIENCE	3.91	0.46	0.03	*"you have to be able to play at all levels"*
ADDING VALUE MEANS BEING PHYSICALLY CLOSE TO THE ISSUE	THE PRIMACY OF PERSONAL EXPERIENCE	3.15	0.61	0.04	*"adding value means being physically close to the issue"*
SKILLS AND FEELINGS ARE BUILT	BUILT STRUCTURE	4.13	-0.33	0.04	*"competence is built"*
MARKETS ARE PHYSICAL OBJECTS	PHYSICAL OBJECTS	3.84	0.47	0.04	*"by being focused your grab market share"*
STRUCTURE NEEDS TO BE APPROPRIATE TO THE MISSION	BUILT STRUCTURE	3.79	0.41	0.04	*"structure drives growth and develops talent"*
COMPANIES AND MARKETS EXIST IN SPACE	SPATIAL LOCATION	3.42	-0.45	0.05	*"companies are located in a market space"*
DEEP INSIGHT INTO HOW AND WHY THINGS WORK	STANDARDS & COMPETENCE	4.5	0.29	0.05	*"you need to have fundamental understanding of what's going on in the business"*

to demonstrate how converging threads of evidence from metaphor and schema analyses, as well from quantitative studies and the overall saturation of data reflect a pattern of discourse suggestive of cognitive structure. I used three different techniques in my analysis and conducted each analysis at different times, and the results show convergence around a subset of the data. For example, only two schema categories are not directly insinuated by the metaphor classification analysis: *STANDARDS AND COMPETENCE* and *THE PRIMACY OF PHSYICAL EXPERIENCE*. Yet examination of the subclasses reveals that metaphors pertaining to *standards* and *physical experience* ("seeing is believing") are represented across other metaphor classes in abundance. Informants used metaphors with source domains related to these two schemas but I classified the metaphors in other ways in order to stay as close as possible to the metaphor source domains.

I caveat these observations by acknowledging my perceptions are informed by my research at IMCO. Much as someone sees a map of a place now visited differently than before he or she journeyed to it, my work on schemas has put some of these observations into relief. I now 'see' these phenomena differently than before I did this research. But from all modes of analysis a storyline emerges. Several distinct cognitive orientations appear within IMCO characterized by a distinct bias towards *personal experience, built structure, standards, competence (or rules), machines,* and *spatial location*. These are not the only cognitive orientations, to be sure, but taken together suggest there are distinct ways in which this sample of IMCO employees think. Much like mapping a new and hitherto uncharted island, or perhaps sequencing a string of DNA, this rather elaborate effort of identifying, labeling and testing the content of mental representations comes to this: The schema, metaphor and factor analyses provide directionally promising results showing shared, cognitively salient and pervasive patterns of language and cognition. It remains to be seen whether these orientations are the result of functional embodiment related to IMCO's strategic task context, and how they manifest in practice. If the answer is 'yes', at least provisionally, evidence for functionally embodied culture may be said to exist.

Notes

1 While it might be tempting to attribute this to the fact informants were all senior executives whose job it is to make decisions based on reasoned judgments and causal logic, I found from my pilot studies with software engineers and HR professionals that these groups employ causal reasoning nearly as much. This type of reasoning appears to be a feature of professional work in general, and is not a function or role or hierarchy.

2 Henceforth I use the following conventions. Metaphor classes are denoted by CAPS; schema categories or individual schemas by *ITALICIZED CAPS* (as in the example). Direct quotes are denoted with quotation marks and italics.

3 *LIVING THINGS* contains schemas such as *CULTURES ARE PEOPLE* (*"have a healthy culture"*) and *LEADERSHIP IS PASSION* (*"resolute, solid, passionate leadership"*). As discussed in Chapter 4, not all schemas within an organization

will be solely the product of unique functional grounding. Much sensemaking in organizations is derived from common business discourse and schemas. This is likely due to the fact all businesses, regardless of industry or mission, share common concerns and interests, such as making money, selling products and services, and managing people. These activities result in a body of highly conventional schemas expressed through common tropes.

4 Strauss (2012) defines conventional discourse as shared schemas expressed in "stock ways" (p. 20).

5 This idea is captured well in Charan and Drotter's (2011) *Leadership Pipeline*. They describe the transition from functional management (e.g. management of sales or engineering) to business management (e.g. managing an end-to-end business) and the "shift," or discontinuity, of mastering new skills while needing to obsolesce old skills.

6 The reason for inclusion of *tools* in this category is that all references to tools were about improving performance or achieving a result through something akin to a machine.

7 I recorded six conversation topics: *Organizations, People, Business Strategy, Challenges and Mitigations, Culture,* and *Leadership*.

8 Polysemy rendered discrete metaphor analysis fruitless beyond a certain point. For example, arriving at a class more precise than STRUCTURE or FORCE or OBJECT (etc.) was a lesson in futility. Consider the following sentences (parenthesis indicate one of two source domain classes in which the metaphor could be classified):

"My plan is to back off a little" (SPATIAL or FORCE)

"I can get to the levels of something fairly quickly" (SPATIAL or STANDARDS)

"You don't have to necessarily be a subject matter expert in all of them" (PHYSICAL OBJECT/CONTAINER or STANDARDS). I took into account what other metaphors informants were using and classified according to my sense of the speaker's overall intent in the passage. But the more important aspect of the metaphor analysis was to identify which classes, in general, were most prevalent, how they related to the schema categories, and then to then look at the function of individual metaphors and metonymies in reinforcing or connecting particular schemas.

9 I used Radden's (2003) definition of within-domain mapping, looking for clear "stands for" relationships of correlation, complementarity, implicature, or category structure.

10 Source domains for metaphors based on people or living things are common in part because organizations are made up of people, and metaphors based on living things or people are, obviously, ready referents. This was also evident in my previous studies of software engineers and HR.

11 The Challenges and Mitigations topic produced the most metaphors in part due to the interview itself—much of it was focused on identifying challenges and discussing ways of overcoming them. But it also reflected the fact speakers were particularly animated by discussing challenges, barriers, and strategies for overcoming them.

12 My familiarity with IMCO's context allowed me to make more informed judgments about informant narrative logic and conventionality than an investigator unfamiliar with this environment. Of course, as mentioned, in many polysemous cases it was this very knowledge that helped the analysis. For example, knowing that the connector business unit was in a turnaround situation helped me make sense of that unit president's interview. Not surprisingly, he spoke at length about the challenges of returning a manufacturing business to profitability. This allowed me to ask more focused follow-up questions in the interview. In the end, I believe my familiarity with IMCO's business and context enabled a more

free-flowing and 'natural' conversation, which, in turn, facilitated the elicitation of richer data. Certainly this knowledge could have also skewed my interpretations. At the same time it may have allowed me to understand certain discourses in ways a culturally naïve (to IMCO) investigator might not have. It remains an open question whether the codings of a researcher unfamiliar with the cultural context in which a discourse is situated offers any value to the analytic process.

13 We used an agreement scale where 1 equaled strongly disagree and 5 equaled strongly agree.

14 'We' here is not the royal 'we': much thanks is owed to David Hayden of the University of California, Berkeley who ran this analyses and patiently worked with me to explain the results.

15 The reason why all schemas were not included was to minimize survey length. Because participation was voluntary, we deemed survey length to be important in encouraging participation.

16 Where there was no identifiable cluster corresponding to a schema category, the cluster was labeled 'Mixed', with the majority category in parenthesis (Table 6.15).

17 It is also conceivable to see the latent factor in this category relating to a general leadership category.

18 Included in these data are respondents from IMCO's sister company created from the same spinoff, 'WaterCo' (not its real name), as well as from other companies.

19 While the two groups answered differently, they did so in ways that was not absolutely 'true' or uniform for IMCO and 'false' for non-IMCO; some members. Some examples: The first schema *"personal experience leads to the best insight"* was 3.93 (mostly agree) for IMCO and 3.21 (mostly neutral) for non-IMCO, clearly more prevalent for IMCO, but there were individuals in the non-IMCO group that also agreed with this schema. The second schema, *"to see how things work you need to be in the middle of it"* was rated 3.37 (weak agree) for IMCO and 2.67 (weak disagree) for non-IMCO: Fairly neutral for both groups but on the plus side for IMCO and minus side for non-IMCO. The schema *"debates about contrary points of view lead to better contributions"* was rated 4.08 (agree) for IMCO and 4.46 (agree/strongly agree) for non-IMCO. In this case the schema was present in both groups but more important among non-IMCO respondents.

Bibliography

Barcelona, A. (2003). Introduction: The cognitive theory of metaphor and metonymy. In: A. Barcelona (Ed). *Metaphor and metonymy at the crossroads*. (pp. 1–30). Berlin: Mouton de Gruyter.

Charan, R., Drotter, S., & Noel, J. L. (2011). *The leadership pipeline: How to build the leadership powered company*. San Francisco: John Wiley.

DeCoster, J. (1998). *Overview of factor analysis*. Retrieved from http://www.stat-help.com/factor.pdf.

Descola, P. (2013). *Beyond nature and culture*. Chicago: University of Chicago Press.

Fleck, L. (1979). *Genesis and development of a scientific fact* (Fred Bradley and Thaddeus Trenn, Trans.). Chicago: University of Chicago Press. (Original work published 1935.)

Martin, J., & Frost, P. (2011). The organizational culture war games: A struggle for intellectual dominance. In M. Godwin & J. Hoffer Gittell (Eds.), *Sociology of organizations: Structures and relationships* (pp. 559–621). Thousand Oaks, CA: Sage. Retrieved from http://scholar.google.com/.

Quinn, N. (2005). How to reconstruct schemas people share, from what they say. In N. Quinn (Ed.), *Finding culture in talk* (pp. 35–84). New York: Palgrave Macmillan.

Radden, G. (2003). How metonymic are metaphors? In R. Dirven & R. Pörings (Eds.), *Cognitive linguistics research: Metaphor and metonymy in comparison and contrast* (pp. 419–445). Berlin: Mouton de Gruyter.

Sinha, C., Sinha, V., Zinken, J. & Sampaio, W. (2011). When time is not space: The social and linguistic construction of time intervals and temporal event relations in an Amazonian culture. *Language and Cognition* 3(1), 137–169.

Strauss, C. (2012). *Making sense of public opinion: American discourses about immigration and social programs.* New York: Cambridge University Press.

Taylor, John, R. (2006). Polysemy and the lexicon. In G. Kristiansen, M. Archard, R. Dirven, & F. Ruiz de Mendoza Ibanez (Eds.), *Cognitive linguistics: Current applications and future perspectives*(Vol. 1, pp. 51–80). Berlin: Walter de Gruyter.

Turner, V. W. (1975). *Revelation and divination in Ndembu ritual.* Ithaca, NY: Cornell University Press.

Urciuoli, B. (2008). Skills and selves in the new workplace. *American Ethnologist,* 35(2), 211–228.

7   Where Culture Comes From
Functional Grounding and Its Affordances

Conglomerates, by definition, exist to diversify and improve competitive position and produce better financial return for shareholders (Smith & Schreiner, 1969). IMCO's nearly 100-year legacy as a diversified conglomerate suggest values characteristic of conglomerates, such as diversification of assets and a portfolio approach to business management would be visible in a study of its schemas. Only two out of my 10 informants joined IMCO after it was spun off from the 'old' conglomerate IMCO, so it would be conceivable to expect more 'conglomerate mindsets' from this sample, such as an orientation to asset diversification and similar investment values and practices. These conglomerate orientations do manifest in some ways in IMCO practices, but, overall, functional embodiment based on a conglomerate task environment was not obvious. What was more in evidence were grounding effects based on IMCO's manufacturing task context, as seen through two strands of evidence. The prevalence of schemas related to ordinary manufacturing tasks and routines, and from the tasks associated with managing a global manufacturing enterprise.[1] How IMCO executives use metaphor is also evidence of functional grounding.

This chapter bridges the results presented in the last chapter with a discussion of IMCO's strategic task context, showing how it functions as the grounding source for schemas. I then elaborate on how IMCO's schemas manifest as culture through shared cultural models, and through what I call affordance structures, which include adaptations to the schemas. I close with a discussion of what else might account for these results.

1. *Manufacturing Realities*: Measurement and Certainty

From the evidence presented in the last chapter, IMCO's most prevalent schemas relate to *STANDARDS AND COMPETENCE, BUILT STRUCTURE, THE PRIMACY OF PERSONAL EXPERIENCE, MACHINE, LIVING THINGS*, and *SPATIAL LOCATION*. With the exception of *LIVING THINGS* and *SPATIAL LOCATION*, which are conventional schemas to be found across many different types of industries and occupational groups, the remaining four types are rooted in the task context of manufacturing. In considering each of these four, a connection to manufacturing tasks, challenges, or mitigation strategies, can be clearly drawn. For example, the grounding for *BUILT STRUCTURE, MACHINE,* and *PRIMACY OF PERSONAL EXPERIENCE* schemas is obvious. IMCO builds things—lots of them—such as brake pads, airplane seat actuators, connectors for cell phone chases, vibration dampening for tanks, and so on, and does so using complex machines. Its largest business actually makes machines (industrial pumps). The grounding for these schemas is the task environment of IMCO's principal means of production, the physical activity of manufacturing. The experience of working on a manufacturing line, even with automation and machining, provides a grounding source for *PRIMACY OF PERSONAL EXPERIENCE* schemas, exemplified—not coincidentally—by the metonymy 'hands on'. Literally, the hand makes the thing. In a pervasive and sustained environment of machines and industrial components enacted and sustained through physical labor, cognitive orientations related to *BUILT STRUCTURE* and *MACHINE* prevail. This grounding source, of course, is not unique to IMCO. Were this claim to be substantiated, similar schemas should be in evidence at other diversified industrial manufacturers. While this is the first study of its kind to examine this question, there is some anecdotal evidence that similar schemas are indeed in evidence at other similar manufacturers.[2]

Meanwhile, *STANDARDS AND COMPETENCE* schemas, I suggest, are less related to the physical task environment and more to the management of the challenges and risks involved in a global manufacturing business, and, perhaps, to IMCO's historical context, or historicity. While the differences between production tasks and their management are subtle, management activities also induce distinct cognitive orientations. A closer look at some of the principal measurement and risk management challenges in global manufacturing management makes this distinction clear.

Measurement in Manufacturing

Manufacturing is a measurement-intensive industry. Given the high costs and risks associated with the production and management of raw materials, supply chains, distribution channels, and labor, the need for close and accurate measurement of processes and productivity in manufacturing operations has been documented in virtually all industrialized and emerging economies. Scholars have studied measurement approaches to manufacturing output and productivity (for example, see Gupta & Goyal, 1989; Kaplan, 1992), supply chain management (for example, see Santos, Gouveia, & Gomes, 2006), quality management (for example, see Arauz, Matsuo, & Suzuki, 2009; Li, Rao, Ragu-Nathan, & Ragu-Nathan, 2005), lean and total quality management (for example, see Fullerton & Wempe, 2009; Li et al., 2005; Shah & Ward, 2007), and change management (for example, see Taskinen & Smeds, 1999). The need for performance measurement in manufacturing is closely associated with the increase in competitive forces resulting from the globalization of manufacturing activities and markets. As manufacturing organizations reorient their strategies, operations, processes and procedures to remain competitive, the need for accurate and improved measurement across all operational performance aspects is paramount (Clinton & Chen, 1998; Schmenner & Vollmann, 1994, in Gomes, Yasin, & Lisboa, 2004). Manufacturing's focus on measurement is one reason why manufacturing organizations were early adopters of standards like ISO 9000 (Singh, Feng, & Smith, 2006). Without the ability to understand and measure performance, benchmarking efforts related to lean, or so-called 'manufacturing excellence' aimed at instilling world-class manufacturing practices, are compromised (Gomes et al., 2004; Mann, 2009).

The creation of standards, and the need to formally define competence—what 'good' looks like—is an established feature of modern manufacturing. Thus it is no surprise that schemas associated with *STANDARDS AND COMPETENCE* surfaced at IMCO. *STANDARDS AND COMPETENCE* schemas are a result of a pervasive orientation by management toward measurement to improve efficiency and productivity. Activities such as Lean, Six Sigma, value stream mapping, or the establishment of appropriate production targets, require benchmarks against a well-defined standard. Lean transformation, for example, is a change to processes and practices based on a targeted standard (Mann, 2009). The basis of any lean transformation usually begins with the establishment of what is called 'standard work'—a definition of common tasks making up unit of work in a production line (Figure 7.12).

A value stream map compares the current with ideal in order to design an optimal process for taking a product or service from inception to production through to the end user (Rother & Shook, 1999). While true in other fields as well, these kinds of benchmarking activities are motivated by the significant potential cost saving such initiatives represent (Mann, 2009). This idea is borne out in IMCO's 2012 annual report:

> While Lean and Six Sigma have been part of our culture for more than a decade, Lean Transformations take it to the next level by involving every employee and touching every part of the an organization in an effort to streamline operations and improve efficiency and effectiveness.
> (IMCO CEO, 2012 letter to shareholders)

As such, benchmarking, or more generally measurement, is critical to establish a standard of excellence in service of maximizing productivity while lowering costs. Sustained over time, the constellation of such activities causes the induction of schemas related to *STANDARDS AND COMPETENCE*.

When particular schemas are well established within a community, they tend to be widely distributed beyond the professional or occupational groups associated with their use or induction. This may be due to the power differential between so-called 'in groups' close to the firm's core means of

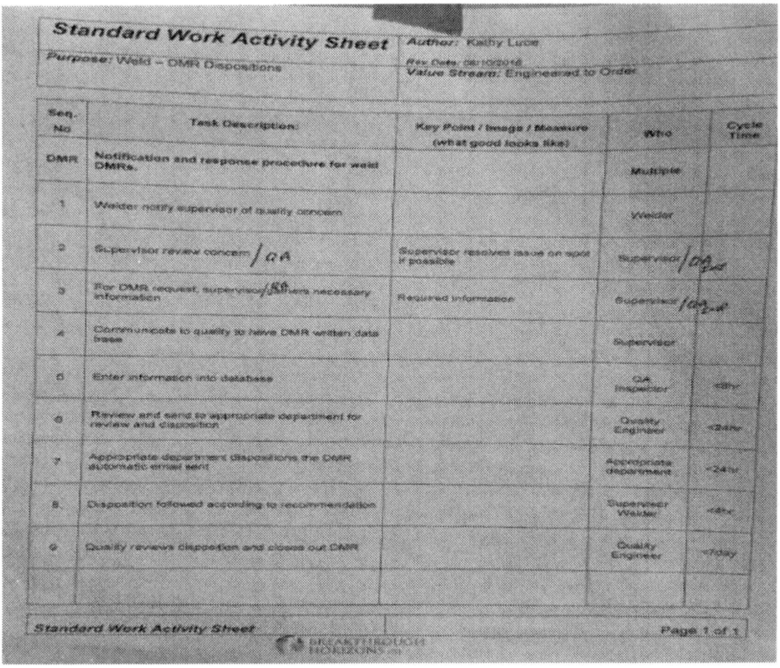

Figure 7.12 Standard Work definition at a lean transformation event (author photo).

production (such as software engineers in a software engineering firm), and those who want to be seen as affiliated with that group, or want to exert influence. This process often involves the tacit appropriation of the schemas associated with the power group. In my own observations at IMCO, *STANDARDS AND COMPETENCE* schemas permeate many functional activities well beyond manufacturing operations, from finance to HR to marketing, such as when a marketing manager told me he was "leaning out" his web design activities. These schemas manifest through both formal and ad hoc efficiency and improvement-oriented activities across many functions.

Historicity: A Collection of Small Businesses

As we saw in Chapter 4, cultural schemas are not learned as rules and precepts but are internalized little by little, without any overt teaching or transmission. Their logic can be traced in some cases through history, as may be the case in Restrepo's compelling study of honor code practices in the Canadian prairie, or in Strauss and Quinn's study of American marriage.

The phenomenon of historicity may also partially account for the grounding of *PRIMACY OF PERSONAL EXPERIENCE* schemas at IMCO. In its 100-year history, IMCO acquired hundreds of companies.[3] While many were prominent national brands, many others were small, family-run businesses, some with employees who began their careers and worked in the same business and location for 25 or 30 years, surviving a series of acquisitions to be, today, part of IMCO. Several of my executive informants 'grew up', as it were, in these businesses. One was the president of the industrial pumps unit containing what is currently IMCO's most well-known brand. In our interview he told me he still "bleeds blue"—he "bleeds" the color of the logo of the subsidiary in which he spent his entire career, and in which his father also worked as well as several family members. IMCO's brake pad business, similarly, consists of a decades' old manufacturer in northern Italy that started as a family-run business whose sole customer for many years was Fiat. IMCO's elastomer business was acquired in 2006 and is over 50 years old. Like most of the companies in the IMCO portfolio, this business runs as a relatively independent entity employing 250 people in western New York.

The fact IMCO's business are all distinct from each other and managed as independent divisions, or independent businesses within divisions, allows many of the prevailing schemas within those organizations to prevail. As a conglomerate, IMCO did little historically to integrate these businesses with others. Thus, while manufacturing-related schemas most likely underpin all of them by virtue of their task environments, in small organizations often it is the case that everyone knows everyone else.[4] This sense of social proximity sustained over many years, if not decades and generations, provides a grounding source for *PRIMACY OF PERSONAL EXPERIENCE* schemas. Social-proximity-induced schemas have been carried into a broader IMCO culture because several members of IMCO's executive team spent considerable time in these small units, including three of my informants. This may account for the fact four *PRIMACY OF PERSONAL EXPERIENCE* schemas in the quantitative study, *PERSONAL EXPERIENCE SOLVES COMPLEXITY* (*"personal experience leads to the best insight* and *to see how things work you need to be in the middle of it"*), and *BREADTH OF EXPERIENCE ENABLES SUCCESS* (*"you have to have breadth of experience* and *you can't go on what people tell you. You need to see for yourself"*) tested as most unique to IMCO (Chapter 6). Not surprisingly, loyalty and 'sense of family' are social norms and practices in evidence within many business units (as opposed to in the corporate office). It is ironic, but not surprising, that IMCO's culture-shaping project is led by corporate headquarters. As expected, it has been met with some skepticism by many in the local units as they perceive an effort to homogenize their own cultures.

The Management of Certainty

Dealing with uncertainty can be said to be a concern of management in all industries, but is of particular concern in industrial manufacturing given the high costs inherent in production, inventory management, and global supply chains (for example, see Bugos, 1993; Newman, Hanna, & Maffei, 1993). As put by Newman and his colleagues, "Manufacturing firms are continually bombarded with unpredictable and uncertain events from both outside and from inside their organizations" (p. 19). Firms have addressed this challenge by attempting to develop flexible manufacturing techniques and systems such as just-in-time production, the focused factory, as well as value stream mapping and lean production (Newman et al., 1993), or by implementing advanced program management methods to assure reliable project completion (Bugos, 1993). IMCO employs many of these standard industry approaches, including value stream mapping and the use of focused factories.[5] These activities represent highly rational ways to deconstruct and organize complex manufacturing environments in order to increase visibility, throughput, and thereby gain greater insight into potential production risks. The quest for certainty, thus, can be said to be the desired outcome of manufacturing management. IMCO is no exception.

The need for certainty in manufacturing I believe provides another induction context for *PRIMACY OF PERSONAL EXPERIENCE* and *STANDARDS AND COMPETENCE* schemas. "*Seeing around corners,*" a frequently heard metaphor (Chapter 6), concerns predicting and thereby attempting to mitigate risk. The *PRIMACY OF PERSONAL EXPERIENCE* schemas listed in Table 7.17 are suggestive of an operating environment where predictability in managing complex supply chains, compressed lead times, far-flung customers, multiple businesses and industrial segments, and a global workforce, are paramount.[6]

Certainty-management, I suggest, is also the induction engine for the most prevalent schema in my data, *DEEP INSIGHT INTO HOW AND WHY THINGS WORK (STANDARDS AND COMPETENCE)*, as captured in the reflection of one informant:

> *So you've got to adjust the lens to make sure you're seeing things clearly. I guess what it comes down to in my mind . . . is just awareness.*

Table 7.17 PRIMACY OF PERSONAL EXPERIENCE Schemas Related to the Management of Certainty

ADDING VALUE MEANS BEING PHYSICALLY CLOSE TO THE ISSUE
BREADTH OF EXPERIENCE ENABLES SUCCESS
EXPERIENCE ENABLES STABILITY
FOCUS ON THE IMMEDIATE PROBLEM FIRST
INFORMATION MUST BE VERIFIED
LEADERS HAVE TO PERSONALLY KNOW THEIR CUSTOMERS
PERSONAL COMMUNICATION SOLVES PROBLEMS
PERSONAL EXPERIENCE SOLVES COMPLEXITY
YOU HAVE TO INTERACT WITH ALL MANAGERS
VISION COMES FROM EXPERIENCE
WE NEED TO SEE THE DATA

> *Constantly be thinking—what should I be doing? Should I be doing this or not? Do I need to work this issue for somebody else take to care of it?*

This executive's almost obsessive quality of thinking is a product of the need to be 'seeing clearly' in order to mitigate risk and successfully manage the business. Table 7.18 lists the many *STANDARDS AND COMPETENCE* schemas related to the desire for greater predictability and certainty in IMCO's business and management practices.

These schemas reflect their origins: an environment of shared tasks related to manufacturing *things*, and a context in which dominant strategic activities of *measuring* and attempting to achieve greater *certainty* are paramount.

Table 7.18 STANDARDS AND COMPETENCE Schemas Related to the Management of Certainty

---

CAPABILITIES NEED TO BE RELIABLE
CLEAR THINKING SOLVES ISSUES
CONSTRUCTIVE CONFLICT LEADS TO BETTER CONTRIBUTIONS
CULTURES HAVE RULES
DEEP INSIGHT INTO HOW AND WHY THINGS WORK
DEVELOPING OTHERS IS KEY TO SUSTAINABILITY
EXCELLENCE REQUIRES STANDARDS
FOCUS IS KEY TO SUCCESS
GOOD MATERIALS PREVENT PRODUCT FAILURE
GOOD PLANNING DRIVES GROWTH
GOOD PLANNING LEADS YOU OUT OF ISSUES
GROWTH REQUIRES GLOBAL THINKERS
KNOWING JUST WHAT IS NEEDED FOR EACH PERSON
MANAGING COMPLEXITY IS BALANCING MANY THINGS AT ONCE
METRICS LEAD TO GOOD OPERATIONS
MODELS ENABLE THE RIGHT DESIGNS
ORGANIZATIONS MUST ALLOW TRACKING, MONITORING AND CONTROL
PEOPLE CAN PERFORM IF THEY ARE GOOD
PERFECT FORECASTING IS ACCURACY
PERFECTING THE BALANCE BETWEEN EFFICIENCY AND PEOPLE DEVELOPMENT
PERFECTING WHAT IS TRIVIAL
PROBLEMS HAVE A ROOT CAUSE—AND ARE SOLVED BY FOLLOWING THE SAME RECIPE
REPITITION YEILDS PROFICIENCY
RESPONSIBILITY REQUIRES AUTHORITY
RULES LEAD TO SUCCESS
SUCCESS IS COMPLETENESS
THE "RIGHT" PEOPLE
VERIFICATION BRINGS CERTAINTY
WE NEED AN OWNERSHIP MINDSET

The Language of Things

Technological grounding can structure a cultural community's use of metaphor, described earlier with the example of Qwest. This is not linguistic determinism, but examples of progressive alignment as described in Chapter 4. When task environments are rich with experiential exemplars from which an abundance of schemas can be induced, such as is the case with manufacturing environments, stronger and more pervasive schemas are created. Metaphor can also function to create better conceptual matches between source domains and targets. The frequency of particular metaphor source domains, therefore, can be evidence of progressive alignment.

At IMCO, the metaphor source domains of PHYSICAL STRUCTURE OR OBJECT, SPATIAL LOCATION and MACHINE, in particular, point to functional grounding in manufacturing: IMCO makes things (objects), and many of its products are, in fact, machines. While obvious and literal, I believe the physical task environment, encountered and enacted over years, provides the context for schema induction. The most frequent schemas and metaphors concern *first-hand experience, structure, standards, competence (or rules)*, and *spatial location*, and actions that relate to *working with, building, measuring* and *managing physical objects* and *machines*. These source domains were not evident anywhere to the same degree in my previous occupational studies of software engineers and HR.[7] Even if the codings were different at IMCO, due to the level of data saturation I believe the sheer volume of schemas adduced and metaphors identified points to manufacturing as a grounding source.

As discussed in the previous chapter, that a high percentage (52%) of metaphors at IMCO are conventionalized metonymies relating to physical structures or objects is additional evidence of progressive alignment. Metonymies denote schemas. When they function as cognitive artefacts this means they are already well understood and adopted in the community, which reinforces and solidifies the conceptual alignment between source and target for members of that community.

2. From Schemas to Culture

Schemas constitute a firm's culture in two ways—through sensemaking based on cultural models and through affordance structures. This section is devoted to a discussion of both phenomena as insinuated by the IMCO data.

Cultural Models for Leadership and Business Success

Cultural models underwrite the majority of group sensemaking activity. These are not models *of* the world, but *for* the world. As reviewed in Chapter 3, more complex schemas, and networks of schemas, make up a cultural model. Schemas and cultural models are appropriated as resources when they prove robust enough for sensemaking; that is, they render meaningful what is happening.

The network of primary schemas described in the last chapter provides the foundation for executive sensemaking at IMCO. These are not the only foundation for sensemaking; managers are capable of drawing from a great number of schemas and cultural models to structure their own sensemaking, and many of these will be conventionalized in the wider sociocultural environment, as we saw with *FORCE* and *SPATIAL* schemas (and see Chapter 4). But some will be rooted in the task context of the organization and (or) the dominant professional orientation of its managers. The more that are, the more distinct a culture will appear.

As described earlier, schemas and models are hierarchically organized, with more primary tacit schemas organizing more complex cultural models. The underlying schemas underwrite and constrain the logic of more complex models. Figures 7.13 and 7.14 provide examples, showing how IMCO's schemas make up two important cultural models for leadership and general business success. The arrows between the schemas show the interrelatedness of the logic within them.

For example (Figure 7.13), *BUILT STRUCTURE* schemas, along with others, comprise IMCO's shared cultural model of leadership: Leadership success derives, in part, from having a solid organizational foundation, from building a culture, from building (strong) relationships, and from having the right kind of organizational structure for the size of the organization. Successfully managing a business at IMCO means conceptualizing these activities in terms of *built structure*, *standards*, *personal experience*, *numbers*, *machine*, and so on.

What is immediately evident is how thoroughly unremarkable these models are. The schemas that comprise them sound mundane and familiar. Anyone who has spent time in a manufacturing environment will likely have a 'so what' reaction to them. And that is precisely the point. Individual schemas, in their experientially grounded tacitness, are taken-for-granted features of cognition.

As presented earlier, schemas anchor as well as *extend* each other. For example the schema *DEEP INSIGHT INTO HOW AND WHY THINGS WORK*, central to both cultural models, becomes figural and meaningful when extended by schemas related to personal experience or built structure (Figure 7.13), or machines and numbers (Figure 7.14). As individual units of cognition, the schemas are trivial, obvious, and incomplete; taken as a network they structure a complex and elaborate model for running a successful manufacturing enterprise. By 'structure' I mean shape and characterize the cultural model in terms of its constitutive features: *Built structure*, *standards*, *personal experience*, *machine*, and so forth shape the logic, narrative and *character* of the model. Most managers, I suspect, when prompted will recognize that organizations are not literally machines (etc.). This does not

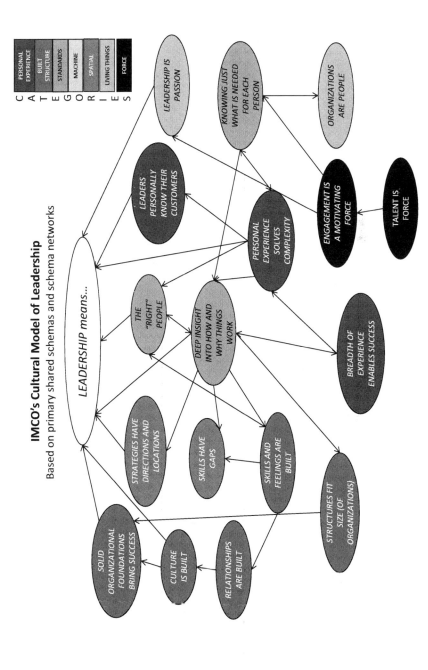

IMCO's Cultural Model of Leadership

Based on primary shared schemas and schema networks

C	PERSONAL EXPERIENCE
A	BUILT STRUCTURE
T	
E	STANDARDS
G	MACHINE
O	
R	SPATIAL
I	
E	LIVING THINGS
S	FORCE

LEADERSHIP means...

LEADERSHIP IS PASSION

KNOWING JUST WHAT IS NEEDED FOR EACH PERSON

ORGANIZATIONS ARE PEOPLE

LEADERS PERSONALLY KNOW THEIR CUSTOMERS

PERSONAL EXPERIENCE SOLVES COMPLEXITY

ENGAGEMENT IS A MOTIVATING FORCE

TALENT IS FORCE

THE "RIGHT" PEOPLE

DEEP INSIGHT INTO HOW AND WHY THINGS WORK

BREADTH OF EXPERIENCE ENABLES SUCCESS

STRATEGIES HAVE DIRECTIONS AND LOCATIONS

SKILLS HAVE GAPS

SKILLS AND FEELINGS ARE BUILT

SOLID ORGANIZATIONAL FOUNDATIONS BRING SUCCESS

CULTURE IS BUILT

RELATIONSHIPS ARE BUILT

STRUCTURES FIT SIZE (OF ORGANIZATIONS)

Figure 7.13 IMCO's cultural model of leadership based on primary schemas.

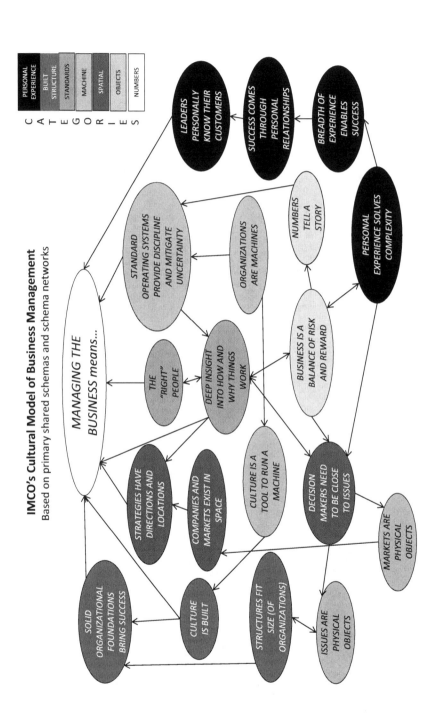

IMCO's Cultural Model of Business Management
Based on primary shared schemas and schema networks

CATEGORIES
- PERSONAL EXPERIENCE
- BUILT STRUCTURE
- STANDARDS
- MACHINE
- SPATIAL
- OBJECTS
- NUMBERS

LEADERS PERSONALLY KNOW THEIR CUSTOMERS

SUCCESS COMES THROUGH PERSONAL RELATIONSHIPS

BREADTH OF EXPERIENCE ENABLES SUCCESS

STANDARD OPERATING SYSTEMS PROVIDE DISCIPLINE AND MITIGATE UNCERTAINTY

ORGANIZATIONS ARE MACHINES

NUMBERS TELL A STORY

PERSONAL EXPERIENCE SOLVES COMPLEXITY

MANAGING THE BUSINESS means...

THE "RIGHT" PEOPLE

DEEP INSIGHT INTO HOW AND WHY THINGS WORK

BUSINESS IS A BALANCE OF RISK AND REWARD

STRATEGIES HAVE DIRECTIONS AND LOCATIONS

COMPANIES AND MARKETS EXIST IN SPACE

CULTURE IS A TOOL TO RUN A MACHINE

DECISION MAKERS NEED TO BE CLOSE TO ISSUES

MARKETS ARE PHYSICAL OBJECTS

SOLID ORGANIZATIONAL FOUNDATIONS BRING SUCCESS

CULTURE IS BUILT

STRUCTURES FIT SIZE (OF ORGANIZATIONS)

ISSUES ARE PHYSICAL OBJECTS

Figure 7.14 IMCO's cultural model of business management based on primary schemas.

stop them from thinking and acting as if they were. In this way cultural models make these activities culturally relevant and meaningful.

Not Just Belief Systems

Which brings us to a key point. Cultural models form the foundation for culture because they collectively comprise what a community believes is meaningful. Cultural models are not to be confused with 'systems of belief'. What makes a cultural model different is that it characterizes the assumptive nature and logic of the belief, whereas a belief system is a consciously held set of ideas and values. Beliefs are built from schemas, to be sure, but beliefs pertain to content; cultural models pertain to content *and* structure. When describing complex problem solving if a manager says "*I looked deeply into that issue*" he is not only describing a belief that looking deeply, or *deep insight*, is important for understanding complex issues, but is also describing what it is like to do so. That is, complex issues require time and depth of insight. The metaphor *deep insight* is constitutive of the schema *DEEP INSIGHT INTO HOW AND WHY THINGS WORK*, which is part of the more elaborate model about managing a business. And because they are borne out of an experiential grounding source, they offer clues as to why the belief is as it is to begin with. Sensemaking in this way is always more than just thinking. It is meaning making retrospectively shaped, structured, colored, and flavored by experience.[8]

As such, these cultural models comprise how IMCO leaders make sense of leadership and business success. Other cultural models could be dynamically derived from the same pool of schemas, resulting in a set of models for all domains of organizational sensemaking. Taken together, they would make up what could be readily identified as culture.

Affordance Structures

Up until now we have been focused on schemas observed through language. Although we showed through our quantitative study the existence of latent factors based on schemas, to obtain these results our survey was of necessity derived from the same language-based codings through which we adduced the schemas. To observe what Descola calls the "structural subconscious" one must be attuned not to only to language but to practice, to how schemas manifest "among the properties of the institution that reveal it to the observer" (2013, p. 93). As stated in Chapter 4, practices to Swidler can be "read" for the schemas they contain. Swidler's use of the term "practice," however, is all encompassing. It subsumes language, whereas I believe language, and semiotic forms in general, are their own domains. Once constituted as such they become eligible as objects of praxis. Schemas power and endow practices with dynamic, particular and often idiosyncratic qualities and features. For these reasons I prefer the term *affordance structures*.

The term *affordance* was introduced by the perceptual psychologist James Gibson to refer to what the perceived environment offers, or *affords*, for action.[9] Donald Norman appropriated the term in the context of design and human–machine interaction to mean action possibilities as perceived by an actor (McGrenere & Ho, 2000). Affordances specify the range of possible activities and relationships among actors and objects (McGrenere & Ho, 2000). It is in this secondary sense I use the term to refer to the possible activities and relationships among actors and actual or imagined organizational structures—practices, processes, routines, behaviors, habits, norms, practiced values, organizational designs, physical layouts, and the like—that manifest schemas. One might, of course, think of affordances as visible 'culture'. But affordances are more. They instantiate schemas within real, or assumed to be real practices actors enact or appropriate in response to inputs at the sensemaking boundary. Some affordances are physical, like the choice of logo or the layout of offices. More often they are patterns of behavior, or sanctioned and expected formal and informal practices, processes, routines, habits, or norms. They extend to *practised* rather than espoused values.[10]

Actors will hold up affordance structures as paragons of their own culture. These will be practices deemed most essential to the firm's functioning or survival, and, unsurprisingly, will tend to be those most vigorously rationalized and defended. Thus, affordance structures are not only *how we do things around here*, but entail an inherent justification, as in *what those things are* and *why we do them to begin with*.

Affordance structures have a dual, or adaptive, function. They manifest as schema-endowed practices, but also as adaptations to those practices, and by extension the schemas that underwrite them. In Steele's language, affordances and adaptations may reflect the "overlearned," indiscriminate and unconscious application of schemas across domains. Thus, in the same way an airline obsessed with efficiency and time reflexively applies time pressure to a merger where time pressure is counterproductive to successful integration, so do many of the schemas identified at IMCO manifest as indiscriminate and unconscious practices across domains. Figures 7.15–7.18 provide examples.

Affordance structures are how cultures come to be recognized as such by their own members. To illustrate, once I achieved over several months what I believed was a satisfactory analysis of the interview data, I presented my findings to the CEO and two members of her staff not part of the original interviews. I used this meeting as a face validation exercise to determine whether the adduced schemas 'made sense' to them. I also used our meeting to present how I had observed the schemas manifest across affordances. The CEO and her team wholeheartedly agreed with the schema findings, but were most intrigued by the affordances because it was through these practices that most of the schemas took shape and acquired meaning. Within them they could 'see' their own culture, not necessarily as they idealized it, but as they perceived how it actually 'operated'.

The rest of this section illustrates a few of the most noticeable affordance structures and adaptations at IMCO. They include a mixture of organized processes and practices as well as informal practices, including normative ones related to social acceptability. The goal here is illustrative, to convey how schemas power practice. Figures 7.15–7.18 are the product of my own observations and field notes over the course of several years of work at IMCO. Methodologically these should be read as the output of an extended case study, as discussed in Chapter 5. The affordances are organized by schema category. To the left in the diagram is the category and most prevalently shared schemas informing the practices. At the center are the practices themselves, and at the right the adaptations to these schemas as observed over time. Like their underlying schemas, affordances are not isomorphic with individual schemas but can be underwritten by several different schemas at the same time.[11]

I noted four general practices through which to trace affordances. I could have identified several more but isolated these for two reasons. First, they are generalizable across all organizations. Second, they provide productive ways for groups to identify schemas. The four practices are *management reporting*, which includes all the formal and informal ways managers monitor and keep up with what is going on in the business, covering everything from monthly and quarterly financial reporting to formal and informal manager–employee one-on-one meetings; *planning and forecasting*, which includes the formal and informal ways of planning, from annual strategic planning processes to ad hoc group planning sessions; *people*, which includes all the formal and informal ways of managing and developing people, including the standards upon which decisions about people are based; and *social acceptance*, which includes the formal and informal ways social acceptability norms manifest and are inculcated.

According to the CEO and members of her staff, the affordances I presented (Figures 7.15–7.18) were a reasonable snapshot of IMCO culture, or at least an operational aspect of it. This was not a surprise. It is through practices and adaptations that schemas and cultural models are most clearly observed.

Adaptations are reactions to prevailing practices and their underlying schemas. They tend to be what actors signal as the undesirable characteristics of their own cultures, as noted in the examples.

As the incarnation of tacit shared schemas, and similar to the metaphors and causal reasoning embedded within discourse that disguise their existence, affordances have the appearance of everydayness. They manifest to its members as perfectly ordinary features of how the organization does business, for example, as particulars of the budgeting or strategic planning process. This quality makes them, like their underlying schemas, grudgingly hard to observe—unless one has the magical luxury of inhabiting a different organization at the same moment in time in order to witness these same everyday processes conducted with startlingly different emphases. In this way

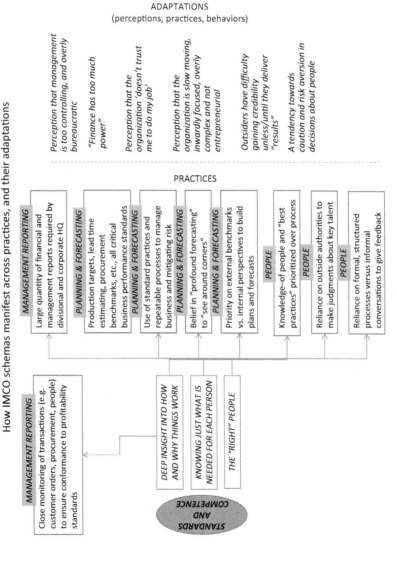

Schema Affordances: STANDARDS AND COMPETENCE
How IMCO schemas manifest across practices, and their adaptations

ADAPTATIONS
(perceptions, practices, behaviors)

PRACTICES

MANAGEMENT REPORTING

Large quantity of financial and management reports required by divisional and corporate HQ

PLANNING & FORECASTING

Production targets, lead time estimating, procurement benchmarks, etc., all critical business performance standards

PLANNING & FORECASTING

Use of standard practices and repeatable processes to manage business and mitigating risk

PLANNING & FORECASTING

Belief in "profound forecasting" to "see around corners"

PLANNING & FORECASTING

Priority on external benchmarks vs. internal perspectives to build plans and forecasts

PEOPLE

Knowledge-of people and "best practices" prioritized over process

PEOPLE

Reliance on outside authorities to make judgments about key talent

PEOPLE

Reliance on formal, structured processes versus informal conversations to give feedback

Perception that management is too controlling, and overly bureaucratic

"Finance has too much power"

Perception that the organization 'doesn't trust me to do my job'

Perception that the organization is slow moving, inwardly focused, overly complex and not entrepreneurial

Outsiders have difficulty gaining credibility unless/until they deliver "results"

A tendency towards caution and risk aversion in decisions about people

MANAGEMENT REPORTING

Close monitoring of transactions (e.g. customer orders, procurement, people) to ensure conformance to profitability standards

DEEP INSIGHT INTO HOW AND WHY THINGS WORK

KNOWING JUST WHAT IS NEEDED FOR EACH PERSON

THE "RIGHT" PEOPLE

STANDARDS AND COMPETENCE

Figure 7.15 Affordance structures based on *STANDARDS AND COMPETENCE* schemas.

Schema Affordances: THE PRIMACY OF PERSONAL EXPERIENCE
How IMCO schemas manifest across practices, and their adaptations

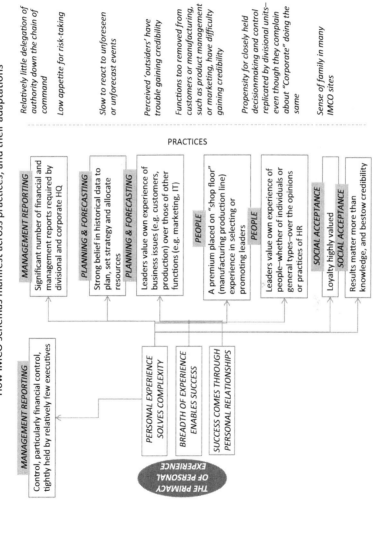

ADAPTATIONS
(perceptions, practices, behaviors)

PRACTICES

MANAGEMENT REPORTING
Significant number of financial and management reports required by divisional and corporate HQ

Relatively little delegation of authority down the chain of command

Low appetite for risk-taking

PLANNING & FORECASTING
Strong belief in historical data to plan, set strategy and allocate resources

Slow to react to unforeseen or unforecast events

PLANNING & FORECASTING
Leaders value own experience of business issues (e.g. customers, production) over those of other functions (e.g. marketing, IT)

Perceived 'outsiders' have trouble gaining credibility

Functions too removed from customers or manufacturing, such as product management or marketing, have difficulty gaining credibility

PEOPLE
A premium placed on "shop floor" (manufacturing production line) experience in selecting or promoting leaders

PEOPLE
Leaders value own experience of people–whether of individuals or general types–over the opinions or practices of HR

Propensity for closely held decisionmaking and control replicated by divisional units– even though they complain about "Corporate" doing the same

SOCIAL ACCEPTANCE
Loyalty highly valued

SOCIAL ACCEPTANCE
Results matter more than knowledge, and bestow credibility

Sense of family in many IMCO sites

MANAGEMENT REPORTING
Control, particularly financial control, tightly held by relatively few executives

PERSONAL EXPERIENCE SOLVES COMPLEXITY

BREADTH OF EXPERIENCE ENABLES SUCCESS

SUCCESS COMES THROUGH PERSONAL RELATIONSHIPS

THE PRIMACY OF PERSONAL EXPERIENCE

Figure 7.16 Affordance structures based on *PRIMACY OF PERSONAL EXPERIENCE* schemas.

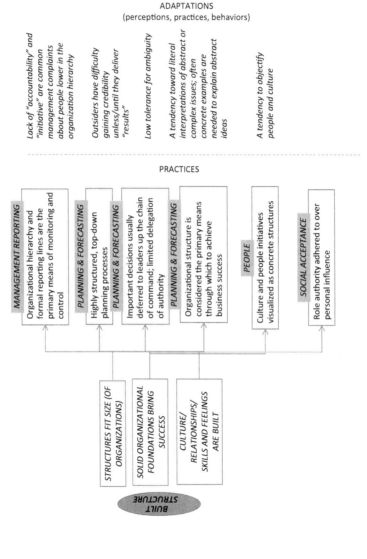

Schema Affordances: BUILT STRUCTURE
How IMCO schemas manifest across practices, and their adaptations

ADAPTATIONS
(perceptions, practices, behaviors)

PRACTICES

BUILT STRUCTURE

STRUCTURES FIT SIZE (OF ORGANIZATIONS)

SOLID ORGANIZATIONAL FOUNDATIONS BRING SUCCESS

CULTURE/ RELATIONSHIPS/ SKILLS AND FEELINGS ARE BUILT

MANAGEMENT REPORTING

Organizational hierarchy and formal reporting lines are the primary means of monitoring and control

PLANNING & FORECASTING

Highly structured, top-down planning processes

PLANNING & FORECASTING

Important decisions usually deferred to leaders up the chain of command; limited delegation of authority

PLANNING & FORECASTING

Organizational structure is considered the primary means through which to achieve business success

PEOPLE

Culture and people initiatives visualized as concrete structures

SOCIAL ACCEPTANCE

Role authority adhered to over personal influence

Lack of "accountability" and "initiative" are common management complaints about people lower in the organization hierarchy

Outsiders have difficulty gaining credibility unless/until they deliver "results"

Low tolerance for ambiguity

A tendency toward literal interpretations of abstract or complex issues; often concrete examples are needed to explain abstract ideas

A tendency to objectify people and culture

Figure 7.17 Affordance structures based on *BUILT STRUCTURE* schemas.

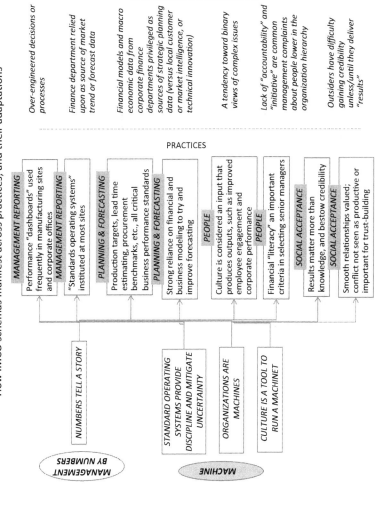

Schema Affordances: MANAGEMENT BY NUMBERS, MACHINE

How IMCO schemas manifest across practices, and their adaptations

ADAPTATIONS
(perceptions, practices, behaviors)

PRACTICES

MANAGEMENT BY NUMBERS

NUMBERS TELL A STORY

MANAGEMENT REPORTING
Performance "dashboards" used frequently in manufacturing sites and corporate offices

Over-engineered decisions or processes

MANAGEMENT REPORTING
"Standards operating systems" instituted at most sites

Finance department relied upon as source of market trend or forecast data

PLANNING & FORECASTING
Production targets, lead time estimating, procurement benchmarks, etc., all critical business performance standards

Financial models and macro economic data from corporate finance departments privileged as sources of strategic planning data (versus local customer or market intelligence, or technical innovation)

PLANNING & FORECASTING
Strong reliance on financial and business modeling to try and improve forecasting

MACHINE

STANDARD OPERATING SYSTEMS PROVIDE DISCIPLINE AND MITIGATE UNCERTAINTY

PEOPLE
Culture is considered an input that produces outputs, such as improved employee engagement and corporate performance

A tendency toward binary views of complex issues

ORGANIZATIONS ARE MACHINES

PEOPLE
Financial "literacy" an important criteria in selecting senior managers

Lack of "accountability" and "initiative" are common management complaints about people lower in the organization hierarchy

CULTURE IS A TOOL TO RUN A MACHINE?

SOCIAL ACCEPTANCE
Results matter more than knowledge, and bestow credibility

Outsiders have difficulty gaining credibility unless/until they deliver "results"

SOCIAL ACCEPTANCE
Smooth relationships valued; conflict not seen as productive or important for trust-building

Figure 7.18 Affordance structures based on *MACHINE* and *MANAGEMENT BY NUMBERS* schemas.

schema-endowed practices are polarities. Every firm, of course, engages in them but with slightly (or perhaps significantly) different emphases. With respect to management reporting (Figures 7.15–7.18), for example, in one firm the emphasis might be on quantity, insisting on many reports each month from each business unit, as is the case at IMCO. In another, the quality of the information within each report might be stressed over frequency. And another might eschew internal formal reports altogether, relying instead on informal feedback, or by management 'walking around'. These differences are a function of the underlying schemas that give these practices their particular quality and character.

Management Reporting

The management of conglomerates is primarily oriented towards balance sheet and investment portfolio management, with the main goal the rapid growth of earnings (Weston, 1969). It follows then that one of the most important competencies for the corporate holding entity is financial management. While this is the case somewhat for all companies, the diverse nature of conglomerate portfolios means they often tend to focus exclusively or primarily on financial management rather than other forms of management control. IMCO's corporate finance group requires 40 to 50 financial reports each month from its divisional units, an amount considered excessive, especially for a company of IMCO's size, according to two of my interview informants and several others spoken to in the course of my work there. Finance departments in the divisional units have staff solely dedicated to producing reports to satisfy headquarter needs for information. Producing financial reports to track unit performance is not unusual; it is standard practice in most large companies. What is unusual is the quantity and frequency of reports at IMCO. As put by one informant:

> One biggest challenge that I see with IMCO as a whole is that we tend to be very inwardly focused and we spend a lot of time trying to explain to ourselves what is happening rather than focusing outside and saying what is it we need to do to keep moving the needle forward . . . in our attempt to figure out what's happening, we can complicate things. We do conduct way more than we need in terms of reviews regarding business reviews, regarding monthly reports . . . any time you need more than 2–3 reports to run a business, then you have complicated your business.

Another example comes from IMCO' connector division. This business maintains a customer order-tracking system for verifying and fulfilling customer orders. As with many IMCO businesses, part of the connector business is based on custom-built connectors; that is, high-volume orders fulfilled not from existing inventory but from tailor-made parts sourced just in time from supply chains. To track where a customer's order is in the manufacturing process, each department involved, such as sales, product management, procurement, and operations registers a status with the order as they 'hand off' the order to the next department as it is readied for production. The finance function, however, does not allow an order to be placed in the order management system until it can verify the order's profit margin will meet its profitability standards. This verification can negate an order, or slow it down so that sales or product management must renegotiate a price with the customer after the sale has been made. These controls often put an order at risk because of delays in fulfillment or because of renegotiations on price. This practice does not appear to be the norm in other manufacturing companies. Margin determination on specific orders is typically a function of sales or product management. Finance plays a monitoring role, but without order veto power.[12]

This may be an example of Steele's organizational overlearning. Financial management and control practices, overlearned from years of managing business through primarily financial means as a conglomerate, are applied to individual customer transactions. Historical management practice based on financial monitoring and control are carried into the present day even though the company is no longer a conglomerate of the same size and scale. What might account for this? IMCO managers, when queried about these practices, steadfastly underscore their importance to their business. From the research presented here, however, the answer is obvious. As depicted in Figures 7.15 and 7.16, IMCO's financial reporting practices are fueled by *STANDARDS AND COMPETENCE* and *PRIMACY OF PERSONAL EXPERIENCE* schemas, in particular *DEEP INSIGHT INTO HOW AND WHY THINGS WORK* and *PERSONAL EXPERIENCE SOLVES COMPLEXITY*. The emphases on quantity and frequency of reports and the detail within them, the fact financial reporting is often duplicative, collected by both corporate headquarters and each division's headquarters, and the bases on which these practices are justified, all, are no surprise. Finance's role in approving margins on customer transactions in the connector business is the product of *DEEP INSIGHT INTO HOW AND WHY THINGS WORK* and *PERSONAL EXPERIENCE SOLVES COMPLEXITY*, schemas inculcated in a legacy task environment applied reflexively to present day circumstances. As a kind of proof that schemas structure these practices, other than the few people who mentioned it in my interviews, there is little awareness by management of these control and certainty-oriented practices. I have not observed nor heard of any discussion about developing faster or more efficient planning and reporting practices based on alternative performance measures, or, for example, phasing in modern reporting alternatives, such as those derived from machine-learning or 'big data' based approaches.[13]

This is the effect of referential transparency. It is hard for IMCO managers to conceive of alternatives because the schemas themselves, borne out of years of operating the business using legacy management and financial reporting practices, constrain the problem-frame and shields actors from the construction of possible alternatives. The reporting practices themselves are not what signal the existence of the underlying schemas. It is the reflexive way IMCO managers undertake financial reporting and management control to apparent excess that reveals their schema-endowed character.

Of interest here as well is the theme of control and its numerous adaptations. The theme, in effect, is replicated across practices, as depicted in Figures 7.15–7.18, largely the result of the pervasive *PERSONAL EXPERIENCE SOLVES COMPLEXITY* schema. Interestingly, control is both a feature of practice and an adaptation to it (Figure 7.16). For example, many of my informants in divisional or 'field' roles railed at the number of management and financial reports required by corporate functions, and yet they themselves would institute similar practices in their own units, justifying them by the need to 'stay on top' of their business, or because a business was in a turnaround situation. By perpetuating the very structures they complain about, they demonstrate the insidious and pervasive nature of schemas. Figures 7.15–7.18 depict similar management reporting practices and adaptations characterized by control, certainty, and standards.

Planning & Forecasting

The best depiction of IMCO's planning and forecasting practices comes from the general manager of IMCO's aerospace components business:

> *How we do that (mitigate uncertainty) is (through) really profound forecasting and modeling, and being proactive. So we build the tools. Every week we look at the outlook of forecasts of orders and sales, and profits and revenue of the business by product, by location. So we have a very good operating system if you will, to look forward, especially being in aerospace . . . So we have a very disciplined process of looking at it, and if there are changes or if there are ups and downs, then this group, my group, my leadership gets together and we would take a look at what actions we're going to take. Whether it's cost reduction, or other changes.*

This passage illustrates how several schemas shape this executive's conception of his division's planning and forecasting practices, and how adaptations result. He is describing practices in part driven by the *PERSONAL EXPERIENCE SOLVES COMPLEXITY* schema, with its emphasis on mitigation through weekly examination of relevant data by leadership (Figure 7.16). These practices are also driven by *SOLID ORGANIZATIONAL FOUNDATIONS BRING SUCCESS* (Figure 7.17), with its emphasis on hierarchy *("my leadership")*. And it illustrates the *STANDARD OPERATING SYSTEMS PROVIDE DISCIPLINE AND MITIGATE*

UNCERTAINTY and *NUMBERS TELL A STORY* schemas with the use of the metaphor *operating system* and the emphasis on *orders, sales, profits and revenue* (Figure 7.18). All of these practices involve minimal delegation of authority, insinuated by the last sentence emphasizing the actions the leadership group takes, as opposed to, say, encouraging or empowering others lower in the organizational hierarchy to do so. The adaptation comes in the form of frequently heard refrains: *Management is too controlling, and overly bureaucratic,* and the organization *"doesn't trust me to do my job"* (Figure 7.15).

Noteworthy here as well is the perception that frequent management review is key to mitigating risk. At the same time, there is a prevailing sentiment that the company is slow to react to unforeseen events (Figure 7.16). This apparent contradiction is reconciled by understanding some practices themselves are adaptations, reactions to perceived 'cultural' shortcomings, much in the same way as with Hutchins' Trobriand myths. Schemas and cultural models can manifest as cultural defenses, including defenses against norms that themselves may be the product of the same schemas. Management practices such as proactive forecasting designed to improve on the perceived shortcomings (slowness) of the prevailing forecasting practices draw from the same tacitly held schemas that make up the cultural artefact of slowness to begin with! Adaptations in this way are delimited by available action repertoires even while appearing to allow for their full enactment. This phenomenon is also seen in relation to external expert authority, discussed below.

The explanation for this is that as cognitive resources for sensemaking, cultural schemas are finite. They are limited by the task and professional environment that enables their induction. Most organizations do not have an unlimited supply of them, as this illustration shows.

People

Figure 7.19 is an image developed by IMCO HR staff depicting two important people-oriented initiatives undertaken by the firm in recent years—an integrated talent management system, and the aforementioned culture work. The graphic shows how these two initiatives support and underpin the overall HR strategy.[14]

What is notable here are not the initiatives themselves, but how they are depicted. Not only has culture been ontologized, it has been concretized, made into a building block situated right beneath the initiatives of job classification and career frameworks.[15] The box depicting culture refers to normative behavior, confirmed in discussion with the author of the slide. But the visual metaphor renders 'culture' as a concrete foundation for other initiatives that 'sit' on top of it. This calls to mind how IMCO characterizes itself as a company that makes things that make other things work, described in the Introduction. In an organization where *BUILT STRUCTURE*

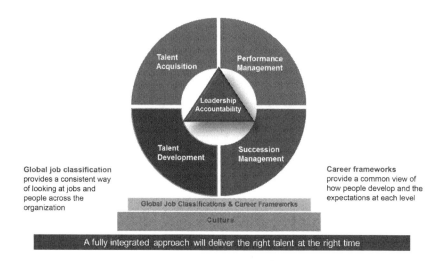

Figure 7.19 IMCO's integrated talent management and culture initiatives.

and *PRIMACY OF PERSONAL EXPERIENCE* schemas predominate, the tendency to render culture and people initiatives as tangible objects is not unexpected. Even though the culture consultants operationalized culture in normative terms (conflating it with personality traits), culture when rendered by IMCO staff turns into concrete building blocks, foundations for statuary. This could simply be coincidence. Foundational HR initiatives in other companies are sometimes rendered in similar fashion. On the other hand, there are many visual metaphors to depict the relationship between a source and its dependencies: Hub and spoke, top-down hierarchy, a timeline with antecedents are a few that come to mind. Why this particular building block metaphor? Given the network of primary schemas making up IMCO culture, the tendency towards concretizing may be inevitable. The new is made sensible by drawing from the familiar—in this case, the prevailing cognitive resources comprised in part of *SOLID ORGANIZATIONAL FOUNDATIONS BRING SUCCESS,* and *CULTURE/RELATIONSHIPS/ SKILLS AND FEELINGS ARE BUILT.* Inherently abstract HRM practices are depicted through the cultural-cognitive resources most readily available. These tend to be the ones that communicate most effectively to the intended audience, the managers and executives at IMCO.

Some practices highlight the complex interplay between schemas and adaptations. For example, while *DEEP INSIGHT INTO HOW AND WHY THINGS WORK* is dominant across a number of practices, including those pertaining to people, it fosters a curious adaptation. The firm is quite cautious and risk averse in its hiring and promotion decisions, especially for senior executives. All executive-level promotion and selection, whether internal or external, is subject to an extensive interview and assessment by an outside firm, Korn Ferry, who uses their own criteria to render a selection decision on each candidate. In spite of the fact of IMCO's investment in the integrated talent management infrastructure that provides behavioral standards (competencies) validated for IMCO executive roles, as well as an interview methodology (behavioral interview questions) that makes interviewing for these roles highly predictive, senior management prefers the assessment of an outside 'expert' rather than rely on their own standards and selection skills, or the expertise of their internal HR staff.[16] Of course, this can be read as caution or prudence, or perhaps as a way to deflect subpar hiring judgments by blaming the assessor. Or perhaps this is simply executive humility. An outside perspective for important senior level hires is surely beneficial. But the point here is not the efficacy of the practice but its contradictions. In a firm where *DEEP INSIGHT INTO HOW AND WHY THINGS WORK* and, to a lesser extent, *KNOWING JUST WHAT IS NEEDED FOR EACH PERSON* prevails, IMCO defers executive selection to outside experts. Rather than see this practice as an anomaly, one can read it as an adaptation: because IMCO executives hold the schemas they do, trusting an outside expert in a domain (executive selection) considered beyond their range of expertise makes sense. In this case, *deep insight* manifests by extension as trust in an expert third party to have that insight, whereas in other domains, such as managing a supply chain or forecasting the profitability of a customer order, these schemas and their affordances result in adaptations of *mistrust* (Figures 7.15 and 7.16). This is another of the many ways in which schemas evidence their transposability across affordance structures to generate complex, context-specific adaptations.

Social Acceptance

Social acceptance practices consist of the multifold ways people in organizations manifest normative behavior. One manifestation at IMCO, as discussed earlier, is loyalty (Figure 7.16), an affordance of *SUCCESS COMES THROUGH PERSONAL RELATIONSHIPS* and *PERSONAL EXPERIENCE SOLVES COMPLEXITY*. These schemas are grounded in the social learning and historical context of social proximity in what are a collection of several small businesses that make up IMCO. This is not the only induction context for these schemas, but adds to those already inherent in the material and physical milieu of manufacturing and its successful management.

An interesting normative affordance concerns the concept of *results*. This theme takes many forms, from everyday discourse to formalized competencies, and as a social norm, as seen in Table 7.19. The refrain *drive for results* is expressed most often as a value and positive attribution (*"he's a driver"*). As Figures 7.16 and 7.18 depict, getting results matters considerably more than generating ideas. I contrast this with my own experience at Microsoft and other software companies where generating ideas and 'intellectual horsepower' are valued and considered paramount for success. At IMCO, those that get 're-sults', that is, achieve success as measured in financial (sales) or other metrical terms, such as managing a manufacturing line within time and budget, accrue personal credibility and over time reap rewards such as promotions and job security. Those that do not, or are perceived to be too conceptual, theoretical, disconnected from 'the business' or not 'hands on' enough tend to be socially marginalized. The affordance is powered by the *PERSONAL EXPERIENCE SOLVES COMPLEXITY* and *ORGANIZATIONS ARE MACHINES* sche-mas, and to a lesser extent by more common *FORCE* schemas.

Manifesting as social norms, these schemas engender complex adapta-tions. One of them is that functions or jobs whose outputs do not readily lend themselves to tangible results, such as product management or market-ing, have difficulty gaining credibility. IMCO, in fact, has for many years struggled to provision these functions with greater resources and authority. The challenge, as put to me by several informants, is that despite added resources and organizational visibility, including hiring a seasoned prod-uct management executive from General Electric, these functions are not granted sufficient authority or resources to be effective. For example, even though leaders acknowledge the company needs to adopt more rigorous product definition, market segmentation and market intelligence practices in order to be more responsive to shifts in markets, all the traditional prov-inces of product management, much of the control over resources and the setting of product or market strategy, reside within finance and, to a lesser extent, sales leadership and the leadership of the four main divisions. Prod-uct managers play a role, but often it is to convey input from sales into a centralized product and strategic planning process. A central coordinating strategic planning function manages the annual process of compiling and reconciling divisional strategic plans, including those concerning products and markets, but this function for the most part is a process coordinator. Ultimate decision-making authority over product and market strategy at the corporate level resides in the finance function and the office of the chief financial officer.[17] Again, like an undertow pulling strong swimmers from shore, even deliberate and well-intentioned initiatives such as attempts to invest in product management capabilities are inexorably drawn away from their intended destination, the result of tacit schemas.

The emphasis on results also has visible manifestation in a formal opera-tions functional competency called *Drive for Results* (Table 7.19).

Positing a competency such as *Drive for Results* is not unusual; drive and initiative are mainstream business values in the United States. What is unusual is the degree to which it is emphasized at IMCO. *Drive for results*, in addition to being a competency is a cultural model for *achieving results*. Several schemas underwrite it, rendering it a coherent and well-understood cultural model. It contains the notions of accountability; ownership; per-severance; modeling espoused values; goals; leading by example; initiative

Table 7.19 DRIVE FOR RESULTS Competency (Operations)

1. Demonstrates integrity, and a sense of ownership and accountability for the outcome of projects or initiatives.
2. Holds others accountable for their commitments.
3. Demonstrates passion for delivering high quality work that achieves customer and business goals.
4. Leads by example, models company values, and perseveres and stays upbeat in the face of obstacles.
5. Resolves process exceptions or unaddressed issues regardless of scope of responsibility.
6. Develops an organizational structure, process framework, and work environment that support core IMCO values and enable business results for IMCO and its customers.

(resolves process exceptions); and structure. All of these themes are underwritten by predominant schemas: *ORGANIZATIONS ARE MACHINES* in the notion of *drive, PERSONAL EXPERIENCE SOLVES COMPLEXITY* through *ownership* and *accountability, SOLID ORGANIZATIONAL FOUNDATIONS BRING SUCCESS* with *structure, THE 'RIGHT' PEOPLE* with *modeling company values.*[18]

Drive for results also appears in the culture-shaping effort describing IMCO's new aspired values (Introduction): "We solve it." The aspired behaviors are framed in terms of problem solving. Whether unconscious or deliberate, the message is clear. The new culture, like the old, is about delivering results.

The same idea is to be found in one of HR's competencies. By virtue of its administrative and risk management role, many HR departments do not ordinarily define their own success in terms of achieving 'results', at least not in an overt way. This is not to say HR is not outcome oriented, but what is unusual is the degree to which this orientation manifests at IMCO given the conditions under which HR operates. To add context, HR has been comparatively underfunded at IMCO with respect to personnel and technology. As a conglomerate, IMCO's focus was extracting as much profitability as possible from its business units; HR was considered an administrative cost. Although this is in the process of changing, one manifestation of this is that until 2015 the company did not have a common HR information system (HRIS), unusual for a company of its size and global orientation.[19] This rendered many basic HR tasks difficult and time consuming: Producing a basic report on who works for the company often took weeks. Thus, for HR to espouse *drive for results* when much of the infrastructure enabling it to deliver basic 'results' is lacking is ironic. And yet the competency was developed and implemented by HR leaders without any self-consciousness, well before implementation of the HRIS.

What accounts for this? Perhaps this was a deliberate attempt by HR leaders to raise standards. One could point to the fact the HR industry espouses achieving results as a way to gain business credibility and a so-called 'seat the table'.[20] Such is the case with a profession that suffers from chronic occupational insecurity about its own value. But I suspect HR's adoption of this competency here has less to do with conforming to industry norms. As we saw with Microsoft HR's use of a lingua franca to curry legitimacy with engineers and executives, I suggest HR's adoption of the social norm of *drive for results* at IMCO is so that it can be more accepted and credible in the organization. Appropriating prevailing schemas by adopting one of its most iconic affordances is a common and effective influence tactic. Again, actors appropriate the cognitive-cultural resources at their disposal. In HR's case, it is to legitimize their own power, at least in relation to those it perceives as more powerful.

Culture's Apparent Clarity

The affordance structures described in the foregoing can be said to characterize IMCO culture, or at least the parts visible to this observer and his informants. Practices and adaptations are manifestations of the firms' underlying reflexive cognitive orientations and predispositions, its structural subconscious. Cultures are rooted in a community's structural subconscious; practices and adaptations are how actors come to see its manifestations, and their reactions to it form the basis of a dialogic relationship. The 'culture' becomes an emergent co-constructed reality as actors perceive and adapt to practices endowed by schemas. Culture in this way is epiphenomena, as Vike characterizes it, but in a dialectical sense. The structural collective unconscious imprints itself on collectively enacted practices and adaptations that actors treat as ontologically real.

This leads to complex but potentially fruitful intervention strategies. Because actors 'see' their own cultures, as was the case with IMCO's CEO and her staff, they have no trouble positing culture as ontological wholes, characterizing them, distinguishing between them, and attempting to manipulate and change them. This is the intuition actors have about their own cultures described in the opening chapter. Actors intuitively but readily identify what makes one practice in one culture appear and feel different than another, even if they cannot tell you why. For example, as most managers know, planning, budgeting or employee promotion in one organization can be conducted in very different ways with very different emphases or definitions of success in another even while the mechanics of these practices are largely the same. Underlying schemas endow practices with their particularity and distinctiveness, rendering affordances as polarities, a tendency to do it this way rather than that way, or emphasize this aspect versus that. Which is why for any given system of affordances, actors will perceive themselves unable to behave differently except perhaps at great personal risk. Affordances circumscribe action even while masking their own delimiting character. Although IMCO managers may be aware that many of their practices unwittingly reify a sense of *control*, they are unaware of the *standards/competence* and *personal experience* schemas fueling them. Schemas are the experiential endowments of practices, underwriting their points of emphases, bases of authority, or the ways they reveal or hide their emblems of power as they are appropriated and enacted.

Affordances are also why culture change holds the magnetic attraction it does for managers and practitioners. In their apparent ontological clarity, practices and their adaptations hold the illusion they are be eligible for change, in the same way a convoluted process cries out for simplification. What remain hidden, of course, are the underlying schemas that give affordances their resonant particularity and ontological clarity to begin with. This duality is what renders culture so pervasive, and so hard to change.

3. Other Possibilities

For some readers I am sure the last two chapters have instilled a growing sense of unease concerning the ontological and epistemic slipperiness of our investigation into the functionally grounded unthought known. That the evidence for cognitive structure independent of language is strong and well accepted may not be recompense for what appears to be an unavoidable circularity in the argument. And while circularity was addressed in previous chapters (see Chapter 4 and 5), it is worth a few more words here given the specific evidence of schemas, models and affordances presented here.

Circularity

On the one hand, asserting that schemas arising out of the grounding context of manufacturing task, operational measurement, certainty-management, and small-firm historicity beget thinking and practice emphasizing standards and competence, personal experience, built structure, machines, and so forth, presents a causality problem. Do the schemas beget the affordances, or is it the other way around? One could argue the kind of reporting, monitoring, and forecasting depicted is just what manufacturing companies do to ensure profitability. And, of course, that is the point. The ecological constraints of the task beget the cognitive orientation.

And yet this kind of circularity poses, at a minimum, a distraction. To address it we must return to the core principle of *interactionism* discussed in Chapter 4. This principle holds that the actor is embedded within a preexisting kinesthetic, task (material), and sociocultural context while also continually interacting with it. In this interaction the actor is engaged in a process of *diachronic dynamism*. Affordances exist in time. At any one moment in time the relationship between schemas and affordance will appear to be circular. But were we to consider that moment as one frame in a movie, the movie would reveal its antecedents and consequences. In the same way a firm may appear underdetermined at any given moment in time, functionally embodied culture may appear endlessly circular when the variable of time is removed from the picture.

What comes first is the plasticity of the embodied human mind and its ability *over time* to mirror and replicate experiential structure and analogically extend it to new instances. The nature of the surrounding physical and social environment, including—and especially—the organizational task context and the social forces inherent in it (including its professionalization) shapes thinking that in turn shapes practice. A guitarist thinks of his own hand as an extension of the guitar only after thousands of hours of practice. In this same way, sustained exposure to the experiential milieu and to successfully operating within it gives rise to practices and habits of thought that, in turn, enact and reify those same practices. Over time this further shapes the minds of those doing the practising.

This is indeed a recursive phenomenon, but also a dynamic one. In the same way an iceberg slowly moving across the Arctic Sea seems permanently etched into its scene but is in fact calving and reshaping itself as it moves, functionally embodied cultures are eligible at any one time to be depicted by the kind of analyses provided here, but are in no way ever static. We do not see the movement, only the iceberg. We think of practices and schemas as circular only because we omit the variable of time and the dynamism that comprises lived experience. Through schemas humans endow affordances with cultural meaning at any one point in time, but at another these same practices and schemas may be altered based on perceived impingements at the sensemaking boundary, and (or) through willful acts of powerful change agents. If the resultant practices are capable of being sustained such that they revise or induce new schemas, those schemas over time will become pervasive and result in new affordances and adaptations. This dynamic is *necessarily* and *essentially* recursive because the embodied mind itself is dynamically situated and ecologically embedded in a physical and social reality that is itself subject to change.

Thus, can it really be a surprise that the finance group in the connector business at IMCO verifies profit margins before a customer order can be approved and manufacturing commence? This practice exists based on pervasive standards and personal experience schemas borne out of certainty-management contingencies, among other task contexts. Over time, based on shifts in the dynamics of the connector business and its leaders endeavoring to change practices based on perceived threats at the sensemaking boundary (such as the need to move more quickly in order to remain competitive), the practice will change. If a new practice is sustained and aligned with other practices, it will serve to modify older underlying schemas.

Thus, to build on what was put forth in Chapter 5, the ontological status of schemas is always contingent upon both their manifestation and inducement in time and space. Circularity is an epistemic limitation: We can only posit the existence of the functionally embodied culture framework by analyzing its effects within one point in time. That said, we can ensure this frame is richly saturated with converging data, as done here.

Language Games Versus Functional Grounding

A second way to explain these data, as suggested earlier, is to suggest what is observed at IMCO is not evidence of functional grounding but instead ungrounded or arbitrary features of language and cognition. One might claim, for example, that schemas in the category *MACHINE* are not unique to IMCO because they appear in other organizational environments, such as in software engineering, among others. Or argued from the opposite perspective, even though a part of IMCO is in the business of making machines, the fact *MACHINE* schemas are not foundational or more dominant might persuade an observer to refute the functional grounding thesis altogether on the grounds the schemas are neither unique nor reflective of task context. This, again, is the 'language games' argument. What is observed is not the result of underlying cognitive structure but of actors consciously appropriating discourse and tropes from the wider business and popular culture.

Underlying this argument is an agent–agency bias. Culture has nothing to do with shared cognitive structures because humans have free will and agency and, culturally speaking, are capable of acting beyond any cognitive-corporeal or ecological constraints. Culture in organizations is not the product of a pervasively structured subconscious indelibly tied to task environments or professional orientation and predisposition. Culture is whatever we want it to be. If a manufacturing enterprise wants to have a culture like Google's, well, it is just a matter of having leaders who can make it so. If a non-profit therapeutic institution serving the disenfranchised poor cares to manage itself like a for-profit business, it is just a matter of learning the right discipline and professional management techniques. Much of the edifice of mainstream culture practice, in essence, claims as much. And while I might argue this claim self-serves the economic interests of a large consulting industry as well as business school pedagogy for the benefit of its consumers, the actual state of affairs is more complicated.

The data from IMCO strongly refutes the language game argument and its underlying agency bias. For one, there is too much data. The convergence of data from three triangulated streams of research—causal reasoning, metaphor, and quantitative analysis—and its sheer volume, negates agent bias. If actors spoke and acted without any underlying ecological cognitive constraint, the data here would be much more random and without discernible pattern. If multiple modes of analysis reveal pervasive patterns, as is the case here, that these patterns have meaning and reality for actors within that community can safely be concluded. Even the most parsimonious reading of these data using only the quantitative analysis shows a percentage of the most frequently adduced schemas are unique and cognitively real for informants. All the data converge on a pervasive set of underlying schemas that play a significant role in underwriting what can be thought of as part, or whole, of IMCO's culture.

Second, the affordance structures, in particular the great many number of practices that manifest the adduced schemas, and the nature of the adaptations signal that the schemas are culturally salient. This has been validated by IMCO informants, including its CEO. That schemas are cognitively real does not by itself qualify them as culture. To make this broader claim, we used the affordance structures as evidence. For example, the perception that *management is too controlling, and overly bureaucratic*, fueled by *DEEP INSIGHT INTO HOW AND WHY THINGS WORK* (Figure 7.15) is a common adaptation to IMCO's management reporting practices. This is not suggestive; like all other adaptations, informants attributed this to pervasive behaviors and practices. It would be harder to suggest IMCO's schemas are functionally grounded if their manifestations were not so widespread and their adaptations not so widely reported.

Functional grounding is not a straightforward mirroring of the task or professional environment. If it were, schemas would be isomorphic with affordances, which they are not. Often the same schema manifests across many practices, as we see with *DEEP INSIGHT INTO HOW AND WHY THINGS WORK*. Grounding, as discussed in Chapter 4, is a highly complex process involving many interleaved dynamics. Qwest's justification of its takeover of USWest was a function of a complex set of frames and narratives grounded not in its fiber optic technology, but in the perceived advantages of that technology. As I show above, the grounding effects in my data are in part related to IMCO's manufacturing task environment, but also to the company's need to achieve certainty in a global competitive context.

The unreflective generation of knowledge is epistemologically problematic; one indeed needs to envision the limits and distortions of one's own investigative modalities. In our case here, more studies are needed to substantiate links between task context and schemas across different organizations and industries. But thought constraints eventually produce facts, as Fleck reminds. The evidence here, I believe, is a productive start.

4. *Summary*: The Transparency of Culture

Our investigative foray into schemas and their affordances illustrates the complexity of untangling cultural practice from its cognitive underpinnings. Their interweaving makes schemas difficult, but not impossible, as objects of inquiry, as this study has shown. Cultures exhibit patterns and tendencies that are intuitively resonant yet remain opaque for most of its members. This returns us to Descola's assertion that behavior in a collective displays consistency and automatism that its members are usually unable to relate back to a system of explicit rules. He goes on:

Such lines of conduct, such routine reactions and choices, and such shared attitudes towards the world and others are distinctive enough to serve as an intuitive indication for gauging the differences between neighboring peoples. However, they are so deeply internalized that they seldom surface in reflexive deliberations.

(2013, p. 92)

It is in these "deeply internalized" recesses that culture resides. Culture in this way is at once more fundamental, and also more mundane. There is nothing earth shattering about *PERSONAL EXPERIENCE SOLVES COMPLEXITY* or *SOLID ORGANIZATIONAL FOUNDATIONS BRING SUCCESS*. That is, until they become fuel for powering how decisions are made or resources allocated, imbuing the organization with an adaptive and pervasive sense of over-control or lack of trust that members palpably recognize as byproducts of their own culture.

Such practices and adaptations, the schematic affordances, are imbued with the patterned residue of the collective structural subconscious. These patterns are discerned as inherent logic, not in the form of a singular foundational schema but as pervasive sets of orientations and polarities that underlie and structure sensemaking. These are the cognitive resources actors collectively draw upon to orient themselves to their worlds and through which to locate meaning. Schemas, or rather their tacit appropriation, in this way are the principal drivers of culture in organizations. They provide an orienting and motivating logic that 'makes sense' because they are inextricably borne out of and tied to the organization's task environment, its dominant professional orientation, or both. They are a kind of cultural DNA, difficult to see and yet all-encompassing, which is precisely what gives culture its beguiling and intuitive sense of normative possibility.

Notes

1 With 30% of my informants having engineering backgrounds, some schema grounding based on engineering professionalization was expected, but this effect was muted (Table 5.5, Chapter 5). Manufacturing operations is also the background of six out of 10 informants. Professionalization effects from manufacturing operations, however, are hard to distinguish from grounding effects from manufacturing *tasks* and *management*. For this reason, I focus my discussion on the latter.

2 This would be in keeping with Gordon's (1991) thesis that companies within the same industry groupings have similar cultures. For instance, anecdotally, there is some evidence that aspects of Honeywell culture are characterized by *STANDARDS AND COMPETENCE* schemas (*The Economist*, April 14, 2012). IMCO's sister spin off, WaterCo, shows evidence of *STANDARDS AND COMPETENCE, BUILT STRUCTURE* and *MACHINE* schemas. Much more work is be needed to substantiate these claims, but the framework of functional embodiment is consistent with an industry-determinants or organizational culture thesis.

3 From 1960 to 1977, IMCO acquired more than 350 companies and had a portfolio that included hotels, car rental, insurance, and baking, as well as industrial products. One of IMCO's most prominent brands today is an industrial pump manufacturer that is over 100 years old.

4 I have spent portions of my career in two start-up companies, the largest one growing to a size of about 125 people.

5 A focused factory (Skinner, 1974) structures its basic manufacturing policies and supporting services to address one explicit manufacturing task instead of many tasks that might conflict with each other.

6 The two schemas not included in this list, *IMCO MOVES TOO SLOWLY* and *MATRIX ORGANIZATIONS REQUIRE DIPLOMACY* are less a direct manifestation of grounding in certainty-management but may be byproducts or adaptations. Organizations obsessed with certainty take longer to make decisions and may require more diplomacy. They are also more risk averse, an affordance described later in this chapter.

7 SPATIAL LOCATION was the most frequent source domain used by software engineers by a factor of almost two to one. In my study of HR, source domains pertaining to people and feelings were most frequent.

8 This underscores Weick's (1995) original "seven properties" of sensemaking, which include the ideas that sensemaking is retrospective, enactive, and social.

9 I owe the inclusion of the term here to Fred Steier, who early on suggested it.

10 Espoused values are often not the result of functionally grounded schemas. They are conventional discourses. They remain espoused rather than practised because the schemas that inform them are not grounded within the socio-technical environment of the firm, thus enacting them as practices is culturally dissonant.

11 Note that *LIVING THINGS* and *SPATIAL LOCATION* categories have been omitted because they do not appear to uniquely inform any affordances. That is not to say the do not manifest in any IMCO practices, only that that I have not observed their effects. This may be due to the fact these schemas are conventionalized in business.

12 Source: IMCO informants.

13 For an example of these alternatives, see "The Watchers" (*The Economist*, August 20, 2016).

14 "Integrated talent management" refers to the linkage of comon HR practices such as recruitment, training, development, succession planning, performance management, and pay to common standards. Standards are usually in the form of competencies, job descriptions, or job families, or variants. Our consulting practice developed some of these standards, called 'career frameworks', through an emic methodology, and played a lead role in developing the integrated talent management strategy with IMCO HR. That said, we were not involved in the graphic referenced in this section.

15 Job classification is a systematic way to organize firm's jobs into taxonomy such that compensation ranges for jobs can be rationalized against market pay.

16 As mentioned, our firm developed these standards, so it is safe to say we have an opinion about this practice. But that is not the point of this example.

17 It is not coincidental that IMCO's CEO was the former CFO of the pre-spinoff entity. This is not to imply that the CEO imposes finance-oriented cultural models. While I was not privy to the decision-making process behind her CEO appointment, it is not inconceivable that IMCO's board appointed her because of her finance experience as a way to mitigate risk for a newly independent IMCO. Such a decision would be entirely consistent with prevailing IMCO schemas.

18 *FORCE* schemas are also in evidence with *drive, perseverance, achievement*, and *initiative*.

19 Information on who works for the company, where, at what level and with what title, and so forth, were maintained on spreadsheets, or scattered in various systems within discrete sites or business units and not connected to one another.

20 A 'seat at the table' is a metonymy that refers to HR's need to gain acceptance by business leaders in order to contribute its expertise in all aspects of business management. For a good orientation to HR's challenge in this area, I recommend Boudreau and Ramstad's *Beyond HR: The new science of human capital* (2007). Should the reader have doubts about HR occupational self-consciousness and confidence (at least in the United States), consider Fast Company's (2005) *Why We Hate HR*.

Bibliography

Arauz, R., Matsuo, H., & Suzuki, H. (2009). Measuring changes in quality management: An empirical analysis of Japanese manufacturing companies. *Total Quality Management, 20*(12), 1337–1374.

Boudreau, J., & Ramstad, P. (2007). *Beyond HR: The new science of human capital.* Boston: Harvard Business School Press.

Bugos, G. (1993). Manufacturing certainty: Testing and program management for the F-4 Phantom II. *Social Studies of Science, 23*(2), 265–300.

Clinton, B. D., & Chen, S. (1998). Do new performance measures measure up? *Strategic Finance, 80*(4), 38.

Descola, P. (2013). *Beyond nature and culture.* Chicago: University of Chicago Press.

Fast Company. (2005). Why we hate HR. *Fast Company.* Retrieved from https://www.fastcompany.com/53319/why-we-hate-hr.

From bitter to sweet: Honeywell International. (2012, April 14). *The Economist.*

Fullerton, R. R., & Wempe, W. F. (2009). Lean manufacturing, non-financial performance measures, and financial performance. *International Journal of Operations & Production Management, 29*(3), 214–240.

Gomes, C. F., Yasin, M. M., & Lisboa, J. V. (2004). A literature review of manufacturing performance measures and measurement in an organizational context: A framework and direction for future research. *Journal of Manufacturing Technology Management, 15*(6), 511–530.

Gordon, G. G. (1991). Industry determinants of organizational culture. *Academy of Management Review, 16*(2), 396–415.

Gupta, Y. P., & Goyal, S. (1989). Flexibility of manufacturing systems: Concepts and measurements. *European Journal of Operational Research, 43*(2), 119–135.

Kaplan, R. S. (1992). Measuring manufacturing performance: a new challenge for managerial accounting research. *The Accounting Review, 58*(4), 686–705

Li, S., Rao, S. S., Ragu-Nathan, T. S., & Ragu-Nathan, B. (2005). Development and validation of a measurement instrument for studying supply chain management practices. *Journal of Operations Management, 23*(6), 618–641.

Mann, D. (2009). The case for lean culture: Sustain the gains from your lean conversion. In Association for Manufacturing Excellence (Eds.), *Sustaining lean: Case studies in transforming culture* (pp. 1–18). Boca Raton: CRC Press.

McGrenere, J., &, Ho, W. (2000, May 15–17). Affordances: Clarifying and evolving a concept. In *Proceedings of graphics interface* (pp. 1–8). Montreal, Quebec, Canada. Retrieved from http://www.graphicsinterface.org/proceedings/2000/ishii.

Newman, W. R., Hanna, M., & Maffei, M. J. (1993). Dealing with the uncertainties of manufacturing: Flexibility, buffers and integration. *International Journal of Operations & Production Management, 13*(1), 19–34.

Rother, M., & Shook, J. (1999). *Learning to see: Value-stream mapping to create value and eliminate muda*. Brookline, MA: Lean Enterprise Institute.

Santos, S., Gouveia, J. B., & Gomes, P. (2006). Measuring performance in supply chain: A framework. In *13th international EurOMA conference* (pp. 18–21). Retrieved from: https://pdfs.semanticscholar.org/ed7c/f47e11612331818c7118a-b45e771b4351f36.pdf

Schmenner, R. W., & Vollmann, T. E. (1994). Performance measures: Gaps, false alarms, and the "usual suspects." *International Journal of Operations & Production Management, 14*(12), 58–69.

Shah, R., & Ward, P. T. (2007). Defining and developing measures of lean production. *Journal of Operations Management, 25*(4), 785–805.

Singh, P. J., Feng, M., & Smith, A. (2006). ISO 9000 series of standards: Comparison of manufacturing and service organisations. *International Journal of Quality & Reliability Management, 23*(2), 122–142.

Skinner, W. (1974). The focused factory. *Harvard Business Review*. Retrieved from http://hbr.org/1974/05/the-focused-factory/ar/1.

Smith, K. V., & Schreiner, J. C. (1969). A portfolio analysis of conglomerate diversification. *The Journal of Finance, 24*(3), 413–427.

Taskinen, T., & Smeds, R. (1999). Measuring change project management in manufacturing. *International Journal of Operations & Production Management, 19*(11), 1168–1187.

The watchers: Measuring companies. (2016, August 20). *The Economist*.

Weick, K. (1995). *Sensemaking in organizations*. Thousand Oaks, CA: Sage.

Weston, J. F. (1969). The nature and significance of conglomerate firms. *John's L. Review, 44*, 66.

8 Functionally Embodied Culture
Possible Limits, or Limitless Possibilities?

William James (2011) wrote in 1907 "a new opinion counts as 'true' just in proportion as it gratifies the individual's desire to assimilate the novel in his experience to his belief in stock." Following James' pragmatism, "truth" here is the intuition of managers, practitioners, and those in management education whose belief in the normative power of culture over the last 35 years has been unshakable in the face of more, shall we say, hard core academic skepticism.

In positing a new framework for organizational culture I join in that skepticism by casting into doubt its many common tropes. The functionally embodied framework and its supporting evidence undermine the mainstream view that culture comes about through the imposition of values, norms or beliefs. Values and such may be what a management team fervently believes to be righteously true or essential, but if this were the case culture shaping would by now be indisputably straightforward given the thousands of enterprises trying their hand at it over the last several decades. Instead, the culture landscape is scarred by academic wars and littered by wasted resources with little evidence of culture-shaping success. The evidence here also casts into doubt that culture is personality writ large, or the product of language games, or a tool of domination and subversion. Cultures may at times exhibit any one or all of these characteristics, but the stuff of culture, as said, is more fundamental, mundane, and deeply rooted.

And yet, beyond management consultants or managers whose interests in advancing culture's causality in profit-making and organizational well-being tend to reduce it to a smartly packaged recipe, there is some evidence to the contrary. Much of it (though not all) comes from smaller enterprises, many of them in the so-called new economy whose primary business is disrupting old business models. Here there is evidence that culture is, in fact, being willfully shaped and imposed. How is this happening? Is this a refutation or limitation of the functional embodiment thesis, a manifestation of it, or simply a feature of organizational size? It is worthwhile to examine these cases to test the limits of our thesis, or, maybe, improve its utility.

As the foregoing has laid out, functional grounding manifests in any task environment or professional milieu where there is sustained collective effort toward a goal. All humans in organizations manifest shared schemas; the extent to which their schemas are unique and dominant within that milieu—versus appropriated from stock cultural scripts or conventional business discourse—is a function of the ubiquity of the grounding contexts described in Chapter 4. As made clear in the last chapter, aligned and sustaining practices are integral to schema proliferation and cultural consistency. They are also key to culture change, to the extent it is possible, as I shall describe below.

In this closing chapter I turn away from theory and evidence to application and implication. I examine the contrary evidence of culture shaping to pressure-test the functionally embodied framework, reviewing three cases where culture shaping appears to be a function of leadership agency. I then review how approaches such as the one at IMCO are undermined by the functional grounding thesis. I close with a return to a discussion about leadership's role in culture change, and provide a short overview of intervention alternatives consistent with the theory and evidence presented here.

1. The Culture Shapers

Spend any time in a start-up company today and it is hard not come away with the belief that creating one's own culture is critical for business success. Certainly this is the case at one of our clients, a San Francisco-based data science firm trying to disrupt the real estate industry. Perhaps it is a function of the age: This company is led by professionals in their late twenties and early or mid thirties, so-called millennials, who, contrary to the prevailing ethos of 10 or 20 years ago when I worked in start-ups, believe culture to be integral and causal to business success.[1] In this particular company, the founding members are convinced creating the 'right' culture is critical not only to success but to everything they are doing, from hiring to making optimal decisions to having difficult conversations. Culture is an avid topic of conversation, almost to the point of obsession. It certainly is considered a resource as precious as financial capital.

This philosophy is described beautifully in Robert Kegan and Lisa Lahey's (2016) *An Everyone Culture: Becoming a Deliberately Developmental Organization*. In it they detail their experiences with companies that epitomize employee development not as a matter of human resource policy or strategy but as integral to business success. Developing capability, indeed human potential, in what they term deliberately development organizations, or 'DDOs', is a business imperative. For DDOs, there is no difference between business and employee development. The two are strategically fused and critical to surmounting the challenges of business in the so-called VUCA world of the 21st century.[2] As they put it, "the relationship between realizing human potential and organizational potential in these companies is a dialectic, not a trade-off" (p. 6). While their focus is on how companies make human development an integral and essential part of organizational life, their underlying thesis is that culture is the enabler, the force for doing so. Culture is the "incubator" and "accelerator" of individual growth (p. 5). To become a DDO, thus, requires engineering one's culture:

> Imagine hardwiring development into your bottom line so that, along with asking whether your culture is fostering the other elements of your business success (such as profitability or the consistent quality of your offering), you ask—demand—that your culture as a whole, visibly and in the regular, daily operations of the company, be a continuous force on behalf of people overcoming their limitations and blind spots.
>
> (p. 5)

In the same way others attribute culture to business success it would be easy to fault Kegan and Lahey for freighting culture with the responsibility of inculcating employee development. But through three case studies focused on the practices of Next Jump, Decurion, and Bridgewater, they render intimate portraits of how leaders are shaping culture to furnish their organizations with the resources to actualize human potential. It is worthwhile to spend a bit of time deconstructing what these DDOs are doing 'with' culture because, according to Kegan and Lahey, it is evidently figural to the success of these companies.

Two things stand out from these cases. First, these organizations are unusual. Second, they are indeed appearing to shape culture. Leaders are actively and consciously shaping their organizational practices and normative behavior to manifest deliberately developmental cultures. Are these companies a refutation of the functional embodiment thesis, anomalous outliers, or, perhaps, best-case examples?

Kegan and Lahey claim each of these companies consciously "nourish" a culture that allows individual development and the attainment of business goals in mutually supportive ways and "at scale" (pp. 3–4). How they do so varies from company to company, but each share what is by now a familiar common feature: *practice*. Culture shaping involves the careful design and sustained enactment of practices that deliberately align and reinforce desired norms and values. While values and philosophy are articulated and clearly matter, it is everyday business practices and routines deliberately architected that carry, inculcate and sustain each organization's developmental ethos.

Take Next Jump, an e-commerce company with about 200 employees that aggregates employee buying power by connecting people in companies with merchants and analyzes the resultant data to make inferences about buying habits.[3] The actions that reinforce its desired culture include espousing and practising rapid development by putting people into jobs for which "they are not prepared to succeed," or proudly advertising their "non-exceptionalist" culture by instilling a peer-chosen company leadership team, or active and ongoing encouragement of "failure" in "the pursuit of excellence" (p. 16). Similar practices include daily check-ins with mentoring partners, weekly situational workshops with groups of such partners, and monthly events where employees give presentations to the rest of the company on their own contributions and receive "on the spot coaching" from senior members (Glassdoor.com). Next Jump's practices, as their CEO puts it, are "carefully designed rituals" (p. 135) orchestrated to create an environment where "working on one's character" (p. 142) becomes habit.[4]

The other two companies appear to be equally practice-obsessed. Decurion, a family-owned business in its third generation of leadership employs 1,100 people and owns a portfolio of theaters, a real estate development firm, and an assisted living facility. It promotes ongoing feedback and performance transparency in a myriad of practices designed to instill community and make people feel joined. Leaders at Decurion, according to Kegan and Lahey, continually practise exposing issues and patterns of thinking in a group environment to let "the problem solve them" (p. 31).

Bridgewater is one of the most successful money managers in its industry, having won more than 40 industry awards within the past five years alone (Kegan & Lahey, 2016). They are privately held with about 1,500 employees and display an intense "idea meritocracy" promulgated by their founder, Ray Dalio (p. 46). Likened to a cross between business and "the U.S. Navy SEALS" (p. 13), Bridgewater's desired culture is expressed in over 200 principles, among them an emphasis on prioritization, diagnosis, analysis, synthesis, logic, and "pushing through pain" (p. 43) all to accomplish results while achieving "excellence through constant improvement" (p. 50). The company practices what Kegan and Lahey term *radical transparency* as a means to get at and "trust in truth" (p. 48). Much if this is enacted in informal practices:

> At any time, routine business conversations can shift into an opportunity for truth-telling and collective learning. It is common to pause for a 'step-back' moment in the middle of a meeting to take stock of errors, to diagnose their root cause in people's habitual actions and thinking, and to identify what people can learn from their own defensiveness . . .
> . . . At Bridgewater, every day is a kind of after-action review, although the process goes much deeper than a typical post mortem. A given conversation of this sort doesn't stop until people have learned something about the person involved.
>
> (p. 51)

Bridgewater even has an equation, "Pain + Reflection = Progress," and an app that employees use to record and "share experiences of negative emotions" (p. 52). Radical transparency extends into open meeting rooms and "no such things as private meetings" (p. 42). Bridgewater's leaders state that their culture, with the transparency ethos at the core, is the source of their success.

In all three companies leaders appear to consciously and deliberately impart beliefs, values and expected norms through formal and informal practices that reinforce and sustain their own cultures. Leaving aside the abundant goodwill they display in transcending traditional business limitations to make development essential to business success, at issue is the question of agency: Can leaders really engineer culture independent of sociotechnical context or constraints? Does task or professional context influence or predispose thinking and action, and thereby culture, or are leaders truly independent actors able to arbitrarily impose beliefs, values, and norms? The theory and data presented earlier suggest the answer is clearly 'no'. So what is happening at these DDOs?

Clues to a possible answer are found within these cases and may indeed have less to do with agency and more with context. These DDOs *do* show evidence of functional grounding. In Next Jump's case, firm size may also play a role.

Starting with the most obvious case, Bridgewater, clues can be found in its co-CEO's explanations for how the company's principles lead to its success:

> The market price is a weighted average view of what is going to happen in the future. The only way you can know something better is to have a better understanding of what can happen in the future . . . We have this notion about the constitution of the company that these are the principles. So that every decision, we are reflecting on "What principles are at play? And how do you take this decision with respect to these principles?"
>
> (Greg Jensen, quoted in Kegan & Lahey, 2016, p. 47)

The co-CEO characterizes the company's principles as a source of " 'compounding understanding', much like compound interest" (p. 47). He also succinctly describes the relationship between task and culture, or to paraphrase Hutchins, the structure of the task is replicated in cognitive structure. Compound interest is framed as "compounding understanding" so that people keep continually learning.[5] Kegan and Lahey acknowledge as much:

> In the algorithms of its proprietary systems, the company has recorded all its technical investment knowledge—a set of principles to guide investing. As many as 98 percent of Bridgewater's financial decisions are executed automatically based on that set of codified market decision rules . . . In contrast, the "Principles" document—the Bridgewater constitution, which all citizens of the company seek to uphold . . . (is) about the ways people act to foster and preserve a culture of truth and transparency.
>
> (p. 47)

Bridgewater's particular strategic task context is uncannily mirrored in its principles, all 200-plus of them. Having a better understanding of the market than the competition is fundamentally predicated on "having better ideas than other people" (p. 47), which means better analysis, synthesis, and learning. These principles are codified and sustained through practices emphasizing constant improvement—the principal of compound interest analogically transferred to the domain of people. Beyond its status as a DDO, what renders Bridgewater unique is that unlike many organizations, the process of transposition appears to be entirely *conscious* and transparent. Far from refuting functional embodiment, Bridgewater is actually a best case for the framework's application!

In any organization there are sure to be principles and practices that are not neat analogs of its strategic task orientation. But the issue here is not to describe Bridgewater's culture in minute detail but to account for how functional embodiment might plausibly explain its culture. Philosophies and practices do spring from leaders, but what accounts for their particularity to begin with, as captured by expressions like *compounding understanding*? Culture does not spring from the minds of actors without cognitive antecedents.

A similar explanation can be found at Decurion. Clues to the origins of Decurion's culture of creating conditions for people to feel joined through practices emphasizing community, feedback and transparency can be located in two places. The first is in its history. ArcLight Cinemas, a subsidiary launched by Decurion's current CEO, was created in 2002 on the principle of reimagining the entire movie-going experience. The guest experience was designed to be different in every way from a traditional movie theater, from reserved seating to concessions to a bar to personalized engagement from staff members. This experience of personal attention to the guest experience finds analogs in Decurion's emphases on individual connection and excellence. More precisely, a second clue is found in the CEO's description of company history. Writing about his return from business school to take a leadership role at ArcLight, he states:

> I came to formulate my purpose as providing contexts for people to flourish . . . And it is animating the purpose of Decurion. I love movies like *Brazil* and the *Hudsucker Proxy* because they capture and warn us of the dehumanizing reality of too many businesses . . . [In those days], the values were present at the company, but I wasn't happy with the ways we were expressing them. Caring about people showed up as paternalism. I saw a lot of loyalty to my family and to people, rather than loyalty to principles. And so, I thought, I am not comfortable with that. It has to change.
> (CEO Michael Forman, quoted in Kegan & Lahey, 2016, p. 35)

This passage shows his commitment to challenging paternalism, but prominent also is the word "loyalty" and the concept of family. His intention is to shift from family loyalty to core principles, but what this meant, according to Kegan and Lahey, was an emphasis on practices that allowed people to "flourish" through communal governance and sharing: Sharing credit, knowledge, wisdom, even jobs, as in the frequently heard saying of "giving your job away" (p. 37). Kegan and Lahey describe learning groups that extoll their members to "hold the whole of the business" (p. 36). What is suggested by these examples is the ubiquitousness of the underlying schema. Where does one first experience the concepts of flourishing, community, sharing, loyalty and holding, but in one's family? These examples point to an obvious grounding context, *family*. Yes, the CEO and leadership teams have made intentional commitments to learning and community, but the schemas giving rise to these beliefs and practices to begin with are already in abundance through three generations of family ownership. It is certainly plausible that the meaning and valance of these principles are already well established, at least tacitly, in the historicity of the strategic context before any deliberate shaping of culture took place.

In the case of Next Jump, evidence in support of functional grounding is less clear. Nonetheless, there may be other explanations beyond acceptance that Next Jump's culture is purely the engineered product of CEO and founder Charlie Kim. One possibility has already been mentioned: there is anecdotal evidence that so-called e-commerce, Internet 2.0 and new economy companies whose primary strategic focus is disrupting older, established business models, apply the same orientation to all facets of their business, including people and culture. The idea is hardly revolutionary. Alan Webber was prescient with this notion in 1993 claiming knowledge as the new competitive resource, and that management's job was to create an environment where learning is a habit. Webber's idea implicates culture at the center of that process. The very act of creating a disruptive technology or business model, as my real estate technology clients in San Francisco are doing, tends to locate all business challenges in a disruption frame. This idea draws from research that shows how technological evolution drives commensurate evolution in industry characteristics, products, capabilities, and value chains (Afuah & Utterback, 1997; Craig-Kennard & Mangematin, 2012). The orientation towards appropriating new technology and skills to disrupt a dominant business model or create a new category, as Kim's Next Jump did, does not stop at customers, markets or technology. The strategic task context, and specifically the differentiated core purpose of *disruption* is experienced and sustained through all aspects of organizational functioning—from writing a business plan to attracting investors to enrolling customers. This induces primary schemas of *newness, innovation,* and *we need to be doing things differently,* and similar. From what we know of analogical transfer, it is entirely plausible that sustained experience in these task contexts begets transposable schemas applied to other domains, such as people and culture. Indeed, these types of schemas are visible as affordances upon stepping in the door of many such companies. Many vestiges of traditional business are gone, from signing in on an iPad instead of being greeted by a receptionist, to open office layouts to free gourmet food at any time of day. There are even changes in the primary modes of electronic communication, with text and technologies like Slack replacing email for in-company communication. In these organizations culture is but another operational category of business to rethink, reimagine, and disrupt. The dominance of the culture narrative in the mainstream business press and pedagogy no doubt also helps, making culture simply another competency for managers to master, no different than marketing, product design, or account management.

Given all this, it is plausible Charlie Kim's focus on culture as *the* enabler of Next Jump's uniqueness draws not only inspiration but its fundamental assumptions from prevailing schemas borne by the strategic task context of disruption and innovation in which he and his team spend much of their waking lives. The strategic task, in essence, is strategic *promise*, the promise at the center of the enterprise's core purpose to change the way the business of employee rewards is fundamentally transacted. As described in Chapter 4, a differentiated core purpose, sustained through aligned practices, can provide sufficient thematicity for schema induction. I suspect this is not only the case at Next Jump but also for an entire generation of new companies across segments who today are harnessing machine learning and data science, among other technologies, to redefine what business looks like.

These cases reinforce the idea that for values or normative beliefs to be imposed by a leader they need to be already present in some form in the system, as discussed in Chapter 1. Functional embodiment explains how this is most likely the case at these DDOs.

Culture and Firm Size

Culture shaping in new economy companies is not only made possible by schema thematicity, but also by firm size. Culture shaping is easier in smaller organizations because schema inducement contexts from similar tasks, routines, a differentiated core purpose, or relatively homogeneous professionalization, will tend to be more prevalent. This facilitates schema sharedness, which allows practices and sensemaking to be readily instituted on widely held assumptions. While it is the case induction contexts need to be in place for some time for schemas to be induced (Next Jump was founded in 1994), it is also the case many founding teams in start-ups often have previous start-up experience. This creates a common foundation of shared schemas (*newness, innovation, disruption, boundary-spanning*, and so forth) that can be readily appropriated in the new venture.

Two related bodies of literature, on social cohesion and network size, support the idea firm size enables homogeneous culture formation. With respect to the former, there is empirical evidence that while task cohesion as compared to social cohesion correlates strongly with small group performance (Carless & De Paola, 2000), social cohesion is a strong predictor of overall system viability (Change & Bordia, 2001). Smaller groups perceive social cohesion more than larger ones, and when culture is conceived as a lever for social cohesion, it is likely to be an object of overt manipulation in a smaller firm.

From an evolutionary anthropology perspective, the study of social networks also supports the firm size thesis. In their innovative study of human networks, Hill and Dunbar (2003) showed that maximum network size averaged at 153.5 individuals, with a mean network size of 125 even when accounting for age, household type and kinship. These findings are close to the group size of 150 predicted by Dunbar's (1993) earlier work on human networks and neocortex size. Here he suggested there may be cognitive constraints on the size of social networks in human and nonhuman primates living in intensely social groups (such as organizations) because the number or volume of neocortical neurons may limit information-processing capacity, and hence the number of social relationships an individual can maintain at one time.[6] Cognitive constraints theoretically constrain culture; beyond a certain size, the effects of a common sense of culture may be muted. In other words, because human social networks may be constrained by an upward limit, it may be easier to engineer a sense of common culture in groups of less than 150.

The evidence from these adjacent strands of research is consistent with functional embodiment. Together, these are equally, if not more, plausible accounts than simple leader agency (independent of context) for why culture shaping might be possible at a Next Jump. Taken to a logical end point, these literatures suggest a single monolithic culture may be impossible in larger organizations. The social cohesion and social network literature draw our attention to the difficulties of culture shaping where no common grounding exists.

The preceding is not intended in away to diminish the remarkableness of these DDOs and their profound orientation to human development. With respect to culture, however, two observations stand out. First, it is obvious these leaders have gone to great lengths to posit culture *qua* culture as *the* enabler of their aspirations. They have invested in the very idea of culture as the vehicle and container for their sterling orientations and ambitions for human development. In doing so they have ontologized culture; they are the extreme case of turning culture into a *thing*. And they have done so deliberately and consciously. This serves to draw energy, attention, and resources to the *idea* of culture as a resource. Culture as epiphenomena becomes culture as physical thing and held up as a symbol of the organization's very specialness and uniqueness.

Second, these companies demonstrate how to sustain culture through the conscious design and implementation of affordances that align and reinforce strategy and espoused philosophy. These leaders are remarkable in how they have gone about this, embedding shared schemas into the social fabric of their businesses to ensure the ongoing sustenance and reinforcement of their values. They may not think of culture as functionally embodied, but they act as if they do. This provides a segue to a discussion about what leaders and practitioners, can, and cannot do to change culture.

2. Functional Embodiment and Culture Shaping

Kegan and Lahey's DDOs make it apparent culture shaping of a certain kind is possible when the values and schemas of leaders are highly congruent with those in the prevailing system, when aspired norms and values are tightly coupled and aligned with the task context, and in smaller enterprises. What remains to be seen is whether culture shaping is possible in larger and global organizations like IMCO. To examine this question it is useful to return to the assumptions underlying the culture-shaping project at IMCO from Chapter 1 and compare these to the functionally grounded approach.

Assumption 1: Culture as Competitive Advantage

The functionally embodied perspective posits that cultural schemas underpin everything we take as 'culture' in organizations. They manifest as cultural models actors use for sensemaking, and power prevailing practices, formal and informal, across all domains of organizational life. Thus, culture may or may not be a source of competitive advantage depending on how much the organization understands this and whether it has the discipline and willingness to adopt or revise their own schemas. It is difficult to argue culture is not a source of competitive advantage for the DDOs. It is also clear how culture became so in those organizations. But whether the DDOs are a useful template for larger and more complex organizations is a more complicated question.

Assumption 2: Culture Can Be Shaped

Rather than assume cultures can be shaped, the better question to ask is where is the locus of intervention, and how systemic is it? The functionally embodied frame on this question is that cultures cannot be shaped except, perhaps, under the conditions described above, but their underlying schemas might be dynamically influenced, provided several conditions are met.

The first condition is that there is sufficient impetus for schema revision at the sensemaking boundary (Chapter 4), such as a significant macroeconomic event or industry shift, a disrupting new technology, a major business challenge, a merger, and so forth. People need motivated reasons to change their own schemas beyond slogans like *we listen to our customers*, or *courage*, or *integrity*. For these words to mean anything they have to connect to values and underlying schemas already resident within the system, and be done in such a way that actors can clearly see how their values or schemas must change. Leaders must connect to what is already meaningful, and do so in meaningful ways. And what is meaningful is usually rooted in the dominant, but often tacitly assumed professional orientation or strategic task focus of the collective.

A second condition is that organizations must ensure their affordance structures are congruent with, rather than adaptations to, their underlying primary schemas. The first step here is to bring the shared schemas into collective consciousness and trace how they underwrite practice. Organizations must then begin to deliberately architect new, schema-aligned practices or induction contexts. In essence, they must try to create a closed cultural system of sustained and reinforcing practices across as many domains as possible. This is much easier in smaller enterprises. In larger ones, cultures are necessarily fragmented based on a myriad of variables, such as strategic tasks that vary by divisional unit; dominant professional orientations; divisional histories and legacies; differing technologies and business models; or regional influences within business units based on history or location of operations. Recall that induction is force-sensitive: When task or social environments are characterized by successful shared task solutions, highly differentiated and meaningful missions, as well as technologies, routines and practices well-aligned to strategic intent, progressive alignment and analogical transfer are more likely. The converse is also true—task solutions, technologies or routines not well aligned or orthogonal to purpose, the product of legacy environments, or not strategically conceived, will result in schemas not widely shared. The greater the number of reinforcing induction contexts, the more unified and cohesive the culture will tend to be.

Thus, a better metaphor than 'shaping' might be one drawn from computer operating systems. When manipulating an operating system, the intervention must begin at the foundational layer of the stack, the shared schema. Is so doing one may begin to appreciate the rigor and discipline involved in culture change.

Assumption 3: Culture Change Must Be Led from the Top

Contrary to the folk belief, and to what is espoused at IMCO, leaders do not 'set' culture. Leadership in the functionally embodied framework is not directly causal in culture shaping. That is not to say leadership does not matter. But it must manifest in more subtle and complex activities. Leaders who undertake culture shaping must do so in much more sophisticated, strategic, multi-modal and sustained ways than what is commonly seen today. Because leaders are most often leading or instigating change, their role in change consists of far more than simply positing a set of values, principles or beliefs, akin to the corporate Ten Commandments, and then waiting for the organizational culture or cultures to magically obey.

Culture change can start from anywhere: the top, bottom, and middle. What is important is for leaders at all levels to recognize the character of their organization's prevailing schemas. Sensemaking organizes itself around primary schemas, thus an organization constituted on a primary schema of control, for example, will invariably seek to suppress any change led from the middle or the bottom. In such organizations the change leader must also be one with positional authority. And leaders must read and influence prevailing power dynamics by understanding the primary schemas at play and how influential actors appropriate them. Then, as stated in Chapter 4, leaders must systematically design interventions targeted at both semiotic and structural practices, and sustain these interventions sufficiently so that they become new schema-induction contexts.

Assumption 4: Culture Change Requires New Behavior

Sustainable behavior change takes place when people become aware of the tacit schemas they hold about how and why things are as they are. When they do, they often become motivated to change them, and this awareness can lead to new behavior (Beckhard & Harris, 1987; Harris, 1994).

Assumption 5: Culture Change Must Happen Quickly

Cultural change will happen when the schemas underlying the culture change. This process is *adverse* to speed. What we know of progressive alignment and analogical transfer is that sustained exposure to grounding contexts is critical for schema induction. Given the tacit and rooted nature of prevailing schemas, expecting change to occur quickly will set false expectations. In many cases, changing prevailing schemas may take years, especially without an environmental stressor acting at the sensemaking boundary.

Assumption 6: Culture Change Must Be Reinforced to Be Sustainable

This is the only assumption supported by the functionally embodied approach. Here, much of the case literature on culture change is in agreement, as demonstrated aptly by Kegan and Lahey's DDOs. Revising and sustaining practices aligned to and reinforcing of the change is usually difficult for organizations to enact, and is usually the locus of culture change failure.

When the shared cognitive structure of groups and organizations are accessed and made visible, interventions based on them are by definition more far reaching, disorienting and impactful because the work takes place amid the layer of widely shared assumptions. For such interventions to have a lasting impact they must be tightly aligned and sustained by practices, and such practices must be in sufficient quantity in the system.

Because primary schemas originate in the organization's strategic task context or dominant professionalization, culture change interventions must target practices close to the organization's core means of production, such as software design and development practices in a software company (including, for example, how customer or market requirements are treated), or manufacturing production and financial control practices in a manufacturing firm. These are not the only affordances to target, but to effect sustained change requires reorienting practices the organization deems most essential to its functioning and survival. Often the reasons for the culture change reside in these practices to begin with, such as with IMCO and their management reporting practices that reinforce prevailing needs to control based on *standards* and *personal experience* schemas. Culture change, thus, has an 'inside-out' quality.

3. IMCO and Culture Change

It is clear by now the 'culture work' at IMCO and the framework for culture put forth here are vastly different enterprises. The terms under which each is constituted are based on entirely different assumptions. What do the results presented earlier say about IMCO's culture-shaping effort?

Schemas, Affordances & Trust

Chapter 1 presented IMCO's desired values and behaviors (Figure 1.1, *We Solve It*), reproduced below (Figure 8.20). To review, these were the aspirations of IMCO leadership based on what they perceived as negative results from an employee survey. The aspired values and behaviors include items such as *we take care of ourselves and each other (Impeccable Character)* and *we challenge the status quo (Bold Thinking)*, or *we are passionate about each other's success and create more success together as a team (Collective Know How)*. On the face of it, these are inspiring personal and group attributes of which few could take exception.

Impeccable character	*Bold thinking*	*Collective know-how*
Our behaviors: • We demonstrate our values of respect, responsibility and integrity in all we do • We are accountable for results and actions • We take care of ourselves and each other • We practice appreciation and gratitude	Our behaviors: • We challenge the status quo and are willing to do things differently • We are curious and agile • We communicate with courage • We are biased for action and speed, while recognizing safety and quality are critical for our success	Our behaviors: • We listen to our customers and create enduring relationships • We continuously learn from each other by valuing different ideas, opinions and experiences • We are passionate about each other's success and create more success together as a team • We contribute to a positive and purposeful environment

Figure 8.20 New cultural behaviors, IMCO (from Chapter 1).

Taken as statements of an espoused culture, a closer read reveals a singular assumption underlying most of them. Consider the *Bold Thinking* column and the statement *we challenge the status quo*. How does one challenge the status quo without a presumption of trust? Or take *we communicate with courage*. What gives rise to courage? Or take *we continually learn from each other by valuing different ideas, opinions, and experiences* or *we are passionate about each other's success and create more success together as a team*. How do these values take root without trust?

The presumption of trust illustrates yet another issue with culture-shaping projects such as this. The espoused values and desired behaviors are taken as faced valid expressions rather than considered in light of the context in which they would need to be enacted. The culture shapers at IMCO want to normatively mold individual behavior, and yet the espoused values and behaviors rely heavily on the presumption of a variable that is in questionable supply. Considering the affordances described in the last chapter, it is difficult to see how trust develops where adaptations to prevailing practices such as *the organization 'doesn't trust me to do my job'; outsiders have difficulty gaining credibility unless/until they deliver "results"; relatively little delegation of authority down the chain of command;* and *lack of "accountability" and "initiative" are common management complaints about people lower in the organization hierarchy* prevail (Figures 7.15–7.18). How does trust develop in a system where PRIMACY OF PERSONAL EXPERIENCE schemas are widely held and lead to practices such as an excessive number of required monthly financial and management reports? It is one thing to espouse the values in Figure 8.20, but what happens to the erstwhile change agent who questions why so many reports are necessary, or the product manager who joins the company from an adjacent industry and lacks shop experience but nonetheless wants to influence the organization with an alternative product marketing process? Or the leader who wants to change forecasting practices to emphasize a more iterative, 'fail fast' approach and comes up against the prevailing DEEP INSIGHT INTO HOW AND WHY THINGS WORK schema and its emphasis on deductive and declarative knowledge over iteration and fast learning? All of these examples are drawn from IMCO cases.

The issue is not intent. The managers at the Leadership Summit were for the most part enthusiastic about these espoused values. At issue is whether such an endeavor is possible when widely held schemas such as DEEP INSIGHT INTO HOW AND WHY THINGS WORK, THE 'RIGHT' PEOPLE, PERSONAL EXPERIENCE SOLVES COMPLEXITY, SUCCESS COMES THROUGH PERSONAL RELATIONSHIPS, SKILLS AND FEELINGS ARE BUILT, and STANDARD OPERATING SYSTEMS PROVIDE DISCIPLINE AND MITIGATE UNCERTAINTY underpin a wide range of practices and cultural models. I do not have any aggregate measure of trust of IMCO. My work there over the past several years suggests levels of trust vary considerably from business unit to business unit.

In general, trust decays the farther removed one is from the object of one's trust. At the site level, trust among co-workers or with site leadership can be quite high, especially given the long tenures among those working in the same site and unit. Trust tends to erode between units and divisional hubs, and more so between entire divisions and IMCO corporate headquarters. These effects can be ameliorated by individual relationships, such as when a manager from the field takes a job at corporate headquarters. But this requires personnel moves; generally trust is not automatically granted between corporate headquarters and field business units.

The same questions can be raised about many of the other aspired culture statements. For example, *we are curious and agile* begs the question of how the organization becomes more agile when many of its management reporting and planning practices are underwritten by *BUILT STRUCTURE*, *PRIMACY OF PERSONAL EXPERIENCE* and *STANDARDS AND COMPETENCE* schemas and fundamentally preclude agility, leading to the adaptations listed in Chapter 7.

In sum, can an organization whose culture (or at least a part of it) is anchored by these schemas change the way it collectively behaves and operates based on what the culture shapers wish to impart? The research presented here suggests this will be difficult. To the extent the schemas identified are more broadly shared throughout the company, top management's desired cultural behaviors will clash with widely held structures of shared meaning conveyed by the schemas.[7]

On the other hand, IMCO employees will also embrace some of the imposed values, namely, those congruent with values already established in the culture and supported by existing schemas, as we saw with Kegan and Lahey's DDOs. For example, *we take care of ourselves and each other* (Figure 8.20) may be accepted in a system where *PRIMACY OF PERSONAL EXPERIENCE* schemas are abundant and norms of loyalty (to 'family' or site) are resident (Figure 7.16). In this way culture shaping becomes an exercise in understanding how imposed values are compatible with prevailing schemas.

4. A Functionally Embodied Approach to Organizational Culture and Change

As one by now might appreciate, the functionally embodied framework is not a recipe for culture change. What may also by now be apparent is the rooted, pervasive and contradictory nature of culture. Tacitly held schemas and their affordances simultaneously obscure and backlight cultural patterns. The functionally embodied approach provides an explication of cultural context and origin while rejecting the notion that culture change is simply a matter of adopting new values, norms or behaviors. It equally rejects the notion that culture is an exclusively semiotic phenomena. Values and such, as well as language and other symbols, are all artefacts in culture and change, but functional embodiment illuminates the shared cognitions that make these artefacts meaningful to begin with. Which is also why functionally embodied interventions require understanding all the systemic interdependencies afforded by the substrate of schemas.

Change the Schema, Change the Culture

For culture change to succeed at IMCO the new culture must draw from its own cognitive heritage—its existing primary schemas. The energy and impetus for change must come from the introduction of new schemas genetically related but distinct from the existing ones, familiar but different enough to anchor new affordances that promote—and in some cases provoke—new behavior. I will not fall prey to my own critique and offer a recipe for how this is to be done. But I can provide a general set of guiding principles for such an approach to consider. The intent here is illustrative and hypothetical, to forward our extended case to help visualize what a functionally embodied culture intervention might look like in practice.

Strategy First

Culture is not strategy, but closely follows it. The schemas that underlie culture may recursively shape it. Fundamental assumptions about what business IMCO is in, and the nature of its markets and competition, will define its core competencies that in turn shape how it organizes itself and goes to market (its *theory of the business*). These activities when sustained will become schema induction contexts, as they themselves are the product of older induction contexts, as depicted in Chapter 4.

IMCO's key to successful culture change might begin with articulating how it conceptualizes its markets, mission, unique value, and core competencies. As a portfolio of industrial engineered product businesses, one of IMCO's strengths is obviously the diversity of its business. The worldwide brake pad business may never have much in common with highly engineered harsh environment pumps for slurry from coal mining, which in turn have little to do with fasteners for smart phone chasses. IMCO's strength undoubtedly resides in its ability to strategically balance its business portfolio to offset dynamic global and local economic and competitive conditions across diverse markets. Privileging decentralized decision making and strategic autonomy so as to quickly respond to local economic variables as they emerge while at the same time leveraging economies of scale in materials, supply chains, and manufacturing processes, and so forth, might therefore be a key aspect of strategy, and key to shaping a meaningful (from a schema-induction perspective) strategic task context.

As one can begin to glean from this back-of-the-napkin analysis, unlike positing a list of attractive values that will likely remain forever espoused, strategic clarity is the first step toward culture change. Clarity is essential because schemas are induced by task context, therefore task and (or) dominant professional orientation must arise out of (but also influence) strategy.

The next question to ask is which schemas support the firm's assumptions and strategy, and which work against it. This exercise could be based on an investigation of schemas and cultural models comparable to what is here, but in less detail (see below). Of course, this is like asking the fish to analyze and change the water in its own tank. The schemas that underlie strategy may be the same ones it does not realize it needs to change. The mitigation is to maintain a meta-awareness of this recursive condition and control for it through a highly iterative and dialogic process, such as one described for a leadership group, below. From this analysis a picture for IMCO might emerge: schemas emphasizing *PRIMACY OF PERSONAL EXPERIENCE* and *BUILT STRUCTURE* might be leveraged in *local* practices that promote autonomous decision making and strategy-setting, customer intimacy, and employee loyalty and engagement. Schemas emphasizing *STANDARDS AND COMPETENCE* and *MACHINE* would be naturally emphasized across all manufacturing activities but also in *specific* reporting and forecasting contexts where the power of IMCO's scale as a global company might be leveraged, such as in procurement, IT, and HR. And note the specificity of these enactments. Schemas and affordances are *selectively* leveraged and implemented that align with and sustain strategy. They are not over-learned reflexive behaviors and practices indiscriminately applied across domains. Thus, schemas like *SOLID ORGANIZATIONAL FOUNDATIONS BRING SUCCESS* do not power all practices related to organizational structure, or manifest as eight levels of authorization for every hire or capital expenditure. Only the ones that promote (for example) local cohesion, agility and customer responsiveness would be privileged. Schemas like *DEEP INSIGHT INTO HOW AND WHY THINGS WORK* could be refocused from practices that today require financial and operational data be funneled to a few individuals who hold all decision-making authority to technologies such as dashboards and practices that synthesize such information to make it available on demand to local managers with decision authority. Or, similarly, the schema could fuel talent management practices that promote hiring and early identification of capabilities so that the workforce *as a whole*, over time, develops better insight.[8]

The above emphasizes appropriating existing schemas through revised affordances. As the company decentralizes and promotes more local autonomy and entrepreneurial decision making (for example), new practices will be conceived. Over time, those practices will induce new schemas that could also be selectively appropriated across the organization.

Practicalities

Our hypothetical IMCO scenario suggests culture change is enacted from a clear recognition of the schemas themselves. This assumes the schemas are known and understood by those enacting the change, which, of course, is often not the case. It might appear easier to enact culture change through affordance that belie the schemas because practices and adaptations are their visible manifestations. However, this is a bit like Lewis and Clark searching for the Northwest Passage. Without at least some sense of what assumptions underlie a given practice, attempting to change culture on the basis of practices alone means wandering in uncharted territory. Thus, the focus of this section is on how to practically investigate schemas so that such ventures might be guided by a kind of compass, however primitive.

Successful and sustained culture change is a complex, multifold two-dimensional process involving, on one axis, interventions at every level of an organizational system: individual, group, and whole system. At the other, it entails changes in language and other semiotic structures (symbols, brands, logos) as well as physical layouts, but, most of all, changes to prevailing practices. But it begins with exposing and making sense of underlying schemas. There are many ways to do this. The most productive from a research perspective have been documented here, but these require training in cognitive anthropological methods, take time, and need to be accompanied by extensive participant observation and action research. For practitioners and managers, therefore, one practical approach involves the use of leadership groups.

Leadership Group Interventions

In culture change, like any change, often it is a leadership group (or groups) that acts as critical coalitions. A leadership group is a body of motivated leaders in a putative cultural community that collectively control or have direct influence over affordance structures.

While there are several ways to elicit and investigate schemas through leadership groups, two promising techniques are described here. One is an approach developed by Etienne, Du Toit, and Pollard (2011) called ARDI (Actors, Resources, Dependencies, Interactions). This approach asks participants in a facilitated group setting to collectively describe how a particular phenomenon works within the four dimensions, along with the causal relationships and interactions between each. This creates a visual representation of a system of causal relationships rendered in schematic form. Participants 'see' their schemas graphically rendered by a facilitator in real-time interaction. This approach has been productive in uncovering schemas and belief frames related to complex, multi-constituent problems like water management (Etienne et al., 2011).[9]

The drawback of this approach, as with similar action-research group techniques, is that empirically it is difficult to separate antecedent cognition from group influences. The facilitator-investigator may not know what represents a pre-existing shared schema from one rendered in the group in the moment, or perhaps rendered as the result of groupthink (Janis, 1971) or social desirability. In addition, this approach focuses on causal relations, which assumes all schemas are causal. Some schemas, as we have seen, are idealizations, expressions of 'should' statements.

Another technique is one we recently piloted with a leadership group and entails what I call 'model reverse engineering.' Set up as a day and a half-long facilitated workshop, we began by asking leaders to collectively document their own practices. We listed the general practice categories outlined in Chapter 7 and asked leaders to write down how they manifested within their own organizations or at their unit of consideration. We also asked them to describe what emotions were evoked with each practice to better understand what adaptations, if any, were being made. Once we had these we asked the group to list what assumptions were implied by each practice.[10] Then, working overnight without the participants the facilitators consolidated the assumptions and created schema statements much like those generated in the tables in Chapter 6. As with the IMCO research, the facilitators endeavored to maintain close fidelity to the underlying assumptions generated by the group while synthesizing them in a way that retained the essence of what was said. This produced a list of 12–15 schema statements, consolidated from the 50 or so generated in the assumption exercise. The next day the facilitators showed the group their synthesis and asked the group to accept, reject, or revise each schema statement. This produced a slightly more consolidated list, but one with high face validity and resonance because the group held veto power over any statement listed. The rest of the exercise was spent reflecting and discussing the implications of what the group had developed as manifestations of their own cultures.

The limitations of this approach are that it is subject to the same groupthink and social desirability issues described above. It also requires trained facilitators to turn raw assumptions into cogent schema statements. As with the any investigation into shared cognition, this introduces a measure of coding bias, albeit one that can be mitigated through participant validation, and through other means such as further interviews and broad surveys. However, this approach bypasses some of the difficulties with antecedent cognition posed by the ARDI research, because all of the practice description and assumptions are emic expressions. What both approaches productively demonstrate is that it is possible to evoke the collective unthought known in a structured and facilitated way.[11]

What these exercises also demonstrate is the dialogic nature of shared schema investigations. The 'reverse engineering' group generated language that described the nature of their own affordances. In effect, they were co-creating their own sense of firm culture as a semiotic artefact. Culture renders action meaningful via its underlying thin coherence, but this coherence is subject to co-creation and construction when illuminated in language. At the same time, it was clear what the group was investigating was real. The practices and adaptations were figural with broad agreement on their existence and consequences. The reflexive process described in the earlier chapters for investigating schemas was replicated at the group level, albeit in a highly facilitated way. The next step would have been to start to link the schemas back to practices and discuss how they might change in line with the firm's strategic assumptions. But as a beginning step, this demonstrates the possibilities for leadership groups offered through emic investigations. The efficacy of making leadership groups aware of the power and salience of their own collective schemas and how they pervasively manifest enables them to develop a meta-awareness of their own, shared tacit cognitive structures. This heightens group-level awareness of cultural phenomena and increases the ability of leaders to effectively intervene in their own systems. Writ large, the promise of this collective awareness and skill holds limitless possibilities for advancing more productive, developmental, and humane organizations.

5. Limitless Possibilities

I have argued in these pages that organizational culture is badly in need of new paradigms, and harvested my experience with IMCO as a research site to make the case. I have argued culture is a largely cognitive phenomenon, cognitive not only in the sense of knowledge but also largely in the sense of situated and embodied *tacit* knowledge in the form of cultural schemas and models. Following Schein, I have argued that organizational culture is indeed a system of *basic assumptions*. And following Sewell, Swidler and others, that these assumptions function as resources for sensemaking and give rise to, pattern and delimit discourse and affordances (in the form of practices and adaptations) across all organizational domains, including the social.

In this way cognition and material culture make each other up. Organizations do things based on the cognitive predispositions of its members and the problems they confront, and these effects delimit and constrain choice, rendering organizational culture the product of collective sensemaking. For these reasons, culture is mostly invisible, acting as a kind of scrim of logic through which belief and action are construed and justified. It is only when the schemas that constitute the scrim are brought into relief through their manifestations in discourse and practice that their pervasive effects can be seen.

Obviously the application of this approach, and its investigative techniques are in their infancy. Much more empirical work is needed, including the development and refinement of the methods used here. A myriad of research questions remain, such as:

- What is the precise model of causality in functional grounding? Professional orientation and tasks shape cognition, but shared cognition also shapes task and professional orientation. A complete model of these effects is needed.

- Why are some schemas shared, and some not? What features and conditions within professional communities and strategic task contexts facilitate the proliferation and appropriation of certain schemas? Is this simply the product of methodological constraint, or a function of schema utility, or something else?
- Under what conditions do environmental factors revise schemas at the sensemaking boundary? Do cultures aid in firm preservation and adaptation, and, if so, what roles do schemas play in this?
- Schemas, and culture, appear to be more easily 'shaped' in smaller organizations, perhaps because of social cohesion or network effects. At what point in organizational size do schemas and cultural models fragment or proliferate? Is 150 the 'magic' number? An investigative modality similar to what is here but controlled by group or organization size could help answer this question.
- The leadership group is a pivotal unit of consideration for schema and organizational culture change research. How do schemas function in groups? How are they sustained or revised?
- Are there alternative ways of detecting and uncovering cultural schemas? For example, do the recent advances in machine learning offer new ways to recognize deep cultural patterns in discourse, thereby making the investigation of organizational culture through the techniques described here more efficient, and therefore more prolific?

Functional embodiment in general, and schema theory in particular as applied to organizational culture, will undoubtedly appear to many as new, complex, recursive, and difficult. This is because the theory is still relatively new, the methods in their infancy, and, perhaps, because modern anthropology is not dominant in the management literature. Although the indirect evidence is abundant, direct evidence of functional embodied cultures beyond this work does not yet exist. Yet cognitive anthropology is well ahead of management science on the topic of culture. Beyond the many ways provided here, the most important is that cognitive anthropology is the only discipline that bridges objectivist–subjectivist dualism by accepting culture's embodied and situated basis while also accounting for its co-constructed, epiphenomenal manifestations. This has far-reaching implications for culture theory.

As Bennardo and Kronnenfeld (2011) put it, "the journey into the cultural mind has only just started" (p. 96). For Hutchins (2005), "the patterns of regularity of interaction with emergent regularities in the material and the social environment provide the basis for whatever truly internal conceptual skills we have" (p. 1575). This regularity is at the heart of culture. And yet because such regularities are not often perceived but instead form the basis for much of our collective unthought known, actors are always exercising their "conceptual skills" in ways indelibly patterned and ramified by their environments. This leads those who wish to understand and perhaps shape culture to posit a kind of illusory coherence for it, an illusion borne by a trifecta of the inertial effects of bureaucracy, the relentless pragmatics of capitalist enterprise, and the human will to self-actualize. Perhaps Sewell (2005) reconciles this tension best when he states:

> Whether we call these partially coherent landscapes of meaning "cultures" or something else—worlds of meaning, or ethnoscapes, or hegemonies—seems to me relatively unimportant so long as we know that their boundedness is only relative and constantly shifting. Our job as cultural analysts is to discern what the shapes and consistencies of local meanings actually are, and to determine how, and why, and to what extent they hang together.
>
> (p. 174)

The project described in these pages, to the extent it might be deemed successful, will have been to do just that: to determine a basis by which local meanings, in certain kinds of contexts at certain moments in time, are capable of hanging together, and why. The ideas and evidence put forward here, perhaps, shed more light on this question.

Notes

1 My experience in Silicon Valley was as part of a software start up in the early 1990s, and again in the latter 1990s with an Internet start-up. In these ventures the focus was solely on survival, and going public. The concept of culture was an afterthought.
2 VUCA stands for volatile, uncertain, complex and ambiguous. The acronym originated from the U.S. Army War College (Whiteman, 1998).
3 And now appears to be dedicating itself to "changing workplace culture" for others (NextJump.com)
4 Interestingly, several reviews on the employee opinion site Glassdoor.com talk about the negative consequences of these practices.
5 Company leaders also view the economy as whole and its own processes as a *machine*. Improving either requires knowing both are inevitably imperfect but can be diagnosed and worked on in a "constant search for the truth about how things are actually going" (p. 50). This has interesting parallels with IMCO's *machine* schema and the manufacturing context of continuous improvement.
6 In his studies of primate social grooming, Dunbar (1993) showed that at a certain point group size becomes too large for social cohesion to be maintained without the use of language. The hypothesis is based on a close statistical analysis of non-human primate neocortex size, group size, and the amount of time devoted to social grooming. From this he predicted humans should live in social groups of approximately 150 individuals. He also used evidence from the ethnological literature as support, since census data from a range of tribal and more traditional societies indicate that groups of about this size are common.
7 Culture change is always possible, however, when done in the most obvious way: by hiring leaders with new schemas. If these new leaders have professional backgrounds overlapping but not identical to the dominant professional orientation, are senior enough in the hierarchy, and have enough personal influence, that is another way to revise prevailing schemas.

8 Interesting, the very title given to the aspired culture, *We Solve It* (Figure 8.20), suggests culture will be 'solved', like a puzzle or a machine. This is yet another example of ontologized culture. On the other hand, it privileges primary *MACHINE* schemas, which may be beneficial in the long run for capturing the imagination of its intended audience, the employees of IMCO.

9 A similar approach has been developed by Sieck, Rasmussen, and Smart (2010).

10 This activity took some guidance from the facilitators; participants had difficulty detaching themselves sufficiently from practices to visualize an underlying assumption.

11 Another approach is to use simulation techniques, such as those that evoke power dynamics.

Bibliography

Afuah, A. N., & Utterback, J. M. (1997). Responding to structural industry changes: A technological evolution perspective. *Industrial and Corporate Change*, 6(1), 183–202.

Beckhard, R., & Harris, R. T. (1987). *Organizational transitions: Managing complex change* (2nd ed.). Reading, MA: Addison-Wesley.

Bennardo, G., & Kronnenfeld, D. (2011). Types of collective representations: Cognition, mental architecture, and cultural knowledge. In D. Kronenfeld, G. Bennardo, V. de Munck, & M. Fischer (Eds.), *A companion to cognitive anthropology* (pp. 82–101). Malden, MA: Wiley-Blackwell.

Carless, S. A., & De Paola, C. (2000). The measurement of cohesion in work teams. *Small Group Research*, 31(1), 71–88.

Chang, A., & Bordia, P. (2001). A multidimensional approach to the group cohesion-group performance relationship. *Small Group Research*, 32(4), 379–405.

Dunbar, R. I. M. (1993). Co-evolution of neocortex size, group size and language in humans. *Behavioral and Brain Sciences*, 16(4), 681–735.

Etienne, M., Du Toit, D. R., & Pollard, S. (2011). ARDI: A co-construction method for participatory modeling in natural resources management. *Ecology & Society*, 16(1). Retrieved from http://www.ecologyandsociety.org/vol16/iss1/art44/

Harris, S. (1994). Organizational culture and individual sensemaking: A schema-based perspective. *Organization Science*, 1, 309–321. Retrieved from http://scholar.google.com/.

Hill, R. A., & Dunbar, R. I. (2003). Social network size in humans. *Human Nature*, 14(1), 53–72.

Hutchins, E. (2005). Material anchors for conceptual blends. *Journal of Pragmatics*, 37, 1555–1577. Retrieved from http://scholar.google.com/.

James, W. (2011). What pragmatism means. (originally published 1907). In J. R. Shook (Ed.), *The essential William James* (pp. 197–214). Amherst, NY: Prometheus Books.

Janis, I. L. (1971). Groupthink. *Psychology Today*, 5(6), 43–46.

Kegan, R., & Lahey, L. L. (2016). *An everyone culture: Becoming a deliberately developmental organization*. Cambridge, MA: Harvard Business School Publishing.

Next Jump company profile. (2016, September 21). *Glassdoor.com*. Retrieved from https://www.glassdoor.com/Overview/Working-at-Next-Jump-EI_IE156468.11,20.htm#WhyWorkForUsTab-22253.

Sabatier, V., Craig-Kennard, A., & Mangematin, V. (2012). When technological discontinuities and disruptive business models challenge dominant industry logics:

Insights from the drugs industry. *Technological Forecasting and Social Change, 79*(5), 949–962.

Sewell, W. H. (2005). *Logics of history: Social theory and social transformation.* Chicago: University of Chicago Press.

Sieck, W., Rasmussen, L., & Smart, P. R. (2010). Cultural network analysis: A cognitive approach to cultural modeling. In V. Dinesh (Ed.), *Network science for military coalition operations: Information extraction and interaction* (pp. 237–255). Hershey, PA: ICI Global.

Whiteman, W. E. (1998). *Training and educating Army officers for the 21st century: Implications for the United States Military Academy.* Carlisle Barracks, PA: Army War College.

Index